Developing with Recreational Amenities

GOLF · TENNIS · SKIING · MARINAS

Patrick L. Phillips
Senior Research Associate
ULI–the Urban Land Institute

ULI the Urban Land Institute

ABOUT ULI– THE URBAN LAND INSTITUTE

ULI–the Urban Land Institute is an independent, nonprofit research and educational organization incorporated in 1936 to improve the quality and standards of land use and development.

The Institute is committed to conducting practical research in the various fields of real estate knowledge; identifying and interpreting land use trends in relation to the changing economic, social, and civic needs of the people; and disseminating pertinent information leading to the orderly and more efficient use and development of land.

ULI receives its financial support from membership dues, sales of publications, and contributions for research and panel advisory services.

James A. Cloar
Executive Vice President

ULI PROJECT STAFF

Frank H. Spink, Jr.	Director of Publications
W. Paul O'Mara	Director, Housing and Community Development Research
Patrick L. Phillips	Project Director
Nancy H. Stewart	Managing Editor
Duke Johns	Copy Editor
Robert L. Helms	Staff Vice President, Operations
Regina Grieb	Production Manager
M. Elizabeth Van Buskirk	Art Director
Helene E. Youstra	Artist
Kim Rusch	Artist
Cynthia Collins	Word Processor

Recommended bibliographic listing:

Phillips, Patrick L., *Developing with Recreational Amenities: Golf, Tennis, Skiing, and Marinas*. Washington, D.C.: ULI–the Urban Land Institute, 1986.

ULI Catalog Number D44

International Standard Book Number 0-87420-664-2

Library of Congress Catalog Card Number 86-61896

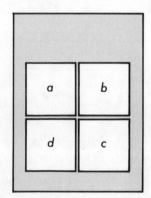

Cover:
a. Plantation Colony Villas, Boca West, Boca Raton, Florida.
Photo by Paul Barton, Pearson, McGuire Associates.
b. Boca West Tennis Center.
Photo by Paul Barton, Pearson, McGuire Associates
c. Chandlers Landing, Rockwall, Texas.
Photo courtesy Realvest, Inc.
d. Deer Valley Resort.
Photo by James W. Kay.

ACKNOWLEDGMENTS

A book of this scope is never possible without the generous contributions of a great many individuals and organizations. Perhaps the most important resource in assembling this text has been the Executive Group of ULI's Recreational Development Council. Among this group, a special note of appreciation should go to Ralph Bowden, J. Richard McElyea, and Erling Speer, each of whom also served on the book's review committee.

In addition to their service on the review committee, Fred Klancnik, formerly of Warzyn Engineering and now with Johnson, Johnson, and Roy, and James Branch of Sno-engineering provided valuable information during the research process. The chapters on marinas and on skiing reflect their respective contributions.

A previous ULI publication, the now out-of-print Technical Bulletin 70, *Golf Course Developments,* was a major influence on this book's treatment of golf course design and construction. Authors Rees Jones and Guy Rando deserve a note of recognition.

In December 1985, ULI sponsored a professional development seminar on the role of recreational amenities in residential and resort development. The presentations and discussions at the St. Thomas seminar provided a substantial boost to this research. Of special note, James Wanless and Bill Wernersback deserve credit for the discussion of disposition issues contained in Chapter 2, which is based on their excellent seminar presentation.

Data provided by various national organizations were invaluable for framing local experience within a larger context. The staff and publications of the United States Tennis Association, the National Golf Foundation, the National Ski Areas Association, and the National Marine Manufacturers Association were most helpful.

Many others graciously donated valuable illustrations, project examples, and case study materials. Robert Grow developed the Otter Creek case study based on an earlier publication in ULI's *Project Reference File.* Robert Page of Kansas State University provided important information on South Seas Plantation. Valuable case study information was also based on earlier contributions by present and former ULI staffers John Cassaza, Kelly Roark, and Dean Schwanke.

Without the contributions of those listed below (and many oth-

Jim Kilday Douglas Dunn	Markland Properties, Inc.
David Howerton Amie Mosher Robert Hart	Robert Lamb Hart Planners and Architects
Dean Kerkling Cliff Simonton	Vail Associates, Inc.
John Grab W. Thomas Hale	Arvida Corporation
Les Boese John B. Dodge	Harbour Ridge
Thomas Hodges Rene Riggan	The Greenbelt Companies
Kathy Gallagher Llwyd Ecclestone	PGA National
Edward Crowley George Parke	Kettler Brothers, Inc.
Susan Capparell Gary Jennison	Corcoran, Mullins, Jennison, Inc.
Ron Kopf	Fairfield Communities
Douglass Norvell	Western Illinois University
Paul Pastoor	John Gardiner's Tennis Ranch
Charles Legler	Port Louis
James Robertson	Realvest, Inc.
Francine Townsend	Sandcastle Associates
Russell Buxton	MacGregor Development Company
Roger Watson	The Eaglemere Group
Lewis F. Payne	Wintergreen
Gary Sandor	The Vintage Club
David Pearson	Pearson, McGuire Associates
B. K. Dawson	Bonita Bay
Brian Silva	Cornish and Silva, Golf Course Architects
Bart Leeds	Naples Bath and Tennis Club
Harry Frampton	East West Partners
Daniel Conway	THK Associates
Patty Doyle	Patty Doyle Public Relations

ers not listed), this book would be far less interesting and useful. The willingness of contributors to subject their projects to close scrutiny has provided the book with valuable, pragmatic examples. ULI hopes that, based on these lessons, readers can more effectively approach their own recreational development challenges.

Patrick L. Phillips

REVIEW COMMITTEE

CONTENTS

Foreword 1

CHAPTER ONE. Amenity-Oriented Development 2
  Recreation and Real Estate 4
  Today's Recreational Development Opportunities 8
    A Rising Affluence 8
    Regional Shifts 10
    Changing Lifestyles 10
    Sensitivity to National Conditions 11
    Development Regulation and Land Supply 12

CHAPTER TWO. Amenities and the Development Process 14
  Developing an Amenity Strategy 15
    Matching Amenities to the Market 15
    Prioritizing Amenity Roles 16
    Balancing Amenity Costs and Benefits 17
    Retaining Developer Control 18
    Transfer of Control and Amenity Disposition 19
  Basic Components of a Disposition Plan 21
    Types of Equity Membership Plans 21
    The Timing and Scope of the Equity Offering 22
    Membership Categories and Classifications 23
    Selling the Equity Certificates: What Price Recreation? 24
    Transferability of Equity Memberships 24
    The Turnover Agreement 25
    Equity Membership Programs: Two Project Examples 25

CHAPTER THREE. Golf Course Development 28
  Golf's Origins 29
  Golf and Real Estate 31
    Private Clubs 32
    Daily Fee Courses 32
    Municipal Courses 32
    Primary-Home Communities 33
    Mixed Communities: Primary, Secondary, Semiretirement 33
    Resorts 34
  Basic Golf Course Types 34
    The Regulation Course 34
    Alternative Course Types 37
    Larger Golf Facilities 38
  Site Selection and Development Feasibility 40
    Course Site Suitability 41
    The Market for Golf 44
    Plans, Policies, and Politics 50
  Golf Course Design and Planning 51
    Development Strategy: The Role of the Golf Course 51

Course Design and Community Development 52
Basic Golf Hole Styles 53
Matching Course Characteristics to the Market 54
Basic Design Principles 56
   The Routing Plan 56
   Tees 56
   Fairways 57
   Greens 58
   Hazards 58
Clubhouse and Related Facilities 60
   Siting Considerations 62
   Program Elements 62
   Practice Facilities 67
Construction Considerations 67
  Clearing 68
  Earthwork 68
  Drainage 69
  Feature Construction 70
  Golf Course Irrigation 71
  Seedbed Preparation and Landscaping 72
  Supporting Infrastructure 73
  Golf Course Development Costs 75
Golf Course Management 76
  The Role of the Developer 77
  Income and Expense Analysis 78
  Maintenance 79
  Programming 81

CHAPTER FOUR. Developing with Tennis 82
Introduction 83
  Origins 84
  Today's Tennis Market: After the Boom 84
Site Selection and Development Feasibility 86
  Physical Requirements 88
  The Market 89
Tennis Facility Planning and Design 92
  Space Requirements 92
  Court Orientation 93
  Selecting a Surface 93
   Porous Courts 96
   Nonporous Courts 96
  Court Lighting 98
  Court Fencing 99
  Indoor Tennis Structures 100
  Practice and Support Facilities 101
  The Tennis Clubhouse 102
Tennis Facility Management 104
  Revenues and Expenses 106
  Facility Maintenance 107
  Marketing and Promotion 109

CHAPTER FIVE. Ski Area Development 110
  Introduction 110
    The Skiing Economy 111
    A Demographic Profile 111
    The North American Ski Area 113
    Skiing and Real Estate 116
    The History and Development of Skiing 118
    The Current Outlook 120
  Site Selection and Development Feasibility 121
    Basic Feasibility Criteria 122
    Site Suitability 122
    Market Characteristics 124
    The Public Policy Context 125
  Ski Area Planning and Design 126
    Trail Planning 127
    Ski Lifts 130
    Base Area Relationships 131
    Snowmaking 132
    Night Skiing 134
    Cross-Country Skiing 135
  Ski Area Permitting: The National Forest System Planning Process 136
  Ski Area Management Issues 138
    Revenues and Expenses 139
    Departmental Operations 140
    Insurance and Risk Management 141

CHAPTER SIX. Marina Development 142
  Growth and Development 143
    A Boom in Recreational Boating 143
    Marinas and Real Estate Development 144
    Marina Development Issues and Trends 145
  Site Selection and Development Feasibility 146
    The Legal and Policy Context 148
    The Physical Environment 151
    The Marina Market 153
  Marina Planning and Design 155
    Basic Marina Types 156
    Spatial Requirements 157
    Functional Relationships 158
    Mooring Layout and Water Circulation 159
      Basic Elements 160
      Floating versus Fixed Piers 160
      Basin Shape 162
      Entrances and Channels 162
      Turning Areas 162
      Slip Sizing and Placement 163
  Engineering and Construction Considerations 164
    Dredging 164
    Breakwaters 166
    Piles 167

Bulkheads 167
Locks 168
Fueling Facilities 168
Access and Circulation 168
Other Facilities 169
Boat Handling Equipment and Storage Options 169
Legal and Regulatory Issues 170
Federal Regulatory Programs 171
State Regulation 173
Local Government Regulation 174
Marina Management and Operations 174
Facilities Management 174
Administrative Management 176
Budgets 176
Organization 177
Financial Case Study: Walden Marina 178

CHAPTER SEVEN: Case Studies 180
Longboat Key Club, Sarasota, Florida 181
Beaver Creek, Colorado 188
PGA National, Palm Beach Gardens, Florida 196
Chandlers Landing, Rockwall, Texas 202
Otter Creek, Little Rock, Arkansas 206
Naples Bath & Tennis Club, Naples, Florida 211
Hidden Valley, Somerset, Pennsylvania 215
Fairfield's Players Place, North Lauderdale, Florida 220
Lochmere, Cary, North Carolina 223
Gainey Ranch, Scottsdale, Arizona 229
Ocean Edge Resort, Brewster, Massachusetts 235
Harbour Ridge, Stuart, Florida 239
Spinnaker Island, Hull, Massachusetts 247

NOTES 253

FOREWORD

Recreational amenities have long been major elements in the design and development of planned communities. They can involve major commitments of public and private financial resources, they can consume (as in the case of golf courses) significant portions of a project's land area, and they are often essential in marketing planned communities as desirable places to live. In the past, however, developers often treated golf courses, tennis clubs, and other amenities primarily as "giveaways," useful for creating real estate value and a marketable image but not as facilities that could yield direct economic returns. Now developers are discovering that if properly structured and carefully managed, such facilities can contribute important sources of revenue.

For any development to be accepted in a market, the type, quality, and number of amenities must be considered. Golf, marina, tennis, and skiing facilities can play various roles in a development venture, depending on their size, overall quality, and the level of services and programs they provide. Too often, the amenities that are selected prove not particularly useful or necessary for the future residents, who generally are the ones who must bear the burden of maintaining them.

The decision by a developer to include or exclude certain amenities should be largely based on six factors: what is being offered in similar local projects; the future residents/users for whom these amenities are being planned; how much money is available for amenities and whether the costs are justified; how the amenity fits in with the total project physically, economically, and as part of its image; what quantity of the amenity should be provided and what the climate will allow; and what the marketing benefits will be.

This book resulted from a belief that these basic questions were often not being addressed by developers of residential and recreational communities, and that too many projects had been developed including amenities that either were promised but never built or built but never used. It also grew out of the need to update two out-of-print ULI publications—*Golf Course Development* (1974) and *Planning and Developing Waterfront Property* (1964)—and to supplement the discussion of amenities in the *Residential Development Handbook* (1978) and the *Recreational Development Handbook* (1981).

Published as a product of ULI's housing and community development research program, this book discusses the social and economic trends regarding leisure and recreation and the role of amenities in the development process, and then focuses on four major amenities: golf, tennis, skiing, and marinas. In addition to a general exploration of the growth of each amenity, its unique planning and design issues, and management considerations, the book features several in-depth case studies of amenity projects.

W. Paul O'Mara
Director
Housing and Community
    Development Research
ULI–the Urban Land Institute

1

CHAPTER ONE

AMENITY-ORIENTED DEVELOPMENT

A well-conceived and carefully timed package of recreational amenities can be a brilliantly successful addition to a development project. These facilities can help a project catch the eye of a particularly coveted market, accelerate sales, and add considerable value to the real estate. By striking a careful balance between amenities and real estate, and by success-fully juggling a wide array of management, maintenance, and other issues, a developer can enjoy considerable payoffs. The unfortunate, but inevitable, corollary is that the pitfalls can be equally considerable.

There are two fundamental reasons why developers include amenities in their projects. The first incentive is to enhance the value of either improved land or real estate products. In a prototypical example, the front-end cost of a golf course can be amortized by the premium prices obtained for lots or homes fronting on the fairways. Although there are countless variations on this scenario, the basic motivation remains the same. Some developers, of course, also intend to create an amenity, such as a marina, ski area, or tennis club, that can eventually be a profitable entity in its own right. Generally, this evolution is likelier in projects that are structured to operate more as resorts and less as primary- or second-home communities.

The Vintage Club

2

The second basic reason for including amenities is to acquire marketing leverage. A well-planned amenity package can help establish a project's overall credibility and image (along with that of the developer), especially in emerging markets or in relatively remote locations. Often, such projects will include resortlike elements, such as a small hotel or a temporary rental program, to cater to the sales prospects attracted by the amenity. Ideally, the increase in sales traffic leads to a faster absorption rate, and the developer quickly recoups his or her wise investment in recreational facilities.

There are other potential payoffs for the developer. One of the most subtle is that recreational amenities, especially in a primary home development, can ultimately become the social focus of the community. In Otter Creek, a 550-acre subdivision bordering Little Rock, Arkansas, a relatively modest racquet and swim club hosts an extraordinary number of events and functions and, because the developer has transferred the facility's ownership to the homeowners' association, it does it on a shoestring budget. By helping to create a thriving, cohesive community out of what might have otherwise been an ordinary subdivision, the amenity serves a purpose far beyond adding value to real estate or selling homes faster. A healthy community like Otter Creek will undoubtedly enhance the developer's credibility and reputation and may help create other spin-off opportunities over the long run.

In addition to these potential payoffs, recreational amenities can carry some significant risks. The most obvious risk, of course, is that the basic strategy might not work. If the facilities fail to attract the market and do not help generate sales, the high carrying cost on the debt required to build the amenities, combined with lower-than-expected created values, could threaten the financial viability of the entire project.

A range of potential factors can exacerbate this gloomy scenario. One is the seasonal nature of many recreational amenities. In many regions, such highly capitalized facilities are only attractive and productive during certain times of the year. Developers of destination resorts often ameliorate this risk by adding multiseason facilities to attract visitors in the so-called "shoulder seasons." Ski areas obviously depend heavily on favorable snow conditions, although modern snowmaking equipment has imparted some flexibility and assurance to that unpredictable business.

Recreational development projects, especially resort and second-home projects, are also subject to fluctuations in the larger economy. Immediately after the November 1984 announcement of proposed tax reforms (including the elimination of the deduction for second-home mortgage interest), sales traffic at many well-known second-home projects withered.

Recreational projects often face a more rigorous and complex public approval process than do other types of development. This requirement is sometimes due to their location in attractive, and often environmentally sensitive, areas. Other times, they face considerable community opposition.

A poorly planned amenity package can saddle a developer (and later, a community association) with excessively high maintenance and operating costs. Many developers are not prepared for the management and operational complexities of amenities. Indeed, the growth of "developer's clubs" associated with real estate developments has spawned a number of professional club management firms that specialize in operating and managing

David Lokey

recreational facilities. Often, the long-term nature of a recreational project requires several transitional stages and midstream adjustments. For example, club facilities may be open to the public in the early years of operation but may gradually become more restricted. Even more complex, resort-like accommodations and services are sometimes used in a project's early years to attract potential buyers. These

Seventh hole, Pebble Beach Golf Links.

project elements may coincide or conflict with other project objectives. One of the most problematic aspects of recreational development is balancing upfront expenditures for amenities with the marketing and sales benefits derived from them. Phasing and timing of amenity development thus become critically important.

Finally, assuming the amenity package has successfully spurred sales and added the expected value to property, the developer must deal with the question of disposition: conveying the facilities to a long-term operating or ownership entity. Unless the developer plans to own and operate the amenities as a profit-making enterprise, control is usually transferred to either the homeowners or some other group. Because the consumers of the amenities have by this point come to expect a certain level of maintenance and operation, the issue of disposition raises a whole host of concerns that are discussed in greater detail in Chapter 2.

RECREATION AND REAL ESTATE

The notion of "amenity," as applied to real estate, is a rather broad concept that can encompass virtually any feature that is attractive to a given market and thus adds value to land. Many amenities are inherent in a site or location: a splendid view, convenient access, or a mild climate. Amenities also include those features added to a particular development that, although nonessential to the project's main function, serve to attract a market. An office park, for example, may offer a daycare center. Similarly, a residential project could include a security patrol.

Today, in the lexicon of residential development, the term "amenities" usually connotes recreational facilities, either natural, such as a beach, mountain, or lake, or built, such as those facilities discussed in this book. In most projects, these facilities produce a major impact on virtually every phase of development, from concept development to financing, land planning, marketing, and management. The premise inherent in the addition of recreational amenities, of course, is that they complement the real estate products. People like to pursue their leisure pastimes near where they live (or where they vacation), and the presence of housing or a hotel can provide a market for the recreational facilities. And in many

cases—golf courses are the classic example—the physical presence of the amenity, even if the facility is not used by the buyer, will impart value to the adjacent real estate.

This relationship between recreation and real estate is nothing new, of course. After all, the amenities at Hadrian's villa, built at Tivoli, Italy, in 124 A.D., included extensive gardens, theaters, and baths. Closer to home, a variety of American resort communities, such as Cape May, New Jersey, were flourishing by the middle 1800s. By the later 1800s, the recreation–real estate connection was evident at a wide range of levels: from the supremely luxurious resort hotels and summer home colonies of Newport, Palm Beach, and Long Island to the crowded, rustic camps and cottages of the Jersey shore and Cape Cod. At about the same time, the first of the recreational land booms was stirring in Florida and California.[1]

For most of these early projects, the key recreational amenities were usually an artifact of location and landscape. Ocean breezes in summer, warm, dry desert air in winter, and pleasant scenery year-round were perhaps the most important amenities; the facilities that are so familiar today—golf courses, tennis courts, marinas, and ski slopes— were virtually unknown at the time.

Not until 1907, for example, at Pinehurst, North Carolina, did an American developer take advantage of the mutually supportive relationship between a resort hotel and a golf course.[2] Similarly, the first major destination ski resort did not appear until 1936, when the Union Pacific railroad christened Sun Valley in Idaho.[3] And, although the roots of pleasure boating are undoubtedly ancient, the term "marina" itself was coined only in 1928.[4]

With the exception of the Great Depression and World War II, however, the story of American recreation in the twentieth century is one of increasingly broad participation and steadily growing demand. Although much of this demand has been satisfied by rising public expenditures for parks and recreation, a strong market developed in the relatively affluent postwar years for recreational real estate. Ski resorts sprouted in the Northeast and West, marinas dotted the coasts and the Great Lakes, and country clubs boasting tennis courts and golf courses appeared throughout the nation, not only as part of resorts and second-home developments, but increasingly as part of suburban subdivisions.

In the 1960s and 1970s, many of these recreational community development projects were made easier through the widespread use of planned unit development (PUD) municipal ordinances and by the popularization of other innovative planning techniques. A key feature of these planning approaches was the value placed on open space and recreational amenities.

The PUD heritage, after all, includes one of the nation's first planned communities: Radburn, New Jersey. At Radburn, 788 units were clustered to enable 15 percent of the total site area to be devoted to an internal open-space network. Recreational facilities included tennis courts, swimming pools, and playgrounds. Perhaps most striking, considering that the first Radburnites moved in 1929, all the common areas and recreational amenities were (and still are) owned, managed, and maintained by a homeowners' association.[5]

By the 1960s and early 1970s, strong demand for recreational property, along with widespread speculation in land, led to a boom in recreational real estate development. Large corporations entered the land sales business, subdividing and marketing huge tracts of lands, often in relatively remote areas with inadequate site improvements.[6] Unwitting purchasers, many of whom were located several states away from the subject property, paid far more for the land than it was worth. As a result, by the late 1970s less than 30 percent of the nation's recreational lots had been built upon. Complaints about misrepresentation and fraud were coupled with charges of excessive soil erosion, inadequate infrastructure, and widespread environmental impacts associated with poorly developed recreational projects.

One response to these abuses was dramatically increased federal and state regulation of recreational land development. In 1969, a watershed year for regulation, both the Office of Interstate Land Sales Registration (OILSR) and the National Environmental Policy Act (NEPA) were established. OILSR requires all projects of 50 lots or more to register a prospectus if they will use interstate commerce to market the land. In response to the more than 3,000 complaints received by OILSR each year between 1971 to 1977, the government pursued a number of indictments against developers and suspended sales at hundreds of projects.

NEPA mandated the now familiar environmental impact statement, a comprehensive review required for all major federal actions significantly affecting environmental quality—a category that includes, for example, the permits required to develop most marinas and ski areas. Fortunately, while "land merchandising" operations and the resulting regulation helped to focus public attention on the abuses of a few large-scale developers, a countervailing trend was gathering steam off the South Carolina coast.

Sea Pines Plantation on Hilton Head Island, started by Charles E. Fraser and the Sea Pines Company in 1957, is widely considered to be the leading prototype of the planned recreational/resort community. According to Fraser, "Sea Pines Plantation's concept made a 180-degree turn away from the prevailing standards of mid-South seacoast development." Among dozens of other innovations, Sea Pines pioneered the now standard use of comprehensive plans, based on extensive ecological research, to guide the project's development. Further, the company made certain the master plan was followed, through extensive, privately administered deed restrictions and protective covenants. This private system effectively replaced the traditional local government role in land use regulation. Although replication of Sea Pines Plantation would today be difficult, the project's influence has been immense, not only in its planning principles but also in its personnel. Virtually a whole new generation of resort developers cut their teeth at Hilton Head: at last count, the leaders of more than 40 other development companies were Sea Pines alumni.

Sea Pines Plantation and its progeny—at Kiawah Island in South Carolina and Amelia Island in Florida, among many others—have helped to underscore the need for recreational developers to maintain a sense of stewardship for the land and its ecological values. Large-scale recreational development today must trade off a wide range of benefits (housing, recreation, and job opportunities) against the potential adverse impacts of development (erosion, loss of wildlife habitat, traffic congestion). Recreational developers, given the locations in which they operate, must recognize competing interests in sensitive resources and must assume a high degree of responsibility and accountability toward the environment. The alternative is to invite a return to the past cycle of shoddy development practices, increasingly rigid regulation, and financial risk.

Since the mid-1970s, recreational real estate has weathered two recessions that together had the effect of shaking marginal development firms out of the industry and of making those who remain more creative in project design. As a result, the variations on the basic recreational real estate themes have broadened considerably. Whereas before, a project could easily be labeled as "primary-home," "second-home," or "resort," today's larger projects are likely to contain real estate products oriented to several specific market segments. Moreover, buyers and investors may face an array of ownership alternatives, from timeshares of varying lengths, to segments of ownership (quarter-shares and eighth-shares, for example), to proprietary or undivided interest ownership. Developers' perceptions of finely segmented markets, usually based on increasingly sophisticated market research, have led to extremely complex projects.

Sea Pines Plantation, Hilton Head, South Carolina.

As a result, the familiar golf-tennis-swimming amenity package, although still the most common, is now being supplemented by a variety of health and fitness facilities, for example. New options for amenity ownership and operations also exist. Developers who traditionally have simply transferred ownership of the amenities to the homeowners' association at buildout now face numerous alternatives for disposition or long-term operation. These can include leasing or selling the facilities to a resort operator or specialized club management firm, or setting up various membership programs or equity offerings to transfer the amenities to the project residents.

Because of this complexity, defining the scope of recreational development in the United States is difficult. One popular, but ambiguous, index used in the past has been the number of recreational lots and second homes, although no comprehensive single source exists for these data. In 1974, industry analyst Richard Ragatz placed the number of recreational lots at between 10 and 15 million.[7] A 1979 search of OILSR registrations showed 21,391 subdivisions with 7.7 million lots.[8] Most recently, a study by Economics Research Associates concluded that about 4.5 million second homes presently exist in the United States,

with about 105,000 added every year.[9] These properties represent an assessed valuation of $306 billion, the study continued, and account for more than $3 billion annually in local property tax revenues. Moreover, the second-home industry employs, through construction, building supply, and service industries, more than 2.4 million workers. These numbers are only useful, however, as a relative index of amenity-oriented development; they do not include, for example, the thousands of primary-home communities that offer recreational amenities.

TODAY'S RECREATIONAL DEVELOPMENT OPPORTUNITIES

Leon Corry

In the last 25 years, in their own inimitable fashion, Americans have resoundingly affirmed the value of outdoor recreation. Consumer expenditures for recreation and leisure pursuits increased in real terms by nearly 250 percent between 1960 and 1979.[10] By 1984, according to a recent survey, four in 10 of us took part in some recreational activity every day. Nearly 70 percent did so at least once a week. Although younger people are generally more active, older age groups are also enthusiastic about recreation. Twenty-five percent of those over 65 participate at least weekly.[11] The Congressional Office of Technology Assessment recently identified the "travel, recreation, and tourism complex" as perhaps the second largest major segment of the American economy.[12]

The underlying reasons for this tremendous growth in the perceived value of recreation are subtle and complex, and they extend deep into the foundations of the nation's psyche as well as its economy. The popular futurist John Naisbitt has suggested that the principal motivation lies in the shift from an industrial economy to a service economy. A nation of computer programmers and clerks, logically enough, needs more exercise than a nation of steelworkers. Probably as important

as the nature of work is the amount of time spent on the job. Americans have seen a steady contraction in the length of the average work week, especially during the first half of the century. While the widely heralded shift to the four-day work week has not widely occurred, as a nation we enjoy more available leisure time than ever. This trend, however, is in flux, at least over the short term. Major factors influencing leisure time include more vacations, retirement age, life expectancy, and overall economic conditions.

Consumer expenditure patterns and participation rates are useful as general indicators of recreation demand, but what other factors are currently shaping opportunities and constraints for developers interested in providing recreational amenities? This section will examine the impacts of a number of issues on amenity-oriented development, including demographic patterns and projections, changing lifestyles, public policy and development regulation, and the influence of larger economic conditions.

A Rising Affluence

In the myriad of population variables and demographic indicators, the most consistently reliable predictor of participation in recreational activities is household income. Although the strength of the correlation varies with the type of activity, the extent of participation generally increases with rising income. To a lesser extent, the rate or frequency of participation also increases with income. For the four activities considered in detail in this book, this relationship is consistently strong. Figure 1-1 indicates participation by income group for several popular sports and activities. The positive correlation between participation and income is especially apparent for sports that require special equipment or facilities, such as boating or skiing, or for those traditionally associated with private clubs, such as golf. Although comprehensive historical data are difficult to find, it is likely that efforts by such groups as the U.S. Tennis Association and the National Golf Foundation, coupled with far higher expenditures for public parks, have made these activities more popular at lower income levels as well. It is revealing, however, to note that the proportion of people who reportedly do not participate in any recreational activities decreases dramatically as income rises. Certainly, income is also strongly linked to education, household type, and availability of leisure time—all factors that influence participation rates.

Figure 1-1

PERCENTAGE PARTICIPATING IN RECREATIONAL ACTIVITIES BY INCOME[1]

Activity	All Incomes	Less Than $5,000	$5,000–$14,999	$15,000–$24,999	$25,000–$49,999	$50,000 and up
Swimming	53%	34%	39%	57%	68%	72%
Bicycling	32	23	24	35	41	42
Boating	28	16	20	27	39	43
Jogging	26	21	20	27	33	37
Tennis	17	12	11	18	22	37
Golfing	13	6	6	13	20	27
No participation	11	28	18	6	4	3
Skiing	9	5	5	7	13	21

[1]Figures represent percent of respondents who participated in activity at least once in the previous year. Based on a sample of 5,757 persons 12 years and older, with interviews conducted from September 1982 to June 1983.
Source: *Statistical Abstract of the United States, 1985.* United States Bureau of the Census.

Because of the strong relationship between recreational activity and income, the demographic trend that portends the most dramatic impact on recreational amenity demand is a widespread, steady rise in household income. After the erosion of household income caused by the1970s' "stagflation," recent projections by Data Resources, Inc. (DRI), suggest that America's average real household income will rise 27 percent between 1980 and 1995. Moreover, this rising affluence is broad-based, holding true for all household types. This "democratic affluence" is largely a result of a transition to a service-oriented economy, a greater proportion of workers in white-collar jobs, and the increasing participation of women in the workforce.[13]

DRI forecasts a median household income of $25,000 by 1995, up from 1980's level of $20,000 (all figures quoted are in 1984 dollars). Most important for recreation demand, however, the number of most affluent households will grow the fastest. The number of households with incomes of $50,000 and up will nearly triple, and will represent 18 percent of all households by 1995. By contrast, in 1980 these relatively high earners accounted for only 8 percent of all households. According to the projections, the number of households with incomes below $40,000 will shrink to represent 72 percent of all households. The proportion of households with incomes above $40,000 will increase accordingly—and dramatically—from 16 percent to 28 percent.

Activity, of course, is also strongly correlated with age, and this rising affluence will be accompanied by an overall aging of households. Just as the baby boom generation swelled the numbers of young households (with relatively low incomes) in the 1970s, it will account for the largest generational shift in the next 15 years. Households headed by persons from 25 to 34 years old, and with incomes of $10,000 to $20,000, will be overshadowed by those ages 35 to 44 bringing in more than $35,000.[14] The number of households headed by 50- to 64-year-olds will grow only slightly, although their average income will show a sizable increase.

DRI projects that 20 percent of these older households will be earning more than $50,000 by 1995.[15] Although the number of households headed by people over 65 will rise by nearly a third, the share of all households represented by the retirement market will remain steady at about 21 percent. This segment will also be better off financially, but their average household income will not rise as much as younger households. Older Americans will also be healthier, and thus more active than ever. An important, and unresolved, question is whether or not recreational habits established early in life will be carried on into later years.

Bohicket Marina Village, Seabrook Island, South Carolina.

Diedrich Architects and Associates, Inc.

The link between increasing household income and recreational demand is far from clear, however. A number of factors cloud the picture. First, the growing number of two-career couples—up 30 percent from 1970 to 1980—coupled with a declining birth rate will mean more households with fewer children. Traditionally, recreation participation has gone up as family size increased. Of course, these families also have a higher household income and per capita income and are better educated and more mobile, all factors that generally mean greater demand for recreation.[16]

Additionally, many younger baby boom families, especially those with only one income, will be less able to afford real estate than their parents' generation or than even older members of their own generation. High inflation and high real interest rates in the 1970s and early 1980s have outpaced income gains for the same period, effectively pricing many families out of the market. This trend is especially true for vacation property and second homes, markets in which projects often include recreational amenities. Consequently, this latent demand for recreational real estate may shift to other, more affordable substitutes, such as membership resorts or new forms of shared ownership.

Regional Shifts

The well-known shift in population from the Northeast and Midwestern states to the Sunbelt is also affecting the demand for recreation. Recreational developments have long enjoyed stronger-than-average markets in locations with genial climates, sizable retirement populations, and strong tourism markets, such as Florida and California. More recently, with greater employment growth in the Sunbelt generally, these strong markets are further segmenting into more specialized markets—for example, for primary housing, second homes, resorts, housing for active younger families or preretirement couples, and traditional retirement communities. Many developers in Florida are targeting more than one of these markets in their new projects (see the Harbour Ridge case study in Chapter 7, for example). Further, areas that might be called the "secondary Sunbelt"—Georgia, Louisiana, Arkansas, Tennessee, and other states—are now experiencing considerable demand for new housing and recreational opportunities.[17] In a trend author Richard Robey calls "diminishing regional differences," areas of strong in-migration in the South and West can be expected to show demand patterns for recreation similar to those traditionally found in the Northeast and Midwest.[18] As one example, the resort community of Myrtle Beach, South Carolina, has benefited from continuing employment growth in the Research Triangle Park area of North Carolina.

Changing Lifestyles

A shifting perception of time will accompany the rise in two-income households and the emergence of nontraditional family structures. Active recreation will be only one option competing for a relatively scarce amount of leisure time. Consequently, these affluent families will be willing to pay for high-quality recreational facilities, especially when accompanied by strong programs and a high level of personal service. Many consumers will focus on project quality, performance, and convenience.

Recent trends show strong growth in individual, noncompetitive activities.

Guy Mancuso

The changing nature of time is also signaled by a general trend toward individual fitness and recreation activities and away from the traditional skilled, competitive team sports.[19] Across the nation, hotels, racquet clubs, and resorts are adding facilities to cater to individualized, noncompetitive recreation. In some cases, these amenities have increased the value of associated real estate, much in the same way as for a lot along a golf course fairway. At Snowmass, Colorado, a $3.5 million health club has boosted summer occupancy levels to 80 percent and has helped revive a sluggish condominium market on the valley floor.[20] Some have noted, however, that fitness clubs are likelier to aid resort occupancy rather than spark major real estate gains, although such clubs can be important additions.

While it is difficult to isolate the causes, today's consumers of recreation are interested in improving themselves through meaningful social and personal experiences. The trend toward individual activities notwithstanding, people are focusing more on activities that enhance personal skills, provide educational benefits, and, most important, offer the most flexibility and personal choice. The revolution in the home entertainment industry, where the consumer assumes greater control, with more choices than ever before, is indicative of a general pattern in personal consumption. Consumers accustomed to personalized prod-

Deer Valley Resort in Utah has elevated personal service to new levels. Here, valets remove equipment from an arriving guest's car.

ucts will demand recreational amenities and facilities that emphasize quality and service. Indeed, it will be the developer's sensitivity to the needs of the market that will determine the value of recreational amenities to a real estate project. The lessons of past projects, says William Wernersback of Pannell Kerr Forster, emphasize that physical facilities themselves are not enough; the market must have access to appropriate membership categories, rights, and privileges, a high level of service and management, and quality programs.

Sensitivity to National Conditions

While many developers would agree that amenity-oriented development will always enjoy a strong market at the highest levels, the demand and supply outlook for recreational amenities at lower, middle, and upper-middle income levels remains highly unpredictable. These facilities, after all, are often considered by developers and buyers alike as luxuries, extras that are expendable except under the best market and economic conditions. This is particularly true in resort and second-home areas, where housing starts almost always nose-dive during national economic slowdowns.

In primary-housing markets, even at middle price ranges, amenities come to be expected during strong economic times. With rising land costs, high interest rates, or slackening growth, however, these facilities can become unaffordable frills for both the developer and the buyer.

Increasingly, developers are turning to health and fitness facilities as recreational amenities.

Equestrian center at Windmill Ranch Estates, part of the massive Weston project near Fort Lauderdale, Florida.

Less direct factors can also influence amenity supply and demand. The fuel shocks of 1973 and 1979 greatly reduced the distance most people were willing to travel to a second home, but increased the demand for recreational facilities close by. One second-home developer, in a savvy marketing move, installed his own gas station to allay the fears of long-distance sales prospects. Now, with a worldwide oil glut and falling prices, the project lies well within the market's traveling range and the developer's gas pumps are closed. As another example, the recent deregulation of the commercial airline industry has resulted in more flights at lower prices, especially to resort areas.

Recently, proposed changes to the federal tax code may prove to be the factor with the most dramatic ultimate impact on the resort and second-home development industry.

Small-scale real estate investors have enjoyed various tax incentives in recent years, from favorable capital-gains treatment to the deductibility of second-home mortgage interest. Although the mortgage interest deduction seems safe, other proposed changes in tax policy would be likely to make resort and second-home property a relatively less attractive investment, although the longer-term impacts are less clear. This shrinking investment pool may be ameliorated in the long run by lower interest rates and an increase in disposable income as a result of lower marginal tax rates. Recreational real estate markets can be highly regionalized, depending on local economic patterns. As one example, in 1985, when sales at most second-home projects were moribund, the market in southern New Hampshire was booming. The reason for this, according to industry analyst Richard McElyea, was a surge in the values of primary homes in the Boston area. By tapping the inflated equity in their primary residences, consumers were able to buy previously unaffordable vacation homes.[21]

Development Regulation and Land Supply

Perhaps the most critical factor affecting the supply of large-scale recreational development projects is the way in which government regulation has affected both the development potential of land and the nature of the development process itself. Projects that include major recreational amenities are often more likely than other types of development to be affected by federal, state, and local regulation. Because they are typically located in attractive and therefore environmentally or politically sensitive areas, they must deal with an additional veneer of regulation or a more complex and more expensive development process. Mountains, deserts, and

Historic boathouse and new marina at Windward Harbor, Lake Winnipesaukee, New Hampshire.

At the state level, coastal development opportunities in Florida have been constrained most recently by the Growth Management Act of 1985, which severely limits development in coastal and wetland areas.[24] Similarly, the state of Maryland's Critical Areas Commission has issued proposals, passed by the state legislature, that will aim to direct new development around the Chesapeake Bay into already built-up areas. Arizona, which passed laws in 1984 that require an assured water supply before allowing development, has spurred developers to come up with some creative angles toward building—and irrigating—a golf course in the desert southwest.

In recent years, development in the Lake Tahoe basin has been at a virtual standstill.

coastal areas provide wonderful opportunities for amenity-oriented development, but these areas are also highly valued for many other uses, including wilderness. As a result of these competing values, the development process in such areas can be particularly arduous.

New residential development in the spectacular but fragile Lake Tahoe basin, for example, has been effectively stopped in the last two years by a host of regulations and political conflicts.[22] Indeed, many of the nation's pioneering resort projects could not be replicated in today's regulatory climate. This holds especially true for coastal area development and marinas. The Coastal Barrier Resources Act, enacted in 1982, virtually precludes development on sensitive barrier islands by eliminating all new federal expenditures and financial incentives within designated units of the Coastal Barriers System. The system of barrier islands subject to the law was slated for expansion in 1985 to include 1,400 additional coastal areas.[23]

Robert Phillips

Loews Ventana Canyon Resort, near Tucson, Arizona.

CHAPTER TWO

AMENITIES AND THE DEVELOPMENT PROCESS

Although recreational amenities by themselves do not fundamentally alter the basic nature of the development process, they can have a profound affect on the relative complexity of various development stages, from concept formulation to sales and marketing. For example, most projects, regardless of scale or type, employ the expertise of a variety of specialized team members who collaborate to realize some overall vision of the project. Including recreational amenities exacerbates this need. Market research, for example, takes on added importance to ascertain recreational supply-and-demand patterns. Site planning, engineering, and construction can be complicated by the addition of a golf course, marina, or other facility. Timing and phasing of capital expenditures for recreational facilities becomes critical. And with a major investment in assets that may gradually lose their value to a developer, he or she must consider questions of long-term ownership, operations, and management.

This chapter focuses on some of the implications that recreational amenities can have for the development process. It does not attempt to summarize all aspects of the development process for residential or resort development (see ULI's *Residential Development Handbook* and *Recreational Development Handbook*), but rather takes a closer look at the strategic aspects of amenities, which a developer must consider early in the process. It also discusses some of the options that exist for amenity disposition.

Boca West, Boca Raton, Florida.

DEVELOPING AN AMENITY STRATEGY

An "amenity strategy" means nothing more (or less) than a clear understanding of the role of recreational facilities within an overall project. Any developer considering adding capital-intensive, land-consuming amenities of the type discussed in this book must carefully consider the strategic aspects of amenities. A successful amenity strategy will:

• Match the mix, quantity, and quality of amenities to the market demand;

• Clearly prioritize the expected roles of the amenities over the project's life cycle;

• Balance the timing and magnitude of capital expenditures for amenities with the benefits derived from them;

• Ensure adequate control by the developer over the operation and management of recreational amenities;

• As the development matures, provide for a rational transfer of control (management or ownership, or both) from the developer to the project residents or to another party; and

• Allow the developer sufficient flexibility to react to changing conditions.

Matching Amenities to the Market

Without question, the fundamental precondition for successful recreational development (or, one could argue, for any development) is a clear understanding of the market. As noted in the previous chapter, markets for recreational real estate are splitting into ever-narrower segments. Because each project is unique, with varying parameters of site, location, and market, it is impossible to generalize in detail about optimal amenity packages. Instead, the case studies in Chapter 7 provide useful examples of amenity strategies. Several basic principles exist, however.

Clearly, an amenity package should reflect the nature of the overall project. A development of predominantly single-family detached houses on fairly large lots would not usually require an extensive amenity package. The same project, however, if it contained a significant percentage of multifamily units, might justify a small clubhouse with a swimming pool or perhaps a tennis club. The addition of a hotel would further boost the amenities required.

In some markets, such as South Florida, demand for recreational real estate is so strong that developers often have to come up with reasons *not* to provide amenities. In such strong markets, high-quality amenities are sometimes added even to relatively modest multifamily projects to set them apart from the competition.

When determining an amenity mix, a developer must first consider the natural qualities of the site that, if protected and enhanced, could serve the same functions as built amenities. A project's site plan, for example, might be oriented to take maximum advantage of existing open space, vegetation, and views—perhaps lending value even more effectively than a golf course. Off-site facilities, if available to the project's prospective residents, may also obviate the need for heavy investment in recreational amenities. These could include not only local facilities, such as public golf courses or tennis courts, but also relatively undeveloped areas, such as public lands for cross-country skiing or hiking.

A developer of a seasonal resort project should also investigate the amenity possibilities for the off-season. Most major ski resorts, for example, as they have matured into real estate development, have added golf courses, tennis clubs, and conference centers in an attempt to attract use in the off-season and in "shoulder seasons."

A key obligation is to include recreational facilities that are of sufficient quality and size to accommodate the expected project population. Later chapters present numerous guidelines for the "carrying capacity" of a typical golf course or tennis court, standards that should be respected under most conditions. If recreational facilities are inadequate for the population, or if the memberships are oversold, the developers can risk their own reputations and that of the project as surely as if their streets were substandard.

Prioritizing Amenity Roles

The two basic roles for recreational amenities reflect the interests of the developer on the one hand and those of the project residents or users on the other. Developers choose some facilities for their marketing value, and others because they will be heavily used. Some, of course, fit both categories. Generally, elaborate clubhouse complexes and golf courses are perceived by sales prospects as highly valuable, yet may in fact be underused (although this is less likely in strong golf markets). Other facilities, including swimming pools, open space, and, in some markets, tennis courts, may be heavily used but not as attractive in marketing efforts.

This dichotomy between marketing orientation and user orientation can carry important implications over the long term. The "developer's" amenity, geared to selling real estate, may prove to be an expensive-to-maintain and underused facility as the project matures. At the same time, the "residents'" amenities may become overused and need expansion.

The needs of the developer may also conflict with those of the user when it comes to qualitative aspects of the amenities. In many retirement markets, a "championship-quality" golf course—frequently designed by a famous professional golfer—is perceived as a strong, even essential, marketing tool. In many cases, however, these long, difficult courses are the last thing the typical retired person (with a handicap of 21) needs for regular play. At the same time, a world-class golf course may be able to put what might otherwise have been only a regional resort on the list of major golf destinations, which is precisely what the Harbour Town Golf Links did for Sea Pines Plantation, according to the project's developers.

A key part of prioritizing the roles of the amenity package is formulating an operational plan that clearly sets out who will develop, own, and operate the facilities and for how long; who will use the facilities and on what terms; and precisely what the expected relationship will be between real estate and recreational amenities, in both the short term and over the long run.

Balancing Amenity Costs and Benefits

Phasing and timing of capital expenditures to match the benefits gained from amenities is one of the principal issues in amenity-oriented development. Conventional wisdom has held that recreational amenities should be constructed at the beginning of the development process, and that virtually all facilities should be complete to draw the market. This principle accounts for a major part of the risk involved in recreational development. Upfront amenity development requires heavy early financing in the face of high initial operating losses as real estate products are delivered. In many cases, these front-end capital costs, high carrying costs, and early operating losses prove large enough to cause the initial return on the total investment to be quite low.

Developers can use numerous strategies either to avoid having to develop all the recreational facilities up front, or to accelerate the revenues produced by amenities built early on. Where a strong existing base of recreational projects exists, as in a resort area, some developers have established cooperative use agreements with other projects. These agreements, which allow residents of one project to use facilities located at another, can work well in some markets to help provide an incomplete project with access to physical facilities and at the same time provide a perhaps underused facility with a group of new users.

One popular strategy is to open up membership or access to the recreational facilities to nonresidents. Ideally, this approach enjoys the twin advantages of exposing the project to a wider audience—and thereby attracting potential real estate prospects—and of boosting the facility's revenues through outside dues and fees. In some projects, usually in strong resort markets, multifamily units are built early in the project (along with a golf course or other major amenity), sold to investors, and then operated on a short-term rental basis catering primarily to real estate prospects. Both of these strategies can work effectively to reduce the financial burden of building amenities up front.

These arrangements also require careful management, however. One potential problem in projects marketed as "exclusive" is that project residents may resent sharing their recreational facilities with outside members or short-term resort guests. Similarly, residents may perceive that the value of the amenities is lessened by the presence of outsiders. In many projects, the developer must ultimately decide how to phase out these outside members.

In the last decade, developers of large-scale recreational projects in some areas have grown increasingly reluctant to anticipate demand by building large-scale clubhouse facilities up front. At Arvida Corporation's Boca West project in Boca Raton, Florida, which was initiated in 1973, the major clubhouse facility was not completed until 12 years later—just before the club was sold to project residents. In the interim, the lack of a clubhouse was mitigated somewhat by a cooperative use at a nearby Arvida-owned club. Erling Speer, the developer of the Mariner Sands project in Stuart, Florida, says he expanded that project's amenities "only in the face of very high demand." (Interestingly, however, in California's Palm Springs area, developers are known for starting big, with extensive clubhouses built up front.)

If all amenities are not built up front, later phasing decisions and amenity siting decisions can send important signals to the market. For example, at Lochmere, an amenity-oriented primary-home community near Raleigh, North Carolina, the developers built a swim and tennis center when the project was about 60 percent complete. The new facility was built toward the eastern edge of the site, even though the western part was more fully developed, as a means to demonstrate the developer's long-term commitment to the whole project, not just the early phases.

Grand Cypress Resort, Lake Buena Vista, Florida.

Diedrich Architects and Associates, Inc.

Retaining Developer Control

One of the most widely accepted principles in amenity-oriented development is that the developer needs to retain control over recreational facilities during a substantial portion of the buildout period. Such "control" means building, operating, and maintaining the amenities at a level commensurate with the developer's overall objectives. In most cases, however, operational control also involves operational responsibility and its attendant expense and risk. If the facilities are intended to help sell real estate, for example, they must be carefully maintained. On the other hand, a developer must also strive to keep operating costs under control.

A developer who trades operational control for a lower operational burden assumes the risk that the facilities may be improperly run or maintained. Yielding control, for example, to a profit-oriented club operator may mean that, when strapped, the operator will fail to properly maintain the golf course or tennis courts; as a result, the image of the whole project can suffer.

In many projects, a substantial number of real estate prospects originate from satisfied early buyers. Aggravating early residents through inadequate amenity operation can thus dampen a project's sales considerably. Also, the developer is the one who conceived of the project, with a presumably keen sense of the market's needs and of the amenities' relationship to real estate. There is no guarantee that an independent operator will manage the facility by the same criteria.

On the other hand, some smaller developers may not be equipped to effectively operate amenities themselves. Moreover, they may prefer to place the operational responsiblity and risk on the shoulders of a separate entity. In such cases, yielding some operational control can make sense.

Peter Runyon

Vail, Colorado.

At Lochmere, a separate limited partnership was formed to build and operate the golf course associated with the project. Lochmere's developers donated the land and made a contribution toward the cost of construction for the golf course, but the course developer retains full operational responsibility. According to the developers, the arrangement has worked well, with the operational control in the hands of those who understand the business of running a golf course. In such an arrangement, a developer must clearly establish the rights of access by project residents to the course to protect its marketing value—after all, a golf course, even if located in the neighborhood, is much more attractive if access to it is assured. One key reason that this arrangement works well at Lochmere is that the project also contains two large lakes, waterfront parks, and a quality swim and tennis center. The golf course is thus less important from a user's orientation, but its presence adds significantly to the project's overall marketing strategy.

The relationship between a developer and early club members or project residents regarding amenity operations can be tricky. Project residents and the developer may have inherently competing interests in recreational facilities. During the recommended period of developer control—which usually lasts until the project is greater than 50 percent completed, but may be shorter for a variety of reasons, including lender requirements—residents need to be assured both of effective operations from their standpoint and also of the amenities' long-term viability. Residents thus frequently expect some say in how the facilities are operated. Many developers have found a club members' or project residents' advisory committee or board a useful vehicle. An advisory board chosen or elected from among the members of the property owners' association can lead to better communication of residents' needs and priorities, many of which do not conflict with those of the developer. Perhaps more important, such an arrangement can lead to generally better relations and can greatly ease the later disposition or transfer of amenity ownership and control. When the Arvida Corporation negotiated the sale of the amenities at Boca West to the project's residents, one of the developer's key concessions involved the appointment of an advisory board to represent the membership during the years prior to the ultimate transfer. At many recent projects, developers have established such a body early in the process.

Transfer of Control and Amenity Disposition

In many resort projects, amenity disposition is simply not an issue, at least not in the conceptual planning. It is assumed for most ski areas, for example, that the developer or a subsidiary corporation will simply retain operational control and ownership of the heavily capitalized ski facilities. Only in struggling resort projects does disposition become important, since these recreational facilities are usually planned to have a positive cash flow on their own terms—if they are making money, there is little reason to sell.

In most residential projects, however, amenity disposition tends to be a central issue, and one that should be addressed early in the development cycle. In most such projects, recreational facilities are transferred (given away, essentially) or sold to project residents, club members, or a third party—often a company specializing in club operations.

PGA National, Palm Beach Gardens, Florida.

Project residents are usually represented by a homeowners' or property owners' association. In most primary-home projects with relatively simple recreational facilities, the developer typically receives a return on his or her investment in the amenities through premium prices obtained for real estate. Periodic assessments or a schedule of user fees are also common to help defray the costs of amenity operation. At an appropriate point the amenities are simply conveyed, fee simple, to the association, which assumes full responsibility and control, although the developer may maintain a limited role.

Extensive club amenities that operate more like commercial facilities, which are found in a variety of project types, including both primary- and second-home projects, can be more problematic. Developers often operate such clubs on a membership basis, with project residents and, in some cases, nonresident club members paying an initiation fee, annual dues, and a variety of other fees—all revenues that go to support the club's operation. Theoretically, this relationship can continue well after the last housing unit is built and sold. In most cases, however, as the project matures, the club facilities are sold either to the members—usually represented by a nonprofit corporation—or to a commercial club operator.

Clubhouse at Mariner Sands, Stuart, Florida.

Why is a developer motivated to dispose of a project's amenities? The answer is simple: the economic value of the amenity package to the developer declines with the sale of each parcel of land or housing unit. In addition, during periods of low inflation the carrying costs on the facilities can exceed the appreciation, so the developer is, in effect, losing money by retaining ownership. Once the last housing unit has been sold, the real estate value of the amenities has been exhausted and the developer has no incentive to retain control or responsibility. The economic value has effectively shifted from the developer to the project residents or club members. And the nature of the value has shifted as well: to a developer, an amenity package is valuable as a marketing tool; to the users—residents and club members—it is part of their community, an important social and economic focal point. According to club analyst Ralph Bowden, "this transfer of perceived value traditionally has been ignored in residential development economic forecasting."[1] The original feasiblity studies, Bowden says, focus on the project's marketing and fail to anticipate an extended role for operating and maintaining the amenities.

The failure to perceive this shift in value can have startling consequences for both the residents and the developer. Too often in a typical project, the amenities have been maintained at high levels, the expense of which has been borne by the developer interested in selling the remaining units. When this cost becomes unsubsidized, but members' and residents' maintenance expectations remain high, the relationship between residents and the developer can deteriorate.

Attempts to deal with disposition issues only at the end of a project's development leave the developer in the weakest possible position, subject to making good on the promises of a long-departed sales force and to keeping the amenities operationally comparable to those offered at the outset.

Disposing of amenities in the middle of a project is not much better in most cases. In midstream arrangements the developer still needs the cooperation of the project residents but must also protect access to the facilities for the unsold units. Residents may balk at making what they view as developer-oriented concessions.

Increasingly, developers are recognizing that disposition should be a key consideration early in a project's financial planning. The rights associated with a typical amenity package can represent significant added value to amenity-oriented real estate. To recapture a share of that value, developers need an amenity disposition plan in place at the outset.

The advantages of an upfront disposition plan are clear. The developer avoids difficult and costly negotiations with an organized (and usually agitated) membership and eases the concerns of sales prospects wary of later uncertainty. Perhaps most important, the sale of a club through an upfront equity offering allows the developer to quickly recapture the investment in the amenities, and often to realize a significant return. Finally, the early transfer of facilities to the membership (with continued developer control, in most arrangements) avoids the possibility of later conveying facilities that need substantial repair or replacement.

BASIC COMPONENTS OF A DISPOSITION PLAN

Structuring an amenity package as a resident-owned club, whether done up front or, less desirably, in later phases, is a complex part of project planning. Planning the amenity disposition program should involve the expertise of a number of development specialists, including appraisers, accountants, lawyers, market analysts, and, ideally, the prospective club's manager. Although numerous specific examples exist, some of which are described more fully in Chapter 7's case studies, this section discusses components of only one disposition strategy: the transfer of club facilities to project residents through the sale of equity certificates. First experimented with in Florida and California, this approach offers several clear advantages for the developer, and is becoming increasingly popular across the country.[2] Clearly, each project presents special problems and opportunities. The following discussion offers general guidelines but is no substitute for qualified expert advice.

At Harbour Ridge in Stuart, Florida, the developer structured an equity membership program during the project's early stages.

Although variations exist, at the heart of most equity membership programs is a nonprofit corporation, established by the developer as an entity to channel funds from the equity investors—the new project residents—to the developer, who uses the money to operate and maintain the facilities. At the end of the agreed-upon period, usually when the project approaches buildout, the developer departs, leaving the members/owners in full control. In the process, the developer will in most cases have recouped his or her investment in the facilities. One key benefit is that the funds received by the developer through the nonprofit corporation are usually tax-exempt, at least initially.

This type of disposition can occur up front, during the development process, or at the conclusion of the project's development. Upfront disposition plans can save the developer major headaches later on, but, as will be presented later, there have been some extremely successful midstream equity sales.

Types of Equity Membership Plans

Membership clubs can offer a dizzying array of membership classifications, each with a variety of use privileges. Equity membership programs come in three basic varieties: tiered, unitary, and convertible.

A tiered program creates several different levels of equity membership, with the price of an equity certificate varying accordingly. The various categories, such as "full," "golf," and "social," for example, will each have different rights and privileges. Each type of member will, in addition, pay some varying level of dues or user fees. This arrangement works well when the size of the amenity package matches up with the number and distribution of project residents. At Stuart, Florida's Harbour Ridge, for example, about 815 homes will surround two 18-hole golf courses, a swim and tennis center, and a sizable clubhouse. Figuring 350 golf members per course as a reasonable standard for a project of this type, this amenity package should reasonably meet the project's recreational demand. Accordingly, developer John B. Dodge has created a tiered equity program, with equity certificates priced from $2,500 to $12,000.

On the other hand, when a project's amenities clearly are not sufficient to satisfy all the demands of its residents—3,000 residences and 18 holes of golf, as an extreme example—a unitary membership plan is more suitable. A unitary program offers only one class of equity membership, at one price; each member then selects a level that varies by the amount of annual dues. A unitary equity certificate, for example, may cost $10,000 for all members, but a full member may pay an additional $2,000 annually in dues, whereas a social member may pay only $250. The equity investment, much like an initiation fee, gives the member in a unitary plan the right to select a suitable membership category each year.

The key difference is that, in a tiered plan, the purchaser of, for instance, a social/tennis certificate cannot be a golf member (although most plans would permit access to the golf course through user fees). In a unitary plan, every certificate holder has the right, usually on an annual basis, depending on the specifics of the plan, to select from among a "menu" of membership options.

A convertible plan offers the developer the option of converting later to an equity program, and alerts project buyers to this possibility. In a convertible program, rather than selling the equity certificates at the outset, the developer will usually charge initiation fees that actually serve as an option on a later equity sale. In the meantime, the initiation fee guarantees the buyer continued access to the facilities and provides the developer with important operating capital.

The Timing and Scope of the Equity Offering

Several other issues related to the timing of the offering also deserve close attention. While less important in upfront plans, where the price of the equity certificate is often built into the real estate's sales price, the length of the initial offering period can be important in projects with a large proportion of residents already using club facilities. The developer is usually interested in selling the amenities to the residents as quickly as possible. In most cases, to create incentives for the buyers, an initial offering price is set at a substantial discount. After 30 days, the price could jump several thousand dollars. In another 30 days, the offering could close, precluding to existing residents the opportunity to purchase an equity share, or even to use the facilities at all. Each such measure aims to give the resident or club member a reason to buy an equity share.

According to many involved in equity programs, one key timing consideration relates to the construction schedule for the amenities. Enticing equity buyers is much easier when tangible results are obvious. The opening of a second golf course or a new clubhouse, for example, may coincide well with an equity offering. To help convince reluctant buyers and establish their own credibility, some developers have phased in the equity sale with the completion of amenities: an initial buyer investment is thus followed by an additional increment upon completion of each major amenity phase.

In seasonal second-home or resort-oriented projects, the timing of the equity offering must relate both to the sales season and to the use season. The optimal moment to make an offering may be toward the end of the use season, when residents are still at the project but when sales traffic is slower.

Clearly, in any such program, success depends upon the effectiveness of communications between the developer and the project residents. Some midstream or end-of-development offerings have attracted lawsuits from disgruntled residents who, in some cases, have established that they already have the right to use the amenities and that, in effect, the developers sold the facilities when they sold the real estate. A developer planning a convertible program or a shift to an equity disposition plan late in the project's cycle must ensure that the initial agreements and documentation do not preclude such an option.

The market for the offering can include both project residents and nonresidents. In most cases, however, equity certificates are reserved for real estate buyers. To boost early membership and to provide important revenues to the club in the early stages, nonresidents are often offered annual memberships, for which they pay dues and user fees. To give these outside members some reassurance, and to make business planning for the club easi-

Gainey Ranch, Scottsdale, Arizona.

er, an initiation fee is sometimes charged to nonresidents. This fee can assure annual members some minimum term of membership before being displaced by a resident equity member.

Membership Categories and Classifications

Determining the total number of memberships and the number of members by type involves trading off a number of quantitative issues against several less tangible ones. Later chapters of this text discuss various planning standards for golf courses, tennis courts, boat slips, and other facilities. These match up the number of members that, in a given set of circumstances, can be supported by 18 holes of golf, for example. Determining the total number of members based on such standards is relatively straightforward. Some projects may have more than enough potential members from among the current or future project residents. Others, with surplus amenity capacity, may have to look to nonresident members. In either case, the total membership is not simply a function of the physical facilities' total capacity. Clearly,

membership size also relates to the overall project concept. In sophisticated markets, developers can gain a distinct advantage by advertising the fact that their club's membership is kept deliberately low. This exclusivity and privacy convey a perceived value in many markets that can more than compensate for the fact that fewer memberships will be sold.

The number of members can be boosted above the standard ratios for a given set of physical facilities by stratifying each membership category's rights and privileges. Just as a reservation system increases the capacity of a tennis court, sign-up privileges, preferred starting times, and the like can enable a club to accommodate more members than one without such tools. Therefore, membership size also relates to how a club is managed. In defining the rights and privileges of each member category, the aim should be to ensure that members feel they are getting what they pay for, and that the price is fair in relation to the other membership categories.

An important additional concern in early equity programs is that the developer often must reserve access to the facilities for any unsold units or for other purposes once the amenities are sold. One technique is to establish a "founding member" or "honorary member" category, which then belongs to the developers or their designees.

Loews Ventana Canyon Resort, near Tucson, Arizona.

Selling the Equity Certificates: What Price Recreation?

Setting a price for an equity membership is a highly sensitive issue, similar to pricing real estate or any other product. Although developers will often use the total assessed or market value of the amenities as a starting point for pricing certificates, a club is clearly more then just real estate. Exclusivity and image are less tangible factors, but their effects on the perceived value of a club membership are genuine. In general, though, the factors that will have the greatest importance in pricing the memberships are the capacity and overall quality of the facilities, and the price of the associated housing units or land. Critical to setting a fair price are accurate representations of the facilities being sold and their condition.

The equity certificate price can be fixed or can be allowed to float upward with the level of demand. Generally, letting the price float can help create an incentive for residents to buy into a club early. Most analysts agree, however, that the degree to which a certificate holder can profit from the resale of a membership at an appreciated price should be limited. While allowing some appreciation and profit upon resale can be an incentive for the prospective buyer, it can also lead to the perception that the equity certificate is a security, to be purchased and sold as an investment. To avoid government registration requirements and other hurdles, developers should carefully package equity membership as a right to use a set of facilities, not as a security. Some areas have seen wide price fluctuations. Equity memberships at one California project reportedly jumped in price from $50,000 to $125,000 in the late 1970s, then fell back to $75,000 during the early 1980s' recession.

One popular strategy is to return to the original buyer upon resale of a certificate all of the original purchase price or 80 to 90 percent of the current market price, whichever is larger. The remaining "profit" (sometimes called a "transfer fee") is funneled back into the club, in the form of a "capital replacement fund," used to maintain and replace the facilities. Some sort of reassurance to the certificate holders while the facilities remain under developer control is absolutely essential for the developer's credibility; a mechanism to fund a sound capital improvement program offers an excellent example.

Depending on state laws, when equity certificates are sold early in a project's development the funds may have to be escrowed. In such cases, the developers may have to carefully define the contractual relationship between themselves and the nonprofit club to permit an adequate flow of funds to operate and maintain the facilities.

Transferability of Equity Memberships

One of the fundamental purposes of including amenities, of course, is to help create value in associated real estate. A key issue for the prospective purchaser of an equity certificate is the transferability of the club membership upon resignation from the club or sale of one's property. It has been clearly established in strong recreational development markets that properties with an associated club membership are worth more than a comparable property in the same project without access to the amenities. Transferability will thus help create real estate value in most cases. Generally, upon a property sale, the previous owner sells his or her membership back to the nonprofit club either at what was originally paid or at some percentage of the market price. Then the club will sell the equity certificate to a new buyer.

In projects with resortlike, short-term rental operations, equity memberships should be assignable to these short-term guests. If the owner of a unit leases it on a seasonal basis, some projects require the seasonal user to purchase an annual membership.

The Turnover Agreement

Two critical components of an equity membership program are the conditions that govern the period between the equity offering and the actual turnover of the facilities, and the conditions under which the turnover itself will occur. The closing itself is usually made contingent upon several thresholds. These can include a minimum number of members or certificates sold, a minimum amount of revenue generated through the offering, or simply an agreed-upon date when the turnover will take place. If the memberships are sold along with each real estate sale, as they would be in most upfront plans, a more logical threshold will occur when a certain percentage of the total number of units is sold.

During this period of developer control, a number of important issues must be managed by both the developer and the certificate holders. One key issue concerns the level of annual dues required to sustain the facilities at a level acceptable to both the membership and the developer. Underpricing dues can lead to a growing developer subsidy of operations and, at the point of transfer, a potentially huge increase in dues as the new owners scramble to raise the necessary funds.

An inadequate level of dues can also oblige the developer to make periodic assessments, which can dangerously undermine the developer's credibility. Also during this period, the developer will typically negotiate a reasonable contribution from the club to the overall property owners' association for the upkeep of streets, security, and other expenses borne by the association due to the club's presence.

Operational control and responsibility can be turned over to the members prior to actual ownership of the amenities, although usually the two coincide. To facilitate member involvement and smooth potentially tense relations between the members and the developer during the period of developer control, an advisory board, as previously discussed above, can be extremely valuable. Such a board can not only work with the developer to solve common problems, but it can also establish a governing board and leadership structure prior to the actual transfer. A final consideration in this interim period prior to the transfer will be the policies regarding nonequity annual members.

Equity Membership Programs: Two Project Examples

Any general discussion of amenities disposition—and of equity programs in particular—must underscore the importance of tailoring an individual program to fit each project. As in almost all aspects of development, each deal differs from the rest. One of the major issues is the point in a project's life cycle at which an equity program is best put into place. Other important questions are the nature and quantity of the housing involved, the permanence or seasonality of the residents, and the character of the facilities themselves.

Nowhere is the practice of converting developers' clubs to member ownership more widespread than in Florida. By some accounts, upwards of 20 resort communities in that state have sold their amenities to their residents. Two Florida projects—Mariner Sands, near Stuart, and Boca West, in Palm Beach County—illustrate the range of options available, the detailed planning required, and the potential pitfalls of these programs.

Mariner Sands. Mariner Sands is a second-home community planned for 825 homes, with a full complement of country club amenities, including 36 holes of golf, a tennis center, a swimming pool, and a clubhouse. Environmental Ventures, Inc., the developers of Mariner Sands, structured the amenity package as an equity club "from day one," according to the company's president, Erling Speer. As a seasonal resort with highly variable use of the facilities, Mariner Sands had a club with little potential as an effective profit center. Also, the developers had little desire to stay in the club management business. According to Speer, the firm saw the upfront equity program as a means of recovering its investment in the facilities, of helping to establish its credibility in the marketplace—Environmental Ventures had taken over from an earlier, troubled developer—and of maximizing the capital-gains treatment of the income from the sale of the amenities.

With a good matchup of residents to amenities, Speer decided on a tiered plan, structured around a nonprofit country club corporation. The developers entered into an option purchase and sale agreement with the nonprofit corporation and will transfer the facilities, debt-free, in exchange for all revenues generated by the sales of equity memberships. Memberships are broken into golf, tennis, and social categories. According to the agreement, the transfer will take place when all of the 700 golf memberships have been sold, or earlier, if the developer can transfer the facilities debt-free. At the outset, in 1979, a golf membership sold for $5,000. In late 1985, the price was $20,000.

Boca West Tennis Center.

The proceeds of the equity sales have been placed in a trust account, the principal of which has secured a loan to the developers for capital improvements and maintenance. Any "profits" from resales of memberships are cycled back into a capital replacement fund. An advisory board, which meets monthly with the developers, was established early in the life of the community.

Mariner Sands is about 70 percent built out, and membership sales are keeping pace with real estate sales. According to Speer, the club arrangement "has been a very positive marketing tool because everybody has known what the situation was up front."

Boca West. Boca West, one of the Arvida Corporation's premier resort communities, contains about 2,600 units in several residential and resort villages. Some 4,000 homes are planned at buildout, which is expected in 1990. The extensive amenities include four golf courses, 34 tennis courts, and a 66,000-square-foot clubhouse. Boca West, since it was begun in 1973, has operated as a primary- and second-home community, as well as a destination resort. For years, the amenities were owned and operated by Arvida as membership clubs.

In July 1985, with the firm's long-term business plans in mind, as well as the community's expressed interest in amenities ownership and control, Arvida presented Boca West residents with an equity conversion offering. As in the case of Mariner Sands, Boca West's offering is structured around a nonprofit corporation, the Boca West Club, Inc. The offering has replaced the previous five annual membership categories with a unitary equity membership. The buyers then select from a series of available membership categories, with annual dues ranging from $500 to $2,600.

According to attorney James Wanless, a member of the team that helped craft the offering, a tiered membership plan, if one had been offered at this stage of the project, could have caused a quick sellout of the most popular category—typically golf—and left the buyers of not-yet-built units at a distinct disadvantage. Thus, given the relationship between the amenities and the planned total number of homes, the unitary plan was seen as the fairer option of the two.

The Boca West offering included provisions intended as incentives for buyers: after the first 30 days, for example, the price jumped from $10,000 to $12,500; after 60 days, the offering closed. Upon the initial offering, Boca West's homeowners' association raised several points about the timing of the eventual turnover, the member involvement before then, and the provisions for capital improvements. After successfully negotiating these points and gaining the association's endorsement of the plan, Arvida sold memberships to well over 90 percent of Boca West's property owners, raising some $24 million.

Events at Boca West since this early success, however, highlight the difficulties of a midstream equity conversion—even a conversion with a well-structured program and a premier project. Chiefly because of contests over the provisions for member participation, and over the procedures for resolving disputes during the time of developer control, the plan has been embroiled in litigation. Arvida's president, John Temple, however, remains optimistic that the program will survive intact. Temple notes that the company, in its future projects, will carefully consider structuring amenities in an equity plan from the very beginning.

Mariner Sands.

Mariner Sands

CHAPTER THREE

GOLF COURSE DEVELOPMENT

PGA National

From world-famous resort courses to lesser-known layouts that enhance residential communities across the nation, today's golf courses are increasingly intertwined with real estate development.[1] Since the late 1950s, booming demand for golf facilities has attracted developers anxious to capitalize on the mutually supportive relationship between golf and real estate.

The number of active golfers has tripled since 1960, yet the number of golf facilities has only doubled in the same period. Today, some 21 million American golfers play nearly half a billion rounds every year on more than 13,000 courses.[2] A game once played almost exclusively on members-only private courses is now played predominantly on courses open to the public. At the same time, golf has maintained a certain social cachet that has helped cement its relationship with real estate development. Moreover, a golf course by its very nature is perceived as an amenity even by those who do not actively participate. A residential or resort developer, it might seem, can hardly go wrong by including a golf course in his or her plans.

The costs of developing and operating a golf course, however, are not insignificant. In the flush of the 1960s, residential and resort developers often included golf as a matter of course, paying little more than passing attention to the long-term costs. The premium prices attained for fairway frontage and the marketing advantage of a golf course community usually greatly exceeded the course construction and operating costs, at least after the first few years. With inflation and rising interest rates in the 1970s, however, the already high front-end costs of golf course development skyrocketed. Rising fuel costs, salaries, and other operating costs also placed a heavier burden on the developer or on the the the subsequent owner—often a homeowners' association.

Today, with real interest rates and operating costs still high, developers are more selective about golf course development opportunities and are searching for ways to make the relationship between real estate and golf more productive. Some strategies focus on the course itself, with greater attention paid to alternatives to the prototypical 18-hole, regulation course. Some developers are striving for a stronger link between golf and other recreational amenities, such as bicycle, running, and cross-country ski trails. Many courses are now designed to minimize maintenance costs, sometimes with dramatic aesthetic and planning implications.

Other strategies look less to the course itself and more to the timing and phasing of development expenditures, the facility's ownership structure, and a wider array of management options. And increasingly, existing golf clubs are turning to real estate development as a means of assuring the survival of the course and club. Although the future of the golf course–real estate connection seems assured, the products and the development process are changing.

GOLF'S ORIGINS

The game we know as golf evolved over a period of about 500 years in Scotland on windswept, barren coastal areas called linksland. These early courses were never "designed," except by nature. Linksland was formed by a receding ocean that left sandy dunes and hollows, combined with areas of rich alluvial soils from adjacent estuaries. Turf, along with any other vegetation, was scarce. The short, stiff grass that did survive was highly adapted to the rigorous seaside conditions.

These ancient golf links had no tees, greens, or fairways as we know them today. Instead, the custom was to "tee one's ball within a club length of the previous cup."[3] Natural conditions determined the sequence of play and the number of holes. Hazards were those left by grazing livestock and burrowing wildlife. Not until the mid-1700s did the thrifty and pragmatic Scots begin to modify these natural conditions by creating more permanent grass putting surfaces—the first greens. Until then, the courses were maintained by nature.

Most early courses were located on publicly owned land. Play was open to everyone, and the courses were easily expanded to suit the demand. There were few standard requirements for a links course. In fact, the standard 18-hole length was not clearly established until

Pebble Beach Company

Seventh hole, Pebble Beach Golf Links.

1764. The great old courses of Scotland and England ranged from five to 25 holes.

The first standard-setting links, still viewed as the quintessential traditional golf course, are at St. Andrews, Scotland. The Old Course at St. Andrews has existed in one form or another since as early as 1414, but its designation in 1834 as "Royal and Ancient" by King William IV helped establish St. Andrews as the standard of comparison for all subsequent courses. Perhaps its major influence, however, emerged in the mid-18th century, when the 22-hole Old Course's four short holes were consolidated into two longer holes, thereby establishing the 18-hole standard. About the same time, St. Andrews enthusiasts began forming private clubs to help run their courses and standardize play.

The sport remained largely unknown outside coastal Scotland, however, until the 1840s, when the advent of the railway began drawing crowds of spectators. The game simultaneously witnessed the first in

a long line of equipment innovations with the introduction of a cheaper, more durable, longer-flying golf ball called the gutta percha. This in turn led to new iron-headed clubs with metal shafts and, ultimately, to longer courses and wider fairways.

Since then, similar improvements in equipment and technology, coupled with increases in the game's popularity, have produced a dramatic effect on golf course design and planning. Innovations have been especially abundant in the United States, where golf is only about 100 years old. The first U.S. course is generally acknowledged to be the somewhat audaciously named St. Andrew's course in Westchester County, New York, established in 1888. Several other clubs were founded about the same time, many with rather rudimentary courses. In 1895, the Chicago Golf Club in Wheaton, Illinois, built the nation's first outstanding 18-hole course.

Wintergreen, Virginia.

The following five years saw the number of courses in the United States multiply more than eightfold. Although the vast majority of these facilities were built quickly and cheaply, one of the exceptions was a course designed in 1907 to support soda-fountain magnate James Tufts's new resort at Pinehurst, North Carolina. Pinehurst not only established a new standard for American courses, but it also for the first time significantly linked golf and real estate.

In the 1920s, the pace of golf course development roared. More than 600 courses per year were built between 1923 and 1929, a pace unmatched until the 1960s. This period produced several landmark courses with dramatic new features. Pebble Beach (1919) and Cypress Point (1929), both on California's Monterey Peninsula, incorporated striking and widely copied oceanfront holes. In 1932, Georgia's Augusta National course included areas specially designed for spectators, a move that foresaw an era of professional tournament play that would not only heighten the game's popularity but would also help establish the long, lush Augusta course as the model for subsequent developments. Pinehurst's number two course, redesigned in the 1930s, emphasized this trend.

By the late 1940s, golf in the United States was poised for its biggest boom. The Great Depression and World War II had greatly curtailed course development. At the same time, however, scientific and technological advances in earth-moving and irrigation equipment, herbicides and fertilizers, and turf management techniques were dramatically influencing course design, construction, and maintenance. Rising postwar affluence, increasing mobility (both off and on the course—golf carts were introduced in the 1950s), and expanded leisure time helped to drive demand for new courses.

The years 1960 to 1973 were record-breakers for golf course development, with the number of new facilities averaging 350 per year. Increasingly, these courses were built as part of land sales efforts, planned communities, or resorts. In 1964, about 17 percent of new facilities were real estate–related. By 1974, when the pace began to slacken, this figure was up to 40 percent. In some areas, including Arizona and Florida, real estate projects accounted for more than 70 percent of the new courses.[4]

In 1984, the National Golf Foundation reported that more than half the new courses opened that year were associated with real estate ventures.[5] The overall development pace, however, has fallen through the 1970s and 1980s. In 1983, for example, only 56 new courses were added to the nation's supply, the lowest such gain in 30 years. The 1984 figures were more promising, however, with a net gain of 84 new courses and 53 additions to existing courses.

In 1975, resort expert John McGrath wrote that developers were "now searching for sound reasons [to] build new golf courses. Capital investment and operating expenses of a golf program have increased to the point where a golf course can rarely be justified except as part of a resort development, a municipal recreation program, or a luxury community."[6] Golf, McGrath concluded, had simply become too expensive as a developer's amenity. High land costs, real interest rates, and operating costs, driven largely by huge increases in fuel costs in the mid-1970s, had combined to make golf courses an enormous financial burden. Tennis's popularity was also rising fast, providing an economical alternative.

McGrath made a convincing case that potential developers should view golf courses with a great deal more flexibility. Courses should be planned to reflect a number of objectives, including economic stability, ease and economy of maintenance and operations, and congruence with the other demands of a real estate project. For too long, he noted, golf's proponents had adhered rigidly to conventional notions of course layout and design. The result, in many cases, was a course that was costly to build and maintain and too difficult for the average player. Citing one well-known model course, he pointed out that "the typical golf course owner does not have the resources to compete with the aesthetics or purpose of Augusta National." McGrath offered an agenda for golf course development through the 1980s, including the following steps that developers should take to ensure the game's future growth:

- Substantially reduce the cost of construction;
- Substantially reduce the cost of maintenance and operations;
- Increase the revenues from operations; and
- Maximize all the benefits that a golf course can provide.

In the years since McGrath outlined these objectives, the growth in the number of new facilities has slowed considerably compared to the halcyon days of the 1960s. Golf course designers and developers are making considerable progress, however, toward reducing high capital and operating costs. Faced with increasingly costly or uncertain water supplies, for example, golf course architects are designing for water conservation, which usually means lower overall maintenance needs. Great strides have also been made in the last decade in water reclamation technology, and in public acceptance of reusing wastewater to irrigate courses. At Scottsdale, Arizona's Gainey Ranch, for example, a sophisticated sewage treatment plant reclaims irrigation water for 27 holes. Courses have also been designed to speed up play, thereby increasing course capacity, rounds played, and revenues. Developers are turning their attention to golf course management to reduce costs and increase revenues. "Developer's clubs" are increasingly viewed in terms of their profitability, not just their marketing appeal. And increasingly popular upfront equity plans for amenities aim to accelerate cash flow to the developer and transfer more of the operating responsibility to project residents.

Capital costs, though, remain higher than ever and continue to increase, and alternative types of golf courses, such as par 3 layouts and executive courses, have not proved much more popular in recent years than they were in the 1960s. In 1985, however, two manufacturers introduced a golf ball that travels only half the distance of a regular ball. This innovative ball has led to so-called Cayman golf, played on 18-hole courses that occupy roughly half the land area of a regulation course. While it remains too early to tell whether Cayman golf will catch on, it is worth remembering how the gutta percha ball revolutionized the game in 1848.

GOLF AND REAL ESTATE

Golf courses are developed for a variety of purposes, including to support various types of real estate projects. The most basic breakdown is between courses that are privately owned or municipally owned. Further, privately owned courses may be limited to play by members

Pinehurst.

Number two course, fifth hole, Pinehurst, North Carolina.

Gainey Ranch, Scottsdale, Arizona.

Courtesy Robert Lamb Hart

of a private club, or may be open to the public on a daily fee basis. Either type of course, private club or daily fee, may be associated with a real estate venture, from a primary-home community to a destination resort. Real estate courses will often combine aspects of both a private club and a daily fee course. Municipal courses, although usually owned and operated by a local government, may also include real estate elements.

Boca West, Boca Raton, Florida.

Paul Barton, Pearson, McGuire Associates

Private Clubs

Until 1962, most golf courses in the United States were built by groups of private individuals, organized to own and operate a club. Clubs are usually composed of between 200 and 500 members who pay an initial fee and annual dues to support the capital and operating expenses. The initial fee can carry with it a portion of the club's equity ownership or may simply be an initiation fee, required for membership but not representing an ownership interest. Clubs are usually organized as nonprofit entities.

In 1953, private clubs accounted for about 60 percent of all U.S. courses. Since then, their proportion has shrunk to about one-third. Many real estate clubs, however, are structured around private ownership, especially as a project matures. In a course's early years, it may be open to the public as a daily fee facility to help market the real estate products. Over the life of the project, such a course may continue to operate on a daily fee basis, owned by the membership as an equity club or owned by the developer (or a third party) and operated as a membership facility. When the recreational facilities are transferred to project residents, however, the golf course will commonly become private.

Some private clubs are now turning to real estate development as a means of saving their aging and increasingly expensive facilities. The venerable St. Andrew's Golf Club in Westchester County, New York, is one such club. Facing the need for more than $5 million in capital improvements and rising operating deficits, club members in 1978 turned to a $100 million development strategy involving the construction of 209 luxury townhouses and the renewal of the golf facilities.

Daily Fee Courses

Today there are more daily fee golf courses than any other type. Relatively few daily fee courses, however, are being built as stand-alone business operations, although such arrangements may be successful in strong markets. Like private clubs, most are associated with real estate projects. In the 1950s and 1960s, when land costs, development costs, and operating costs were all relatively low, it was often feasible to tap the growing demand for golf with a daily fee course. Owners received revenues from daily green fees and golf cart rentals, pro shop sales, and food and beverage operations. While many of these businesses remain successful, rising costs and stabilizing demand have made the daily fee golf business much less feasible in most areas without some sort of real estate operation to help generate revenues and offset expenses. In some areas, however, sharply higher green fees and cart rental fees can help produce profits.

Municipal Courses

For the last 30 years the municipally owned share of all golf courses in the United States has remained steady at about 15 percent. Most of these facilities are independent entities, sometimes combined with tennis courts, community centers, or other public recreational facilities, usually operated by a city or county parks and recreation department.

Increasing costs, however, are outpacing growth in public budgets for recreational facilities and programs. Some municipalities, faced with the high capital and operating costs of golf courses, have also turned to real estate development as one way of helping to finance these facilities.

The resort town of Breckenridge, Colorado, for example, agreed in 1982 to annex a large, master-planned parcel located just outside the town boundaries. In exchange,

Garden apartment units at Harbour Ridge, Stuart, Florida.

the developer donated a portion of the land for use as a municipal golf course. The town financed the course's design and construction with a bond issue, and the developer retained the right to build up to 250 housing units adjacent to the golf course, without having to operate or maintain the course. The donated land saved the town a significant portion of the golf course development costs. A subsequent landowner has since offered to build extensive course improvements, including a clubhouse, in exchange for town approval of a special metropolitan district. Whether or not this kind of negotiation is sound public policy, in this case Breckenridge obtained a golf course for far less than if the town had purchased the land outright. Once the project is built, the developer should realize premium prices for his golf-frontage lots.[7]

Primary-Home Communities

The prototypical golf course community, with single-family primary housing lining the fairways, has largely been supplanted by projects that also include some multifamily housing.[8] For developers, the incentive to include a golf course remains the same: premium prices attained for golf course lots and housing units, plus a distinct marketing advantage. Assuming a strong match between the golfing market and the housing market, additional housing units also help ensure activity and revenues for the golf course. A course may also be a suitable use for an otherwise difficult portion of a site. At Lochmere, a primary-home community near Raleigh, North Carolina, for example, the developer located a course through a floodplain area unsuitable for housing. This approach is common in many areas.

In the most common strategy, the developer builds a golf course—and often other recreational amenities as well—early in the process. This phasing aims to provide a strong image for the project in the local

market and to assure early buyers that the planned amenities are on schedule. The developer owns and operates the course, retaining control over its maintenance and management. As the project approaches buildout, the facilities are typically transferred or sold to the residents, often represented by a homeowners' association. This process usually includes some transition period during which the developer will gradually yield operational control to the residents.

Mixed Communities: Primary, Secondary, Semiretirement

In the last 20 years, increasingly segmented housing markets, more progressive local development policies and regulations, and improved consumer acceptance of alternative housing products such as condominiums and timeshare units have encouraged much more complex development projects. The connection between golf and real estate has consequently become more sophisticated and challenging. Today it is an unusual golf development that contains only single-family homes, for example, or only garden apartments. In southeast Florida and other areas, a project will commonly contain primary homes, vacation residences, a resort hotel, and luxury condominiums sold to investors and rented on a seasonal basis.

This kind of project's market might include retired persons, young professional couples, "empty nesters," and hard-core resort golfers. Moreover, the project may be built over a period of 20 years.

Clearly, such a prospect can be daunting for a developer. Assuming a golf facility is the straw that stirs a project's drink, nearly unlimited options exist for development phasing, course planning and design, management, and long-term ownership and operations. The traditional model—build the course early, amortize the cost by releasing prime course frontage, assume the operating burden for the first few years, then turn over the whole bundle to the project residents—is clearly inappropriate.

Faced with this new complexity, the successful developer will limit a course's front-end costs, maximize both marketing impact and cash flow, and provide for an orderly, predictable transition of ownership. Meeting these criteria, of course, requires sound, continuous planning and much greater attention to management.

Eighteenth green at Pinehurst's number two course, with Pinehurst Country Club in background.

Resorts

A resort golf course may supplement either another recreational facility, such as a ski area or marina, or a major natural attraction like a beach. Golf, of course, can also be the main attraction, either on its own or as part of a concentration of golf resorts, as in the area around Myrtle Beach, South Carolina, which boasts nearly 40 courses.

Golfers travel to such resorts expecting not only premier facilities but also a high level of service and accommodations. The connection with real estate therefore differs from the primary- or second-home community. At a resort, a golf course must be more of an attraction in its own right, rather than serving primarily to enhance the value of adjacent real estate. Development along the course frontage, for example, will be less important; to ensure a high-quality course, such development might even be precluded. When high lot values or other site requirements dictate development close to the fairways, as at Beaver Creek, Colorado, and Harbour Town, at Hilton Head Island, South Carolina, carefully devised architectural controls are often used to encourage compatible development.

Resort courses tend to be spacious, memorable, and image-conscious. On some spectacular sites, the most desirable land may in fact be given over to golf. The oceanfront holes at Pebble Beach may not be economically viable in most projects today, but a first-class golf resort will be expected to devote similarly valuable land to the game rather than to building.

Many golf resorts, of course, will also cater to different markets with many different products. Scottsdale's Gainey Ranch, for example, uses 27 holes of golf to unify a 640-acre mixed-use community that includes a resort hotel, single-family homes, multifamily housing for a variety of markets, and commercial retail and office space. PGA National in Palm Beach Gardens, Florida, also combines world-class golf with a resort hotel and a primary- and second-home community.

BASIC GOLF COURSE TYPES

All courses are based on one or a combination of five basic models. The appropriateness of a particular configuration for a given project depends on a number of factors. A developer should consider the overall project objectives, the operational requirements, and the site's orientation, shape, and existing patterns of soils, vegetation, and topography. Like most prototypes, pure examples of each of the five basic courses seldom exist. Instead, characteristics of each type are combined to suit a particular project on a specific site.

Each basic course prototype is based on the concept of the regulation course, which in turn stems from the notion of par. Par represents simply the score for a given hole produced by error-free golf, or the score an expert golfer would be expected to make. Par assumes ordinary playing conditions and allows two putting strokes. This assumes, for example, that an expert golfer would reach the green of a par 5 hole in three strokes. The United States Golf Association has established standard guidelines for computing par values based upon distance (see Figure 3-1).

The Regulation Course

In the past 30 years, the regulation course has emerged as the standard golf facility, a result of both the game's growing popularity and a more general trend in sports toward standardization and uniformity. Beneficial byproducts of the standardization have included an increased comparability of scores from course to course and a more certain definition of player handicap. Both outcomes are popular with players. Some, however, have questioned the wisdom of unwavering adherence to regulation course standards, arguing that the true heritage of golf should be flexibility and adaptability.[9]

Generally speaking, a regulation course will play to a par of between 69 and 73, with par 72 considered the ideal. The standard length for such a course averages between 6,300 and 6,700 yards from the middle tees. Assuming three sets of tees, a standard regulation course could effectively be played from 5,200 to 7,200 yards long.

The basic mix of holes for a par 72 course is ten par 4s, four par 3s, and four par 5s. Ideally, these holes should be evenly distributed along two circuits of nine holes each. Par can be reduced to 71 or 70 by replacing a par 4 with a par 3, or, more desirably, by reducing a par 5 to a par 4. Clearly, the site and the program will determine an appropriate hole mix and total par. Par or total yardage, taken alone, are not indicators of overall course quality or difficulty. In 1975, one popular list of America's top 20 courses included five courses with par 70 and five with par 71.

Regulation courses are sometimes referred to as "championship courses." This overused term means little except that championships may be held there. In most cases, a championship course thus refers to a particularly high-quality regulation course, although the term carries no objective meaning of its own.

Figure 3-1
PAR AND DISTANCE STANDARDS

Par	Men	Women
3	Up to 250 yards	Up to 210 yards
4	251–470 yards	211–400 yards
5	471 yards and up	401 yards and up

Source: United States Golf Association, *Golf Committee Manual and USGA Golf Handicap System* (New York: U.S. Golf Association, 1969).

Each of the following prototypes illustrates alternative ways to lay out a par 72, 7,000-yard-long regulation course. Although this would be a long golf course, the numbers are rounded for simplicity in making comparisons among the alternative course diagrams. The hypothetical course contains four par 5s of 500 yards each, ten par 4s of 420 yards, and four par 3s, each 200 yards long. Also included in each example is a 10-acre clubhouse site and practice area.[10]

The Core Golf Course. The core course constitutes the oldest and most basic type of design. In a core course, the holes are clustered together, either in a continuous sequence, starting with number one and ending with number 18, or in two returning nines. In a returning-nine layout, each nine-hole sequence begins and ends near the

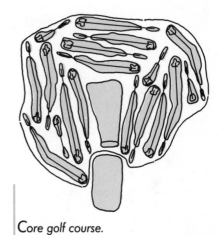

Core golf course.

clubhouse. A continuous layout may locate the ninth hole far away from the first and last holes.

Because it consumes the least amount of land, the core course is usually the least expensive to build. Infrastructure and maintenance costs are also minimized because the holes lie close together. Since all the fairways are located next to other fairways, however, the only sites for real estate development along a core course will lie at its perimeter. This lack of development potential also means that a core course can generally offer the best golfing experience. A core course is most adaptable when used on tight, bowl-like sites with higher-density housing at the edges.

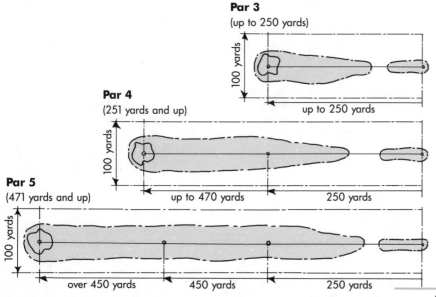

Par 3
(up to 250 yards)

100 yards

up to 250 yards

Par 4
(251 yards and up)

100 yards

up to 470 yards   250 yards

Par 5
(471 yards and up)

100 yards

over 450 yards   450 yards   250 yards

Golf holes in relation to par.

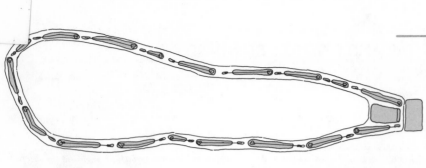

Single fairway continuous 18-hole course.

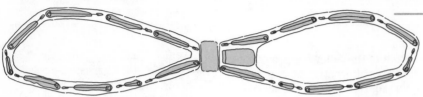

Single fairway 18-hole course with returning nines.

The Single Fairway Continuous Course. This type of course is composed of individual holes strung more or less end to end, played in a long loop from the clubhouse. The single fairway course consumes the greatest amount of land of any of the prototypes, and, if continuous, offers the least amount of operational flexibility. A short round of nine holes, for example, may be inconvenient or even impossible on a continuous course. A continuous course will also limit the overall course capacity. Only one foursome at a time can start on such a course. On a continuous course, it may take up to four hours to get players on all the holes.

Single fairway courses offer the greatest amount of fairway frontage for development sites, although buildings closer than about 150 feet from the fairway centerline can diminish the course's quality. These courses may also be more difficult and slower to play, because the golfer must avoid out-of-bounds areas on both sides of a fairway. (Hitting into an out-of-bounds area carries a two-stroke penalty.) Unlike the core course configuration, the single fairway course can be designed to wind

its way through even fairly difficult terrain. A continuous single fairway course is also extremely flexible, since the only fixed elements are the clubhouse and the starting and closing holes. Pebble Beach, on California's Monterey Peninsula, is one of the most famous courses of this type.

Single Fairway Course with Returning Nines. This configuration offers nearly the same amount of fairway frontage as the continuous single fairway course, but it can be played much more efficiently because of the returning nines. The slightly lower amount of frontage is due to the concentration of tees and greens for holes 1, 9, 10, and 18 in the clubhouse area. In exchange for a small loss in development potential, a returning-nine course maximizes daily play and thus course capacity. With two starting holes and two finishing holes, two foursomes can start simultaneously, then "cross over" after nine holes. The entire course can be in play in only two to two-and-a-quarter hours. Like any single fairway course, however, maintenance costs will be relatively higher than core or

double fairway courses because tees and greens are dispersed over a larger area.

Double Fairway Continuous Course. A double fairway course conserves about 17 percent of the land occupied by a single fairway course. It also offers about 40 percent less frontage for development sites. The side-by-side fairways, however, will provide some savings on maintenance costs. This type of course is particularly suited for long, narrow valley sites, such as at Beaver Creek, Colorado, where, in the course of playing the front nine, the golfer drops 450 feet in elevation (climbing back up on holes 10 to 18). Because the distance between fairway centerlines should be at least 200 feet, it is more difficult to work within existing patterns of topography and vegetation. From the golfer's standpoint, a parallel fairway continuous course, if poorly designed, can be like walking down one side of a street, crossing over to the other side, and walking back. Well-conceived individual holes can help avoid this consequence.

Double Fairway Course with Returning Nines. Like the single fairway layouts, returning nines will mean faster, more varied play in a

Double fairway continuous 18-hole course.

Double fairway 18-hole course with returning nines.

parallel fairway course, when compared to a continuous layout. Returning nines will also slightly decrease the amount of available frontage. Next to a core course, this layout will be the most economical to maintain. Since the distance between potential building sites will total at least 500 feet, assuming 150-foot wide fairways and 200 feet between centerlines, a double fairway course also provides more integrity and identity as a golf course than would a single fairway lined by development. These courses can also accommodate taller buildings along the fairways, which, in a single fairway course, could create an undesirable "alley" effect.

Most contemporary courses combine elements of each of these prototypes to arrive at a satisfactory plan for a particular project. Most, however, are predominantly of one type. Some layouts, for example, will economize with predominantly parallel fairways, but may include four to six single-fairway holes to respond to a dramatic cluster of trees, to skirt a wetland, or to create especially desirable building sites.

Assuming all other factors remain equal, continuous layouts offer maximum frontage but minimum flexibility in operation. Returning nines increase capacity and flexibility at a small loss of developable frontage. Single fairways offer greater design flexibility and maximum frontage but involve higher maintenance costs and, possibly, lower quality of play. Double or parallel fairways economize on maintenance and improve the golf course integrity at some loss of development potential. Finally, a core course remains the most economical and efficient to operate but yields the fewest building sites.

Alternative Golf Course Types

The vagaries of particular sites and particular development objectives may combine to make an 18-hole regulation course infeasible. In such cases, several alternative types of courses may be attractive. Any decision to develop a golf course, and especially a nonregulation facility, should be based on a careful analysis of golf's role in an overall project. A developer must consider how much land is available and the land's suitability for various uses, including golf. Further, the cost of the land should be compared to the expected cost of the real estate products, and the marketability of those products with and without golf should be factored. The developer should also compare golf with alternative recreational amenities that may be less costly but would still provide an acceptable marketing incentive.

If a shortage of land or money precludes upfront development of an 18-hole regulation course, a developer may decide to build a nine-hole regulation course, with or without the intention of adding another nine holes later. Executive courses and par 3 layouts may also be feasible alternatives. In a larger project where land and budgets are ample and the golf market is strong, a developer may choose to plan a 27- or 36-hole layout or may opt for an even more extensive facility.

The Nine-Hole Regulation Course. In 1984, nine-hole courses of all types accounted for about 46 percent of all golf facilities in the United States.[11] This total, of course, includes a wide range of course types, from rudimentary municipal park courses to resort courses that differ little from the best championship layouts, except for the fact that they are only half as long. Nevertheless, most real estate–related courses built in the last 30 years include 18 holes, since this standard remains by far the most popular. A nine-hole course can, however, mean a lower initial investment that easily allows for the addition of a second nine when conditions warrant.

Figure 3-2
18-HOLE REGULATION COURSE DESIGN OPTIONS: RELATIVE PERFORMANCE ON SELECTED CHARACTERISTICS

Design Options	Land Consumption	Frontage Opportunities	Flexibility/ Capacity	Maintenance Cost	"Integrity"[1]
Core	Low	Low	Low[2]	Low	High
Single fairway continuous	High	High	Low	High	Low
Single fairway with returning nines	High	High	High	High	Low
Double fairway continuous	Medium	Medium	Low	Medium	Medium
Double fairway with returning nines	Medium	Medium	High	Medium	Medium

[1]Performance levels indicated are relative and assume a fixed, hypothetical case. A good site and clever design, for example, can produce a single fairway course with stronger golf "integrity" than a run-of-the-mill core course.
[2]Low if continuous, high if returning nines.

Shorter courses may also be more popular in certain regions. At the Villages at Ocean Edge project in Brewster, Massachusetts, the developer refurbished an existing nine-hole course, began real estate development and sales, and then expanded the course to 18 holes. A nine-hole course proved perfectly suitable for the early stages of this project. On Cape Cod, nearly a quarter of the courses are only nine holes, including some of the finest shorter layouts in the nation.[12]

A regulation nine-hole course will run about 2,600 to 3,500 yards long and will play to a par of 35 or 36. With a practice area, such a course will occupy from 75 to 90 acres. Typically, a golfer seeking to play a complete round would play the course twice, which can lead to congested conditions and a less than exciting golfing experience. An alternative to increase the course's playability is to design the holes with multiple tees. By adding nine to 12 additional tees, fairway landing areas, and multiple pins in the greens, each hole can be played several different ways.

According to its advocates, Cayman golf can offer an important new option for golf course developers. Others, however, are not so sure.

The Executive Course. Executive courses of nine or 18 holes first became popular in the late 1950s as a means to both conserve land and to allow for a round of golf in about half the time it would take on a regulation course. (In practice, however, an executive course filled with less experienced players may take as long to play as a regulation course.) An 18-hole executive course will contain four to six par 4 holes with perhaps one par 5. The rest of the holes will be par 3, for a total par of 58 to 60. With a practice fairway, this type of course will fit on about 45 to 60 acres, depending on the site and the layout. Executive courses, which make up about 6 percent of U.S. golf facilities, have been widely successful as supplemental courses in real estate ventures.

The Par 3 Course. As its name implies, this nonregulation course contains only par 3 holes, which range in length from 70 to 250 yards. Such a range will help alleviate the monotony of playing all par 3s, and will encourage a wider club selection. Par 3 courses account for about the same proportion of golf facilities as executive courses. Their popularity seems to have stabilized over the last 15 years. An 18-hole par 3 course will consume the least amount of land of all 18-hole course types. A course 2,000 to 2,500 yards long would fit within 35 to 45 acres.

Cayman Golf. In 1985, the Mac-Gregor sporting goods company introduced a golf ball that travels only half the distance of a regular ball. Theoretically, then, a par 72 course for the new ball could run only half as long as a regular course. Although the resulting game is also referred to by its supporters as "modified golf," the more popular term derives from the site of its introduction, the Cayman Islands' Brittania Resort.[13] The resort's

course was designed specifically for the new ball, which can also be used on par 3 and executive courses. According to its proponents, a Cayman golf course can save up to two-thirds of the land required for a regulation course. As with executive and par 3 courses, this can mean substantial savings in areas with high land costs. Since a developer will still have to build 18 tees and greens, however, the capital cost savings will not be quite so favorable when compared to a regulation course. Nor will maintenance costs be cut by as much, since tees and greens are the maintenance-intensive components of a golf course. Nevertheless, the game could result in a new option for the developer on small sites or as a supplemental attraction for a regulation course. Experience thus far, however, is quite limited.

Larger Golf Facilities

At the other end of the golf facility spectrum are those projects with enough land, a strong enough market, and a big enough budget to permit a larger golf configuration. These amenities usually take the form of a 27- or 36-hole layout, although some major projects, such as Florida's PGA National or Pinehurst, may offer 72 holes or more.

A 27-hole regulation course can be laid out in three returning nines or as one continuous 18-hole course and one returning nine.[14] The former configuration, with three starting and three finishing holes, offers the greatest capacity and the most flexible play. This can be especially desirable at resorts, where play tends to be concentrated in the morning hours. After playing the first nine, a foursome can be directed to the nine with the least congestion for the remainder of the round. Usually, each nine-hole segment will be of similar difficulty to help ensure that all parts of the course are used equally. Sometimes one segment will be easier than the other 18 holes and will be targeted for novices or high handicap players. Similarly, the extra

PGA National

PGA National, a community built around golf, contains four regulation courses.

nine holes may have a different relationship to real estate products than the main course, with a single-fairway nine-hole loop to provide fairway frontage, for example, and an 18-hole core course for playability.

A 27-hole layout also offers exceptional operational flexibility, with almost as much overall playing capacity as that of a 36-hole course. During slack periods, a nine-hole circuit can easily be closed for maintenance or construction. Similarly, the course can be used for tournaments while still allowing member play. One of the greatest advantages of a 27-hole course is that a 50 percent higher capital cost can yield a 65 percent increase in course capacity.

A 36-hole facility can also be designed for flexibility. Two 18-hole regulation courses can be laid out in three basic ways: as two continuous courses, as two courses with four returning nines, or as one continuous course and one course with two returning nines.[15] Two continuous courses are not suitable for most projects, since this configuration will be the least efficient and

will have the lowest course capacity. At private clubs that receive skilled but limited play, however, such as at Springfield, New Jersey's Baltusrol Golf Club, this layout may be satisfactory.

In contrast, four returning nines will produce the greatest course capacity and the fastest play. By combining a continuous course with two returning nines, however, all options are open to the golfer. This

The Vintage Club

The Vintage Club in Indian Wells, California, boasts two distinctly different 18-hole layouts. Shown here, the ninth hole on the Desert Course.

Manley Studios

The view from the third tee, Loews
Ventana Canyon Resort.

SITE SELECTION AND
DEVELOPMENT FEASIBILITY

Questions of golf course feasibility must obviously be considered
within the context of a potential
project's overall concept. This concept, at least in most projects' earliest stages, is an outgrowth not of
exhaustive market research and
economic analysis, but rather of an
individual developer's particular circumstances and intuition. For this
reason, every feasibility analysis
should be considered unique not
only to a particular location, but
also to a particular project concept
or set of assumptions.

In golf-oriented real estate projects, the course is often difficult to
separate from housing units or
other real estate products when
considering feasibility. Developers
will often prepare feasibility studies
based on an assumption that the
project will include a golf course as
an integral component. A market
study or financial analysis for a golf
resort or a golf-oriented second-
home community will not usually
attempt to separate the amenity
from the real estate, except in a financial analysis.

Sometimes, of course, especially
in primary-home communities, a
developer will have already pack-
aged a feasible real estate venture
and will be interested in the question of whether or not to include a
golf course as a recreational amenity. The potential site may include,
for example, some areas not suitable for housing development, such
as a floodplain, that may be useful
as a course. Other developers may
face the possibility of acquiring an
existing course with the intention
of remodeling the layout and developing new real estate products.

layout, used at Harbour Ridge in
Stuart, Florida, is quite adaptable to
a master plan and enables the
course to be integrated with a
greater proportion of the overall
project site. By not having to loop
all the nines back to the clubhouse,
the architect can extend the course
farther into the site and can reduce
the amount of land needed for the
clubhouse site.

Premier golf communities with
more than 36 holes provide examples of the advantages of alternative
layouts. At PGA National in Palm
Beach Gardens, Florida, for example, each of the four 18-hole courses is slightly different, since they
each respond to differing development objectives. The flagship
course, set in the heart of the
2,400-acre community, was designed as a core course to provide a
world-class tournament facility.
Only four development sites front
on this course. A second course,
planned to create the greatest value
in relatively large, single-family lots,
is a continuous, single-fairway
course. In an area of smaller single-
family lots, a third course uses a
mix of single and parallel fairways
for its two remaining nines. The
newest course, which complements
a number of multifamily housing
projects, is designed with parallel
fairways.

At Pinehurst, five of the seven 18-
hole courses are played out of a
central clubhouse. The courses ra-
diate outward from the clubhouse
like the spokes in a wheel, forming
a golf complex with few rivals.

A golf course feasibility analysis can reflect a multitude of different approaches, but each study, no matter what the purpose, should include an analysis of the potential site's physical characteristics, a critical look at the existing and potential local golfing market characteristics, and some consideration of the local planning and policy context.

Course Site Suitability

The most critical site requirement for a golf course, at least for an 18-hole regulation course, is adequate land. Not counting acreage allotted to real estate, a site of less than about 110 acres will not be suitable for an 18-hole regulation course, although one of the alternative course types may be quite adequate and highly successful. The shape of the property is also important. Long, narrow sites may excessively restrict the layout options, resulting in an unsatisfactory facility. Other relevant limitations can be easily spotted. Numerous roads crossing the site, for example, are clearly undesirable.

Assuming a candidate site meets such basic criteria, the developer must undertake a more detailed evaluation of additional site characteristics, including topography, drainage, soils and vegetation, and water availability. Many individual site characteristics, given enough investment, can be made suitable if otherwise deficient. A flat site, for example, can be graded to create interest and improve drainage. Likewise, barren sites can be landscaped and irrigated. Every such effort, of course, carries a cost, and the developer must carefully weigh the corresponding benefits.

Topography. From the qualitative standpoint of course architects and golfers, the most important site characteristic is topography.[16] Courses can be designed for a wide range of topographical conditions, as long as there exists a combination of sloping and flat areas, where tees, greens, and fairways can be fitted to the contours. Steep, continu-

At Gainey Ranch, the developers transformed a flat, barren site into a lush oasis.

ous grades can make a site unsuitable for golf, but if flatter terraces are present or can be graded, the site can be made workable, although this kind of grading can be quite expensive. Steeper slopes will, however, generally increase the acreage required for a course development.

Architects typically begin laying out a course by examining the existing contours for appropriate locations for tees and greens. Nearly as important are suitable fairway landing areas, where a properly hit shot will come to rest without rolling out of bounds or into the rough. The best holes will drop in elevation from tee to landing area and from landing area to green. Such easy visibility for the golfer will result in faster, more enjoyable play.

Relatively flat sites, particularly in areas of high rainfall or shallow water tables (or on floodplains), may be poorly drained, which can lead to maintenance headaches and interruptions in the use of the course. Flat sites may also offer little interest to the golfer, although this limitation may be at least partially overcome by carefully designed individual holes. Because most golf courses include excavated lakes and ponds to serve as hazards

and irrigation reservoirs, the dug material is often suitable as fill to create topographic relief.

A site's topography is also critical in relation to associated real estate. Most often, building sites with the most expansive views of the golf course are the most valuable. A course along a ridge top, for example, with housing sites down the slope, would not impart as much value to those lots as a course in a bowl-like depression or a valley floor, directly visible from the housing. In addition to the gradient or steepness of the slopes, orientation can also affect a course. A long, narrow site oriented northwest and southeast, for example, will mean that holes will be laid out facing the morning or afternoon sun, which can make play difficult. For individual holes, an orientation north and south is best.

Drainage. Slope, of course, is inexorably linked to drainage, another common site limitation. Various types of land not usable for development, such as wetlands, floodplains, drainage channels, and dry streambeds, can make suitable golf course sites. At Scottsdale, Arizona's Gainey Ranch, one of the nine-hole circuits has been dubbed the Arroyo Course, after the seasonally dry watercourses that lace its fairways. Similarly, the course at Stuart, Florida's Harbour Ridge is skillfully integrated among wetlands, not only to make more efficient use of the site but also to add tremendous visual character.

In each of these cases, however, course construction costs have been proportionately higher. Among the features required in wet areas are crowned fairways that shed runoff, drainage swales, and costly drainage structures such as headwalls, drop inlets, and subsurface tile systems.[17]

Inadequate attention to drainage, however, can cost a developer even more, especially in the long run. Chronically wet conditions will reduce the rounds played on the course, with a corresponding drop in revenues, and will make the course less enjoyable to play and more expensive to maintain.

Vegetation. Vegetation ranks second only to slope in its influence on overall site character. Courses can be built on heavily wooded sites as well as on land that has been cleared or that otherwise does not support woody vegetation, such as in the desert. Each site type presents certain advantages and drawbacks.[18]

A wooded site, when fairways are cleared and the course established, can yield the impression of age and maturity in a comparatively short time. Moreover, fairways can be separated by existing vegetation, enhancing the course's safety and playability. Wooded areas between fairways can also serve as locations for other recreational uses, such as walking, cross-country skiing, or bicycling. The principal disadvantage of a heavily wooded course is the high cost of clearing land and, in some areas, of disposing of the cleared material. In settled areas, substantial clearing can sometimes incite community opposition to a golf course project. Often, however, clearing and course development can help increase an area's ecological diversity. While it is true that insensitive course management, including excessive use of chemical herbicides or fertilizers, can adversely affect the environment, more typically a course can be environmentally beneficial. Clearing

Trees help buffer patio homes from the golf course at PGA National.

PGA National

42

operations, for example, can create edges between open and wooded areas, where opportunities for wildlife habitat are greatest. Moreover, a course can help ensure the subsequent preservation of the wildlife habitat.

Abandoned farmland, already cleared but sometimes infertile from agricultural operations, is popular for golf course sites in growing areas. The advantages of a cleared site are that site preparation costs are lower and that potential community opposition is minimized—although a developer may be opposed by those who favor the look of fallow fields over a manicured course. While the costs of clearing will be lower, the savings will be at least partially offset by higher landscaping costs. In addition, for several years such a course will look raw and new compared to a course blessed by larger, mature trees.

Soils. Soil conditions on a candidate site will also affect golf course feasibility.[19] A key ingredient of a course, after all, is vigorous, healthy turf that can be maintained at a reasonable cost. Well-drained, sandy loam soils are most conducive to course construction and maintenance. Alluvial soils in coastal areas, similar to those found on ancient Scottish linksland, can make for particularly cost-effective development. Easy-to-work soils can help minimize costs for earth-moving and stockpiling, drainage structures, and irrigation systems. Peat and muck soils, unstable and high in organic material, on the other hand, can severely constrain development. Clay soils can also be problematic if percolation rates are insufficient to provide adequate drainage, a deficiency that will lead to turf problems and higher maintenance costs. High percolation rates, on the other hand, can increase irrigation and fertilization needs. Clay soils can, however, make construction of lakes and ponds much easier and less costly.

Rocky soils can support course development, but usually such a course will be more expensive to develop. Large areas of ledge rock can be particularly troublesome, often requiring blasting and importation of adequate fill. (Rock outcroppings and boulders can also present unusual design opportunities.) Smaller rocks found throughout the soil will often require removal and disposal, although they can often be used on-site. If a site contains gravel beds, this material must be covered with an adequate layer of topsoil to support turf. It is axiomatic in golf course development that there can never be too much topsoil. Developers will wisely go to great lengths to conserve the existing topsoil on a prospective course site.

Water. For today's golf courses, an adequate supply of water for irrigation constitutes an absolutely critical requirement. A regulation 18-hole course will need a water supply of between 1.5 and 3.5 million gallons per week, depending on the amount and type of turf, the irrigation system, and the climate.[20] Courses can be designed to minimize water consumption. In hotter, drier climates, where golf is often an important recreational activity, water needs can rise dramatically. At Scottsdale's Gainey Ranch, a wastewater treatment plant has been designed to provide up to 1.7 million gallons per day of treated effluent to irrigate 27 holes of golf and a small public park.[21]

Any potential water source should also be examined for its quality. The most important qualitative limitation is the amount of soluble salts. A supply with a concentration of soluble salts greater than 2,000 parts per million will be inadequate to support most grasses.[22]

Water for irrigating a golf course can come from a variety of sources, including wells, existing watercourses, built or natural lakes, or canals. Treated wastewater offers an increasingly acceptable source. In some areas, where course development would otherwise be precluded, irrigation water may also be purchased, although this solution may be quite costly.

Many Florida developers have taken great care to mitigate the impact of golf course development on adjacent wetlands—as shown here at Bonita Bay.

Figure 3-3
SOURCE OF GOLF FACILITY IRRIGATION WATER BY REGION AND PERCENT

Source	North-east	North Central	South	West	Nation
Lakes and streams	55.5%	41.0%	46.6%	32.1%	44.2%
Wells	21.4	39.3	32.6	38.4	33.7
Local potable water	19.6	16.4	12.0	21.3	16.6
Effluent water	2.6	1.7	7.9	7.2	4.6
No irrigation	0.5%	1.6%	0.9%	1.0%	1.0%
No. reporting	457	815	669	368	2,309

Source: National Golf Foundation/Golf Course Superintendents Association of America, *Golf Course Maintenance Report: 1985 Biennial Review* (North Palm Beach, Fla.: National Golf Foundation, 1985), p. 8.

Dug wells, which are the most common source of irrigation water, are also the oldest: by the late 1800s, each of the greens at St. Andrews Old Course boasted its own well.[23] Today, well water is most commonly routed into one or more reservoirs, which are usually carefully integrated into the course design. These artificial ponds and lakes serve as water hazards and, significantly for the proper operation of an irrigation system, help to settle out suspended solids.

Similarly, streams and rivers are often tapped by using a bypass pond adjacent to the existing watercourse. Water is fed or pumped from the stream or river into the pond, where it flows into the irrigation system.[24] The limiting factor in this type of arrangement is the period of lowest flows in the stream's watershed. These dry periods may be supplemented, however, by a well system.

A lake's suitability as a water source depends primarily on the vertical difference between the mean elevation of its surface and the highest point on the golf course. Pumping large amounts of water long distances can be extremely costly.

In some areas, existing canal networks provide the primary water source for a variety of uses. For golf courses, these supplies may be suitable as a backup. Southeast Florida, for example, is laced by a series of canals dating from 1881. Used to drain wetlands, the water level of these canals is approximately equal to that of the water table. Hence, many developers prefer to use a well system as an irrigation source. At Harbour Ridge, near Florida's east coast, a nearby canal serves in conjunction with wells and treated effluent as a backup water source for the project's 36 golf holes.

In many cases, including Harbour Ridge, one limitation of effluent is that it is available only in small quantities until a project approaches buildout and becomes occupied. In a project's early stages, an interim source may be required. At Gainey Ranch, the developer circumvented this constraint by relying on influent from Scottsdale's municipal sewage collection system.

The project, even though it had no on-site producers of wastewater, was thereby assured a steady supply of wastewater ready for treatment and use for irrigation. The solution was also politically expedient: it reduced the load on the city's municipal treatment plant by 1.2 million gallons per day.

Use of treated effluent for irrigation may also affect the placement of housing units. Some communities require a minimum setback distance between residences and the irrigated turf. If improperly designed, treated effluent storage ponds may also foster unsightly algae blooms.

It is difficult to overstate the importance of an adequate water supply. The relative availability of irrigation water may indeed pose one of the major future hurdles to golf course development from the standpoint of public policy and development regulation, which is discussed in greater detail later in this chapter.

The Market for Golf

Any developer considering the feasibility of a golf project should review a wide range of market variables, from employment and income data to recreational preferences. Moreover, the analysis should incorporate information at several different levels of specificity. While local ratios of golf holes per capita, for example, are useful, similar data for the nation as a whole and for selected regions are needed to put the local data into a larger context.[25] Nearly every category of market information should be examined at such multiple levels, usually with a closer look and a finer grain of data as one focuses on a candidate site's immediate area.

Working backward in scale from information on national golfing trends, such as those presented earlier in this chapter, a developer will typically examine trends in different regions of the country on the way to considering statewide patterns, intrastate or metropolitan areas, local communities, and finally

The water reclamation plant at Gainey Ranch represented a considerable upfront investment for the developer, but quickly bolstered the credibility and overall viability of the project.

the primary trade area anticipated for the project. From a developer's perspective, of course, local supply-and-demand information is the most compelling data for a feasibility analysis. At the same time, however, the perceptive analyst may find nonlocal data extremely useful for identifying important trends or highlighting unforeseen opportunities.

Golfing Demand. The most immediate hurdle in determining the market feasibility for a golf course is determining the boundaries of the primary market area. This process requires at least a cursory examination of the project concept in view of national and regional golfing trends. Most likely, the expected market area boundaries will be redrawn several times on the way to a "go" or "no go" decision. In a real estate venture, this determination may of course remain subordinate to the marketing concept for the entire project. In such cases, it is often simply assumed that the targeted market for real estate will

also demand a golf course. Sometimes this market will be quite distant from the project location, as in resort/second-home developments and retirement communities. In these projects, national golfing market data may take on additional importance. In many instances, however, local trade-area characteristics will provide the most valuable insight. An analysis should at least examine local population patterns, age distribution, income levels, and recreational preferences.

Golf demand characteristics can vary widely by region.

45

An often cited rule-of-thumb standard for golf courses is that between 20,000 and 30,000 people will support a single regulation 18-hole course, on average.[26] This ratio assumes that about 8 percent of the population plays golf at least occasionally. That works out to about 2,000 golfers per course. According to the National Golf Foundation (NGF), the nationwide average population per 18 holes is approximately 23,000.

Averages, however, can be deceiving. On a statewide basis, the ratio of population per course ranges from a low of 11,624 to 1 in North Dakota to a whopping 155,750 to 1 in the District of Columbia. Excluding the District and Alaska, the most golf-barren state is Louisiana, with nearly 42,000 residents per 18 holes. Regionally, the South offers the fewest golf courses per capita (when the Alaska figures are discounted for the Pacific region). Somewhat surprisingly, given the short playing season, the upper Midwest states boast the most plentiful supply of courses.[27]

Rules of thumb, of course, are made to be broken, and the ratio of golf courses to population is no exception. Golf play is strongly related to climate. In areas where the weather is temperate for a substantial portion of the year, one can expect to find more than the average number of golfers. In these areas, according to representatives of the real estate appraisal industry, a population as small as 10,000 can support a regulation course.[28] In favored resort or retirement areas, where the weather is good and residents enjoy a larger-than-average amount of available leisure time, the ratio can drop to as low as 2,500 to 1.

Other useful statistics are the number of rounds played nationally and by region. In 1983, the NGF estimated that 17.8 million golfers played about 434,000,000 rounds of golf, or more than 24 rounds per golfer per year.[29] In 1985, the NGF classified about 25 percent of all participants in the sport as "avid" golfers, or those who play more than 25 times annually. Figure 3-4 summarizes characteristics of these golfers as compared to a sample of all golfers.

Figure 3-4
DEMOGRAPHIC CHARACTERISTICS OF GOLFERS, 1985

		Avid Golfers[1] %	All Other Past Year %	Infrequent Golfers[2] %	All Other Past Year[3] %
Sex:	Male	79	77	74	80
	Female	21	23	26	20
Age:	Under 20	7	13	11	11
	20–29	13	28	28	24
	30–49	32	38	46	34
	50 and over	48	21	15	31
Region:	Northeast	19	23	21	22
	North Central	34	38	41	36
	South	26	21	20	23
	West	21	18	18	19
Income:	Under $20K	20	24	29	21
	$20K–$40K	41	44	45	43
	$40K and over	39	32	26	36
Share of rounds at course type:	Municipal	26	28	24	27
	Private	35	19	21	31
	Daily Fee	39	53	55	42
Average strokes over par:		19.4	26.3	29.6	23.1

[1]Those players playing 25 or more times during the past 12 months.
[2]Those golfers playing once or twice during the past 12 months.
[3]Those golfers playing from 3 to 24 times during the past 12 months.

Source: National Golf Foundation, *Golf Participation in the United States 1985* (North Palm Beach, Fla.: National Golf Foundation, 1986), p. 19.

Although these national data can provide a valuable starting point, a well-informed feasibility decision depends upon a clear understanding of the status and dynamics of the local community or the applicable resort market. A developer should examine employment growth and decline as indicators of overall economic patterns. Similarly, building permit data over several years can be useful indicators of growth. The diversity of the local economy is also important, as is the composition of major employers. Together, these two factors can greatly influence the amount of leisure time available to residents. And leisure time, because of the time-consuming nature of golf, can be a major determinant in demand.

Age and income are key demographic variables in assessing the local market. Although golf is played across a relatively wide age spectrum, golfers between the ages of 19 and 64 account for about three out of every four rounds played nationally. Among avid golfers, nearly 50 percent are over age 50; 80 percent are over age 30. Although sex is a less important variable than one might expect, especially in private clubs, where women may account for nearly half of rounds played, women do tend to start playing golf later in life than men. On public courses, men outnumber women both in absolute numbers and in rounds played. According to the NGF's 1985 survey, nationwide incidence of participation was about four times greater for males than for females.[30]

According to the NGF's 1983 survey, the annual household income for private-club golfers averaged about $44,5000, or roughly double that of the nation as a whole. For golfers on public courses, the figure was about $10,000 lower. As might be expected, household income is strongly correlated to education levels. Golfers, on the whole, are better educated than the average American.

The Vintage Club

Desert courses are often most expensive to maintain during the off-season.

Since climate can greatly influence a course's feasibility, a prospective developer should include a survey of average temperatures during various seasons, wind patterns, and average number of days with rain and snow to estimate the expected length of the local golf season. Season length will affect both the revenue side and the cost side of the feasibility equation. While a southern course may accommodate more than twice as many rounds per year as its northern counterpart, the northern course will incur sharply lower expenses for maintenance and operations in the cold season. The southern course, although it, too, will experience an off-season, will continue to have relatively high costs for maintenance year-round. In the Palm Springs desert, for example, the greatest need for costly irrigation occurs in the off-season.

For a course expected to generate players from a local area, a critical step in the feasibility process will be defining the boundaries of the primary trade area—that area from which the course will draw the majority of players. The greatest influences on these boundaries are time and distance. According to one study, golfers travel a mean distance of about four miles to their "home" courses, although this figure will likely be higher in the West or where golf courses are in short supply.[31] Although acceptable travel times and distances will vary tremendously based on local conditions, competing courses, and many other factors, a common estimate presumes a 15-minute journey to play golf. The type of course, however, will also influence this factor. Players will seek out a high-quality course, and tend to avoid a marginal layout even if it is located next door.

ST. ANDREW'S: A PROTOTYPE FOR SAVING OLDER GOLF COURSES

Like many older golf clubs in the United States, the St. Andrew's Golf Club, established in 1888 in Westchester County, New York, could only look enviously at newer courses, where most improvements were financed as part of major real estate ventures, and where an associated group of property owners had a stake in the golf course. However, St. Andrew's assets of land, location, and heritage finally suggested a way to solve the club's need for over $5 million in capital improvements and interim operating deficits. Why not redevelop St. Andrew's into a modern residential golf community and strengthen the traditional character of the club in the process?

For the last seven years, the St. Andrew's Golf Club has been involved in a $100 million development strategy to rebuild its golf facilities in conjunction with the construction of 209 luxury townhomes.

By the mid-1970s, St. Andrew's was facing serious questions about its future. Oriented toward male membership, the club had incorporated no family facilities. Membership had declined gradually from 275 to 125. The facilities and infrastructure were old, and enormous maintenance requirements could no longer be deferred.

By 1979, unable to finance improvements and realizing that immediate action must be taken, St. Andrew's members decided that, first and foremost, they would preserve the club. Instead of selling the land to the highest bidder, they sought a development organization that would given them a "new" club as a "fee" for adding a real estate component to the property.

The club's president secured for the club options on an adjoining 26 acres of land that could be assembled with the club parcel. This acreage, together with the existing zoning—which permitted single-family lots of 30,000 square feet—and the club's willingness to negotiate, placed St. Andrew's in a strong position to deal. Also reinforcing was the fact that the town wanted to keep the club operating; the golf course was an important part of its stock of open space. The club invited developers to submit proposals, from which was chosen the proposal by Jack Nicklaus and Associates, a joint venture of the Jack Nicklaus organization and Tulsa-based FRACORP, Inc. (now called Realvest, Inc.). The Nicklaus name and organization were overwhelming factors in the selection.

The club sold the property to Jack Nicklaus and Associates for $1, in return for $5 million of improvements on the course and the clubhouse, and for absorbing the operating deficits until the club returned to full membership.

The new owner also agreed to cover the club's standing deficits of $120,000. The St. Andrew's Golf Club would stay intact, and would lease back from the new owners the use of the golf course and related facilities for 99 years (for a total cost of $2). The developer would control the new development phase on prearranged terms with the club. Nicklaus and Associates would provide the capital necessary to complete the deal and would buy the abutting 26 acres held on option. To bridge the remaining financing, Chemical Bank agreed to provide a construction loan.

Development was planned around the construction of townhomes and the redevelopment of the golf course and related facilities. The final plan was approved in April 1981, six months after first being submitted. The town had opted to grant PUDs on a site-by-site basis, and St. Andrew's was the first applicant to go through the new process. A covenant with the town keeps the open land "forever green," says project manager Stuart Polly. "The golf course, owned by St. Andrew's homeowners and subject to the lease to the club, cannot be developed."

The two- and three-story townhomes, designed by architect Robert A. M. Stern, are styled after the Dutch colonial design of the historic St. Andrew's clubhouse. Eight basic layouts, ranging in size from 2,500 to 4,700 square feet, give the residences a relaxed, rambling, detached style, an image of suburban architecture familiar to many potential buyers.

The townhome development will have its own recreational center, designed around a restored 4,000-square-foot summer cottage built by Andrew Carnegie in the 1880s. It will encompass a swimming pool, an exercise facility with saunas and a hot tub, five tennis courts, two paddle tennis courts, and social rooms. In addition, every homeowner has the right to join the St. Andrew's Golf Club.

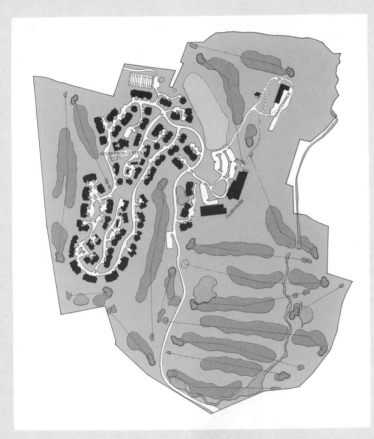

Over $1 million is being spent on restoring the 5,000-square-foot clubhouse to its original style. Of a total of $5 million allocated toward club improvements, $1 million was spent to cover deficits incurred in operating the club during the six-year period of development.

Under the terms of the 99-year lease, the golf club has no mortgage or carried-over deficits. Membership is made up of the added residents and of those club members who have remained during the club's restoration. Total membership is limited to 350, although 275 is considered the number that will make the club self-sustaining. In 1979, the Nicklaus management company contracted to operate the club for 20 years.

Undoubtedly, hundreds of other established golf clubs face problems similar to those at St. Andrew's. They may lack the combined attractions of St. Andrew's, or they may have to contend with zoning problems, but if they have the right resources, they may benefit from incorporating a well-planned real estate development. Older golf courses not only have special environmental attributes, but also often occupy close-in locations in prime neighborhoods—giving them an added advantage for potential development.

A longer version of this text appeared as an article in the December 1983 issue of Urban Land.

The original St. Andrew's course was only 6,000 yards long and lacked modern infrastructure. It was lengthened to 6,500 yards and redesigned in 1983 at a cost of $3 million, approximately what building a new course would have cost. The redesigned course and facilities have been carefully restored to their original turn-of-the-century Scottish style, with links and punchbowl greens.

Noting that the original creek had been straightened and channeled, Nicklaus decided to reopen it and allow it to follow its former bed, wandering among the fairways and forming several new ponds. So that sufficient water would be available for the creek and pond systems, even during dry spells, a separate well and pump were installed at an approximate cost of $100,000.

Clearly, an assessment of local demand cannot be made like a snapshot, a portrait of local economics and demographic conditions frozen at one point. Such an analysis should be based on a forecast of likely future conditions, and should take into account local economic development plans and programs, projections of new industry, highways, or other infrastructure; and overall growth patterns.

Supply Factors: Examining the Competition. The existing golf courses in a region should be critically examined both on their own merits and in view of demand patterns. Simply counting the number of existing holes and dividing that figure into the local population is not particularly useful in determining a future course's feasibility. A comprehensive survey of existing facilities should be supported by a qualitative evaluation of the balance of supply and demand. A prospective developer may discover, for example, that private clubs are suffering because of competing high-quality public courses, or that a

shortage exists of par 3 and executive courses. Similarly, demographic patterns and interviews may reveal an unmet demand for high-quality membership clubs, or patterns of rounds played may indicate that difficult courses are suffering from underplay.

Starting at the metropolitan or subregional level, a feasibility study should include a review of the growth of golf facilities over time and the relationship between facility growth and population expansion. An inventory of existing and planned facilities might include, in addition to the distribution of facilities by size and type, aggregate data on rounds played by course type and average costs by type (private, public, daily fees), including green fees, cart rental, dues, and so on. Course capacity figures by type and current percentage of course capacity used will also be useful. Such an array of data will yield a preliminary indication of the overall characteristics and performance of the area's courses. From this information a developer might determine, for example, that alternatives to regulation 18-hole courses are in great demand.

Further, a developer should closely examine individual facilities, particularly those in the primary trade area or those that cater to the expected target market. A preliminary list of necessary data might include each course's type, length, age, quality or rating, and supporting facilities. Membership or player profiles should also be assembled, and should include membership size, the various membership categories, and costs for each type. The course capacity should be examined in view of rounds played over the last several years. Also useful is operational information, such as staff size by season, waiting times or type of reservation system, and additional services and facilities offered (practice range, pro shop, tennis or other club sports, and so on). Finally, whether or not expansions, improvements, or modifications are planned will give a prospective developer clues to the future supply.

Plans, Policies, and Politics

Like any development project, a resort or residential community that contains a golf course will be subject to the influence of the public interest as it is expressed through a variety of plans, policies, and development regulations. The extent to which these considerations affect a project's feasibility should be identified as early as possible. In many areas, the inclusion of a golf course in a real estate project will neither increase nor decrease the rigors of development regulation. In other locations, however, the facility will have a major effect on the approval process, an effect that can be either positive or negative.

Charlan, Brock, and Young Associates

A comprehensive review of the competition will include a look at support facilities and services.

Traditionally, golf courses have been viewed as rather benign, or even desirable, uses by most communities. After all, their physical characteristics are not unlike those of large parks. The golf course development literature often refers to a course's community benefits, implying that a course will help grease an otherwise squeaky regulatory wheel.[32] In some locations, a course may indeed help speed a project through the approval process, especially if it will be open to the public and demand for public courses is high. Sometimes communities will say as much in the recreation component of their comprehensive plans.

In other places, courses are increasingly suspect, often for rather spurious reasons. In its early manifestations in the United States, golf was a notoriously elitist game. In its Scottish origins, however, and its more recent boom in popularity, the game has displayed a broadly democratic appeal. Nevertheless, an elitist image continues to haunt the game. This image is frequently the usually unstated source of opposition to course development plans. As golf course architect Robert Trent Jones, Jr., has said, "golf courses are an easy 'hit' politically because of an outdated elitist image."[33]

On the local level, the developer of a golf course project will face hurdles not unlike those of any other residential project: zoning, subdivision, and building permit regulations. Often, because courses constitute open space that may be owned or managed by a homeowners' association, golf projects will be appropriate for development under planned unit development ordinances. A course developer may also benefit from an investigation of local property assessment and taxation practices; some communities have established programs that tax golf courses at lower open-space assessed values.

Objections to course development may also be made on environmental grounds. Clearing operations on wooded sites and fill operations in wetlands are particularly visible impacts. Courses may also be perceived as aggravating erosion or sedimentation problems or, through the use of pesticides and fertilizers, as posing a threat to water quality.

The principal objection to golf courses from an environmental standpoint, however, is the use of water for course irrigation. Although the economics and politics of water use, especially in arid regions, are highly complex, courses are often viewed as a relatively low priority when it comes to allocating water resources. Although such concern may be only localized, increasingly state legislatures and regulatory agencies are also questioning irrigation-intensive residential development. In Arizona, for example, legislation greatly restricts land development without an assured water supply. This measure has in many instances substantially increased the costs of building a golf course.

Other regulatory constraints may also increase the costs of development. Pesticides and fertilizers, for example, often require special storage measures under Environmental Protection Agency rules, which may affect the design of a maintenance facility.

At the feasibility stage, this planning, policy, and regulatory context should be evaluated in view of the ideal project concept and the trade-offs or compromises that will be acceptable to ensure government approval. The decision to build a private club as opposed to a daily fee facility may, for example, engender additional community opposition, while special environmental impact mitigation measures may raise development costs. As in most development projects, the primary cost of regulation is time. Unanticipated delay as a result of a zoning battle or permit process may result in an ill-timed release of the project to the market, especially in seasonal markets, and will at the least mean higher carrying costs for the developer. An early reconnaissance of a prospective project's accord with public policies can help avoid such consequences.

GOLF COURSE DESIGN AND PLANNING

A golf course can play a number of important roles in a real estate development project. The relative significance of each role is something the developer must determine at the outset, based on the overall project concept and the preliminary results of the feasibility study. The relative prominence of each role may vary over the life of the project; marketing and image may be most important early on, while playability and ease of maintenance may become the key factors as the project approaches buildout. Nevertheless, a prospective developer should enter the golf course design and planning process with a clear understanding of the course's strategic role within the overall project.

Development Strategy: The Role of the Golf Course

Three prominent golf course objectives are to add value to real estate, to enhance a project's image and accelerate the marketing period, and to provide a quality, user-oriented recreational facility. Each objective carries different implications for a wide range of factors in course development: the course layout, the design of individual holes, the phasing of the construction, maintenance, management, and so on. Many projects, of course, will have multiple objectives, or will seek a balance between, for instance, marketing appeal and long-term real estate value. Other objectives will often be complementary; for the avid golfer, a highly playable course will be a big marketing plus.

Resort courses, as here at Loews Ventana Canyon Resort, are designed to be both memorable and challenging.

Course Design and Community Development

The favored configuration for golf courses in the United States has evolved simultaneously with the relationship between golf and real estate. The classic courses of the first half of this century were essentially core courses, built on a quarter section (160 acres) of land. These were the descendants of both coastal Scottish courses and inland English layouts. Because they existed only for the game of golf, the design of these early courses was not compromised by the demands of real estate value.

Later, as developers began to exploit the economic advantage that a golf course could lend to a real estate project, the prototype shifted to a spread-out course, where single or double fairways offered choice housing sites. Taken to their extreme, many of these layouts paid scant attention to the needs of golf. Value added to land often resulted at the golfer's expense. These layouts were also costly to construct and to maintain, with infrastructure expenses particularly high due to the dispersed nature of the course.

Over the last 15 years or so, the relationship between golf and real estate has matured to the point that many recent designs have struck a mutually supportive balance, where both the efficiency of land use and the playability of the course are emphasized. As a result, contemporary courses are more likely to exhibit characteristics of both a core course and a single- or double-fairway layout. Both housing sites and the fairways are likely to be more compact, making each less costly to develop and maintain. The course still creates real estate value, but not simply because of the frontage relationship; golf values are also emphasized.

Projects in which the course's primary purpose is to create real estate value are often designed to maximize the amount of fairway frontage.[34] The developer of such a project will pay strict attention to the siting of buildings to take advantage of course views. Water will often play a prominent role in the design, not just as a golf hazard but also as a scenic amenity. Where real estate values rank as the prime concern, it is unlikely that the most valuable land, such as an oceanfront, will be devoted to golf.

A course designed primarily to create a memorable image for a residential or resort project will typically be built early, prior to the construction of hotels or housing. For marketing purposes, these courses tend to be designed to support tournament play and will thus be longer and more difficult than the average course. The designer will take advantage of spectacular site features to create memorable, photogenic holes. Every resort course should have at least one "signature" hole. Such an image-conscious course is likely to be substantially more expensive than the average, both to build and to maintain.

In residential communities a golf course may constitute an important element of the project because residents or club members like to play the game. A course designed primarily to appeal to the average player will emphasize playability and the integrity of the course. Although virtually every real estate project golf course will take advantage of some fairway frontage, in a course designed for high-quality, regular play this relationship is less likely to be emphasized. This type of course, when properly designed and constructed, will probably be less expensive than most resort courses. If the course will eventually be owned by project residents, it may be designed with closer attention to lowering maintenance requirements and costs. Since its image-building role is less important, such a course might be built in phases, or may be constructed concurrently with housing products.

Clearly, in any golf course development, the greatest value will be obtained when the course's design characteristics coincide with the market's needs. Significantly, however, the "market" refers not only to golfers, but also to potential real estate buyers or resort guests who may be attracted by the course.

Strategic hole design by golf course architect Tom Fazio. Note the widely varying shot values with differing tee positions.

Tony Roberts, Pearson, McGuire Associates

Basic Golf Hole Styles

Unlike most other games or sports, golf is not played on a standardized field. Indeed, much of golf's attraction is due to this characteristic. Every course is truly an individual, a product of a complex mix of site conditions, weather patterns, local customs, and patterns of play that cannot be fully duplicated elsewhere.

Although the concept of par does much to ensure some comparability of play over a myriad of courses, par values can also be misleading, especially when presented as simply a function of hole length. Perhaps a better, although less precise, criterion for course quality is the term "shot values," which is often used by golf course architects to describe the degree to which a course fairly challenges a golfer. Shot values reflect both the difficulty of the shots required and the relative penalty or reward that results from either a well-played or an errant shot.

Individual golf holes can also be described or evaluated in terms of "style." The three broad categories of hole style that have developed since the days of St. Andrews are penal, strategic, and heroic. These styles can best be differentiated on the basis of the type, placement, and number of hazards.[35]

Penal golf holes characterized the early courses both in the British Isles and in the United States.[36] This type of hole requires play directly across hazards: sand, water, rough, woods, or a combination of potential hazards. Difficult and often frustrating for the average player, penal holes require long, accurate tee shots over hazards to a fairly small landing area. Greens on such holes are often small islands protected by water traps or hidden

from view. Almost every errant shot is severely penalized, resulting in slower play for all but expert golfers. For this reason, penal holes are generally not suitable for a development course, except in the case of a course designed for professional tournaments.

The *strategic* style of golf hole provides alternative routes to a green, with each route offering a commensurate degree of risk and reward. In the United States, the strategic school represents a mid-20th-century refinement in course design pioneered by Robert Trent Jones, Sr. The roots of strategic design, however, can be traced

A heroic hole, number four at Lake Nona, Orlando, Florida. A considerable gamble, if successful, will mean a big payoff. If unsuccessful, however, the loss can be even greater.

Tony Roberts, Pearson, McGuire Associates

back to modifications made to the Old Course at St. Andrews around 1848; increasing play on the venerable course led to widened fairways and larger greens, which, intentionally or not, introduced the element of strategy. With the wider fairways, a player could, instead of carrying every hazard, opt for a longer, but safer, route to the green. Usually, hazards are located so that a golfer who takes a risk with a tee shot will be rewarded with an easier shot to the green. A safer path will typically cost the golfer a stroke or two, but errant shots will not be severely punished. Strategic holes appeal to a wide variety of players. Since they locate the hazards to challenge more accomplished golfers while offering what Robert Trent Jones, Jr., calls a "bail-out" position for duffers, they are particularly suitable for most development courses.

Heroic golf holes blend the characteristics of the penal and strategic schools. Designed mostly for long hitters, these holes also offer the golfer a choice of routes. Unlike the strategic hole, however, the costs of failure are high. Heroic holes often involve a water carry from the tee or to the green. The truly "heroic" strategy, if successful, will mean a substantial reward—usually in the form of a birdie or eagle opportunity. An unsuccessful heroic attempt will cost more than a stroke or two, however.

Today, most courses are designed with predominantly strategic holes with a few heroic holes added, usually around water features. The course architect aims to find a mix of holes that is challenging without being frustrating or boring. For most real estate-related courses, the holes must provide this comfortable challenge at many ability levels. Otherwise, a developer would be unnecessarily limiting the number of potential club members, real estate purchasers, or resort guests. The properly designed combination of holes will offer both flexibility and fairness.

Matching Course Characteristics to the Market

Beyond basic hole styles, a number of other design criteria will be governed by a course's intended market. The market, of course, will be determined by the nature of the project: a community composed of detached, single-family, primary homes will demand different course attributes than will a resort community. Among the important market considerations are the relationship within the project between golf and real estate, the ability levels and diversity of the anticipated players, the overall level of demand for the course, and the frequency of play by project residents or club members.

As discussed briefly in this chapter's opening sections, the type of development will largely determine the optimum course layout. Because one of the primary objectives of a course in a primary-home development is to create value for building sites, such a course is likely to be designed with single fairways (assuming the site permits them) in order to create maximum fairway frontage. At the other extreme, the basic purpose of many resort courses is to attract guests, many of whom will be serious and accomplished players. The integrity of the course may therefore be more important than adding value to sites for housing. A resort course, then, is more likely to be designed as a core layout or with parallel fairways, with special attention to maintaining high quality, creating a special character and image.

Between these relative opposites, of course, lie any number of hybrids and variations. Conceivably, a project could contain primary residences, second homes, a resort hotel and conference center, and investor-owned timeshare units. As the principal amenity, a golf course would thus need to cater to an enormously wide range of players. In such a case, perhaps the best solution would be to develop multiple golf courses, such as at PGA National, that each cater to a different group of users. With a more narrow spectrum of golfers as a project's market, however, a single course can be designed to accommodate a fairly wide range of ability levels.

One means of accomplishing such flexibility is to incorporate long, multiple-position tees that can offer a variety of playing positions. Shot distance is the category of golf performance that most often separates the skilled golfer from the average player, and multiple tee positions offer perhaps the most efficient way to ensure playability for a range of skills. Most modern courses include three or four sets of tees, usually on a carefully manicured surface of about 4,000 to 8,000 square feet. On courses that are played repeatedly by the same golfers, additional variety can be contributed by designing more than one tee area on some holes. These multiple tees can also make par 3 layouts and nine-hole courses much more interesting.[37]

Golf courses associated with real estate projects should be both fair and flexible.

Mariner Sands

Courses oriented to older players can be shorter, flatter, and easier to play than the average regulation course.

Golf courses that are played regularly by the same group of users, such as the members of a private club or the residents of a primary-home community, should be designed to help sustain interest. In most courses, for example, visibility of the green from the tee and of all hazards is maintained to ensure fairness. In a frequently played course, visibility is a less important criterion, because hidden hazards and less predictable shot sequences will become more familiar over time. At resorts and on other courses that are played infrequently, such unpredictability may be considered unfair.

Similarly, a regularly played course might incorporate larger greens that permit a greater variety of pin positions, or more contoured greens that make putting trickier. On courses that experience a high level of demand, however, tricked-up greens and hidden hazards will slow down play, resulting in congestion and long waiting periods.

Because the characteristics of the various golf markets are fairly predictable, the following generalizations can be made about course design and community development. In a primary-home community, a developer should aim to create a course that will sustain the interest of project residents and club members over a relatively long period. Because there is likely to be a large number of golfers, it should be designed to encourage fairly speedy play. Fairways should thus be relatively generous in width, from 150 feet to more than 200 feet. With several sets of tees to accommodate skilled play as well as heavy play by women, juniors, and other shorter hitters, a course can play from about 5,600 to 7,000 yards long, depending on particular site conditions.[38] Players should be able to use every club in their bags. Greens should be relatively spacious. Because this type of course is likely to be eventually owned and maintained by its members, maintenance costs should probably be a key concern.

Courses that cater to older players, as in a retirement or semiretirement community, can be shorter, flatter, and easier to play than the average regulation course, but should still offer challenging golf through strong shot values.[39] Depending on the site, a suitable alternative to a standard regulation course is a par 70 course that ranges from 5,800 to 6,400 yards long, depending on which tees are played. These courses will often offer four sets of tees and fairways that average more than 180 feet in width.

The design of a second-home community's golf course is much like that of a primary-home community, except that it will probably be played less often by project residents. Good tee-to-green visibility, relatively smooth green surfaces, and fairly generous fairways will produce a round of golf more enjoyable for the infrequent player.

Golf resorts should offer challenging, spacious, and beautiful courses maintained in top condition. Although several successful resort courses have incorporated a single-fairway layout, a more popular and usually more appropriate configuration is the core or double-fairway course with at least 600 feet between boundaries. Most resort developers will seek to develop those building sites that offer the greatest return without compromising the course's quality. Resort courses may be played intensively by an individual player, albeit for a limited time. For this reason, they should offer a fair amount of variety, with multiple tees and fairly large greens. A challenging course is essential at a resort. But unless a resort offers several courses or is catering exclusively to expert players, the course should be designed to be both fair and flexible. If a resort has two courses, most designers agree that one course should not be substantially easier to play or less prestigious than the other. If so, golfers might shun the easier layout, even though it might be more suited to their level of play.

Basic Design Principles

Few hard-and-fast rules apply to golf course design, but most modern courses adhere to a general set of design principles developed over the last several decades. These fundamental design guidelines are not inviolate and should be modified according to the demands of a particular site or development concept.

The Routing Plan. The first and foremost course design principle is that a golfer, through the sequence of a round, should experience as wide an array of shots and holes as possible that collectively form a satisfying golfing experience. To accomplish this objective, a golf course designer usually starts by determining the basic hole sequence and relationship of each hole to other project elements such as the clubhouse, water features, housing, and so on.[40]

Typically, the clubhouse and all its associated facilities, along with the first, 10th, and 18th holes, are located first. Holes 1 and 10, as starting points for each nine-hole circuit, assume particular importance. These holes should generally be of medium-difficulty par 4 or par 5, measuring about 400 and 520 yards, respectively. One objective in the design of these opening holes is to avoid slow play off the tee and at the greens. The holes should thus be designed for maximum visibility; water, excessively narrow fairways, and multiple traps near the green should be avoided.

The rest of the holes will take shape after natural locations for tees and greens are located. For tee areas, course architects seek elevated, relatively flat areas. Greens are often located at the base of slopes, which form a natural backdrop, or near creeks, ponds, or other special features.

Figure 3-5
TEE PLACEMENT GUIDELINES

Tee	Drive	Maximum Second Shot
Gold	250 yards	225 yards
Blue	225 yards	200 yards
White	175 yards	150 yards
Red	150 yards	125 yards

Source: National Golf Foundation, 1981.

A popular sequence of par for a nine-hole series is 4–5–4–3–4–5–4–3–4, which yields a par of 36, or 72 over 18 holes. The principal advantage of this mix is that it avoids two consecutive holes of the same par. Simply adhering to this sequence, however, will hardly guarantee an adequate round of golf. The designer must also achieve a balanced distribution of length, difficulty, style, and shot values. Similarly, exceptional site conditions may make breaking the rules imperative. For example, course architects usually try to avoid ending up with consecutive par 3s or par 5s. Springfield, New Jersey's Baltusrol Golf Club, the site of five U.S. Opens, however, closes the back nine with two consecutive par 5s. Similarly, Denver's Cherry Hills Country Club, which has hosted three U.S. Opens, has a front nine with eight par 4s, and a 400-yard differential between the front and back nines. Many of the nation's finest courses exhibit similar anomalies.[41] Since these often reflect the course architect's response to special natural opportunities—a spectacular oceanfront or a stand of specimen hardwoods—they add an extra measure of character and quality.

A round should generally become progressively more challenging as golfers play their way around a course, although, as noted, a relatively easy 10th hole will help speed up play entering the back nine. A striking characteristic of many first-class courses is a strong sequence of finishing holes. As at Harbour Town Golf Links on Hilton Head Island, South Carolina, these sequences often involve heroic holes and water carries. One advantage of heroic holes late in a round is that golfers that successfully take chances can recover several strokes in match play. Water around the finishing holes will also help create a pleasant setting for the clubhouse.

Tees. As the control points for each hole, tees serve a critically important function, one that indicates to golfers the quality of the hole they are about to play. Once simply small starting areas, tees are now large, with turf often equal to that of greens. They can accommodate several starting points, in order to allow play by golfers of varying abilities.

Placement of individual tees on a large tee area is based on the average shot length for various ability levels. Professional golfers routinely make tee shots of up to 270 yards. Most country club players, on the other hand, average about 180 yards off the tee, and juniors and many women players hit the ball from 120 to 150 yards. As a result, the guidelines in Figure 3-5 may be suitable for tee placement.

A closer look at these figures, however, reveals that a tee area would need to be more than 100 yards long to accommodate these four tees. Modern tees are big, but usually not that big. It is difficult in the space of a standard tee to allow for all playing abilities. Usually, three or four sets of tees are arranged in an area about 50 to 90 yards long. Some courses, especially those with four sets of tees or that are designed for a wide range of abilities, will have tee areas up to 150 yards long. Many holes are designed so that tees work closely with sand, water, or other hazards to introduce differing levels of difficulty that are not solely a function of shot length. One strategy, for example, is to position an angled tee area in conjunction with a water hazard so that the players from the front tees have an easier time of it, but only because the water is a lateral hazard, not because the hole is that much shorter.

Tee size is also a function of the level of demand. Heavily played courses will need larger tees to avoid excessive soil compaction and turf damage. A common rule is that the golf course designer should allow 100 to 200 square feet of tee surface for every 1,000 rounds played per year. Thus, a course that expects to host 40,000 rounds annually should design tees of 4,000 to 8,000 square feet.[42] Along with undersized greens, a common symptom of an inadequate course is tees that are too small. Some holes need extra room on the tees. First and 10th holes take heavier use because of practice swings. Par 3 holes, on which the tee shot is played with an iron, are also more susceptible to wear and should thus have proportionately larger tees.

Fairways. Fairways are the playable area from the tee to the green, not including hazards, that are usually defined by rough areas on both sides. Most longer golf holes are designed so that the player hits a full tee shot. Some holes, however, require the golfer to "lay up" the tee shot, or play to a shorter distance. Landing areas on both hole types

Golf course architect Tom Fazio created a strategic hole with the dramatic use of sand at Lake Nona, Orlando, Florida.

should be broad enough and flat enough to provide a fairly predictable finish to a well-hit tee shot. A par 4 hole designed for the better player, for example, would locate the landing area about 225 yards away from the blue tee. A par 5 would add a second landing area (also called "dogleg points," even if the hole is dead straight) about 425 yards from the tee. Under most circumstances, these areas would measure about 120 to 150 feet wide. Wider fairways, up to 180 feet or more, may be more desirable if the course is played by less experienced players or if slow play is a problem. On championship courses or on shorter holes that demand unusual accuracy, landing areas may be as narrow as 100 feet.[43] A single hole can also be designed with wider fairways at a point 150 to 200 yards away from the tee to satisfy the shorter hitter, and a narrow landing area 250 to 300 yards down the fairway for the accomplished player.

On wooded sites, most holes should feature cleared areas of fairway and rough at least 175 to 200 feet wide. Rough, which is usually played as a hazard rather than as out-of-bounds, should generally get deeper as one moves away from the fairway edge. This practice, however, is hard on the duffer, who is more likely to hit deeper into the rough and less likely to escape easily. Also, if the rough plays a strategic role in the design of the hole, maintenance practices must be consistent and reliable. Although larger areas of rough can save on maintenance costs, they can also slow down play.

Numerous tee positions can make a course more flexible and adaptable. Note cart paths running the full length of this hole at The Vintage Club.

This green at Bonita Bay, although virtually flat, is guarded by an enormous bunker.

Greens. Like tees, greens can have a substantial impact on the individual golfer's perception of a course's quality. They can be simple, flat, and small, or wildly undulating, highly contoured, and a quarter-acre in size, all depending on the characteristics of the individual hole, the type of course, and many other factors. Greens are most often located downhill from the tees to ensure adequate visibility, although the greens themselves are usually elevated from the surrounding area due to construction techniques. The most desirable settings for greens are those with natural or created backdrops: a hillside or slope, a stand of mature trees, or a creek.

Most greens on today's courses range from 5,000 to 8,000 square feet. A busy course should have greens of at least 6,500 square feet.[44] Each green should be large enough to allow for four to six potential hole positions. These should be changed regularly to ensure even wear on the green's surface and to create a variety of playing positions. Green size should not be merely a function of the maintenance budget, but should also relate to the nature of the hole. A longer or more difficult approach shot should usually dictate a larger green. Conversely, a golfer hitting a short approach can be challenged by a smaller target. A large green designed to handle heavy play can also be subdivided into smaller areas by bunkers, terraces, or mounding. This technique could be used, for example, to provide both a fairly generous target for the average golfer and a challenge to get in the optimum putting position.

Greens usually slope from the back (away from the tee) to the front at a gradient of at least 2 percent. Average slopes on a green can range from 2 to 4 percent, and small areas can be as high as 20 percent. Short par 3 and relatively easy par 4 holes generally are de-signed with a more difficult putting surface. The trade-off inherent in a difficult green is slow play. Putting is the slowest aspect of golf, especially when compared to the time required to hit a chip shot onto the green.

A sloping surface not only increases the visibility of the green from the tee, it also helps to hold the golfer's approach shot on the green. Most greens will be elevated about one to three feet above the surrounding area at their front edges.

Hazards. Course architects employ a variety of features to define the strategic aspects of a golf hole. The most traditional material, sand, is usually supplemented by water, trees, and rough. Some courses also use mounds, retaining walls, or other elements as hazards. At one course in Stevens Point, Wisconsin, Robert Trent Jones, Jr., has created a beautiful hazard out of 90,000 flowers on a 150-yard par 3. Wind conditions can also be considered a hazard. The basic principle of hazards is to allow the golfer a reasonable chance of recovery. A "reasonable chance," of course, depends upon the nature of both the individual hazards and the course itself. A more challenging course can be expected to present more difficult hazards. Water is a more punitive hazard than sand. Thus, on most holes a golfer will stand a greater chance of landing in a bunker than in a lake.

Sand is a traditional part of golf, carried over in most modern courses from the seaside links of the past, where bunkers were said to have been formed by livestock huddling against the dunes for shelter from the wind. Today, sand is used when other natural hazards are absent. Sand bunkers also serve a variety of visual purposes. They help define greens and fairways and offer a white contrast to a mostly green environment. Since sand usually

stops a golf ball, bunkers are also useful for protecting adjacent areas from errant shots. As hazards, they can also serve in a development course to help direct play away from residential areas.

The most attractive sand traps, which often form the foreground in handsome photographs of spectacular golf holes, combine upward-sloping sand surfaces with heavy, overhanging turf edges. Such bunkers are often designed to resemble those on links courses. Under artificial conditions, however,

this type of trap is also the most expensive to maintain, because its edge requires hand mowing. A common compromise is to landscape less pronounced curves and slopes on a bunker built at or slightly above grade. These can be maintained more easily by riding mowers and raking machines.

In recent years, course architects have adopted another Scottish element: deep bunkers with a front slope retained by boulders, railroad ties, or other structural materials. Although these bunkers can pro-

vide some needed diversity, if overused they can become gimmicky and contrived.[45]

Sand bunkers generally measure about 1,000 to 3,000 square feet if located near a green, and slightly larger, up to 4,000 square feet, if on a fairway. Like all course elements, the design of hazards can involve major consequences for future operations. Hazards are intended to make a course challenging, but if poorly designed they can slow play and greatly increase maintenance requirements.

Although ponds, lakes, and streams do not occupy the traditional position of sand in golf's heritage, water has become an integral element of most modern courses.

Sand is an integral and traditional part of the game.

This is partly due to the fact that water bodies are now required as irrigation reservoirs, but it is equally true that water contributes perhaps more than any other single element to a course's appearance.

Water offers a useful hazard in strategic design, but it is also quite strict. A shot in the water means a penalty stroke, rather than simply a difficult shot. From an operator's perspective, however, this is not all bad. An abundance of sand and rough can greatly slow play. Water, although it offers no chance of escape, can mean faster play, and it does not have to be mowed or raked (although lakes and ponds may involve other maintenance concerns).

Trees constitute an important hazard on many courses. As the only vertical feature on most courses, they are also an integral design element. Wooded sites offer an opportunity to create a variety of enclosed and open spaces that can be used to particular advantage.

In some areas, wind will operate as a hazard, if it is of sufficient strength and is relatively predictable. Prevailing winds on oceanfront sites are a key consideration in the layout of hole sequences. Generally, course designers take care to avoid consecutive holes into the wind. As with most hazards, a variety of conditions is important to maintain, and a sequence of tailwind, headwind, and crosswind may be most desirable.

In real estate development courses, many of the fairways will have staked boundaries that mark the limits of play. Beyond the boundary will lie a buffer zone and development sites. A single-fairway layout will have boundaries on both fairway sides. A golfer landing out of bounds must take a penalty stroke and hit again from the original spot. In effect, hitting out of bounds costs two strokes. Since most average players have a tendency to slice the ball, a closer boundary on the fairway's right side (as one looks toward the green) is usually more punitive than one on the left. For this reason, fairways in relatively dense development courses can be asymmetrical.

Clubhouse and Related Facilities

To developers, clubhouses often seem like necessary evils. Indeed, the most brilliantly conceived project can easily be sunk by a costly, overblown, management-intensive clubhouse. Erling Speer, the developer of the highly successful and influential Mariner Sands development in Stuart, Florida, once said that a golf course can be an enormously profitable entity in its own right—if it can be run out of a tent.[46]

What were once fairly spartan facilities designed primarily to support the immediate needs of golfers have become highly complex and often lavish structures that must cater not only to golfers, but also to community residents engaged in a wide variety of social, athletic, and civic activities. In addition, many developers use golf clubhouses to showcase their projects, with the facility playing a prominent role in marketing efforts. A clubhouse's design can be a valuable tool to help lend a project a desired image, identity, and character. With the agglomeration of these multiple functions, clubhouses can pose complicated programming and design problems; one clubhouse architect likens their complexity to that of a hospital.[47]

The design and planning of a clubhouse carry significant implications for the management and operations of the golf course and, by extension, for the financial viability of the entire project. In many projects, course operations are heavily subsidized for the first few years as the real estate is developed and sold and as the club membership grows. The point at which the golf course breaks even can often be hastened or delayed by decisions made in the design and planning phases. While an underdesigned clubhouse can discourage potential buyers of real estate, an overly elaborate facility can require high capital costs and excessive fixed operating expenses. A developer should

Native vegetation provides a foreground for the golf course, as viewed from residences at Gainey Ranch.

60

carefully balance the resources committed to a clubhouse with the expected returns—both direct and indirect—that the facility will provide.

Clubhouses can incorporate a wide range of facilities and services and can vary tremendously in the space devoted to each element. Whereas a resort clubhouse may be comfortable with a total usable area of 4,000 square feet, an elaborate clubhouse in a primary-home community can easily approach ten times that size. The Vintage Club in Palm Desert, California, boasts an 85,000-square-foot, $25 million clubhouse to support its two golf courses and 400 members.[48] Major variables that will affect clubhouse design include:

- The overall project objectives;
- The project's ultimate size, and the expected phasing or pace toward buildout;
- Sales techniques and marketing program;
- Housing types included;
- Seasonality of use;
- Other project amenities; and
- The number, organization, and diversity of the membership or project residents.

Clearly, each of these factors can be of considerable importance in clubhouse planning, but the nature of the membership will have perhaps the greatest impact. Membership plans and programs, discussed in greater detail elsewhere in this text, must be carefully considered in clubhouse planning. For example, many second-home projects today use limited resort operations, usually offering investor-owned condominiums as guest lodging, in the project's early phases. These visitors, who are also potential real estate buyers, are entitled to use club facilities. This strategy offers one effective way to attract outsiders to

Robert Lamb Hart Planners and Architects

In many projects, clubhouses form the social and symbolic focus of the community, on a grand scale, as at Gainey Ranch . . .

the project, which in some cases may be located in a relatively remote area. As the community matures and the club membership grows, these resort operations are usually scaled back or eliminated. Nevertheless, during some periods the clubhouse will have to effectively support two distinct groups: resort visitors and project residents, who may have widely differing perceptions and needs. Project residents, especially in primary-home or semiretirement projects, will tend to view a clubhouse as the community's social nexus. Resort

visitors will be less likely to see it this way; for them, a clubhouse is basically a place to support golf. They have little use for the card rooms and dining rooms that residents often demand.

Charlan, Brock, and Young Associates

. . . or more modestly, as at Sabal Point Golf Club in Longwood, Florida.

Siting Considerations. On most courses, the most important elements are the holes themselves. The clubhouse, however, plays nearly as influential a role. For many residents or club members, the clubhouse will be the focus of the project, an attractive and comfortable place that will support a variety of activities beyond golf. Because a clubhouse can help establish a project's image early in the development process, an architecturally distinguished facility on a dramatic site can be a strong selling point.

For these reasons, clubhouses are often sited on highly visible, centrally located sites. In the popular returning-nine course layouts, the clubhouse often overlooks as many as four holes and the practice range. In warm climates, a variety of functional considerations, including the need for centralized cart and club storage, will often lead to elevated clubhouses, which tend to take greater advantage of views.

On hilly sites, clubhouses are frequently sited to overlook the entire course, with the facility occupying the highest point. From the golfer's perspective, of course, on continuous layouts this means that playing out on the front nine is downhill, with a grueling climb up the back nine. On many hilly courses, the clubhouse may be best located roughly between the highest and lowest points. Particularly tricky course sites, however, such as at Beaver Creek, Colorado, may dictate a hilltop clubhouse site.

A number of other factors should be considered in siting a clubhouse, including pedestrian and vehicular circulation, the prospective location of maintenance facilities and storage areas, and the relationship between the course and various planned real estate products. For this reason, it is usually advisable for a developer to bring the clubhouse architect into the planning process early.

Program Elements. The largest and most complex clubhouses are built in projects that receive the heaviest, most regular use of the recreational facilities: primary-home or semiretirement communities, where residents occupy their homes virtually year-round. Second-home recreational communities in most markets usually feature more modest clubhouses, but these can also be fairly large, depending on the number of members. Clubhouses in these projects tend to include flexible, multifunction spaces that can adapt to seasonal use demands. Resorts generally have the smallest facilities, often restricted to a modest pro shop and lockers. Because the resort's hotel will usually cater to most of the guests' other needs, the clubhouse will typically be limited to supporting the particular requirements of golf.

Clubhouse program elements can be organized into three basic categories: those that support golf and other physical activities (a squash court or an exercise room, for example); those that support various social functions, including facilities for eating and drinking; and those that are service-oriented, including administrative offices, storage, receiving, and so on. A refinement of this organization that details the spatial requirements of several prototypical clubhouse programs is shown in Figure 3-6. Virtually all clubhouses, beyond the most rudimentary facilities, will include the following elements:[49]

- Men's and women's locker rooms, restrooms, and showers;
- Dining room or snack bar;
- Kitchen or grill and associated storage;
- Office;
- Pro shop with pro's office and associated storage;
- Cart and club storage areas (carts may be stored in a separate building); and
- General storage.

The most common additions to this basic list are a bar or lounge area and rooms for playing cards, which are sometimes incorporated into locker rooms. In addition, a variety of other spaces can help a clubhouse function better, including a lobby and coat room, a waiting

Figure 3-6
PROTOTYPICAL CLUBHOUSE PROGRAMS

SAILFISH POINT
COMMUNITY   Second homes; 550 acres planned for 765 dwelling units
LOCATION   Barrier island, east coast of Florida, north of Palm Beach
AMENITIES   Ocean, lagoon, 18-hole golf course, marina

PROGRAM ELEMENTS

Reception/Administration	No./Type	Square Footage
Lobby & coat storage		1,200
Porte cochere[1]		1,040
Food and Beverage Service		
Dining room		5,330
Grill	250 seats	800
Lounge		840
Kitchen		1,550
Kitchen storage receiving		830
Patio deck/spa[1]		2,430
Activity Support Space		
Golf pro shop		1,250
Tennis pro shop		430
Lounge		300
Men's locker room	Golf	2,100
lounge & toilets	Spa	700
Women's locker room	Golf	1,000
lounge & toilets	Spa	700
Bag storage, club & shoe cleaning	408 bags	600
Golf cart storage[1], cleaning, & maintenance	40 carts	4,500
Lockers—half size	434	
Indoor Activity		
Men's exercise room		440
Women's exercise room		3,480
Men's spa facilities		400
Women's spa facilities		400
Meeting rooms		800
Building Support Space		
Mechanical/electrical/elevator		2,520
Employee lounge, toilets, & lockers		540
Maintenance		300
Laundry		220
Circulation		1,160
Building storage		800
Conditioned Total		31,400
Unconditioned Area Total		7,970
TOTAL BUILDING AREA		39,370

1,108 TSUBO

Outdoor Activity		
Pool Adult		2,420
Whirlpool		80
Pool deck		9,500
Tennis courts	5	
Auxiliary Facilities		
Starter building		650
Chandlery		3,940
Heliport		
Parking spaces	161	

Sailfish Point clubhouse.

Diedrich Architects and Associates, Inc.

PORT ROYAL

COMMUNITY   Second homes and resort planned for 1,000 dwelling units (single-family, cluster, condos); 416-room oceanfront hotel

LOCATION   Hilton Head Island, South Carolina

AMENITIES   Beach club on ocean, additional amenities associated with hotel

Port Royal clubhouse.

Diedrich Architects and Associates, Inc.

PROGRAM ELEMENTS

	No./Type	Square Footage
Reception/Administration		
Lobby & coat storage		1,800
Club administration		
Guest house		3,140
Club manager		200
Catering manager		160
Bookkeeping		180
Men's toilet		500
Women's toilet		540
Office		100
Food and Beverage Service		
Dining room		7,000
Lounge		2,000
Kitchen		3,040
Kitchen storage receiving		1,385
Verandah[1]		5,110
Activity Support Space		
Golf pro shop		2,820
Men's locker room, lounge, & toilets		2,130
Women's locker room, lounge, & toilets		1,260
Bag storage, club & shoe cleaning	306 bags	810
Golf cart storage[1]	206 carts	10,040
Lockers—half size	394	
Lounge		1,432
Indoor Activity		
Men's spa facilities		300
Women's spa facilities		240
Meeting rooms		720
Building Support Space		
Mechanical/electrical/elevator		1,200
Employee lounge, toilets, & lockers		270
Maintenance		390
Receiving		320
Laundry		290
Circulation		580
Building storage		660
Conditioned Total		33,861
Unconditioned Area Total		15,150
TOTAL BUILDING AREA		49,011
Auxiliary Facilities		
Real estate sales		5,176
Parking spaces	379	

PELICAN'S NEST

COMMUNITY   Residential golf course community, 370 acres, 175 dwelling units
LOCATION   Bonita Springs, Florida
AMENITIES   This club serves an 18-hole golf course to supplement the original
                   Pelican Bay facilities

PROGRAM ELEMENTS

Reception/Administration	No./Type	Square Footage
Lobby & coat storage[1]		200
Club administration		100
Food and Beverage Service		
Dining room		780
Kitchen		220
Kitchen storage receiving		30
Patio deck[1]		940
Activity Support Space		
Golf pro shop		980
Men's locker room, lounge, & toilets		340
Women's locker room, lounge, & toilets		240
Bag storage, club & shoe cleaning[1]	(rack) 156 bags	290
Golf cart storage[1]	72 carts	2,720
Golf cart cleaning & maintenance[1]		210
Lockers—shoe	228	
Building Support Space		
Building storage		110
Circulation		140
Conditioned Total		2,920
Unconditioned Area Total		4,380
TOTAL BUILDING AREA		7,300
Auxiliary Facilities		
Parking spaces	55	

[1]Unconditioned area.
Source: Diedrich Architects & Associates, Inc., Atlanta, Georgia.

room, additional office spaces, a laundry or linen room, an employee locker room or lounge, and additional storage space. Increasingly, exercise and fitness rooms are being included. Unless it is located elsewhere on the project, a real estate sales office can be a useful addition in a project's early stages.

Naturally, the relative size and the design criteria for each of these elements will vary depending on each project's specific needs. Every clubhouse is unique. As a general rule, however, the relationship discussed above will hold true: year-round, primary-home communities will require the largest and most elaborate clubhouses, while second-home projects and resorts will usually have more modest facilities. The degree to which specific program elements are affected by this relationship varies, however. A good example is the pro shop.[50]

Traditionally, golfers have purchased most of their clothing and equipment from the pro shop at their "home club." A club in a primary-home community will obviously fit this category. These clubs, where the pro is usually familiar with an individual member's needs and the golfer is familiar with the shop's merchandise and prices, can sell a relatively high volume of clubs and bags. This merchandise is expensive equipment that requires a generous amount of display space. Both the higher sales volume and the larger space requirements mean that a primary-home community's pro shop should be relatively large. Increasingly, however, golfers are purchasing major equipment at discount houses and other retail outlets. In such a market, pro shop sales may be much lower.[51]

Sales can vary widely in a pro shop at a second-home community, because of its seasonal nature. As the population of the project grows, however, in-season sales may not differ markedly from a pro shop in a primary-home community of comparable size. In addition, for many golfers the second-home golf club may in fact be their "home club," where they purchase a wide range of equipment, including clubs and bags. Also, many second-home buyers may be newcomers to the game who need a complete set of equipment. The second-home club pro shop may thus approximate the same size as that in a first-home community.

At a resort, the pro shop often encompasses the largest area of the clubhouse, although the shop itself may be smaller than those in other project types. Resort pro shops are usually the center of golf activity. But most of this activity involves services and sales of small, soft goods. A resort course will not sell large quantities of hard goods, but will do a brisk trade in clothing, balls, gloves, and other accessories, often imprinted with the resort's logo. Because these goods can be stored and displayed in a relatively compact area, the resort pro shop can be smaller. On a sales-per-round-played basis, resort pro shops usually far outpace primary-home community pro shops.

Food and beverage services will be found in varying degrees as part of nearly every clubhouse. While these operations are generally essential, they can greatly complicate clubhouse planning. Commonly, a clubhouse program will include a dining room, a grill or snack bar, an outdoor deck or patio, and perhaps a lounge or a men's grill. Circulation between the kitchen and three or more serving areas can become problematic, especially at peak serving times. Moreover, these facilities require extensive service areas: receiving areas that may require larger driveways or service access, trash storage areas (which in warm climates may need to be air conditioned), and larger amounts of storage space. In addition, a larger kitchen staff will require separate areas for changing clothes, taking breaks, and eating.

One of the most complex issues in clubhouse design is the separation or buffering of various groups of users. Some projects may have a clearly identifiable, relatively homogeneous group of users. A private club restricted to project home-owners where the only recreational facility is high-quality golf, for example, will enjoy a relatively conflict-free clubhouse program. At the other extreme, a club that caters to homeowners, resort guests, and nonresident members will face some likely conflicts, only some of which can be addressed by careful planning and design. Within these broad groups may be other categories of clubhouse users with different needs: tennis players, children using the pool, community groups, and so on.

Essentially, two strategies exist to help mitigate the conflicts between user groups. One is to isolate them spatially, with separate locker rooms, for example, for golfers and tennis players, or with a separate, members-only dining room not open to resort guests. Many such strategies will, of course, require a larger and more complex clubhouse. Another strategy is to attempt to manage the activities and relationships between user groups. For example, some daily fee courses associated with real estate projects will give project residents preference in starting times and advance reservations. Outside members may have more limited access to the course during peak demand periods. The effectiveness of either strategy—spatial separation versus managing access—will depend upon the specific situation in a particular project, but it is essential for prospective developers to design their clubhouses with the composition of the user group—both at the project's early stages and at build-out—firmly in mind.

To facilitate use by different groups of users, the clubhouse plan at Gainey Ranch includes specific areas for both club members and resort guests.

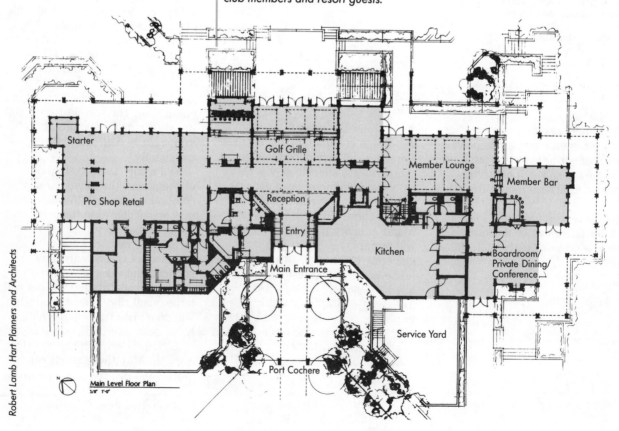

Robert Lamb Hart Planners and Architects

Starter

Pro Shop Retail

Golf Grille

Reception

Entry

Main Entrance

Member Lounge

Member Bar

Kitchen

Boardroom/ Private Dining/ Conference

Service Yard

Port Cochere

Main Level Floor Plan

All real estate projects have a life cycle, during which they experience a number of different levels of activity and use. Phasing and expansion in relation to changing needs should be important considerations in clubhouse planning. Developers receive the most marketing value from a clubhouse when it is an active, bustling place where residents and club members are clearly enjoying themselves. In a project's early stages, when the marketing advantage is needed most, such an image may be problematic. After all, the project is just getting started and not many people will be living there yet. Some developers therefore try to generate activity (and additional revenues) by opening membership to outsiders in the early stages. Another tactic is to design the clubhouse so as to maximize the impact of a less active membership. For example, a facility can be designed to grow along with the project's population. Clubhouse architect Richard Diedrich often designs decks and other open spaces with the expectation that these will evolve first into pavilions, then into fully enclosed, integrated rooms as a project grows. He has also used a modular approach to clubhouse design, with new modules added when needed. This strategy essentially concentrates activity into areas no larger than actually required. Beyond helping to give the impression of greater activity, this approach also helps the developer to control unnecessary capital expenditures.[52] In some cases, a two-stage clubhouse has worked effectively. At Harbour Ridge, developer John B. Dodge used a relatively small but carefully designed clubhouse to accommodate both tennis and golf members in the project's first few years. As the membership grows, he intends to build a much larger and more complete facility, with the smaller building then oriented to tennis.

Practice hole at Bonita Bay.

Practice Facilities. Most clubhouse areas on today's courses include a set of practice facilities, usually designed to permit players to practice all golf shots. A typical practice range includes a driving area, one or more practice putting areas, target greens designed for chipping and iron shots, and practice bunkers. On most courses, this area occupies about four to six acres, or about twice the area of the average hole. The size of practice areas varies, however, depending on the size and skill level of the course's users. A general rule for a driving range is that it should measure about 300 yards by 150 yards. Orientations directly east and west should be avoided. Sometimes these facilities can be quite extensive, with circular driving ranges and numerous target greens. The acclaimed Desert Highlands course in the Arizona desert has a $500,000, 18-hole putting course that, according to the developer, has been extremely well-received by the club members.[53]

Generally, practice areas should be located close to the pro shop to control access and offer convenience to the starting holes. Some measure of buffering between the practice range and other clubhouse areas makes the area safer and will afford golfers on the range some privacy.

CONSTRUCTION CONSIDERATIONS

The process of building a golf course is similar to any construction project, although some elements are fairly specialized. Unlike building construction, many design decisions and refinements can be made by the builder, the developer, and the architect in the field during the construction phase. Since the relationship between these parties is important and can be delicate, a developer should carefully consider in advance the various options for course construction.

An experienced course contractor, for example, can be hired to build the course, alone or with varous subcontractors. Some developers act as their own general contractor and work with a variety of specialists. In other cases, the course architect serves as the general contractor, delivering a complete range of services to the owner, from initial feasibility work to ongoing inspections and maintenance consultations after the course is opened.

Experience is essential in course construction, no matter who performs the work. With the exception of greens and tees, the basic elements of a golf course—clearing, earth-moving, drainage, irrigation, and landscaping—present no unique demands on a contractor, unless unusual conditions are encountered. But the combination of elements, along with the need to make on-the-spot design decisions and judgments regarding the quality of materials, require an experienced construction supervisor.

The following section discusses issues associated with the various stages and elements of course construction as they are encountered on most sites.[54] Construction of each course will vary, depending on individual site conditions, the length of the construction and growing season, the distance from suppliers, and so on.

Clearing

The costs per acre for clearing a site can vary tremendously, depending mainly on the available means for disposing of the cleared material, and on the nature of the vegetation to be cleared. The least expensive location for clearing will be where an active pulpwood industry exists and burning of the remaining brush is permitted. Loggers will frequently pay a developer for the right to remove all marketable trees. The developer must then remove the remaining small caliper trees, undergrowth, stumps, and roots and dispose of them by burying or burning. If pulpwood operations are nonexistent and burning is prohibited, clearing can be quite expensive. Cleared trees must then be buried, chipped, or transported off the site.

Poppy Hill, a new course on the famous Monterey Peninsula in California, cost five times the amount spent on nearby Spyglass Hill, opened 25 years earlier. Although much of the increase can be attributed to inflation and changing construction methods, the new course was developed under strict environmental regulations that preclude burning. All cleared vegetation was therefore chipped and hauled away from the site. Such costs, up to several thousand dollars per acre, may significantly affect the feasibility of developing a course on a heavily wooded site.[55]

After clearing, a site must be restored to its natural grade, with all pockets and ruts filled. Burial areas for logs and stumps should be located away from prospective locations for drainage, irrigation, or utilities. Whenever possible, these burial areas should be located in the rough rather than on fairways, because settling may occur.

Earthwork

Major earthwork on a golf course consists of stripping and stockpiling existing topsoil, mass grading cut-and-fill, final shaping, pond excavation, and topsoil respreading. Although the most cost-effective methods will depend on local site conditions and practices, in general the largest possible equipment will be the most efficient.

Open sites that have been previously cultivated usually contain more available topsoil than heavily wooded sites, since clearing operations often result in a loss of topsoil. Topsoil is critical for the maintenance of healthy turf, and course developers are commonly faced with a shortage of this crucial material. Great care should therefore be taken during grading operations to conserve as much topsoil as posssible. Fairway areas that require substantial grading should be stripped of all topsoil until all the earthwork is completed. This stripping is usually accomplished with bulldozers or scrapers. All stripped topsoil should then be stockpiled as close as possible to the areas where it will be respread. If topsoil is scarce, such high-use areas as tees, greens, mounds, fairway bunkers, and steep slopes should take priority over

Clearing on Cape Cod.

Brian Silva

other areas receiving topsoil. Topsoil handling, as a two-step operation, usually costs from one-and-a-half to two times the cubic yard price for bulk excavation.

Cut-and-fill grading on fairways using scrapers or bulldozers aims to increase the visibility from tee to green and to shape feature (tee, green, and bunker) sites. In some cases, fill is borrowed from areas off the course or from fairway areas, or is produced by excavating lakes and ponds. Because this fill is usually transported a long distance, scrapers are generally used.

Lakes and ponds can also be excavated with bulldozers and scrapers if conditions allow. In areas with a shallow water table or unstable soil conditions, a dragline will usually be used, and the costs will be commensurately higher.

Other complications during earthwork operations occur when a site contains large boulders or ledge rock, or has a severe shortage of topsoil. Rock must either be pushed or otherwise transported to a suitable area off the course, sometimes after expensive blasting operations. Topsoil may be available from building sites or areas slated for roads or parking lots, although in some cases a developer will have no choice but to purchase and import topsoil, which can be extremely expensive. In any event, the combination of limited topsoil, extensive rock, or dense woods can increase costs dramatically.

Drainage

Adequate drainage is essential to ensure a course's quality and playability. On low sites or in areas such as south Florida with a relatively high water table, providing sufficient drainage can account for a significant portion of development costs. Of particular concern in real estate project courses is that future development near the course will be likely to increase the amount of runoff to the stormwater drainage system. The course's drainage system should thus be scaled to accommodate this future runoff.

Building a golf hole at Stratton Mountain. From top to bottom, clearing operations complete; rough grading complete; irrigation system installed; fairway ready for seeding, tee ready for soil mix; early growth.

Most courses employ a combination of surface and subsurface drainage features to handle runoff. The cheapest and easiest means is a series of drainage swales linked to the existing site drainage patterns and natural watercourses. These features should be designed with both maintenance and playability in mind. For example, a swale's contours should blend with the existing topograpy to permit the resulting turf to be cut by gang mowers. Similarly, ditches, while effective and cheap for drainage, create unfair golf hazards and are difficult to maintain. Existing streams, creeks, and rivers offer an effective discharge point for swales and subsurface elements. Although their course may in some instances need to be modified, a disturbed watercourse can greatly exacerbate erosion problems.

Most courses will require some subsurface drainage elements. Subsurface pipe can be used to collect surface water in catch basins or drop inlets and channel it to a stream, lake, or other outlet at a lower elevation. A properly sized system of subsurface pipe can accommodate runoff from adjacent watersheds both in the grow-in period to help prevent erosion and later as adjacent real estate is developed. The cost of installed pipe will vary with the material, the size, and labor costs. The most popular materials are concrete, asphalt-coated corrugated metal, and plastic.

Brian Silva

Drainage features often form important design elements.

Tile fields are also used to drain areas that cannot be effectively drained by swales, and to intercept seepage from springs. Four- to six-inch perforated tiles are installed in a trench that has been backfilled with crushed stone or gravel. Tile drains are also often used to lower a shallow water table in low-lying areas.

Feature Construction

Golf course features—tees, greens, and bunkers—are the best indicators of a course's quality of construction. The proper construction of these features has been the focus of much research and innovation and requires some degree of experience by the contractor.

Although numerous greens construction methods exist, the most popular technique is that prescribed by the U.S. Golf Association (USGA). Most course architects and superintendents follow the basic principles of this technique but may modify some aspects depending on local conditions. The aim of any greens construction method is a putting surface that drains well, resists soil compaction under heavy play, holds an approach shot, and putts true.

In a USGA green, the subgrade is carefully shaped by bulldozers to the contours of the finished product. After drainage trenches are cut into the subgrade, a drain tile network is laid in a herringbone pattern. About 100 lineal feet of tile are required for every 1,000 square feet of green surface. The drainage tiles discharge water away from the green to a swale, pond, or larger underground storm drain. The drainage trenches are filled with gravel, and a four-inch layer of gravel is placed over the entire surface of the green. Sometimes a two-inch layer of coarse sand follows, but this step is often omitted.

The seedbed itself consists of a 10- to 12-inch layer of sand and peat (sometimes combined with native topsoil or other organic material) placed atop the gravel layer. After the seedbed is prepared, the surface is seeded or stolons are planted.

An alternative to this elaborate technique is simply to cover the finished subgrade with an eight- to 12-inch layer of topsoil and then to plant. The key advantage of the USGA and similar types of greens is that they help to ensure durable, high-quality turf. These greens are carefully devised to drain well yet to retain a certain amount of water with regular irrigation. As a result, the turf is more resilient and resistant to disease. A golf course green, although it may look utterly "natural," represents one of the most carefully controlled monocultures imaginable. Poorly constructed greens, although they may be initially cheaper, are sure to cause maintenance headaches later.

Tees are difficult to build correctly. As the starting point for a golf hole, intended to play equally for all players, the grade on the tee must be nearly perfect. Golfers are particular about their stances, and hollows, mounds, or pockets of poor drainage will be unacceptable.

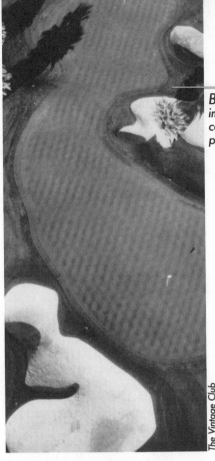

Because of their special use and their importance to play, tees and greens can pose especially tricky construction problems.

Tees are generally sloped to the back, or to the left side as the golfer faces down the fairway, at a grade of about 1 percent to ensure positive drainage. The subgrade should be perfectly uniform and covered with a well-drained sandy loam soil. If the tees are to be maintained at a high level like greens, they should receive a top course of the same seedbed mixture to a depth of about four inches.

Bunkers or sand traps are not especially difficult to build but may be expensive items if they are particularly large, deep, or located in certain areas. In most bunkers, the floor lies above the surrounding grade and is sloped slightly upward for visibility. Under most conditions, this design permits positive surface drainage along the subgrade and out of the trap. This can, however, sometimes lead to sand being washed out onto the fairway. To avoid this washing, or to prevent standing water, tile drains can be installed in the bunker subgrade, with the water redirected into an out-of-play area.

Golf Course Irrigation

Since the late 1800s, when irrigated turf on golf courses was introduced, course irrigation systems have become increasingly important and complex. For a developer, the major variables in an irrigation system are the amount of coverage and the degree of automation. If the system is fully automatic, it can be controlled either electrically or hydraulically.

The amount of coverage depends on the demand for irrigation and on the acceptable cost of the system. In desert areas, a "wall-to-wall" system that covers the entire fairways as well as the tees and greens is generally essential for adequate turf. Some desert courses—like that at Desert Highlands in Scottsdale, Arizona—have been designed with lush turf restricted to landing areas, tees, and greens to reduce dependence on irrigation. In more temperate areas, single-row or double-row fairway systems are adequate. A single row of sprinkler heads, usually located down the center of the fairways, is less expensive due to

lower piping requirements and fewer sprinkler heads, but it will irrigate a smaller area of turf less evenly than would a double row.

All rotary sprinkler heads distribute water unevenly within their pattern of coverage. For this reason, systems are designed with a certain amount of overlapping areas between heads. For example, sprinkler heads with a specified coverage diameter of 150 should be spaced at 75-foot intervals to ensure adequate coverage. With narrower fairways in a relatively moist climate, a single-row system is certainly adequate, but under most conditions a double-row system will prove superior. Generally, wall-to-wall systems with small sprinkler heads and a short trajectory are used in areas with little rainfall and high winds. The greater capacity in a double-row or wall-to-wall system will also increase the size, and therefore the cost, of the pump required. A typical single-row automatic system, for example, will use about 800 gallons per minute (gpm), while a wall-to-wall arrangement could demand up to 1,600 gpm.

Installing a special impervious pond lining.

In recent years most developers have installed fully automatic irrigation systems, the latest of which incorporate extremely sophisticated, microprocessor-based control and monitoring systems. Manual systems, while initially less expensive, are more labor-intensive and less reliable than most automatic systems. Many older courses, however, still rely on manual quick-coupling systems for fairway irrigation, while tees and greens are on automatic systems. In many cases, the renovation of such a course will include upgrading the irrigation system.

Automatic systems are controlled either by hydraulically or electrically operated valves. In some regions hydraulic systems offer some initial cost savings. Over the longer term, however, electric systems are considered more reliable and easier to maintain. Installation costs for an irrigation system will depend on the nature of the site, the ease of trenching and type of materials used, local labor costs, and the contracting arrangement. Additional costs will often include a pumphouse or shelter.

Seedbed Preparation and Landscaping

High-quality golf depends upon high-quality turf. And high-quality turf depends on careful preparation of all areas to be sodded or seeded in grass. Correct seedbed preparation, proper selection of grass for various areas of the course, and good timing all represent important factors in developing healthy turf.

To prepare a seedbed, the area should first be disked to smooth the surface and loosen the soil. After raking to remove sticks, roots, and stones, the seedbed should be graded smooth. At this point the surface should be carefully checked for positive drainage. The area can then be limed and fertilized, based on the results of a soil analysis.

The selection of a type and strain of grass will depend upon expected temperature and precipitation patterns, presence of salt or shade, expected traffic patterns, and resistance to disease and weeds. Developers will also be concerned with a grass's grow-in time and color.

In cooler climates, fairways are generally seeded with various strains of bentgrass or bluegrass. Bentgrass, which can be cropped quite closely, is the usual choice for northern greens. Common Bermuda grass or Bermuda grass hybrids are popular for fairways in warmer climates. Bermuda grass offers good drought tolerance and a durable, highly playable surface. As a warm-season grass, however, Bermuda grass goes dormant in winter and requires an overseeeding of ryegrass to keep turf areas green.

The optimum time to plant northern grasses is from early August to mid-September, although early spring is a preferable planting time in desert and mountain areas that may experience fall temperature extremes. Bermuda grass is best planted in late spring or early summer. The grow-in period, or time required to establish the turf to the point where it is durable enough to played, can range from an entire growing season in New England to as little as 90 days in Hawaii. During this period, maintenance costs will be much higher

than normal due to the need for erosion control measures and reseeding. Significantly, these expenditures must be made while the course is not bringing in any revenues, except indirectly from hopeful real estate buyers.

Additional landscaping costs will be highly variable, depending on the particular site characteristics, the pace of development, the desired effect, and the budget. Although a course cannot be played without grass, other landscaping can be added over a period of years, unless marketing objectives dictate otherwise or unless the design of the course depends heavily on landscaping elements. If a landscaping program is planned, trees should be planted after the turf is established, and then in clusters to separate fairways and to frame greens and other vistas. Besides greatly improving the appearance of the course, trees protect surrounding homesites and give them privacy, which can increase values significantly.

Bonita Bay

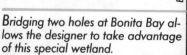

Bridging two holes at Bonita Bay allows the designer to take advantage of this special wetland.

Supporting Infrastructure

As in any major facility, a variety of elements must support the operations of a golf course and clubhouse. Foremost among these is a maintenance building replete with an array of specialized equipment. A properly equipped maintenance center is essential, and can be as elaborate or as spartan as desired. The least expensive and most popular type of course maintenance building is of prefabricated, steel-frame construction. These structures are readily available, easy to build and expand, and flexible in design. Depending on the manufacturer selected, they can usually be built in 10- or 20-foot increments. Most 18-hole courses will require a 6,000- to 8,000-square-foot maintenance building. Thirty-six holes of golf will require about 10,500 square feet.

Most maintenance buildings contain storage areas for materials and equipment, a repair shop, and locker rooms, restrooms, and showers for employees and the superintendent. The array of maintenance equipment required for a typical 18-hole course is presented in Figure 3-7. Although most of this equipment should be purchased in advance of a course's opening, the superintendent will undoubtedly encounter additional equipment needs during the first few years of operations. Provisions should therefore be made in the budget to permit these later purchases as well as expected replacement costs.

Figure 3-7
TYPICAL EQUIPMENT LIST FOR 18-HOLE GOLF COURSE

Items	Use
Tractors & Trucks	
2 Tractors with 3-point hitch	Pulling mowers, general purpose
1 Tractor with front-end loader backhoe	General construction—trap maintenance
1 Compact pickup truck	Transportation for superintendent
2 Trucksters	Crew transport and job mobility, spraying, etc.
2 Trailers, 2-yard capacity dump type	Hauling materials
Mowing Equipment	
2 Triplex greens mowers with verticutting attachments	Mowing greens and tees
2 Triplex trim mowers	Mowing aprons, trap slopes, trimming
1 7-gang fairway mower, tractor mounted, hydraulic lift	Mowing fairways
1 5-gang frame, tractor drawn, with no mowers	Back-up means of mowing, in case hydraulic lift tractor is inoperative
1 5-gang rough mower, pull type 5-blade reels	Mowing roughs
1 72″ or 80″ rotary mower or flail type mounted on PTO (Power Take-Off)	Maintaining roughs and banks

Golf Course Equipment & Tools	Hand Tools
2 Hole cutters	5 Shovels
36 Hole cups	4 Sod lifters
2 Cup extractors	4 Hand edgers
2 Cup setters	2 Ladders
18 Poles & flags	2 Wheel barrows
18 Practice green markers	2 Soil probes
18 Practice green cups	2 Pitchforks
3 Sets tee markers	3 Lifting bars
18 Golf ball washers	2 Sledge hammers
144 Tee towels	
18 Waste retainers	Adequate plumbing, carpentry, mechanic and masonry
18 Tee benches	tools, lapping machines, reel grinder, and bedknife grinder
2 Divot repairers	
2 4″ Pluggers	
1 8″ Turf repairer	
6 36″ Trap rakes	
2 Lawn rakes	
20 14″ Trap rakes	
200 Small trap rakes to be kept in sand traps	

Most courses today allow the use of golf carts (or as they are sometimes called, golf cars). Many private courses and resort courses—where cart rental fees provide a strong source of revenue—require golfers to ride. Some even resort to promoting "walk-only" days as (literally) a change of pace. The use of golf carts is hotly debated by course architects and decried by purists, but the fact remains that they have made the game more popular and more economically feasible and have opened up a wider range of sites for course development.

Golf carts come with a set of requirements. First, they must be stored somewhere. Often, the clubhouse program includes a golf cart storage area. A popular location is underneath the main clubhouse, opening to the rear at a staging area near the pro shop. Carts may be electrically or gasoline powered. If they are electric, the storage area must include access to adequate power for recharging. Likewise, the more powerful, but noisier, gas carts also require a service area.

Many courses that use carts have paths only around high-traffic areas such as tees and greens. With this arrangement, the length of paths would total around 10,500 lineal feet. A more recent trend is to extend cart paths the entire length of the course to avoid excessive wear and to help control cart traffic, although this is considered less desirable for the golfer. These paths, which may total up to 25,000 feet long, help minimize fairway damage and enable the carts to return to the course soon after a heavy rain—an important consideration

Figure 3-7 (cont'd.)

TYPICAL EQUIPMENT LIST FOR 18-HOLE GOLF COURSE

Maintenance Equipment

1	30″ riding rotary mower	Manicuring in vicinity of trees and shrubs
3	20″ commercial rotary mower, air cushion type	Light mowing
1	300-gallon power sprayer (boom and hose attachment)	Large area spraying (fairways)
1	100-gallon truckster self-contained power unit, mounted sprayer, boom and hose attachment, mechanical agitator	Spraying of greens and tees
1	Sod cutter	Removal of sod
1	Greens aerifier	Renovation and reconditioning of established turf to improve aeration reduction of compaction and increase percolation
1	Soil shredder	Soil preparation
1	Soil screen	Preparation and mixing of soil amendments for topdressing
1	Power portable centrifugal pump with suction hose	General purpose pumping
1	Rotary tiller	Thorough mixing of soil on green sites and other areas in preparation for planting
1	Power spiker	Recondition surface soil, reduce crusting, and seedbed preparation
1	Power hedge trimmer	Hedge grooming
1	Power edger	Edging traps and planting beds
1	Power topdressing machine (Sod Master)	General purpose topdressing
1	Power drag mat	Leveling large areas, preplanting, and follow-up of renovation work
1	Large rotary spreader (Lele Model 2500)	Seeding and spreading of fertilizer
1	Small rotary spreader (Cyclone M-3) truckster mounted	Seeding and spreading of fertilizer on greens and small turf areas
2	Small rotary spreaders/seeders	Seeding and spreading of fertilizer on small areas.
2	Tractor-drawn aerification machines	Fairway aerification
1	Hand lawn roller	For cart paths, roads, greens, etc.
1	Fairway sweeper	Sweeping and verticutting fairways
1	30″ power vacuum	Removing debris from greens after renovation
1	Disc-type planter (3-point hitch mounted)	Planting

Source: Rees Jones and Guy Rando, *Golf Course Developments* (Washington, D.C.: Urban Land Institute, 1974), pp. 68–69.

when a course depends heavily on golf cart revenues.

Although concrete is more durable, cart paths are most often built of less expensive asphalt. A width of six feet is usually suitable. If maintenance vehicles will share the paths, the paths should measure at least eight feet wide.

Most courses will also need rest stations or shelters on each nine. These facilities can be quite simple, prefabricated structures or elaborate, custom-designed buildings with restrooms and space for several golf carts. Clearly, the quality of these elements should be commensurate with the course's overall image. Rest stations are often best located where several holes meet, for more convenient access for the greatest number of players.

Golf Course Development Costs

Cost information carries a limited life span. Moreover, the tremendous range of potential course sites and facility characteristics makes generalized costs inherently suspect. In presenting such data, any author assumes the risk of inviting exception, because exceptions to generalizations abound. Nonetheless, the following costs are intended to present some sense of the financial requirements of golf course development. They are based on the experience of the case study projects summarized in Chapter 7 and on interviews with course architects and knowledgeable developers.

For years, the rule of thumb was that a course would cost about $100,000 per hole, exclusive of land costs. For 18 holes and a practice range, this ratio predicted that course construction costs under

general conditions would approach $2 million. There is no doubt that many sound courses could still be built today for well under this figure. According to the National Golf Foundation in 1984, a reasonable range for a total course construction budget, including a fully equipped maintenance building, was from $885,000 to $1,900,000.[56]

Supporting infrastructure: exposed aggregate cart paths . . .

. . . subtly dramatic bridge . . .

. . . and welcome facilities, all at Gainey Ranch.

These figures do not, however, include the cost of the land, the clubhouse, or the architect's fee.

For many regions today, and especially for real estate development courses, these figures are quite low. Actual cost data for several courses are presented in this book's case studies. Based on this information, gathered through the summer of 1985, a more typical range for course construction of the above description would be from $1.8 to $3.2 million.

According to course architect Robert Trent Jones, Jr., in late 1985 a regulation course could be built for a minimum of $1.5 to $1.7 million.[57] The upward limit of the range can easily approach $10 million, as in the case of PGA West or Gainey Ranch.

Maintenance costs are a perennial concern for golf course developers and operators.

Jones estimated that a maintenance building would cost an additional $300,000 to $400,000. At Mariner Sands in Stuart, Florida, a maintenance building was added in 1985 at a cost of $350,000. Maintenance equipment, according to Jones, will cost an additional $400,000 to $450,000. A 1984 survey by the National Golf Foundation placed the median value of capital equipment inventory for a nationwide sample of more than 2,300 courses at about $246,000.[58] The survey also found that the average course spends about $17,500 annually on maintenance equipment. Finally, costs during the grow-in period will run to $250,000 and up, depending on the site and the climate.

In packaging a feasibility proposal for presentation to a lender, the bottom line is what counts. According to recent estimates by developers and lenders, a fully equipped, regulation course built as part of a typical residential or resort project in the southern states will cost between $3.5 and $4 million to open for play.

GOLF COURSE MANAGEMENT

For years, the benefits of a golf course to a real estate project so far outweighed its costs that management issues were often neglected. If a club operation racked up large losses for several years, it was relatively easy for developers to write the losses off to real estate marketing or other departments. Cost control for food and beverage operations or for golf course maintenance was less important than the large profits generated from real estate sales because of the golf course.

As both capital and operating costs have risen, however, course and club management have taken on additional importance. For several years in the 1970s course development slumped in response to rising expenses and uncertain benefits. In the last several years, however, more developers have turned their attention to management issues as a means to recover the profitability of a golf course operation. This trend has led to an increasingly wider range of organizational arrangements for management as well as new techniques for operations and maintenance practices designed to control costs and increase rounds played. Many developers have begun to view courses as potential profit centers in their own right.

A course remains largely a fixed-cost operation. If operated on a daily fee basis, with a marginal increase in revenue for every additional round of golf played, management can have tremendous implications for profitability: timely and effective maintenance operations can be designed to minimize down time; an efficient starting system can help reduce waiting times and maximize the number of rounds played; controlling costs for food and beverage operations can help obviate the need to recover losses from real estate operations, and thus ease pressures to cut essential course maintenance expenditures or to raise greens fees or rental rates.

The Role of the Developer

The most typical organizational arrangement for a real estate project golf course is for the developer or owner to retain full operational control. The course will be structured for accounting purposes as a separate cost or profit center, usually with procedures to accommodate both direct and indirect expenditures. The golf operation may be separated from or combined with other club operations. Operational responsibility will rest with a club manager, a staff of golf professionals responsible for the pro shop as well as instruction and programs, and a course superintendent. The principal advantage of this arrangement is that the developer will be assured of ongoing control over the operations of the club and golf course. This type of control is usually quite valuable when it comes to assuring both lenders and real estate prospects of the project's viability.

The disadvantage is that a developer, especially if his or her firm is small or inexperienced, may not have access to the kinds of superior managers needed to make this arrangement work. Various organizations exist, however, to help assure a developer of the professionalism of their managers. Course superintendents, for example, can be members of or certified by the Golf Course Superintendents Association of America (GCSAA). Golf pros are often members of the Professional Golfer's Association of America (PGA), and club managers are eligible for membership in the Club Management Association of America. Although the presence of these credentials is no guarantee of finding the best personnel, most top-

flight managers belong to these and similar organizations.

A trend that has become much more prevalent in recent years is for the developer to contract with a full-service management firm. This arrangement, based on the proposition that land development and golf course management are not necessarily compatible or complementary fields, is often most suitable for less experienced developers or for those clubs that have been transferred to member or resident ownership. Proponents of contracted management, which is also sometimes called lease management, argue that it enables clubs to have access to a

If space is available, an on-site nursery can help conserve native vegetation and reduce landscaping costs.

wider variety of skilled personnel. Most of the larger management organizations operate nationwide, with coordination at a regional level and specific managers assigned to each club. Individual managers are responsible both for their own clubs and for regional cooperation. This arrangement could provide an individual club, for example, with access to skilled accountants and personnel managers as well as agronomists and turfgrass experts.

The trade-off for the developer, of course, is that a contracted arrangement inevitably involves some loss of operational control. For an established club, however, this factor may be less important than for a club in the early development stages, when relationships between real estate and other aspects of the project remain critical.

Income and Expense Analysis

Golf income varies in source and magnitude based on the type of course (private, public, or daily fee), the location, the market, and the length of the season. For private clubs, the primary sources of revenue include membership fees and dues, food and beverage sales, initiation fees or assessments against real estate, and guest fees. Municipal and daily fee courses will rely heavily on green fees and, in some cases, on annual memberships. The breakdown of member-related income depends on the membership structure.

All types of courses will also look toward merchandise sales, lessons and tournament revenues, and rentals and fees for lockers, golf carts, and other equipment as important sources of income. Food and beverage operations or a driving range may bring in a large proportion of a club's revenue, but will also typically be the source of its principal expenses. Most developers agree that while bar operations can be highly profitable, food services will almost always operate at a substantial loss. According to Erling Speer, a developer will do well to merely balance this profit and loss. A breakdown of income and expenses for a nationwide sample of country clubs is shown in Figure 3-8.

Course expenses can be arranged into four basic categories. The largest category is personnel-related, which includes payroll expenses and related taxes and benefits. These items alone account for nearly half the typical club's expenses. Also included in the operating cost category are expenses for maintenance and repairs, funds reserved for capital equipment purchases, dues, and so on.

For the average club, the cost of goods sold, including food and beverages, makes up the second largest expense category. Fixed charges, such as those for rent, taxes, fees, licenses, and interest costs, constitute another important category. Finally, depreciation and rehabilitation of capital facilities and equipment must be included in the expense picture.

Figure 3-8
COUNTRY CLUB INCOME AND EXPENSES BY CATEGORY

Ratios to Total Income	All Country Clubs
Sales and Income (Except Dues):	
Food	50.8%
Beverages	20.6
Rooms	2.0
Minor-operated departments	4.1
Sports activities	17.4
Other income	5.1
Total Sales and Income	100.0%
Departmental Expenses:	
Food and beverages	66.5%
Rooms	.9
Minor-operated departments	5.5
Sports activities	37.8
Total Departmental Expenses	110.7%
Net Departmental Loss	10.7%
Less Unapportioned Expenses:	
Clubrooms	7.8%
Entertainment—net	1.3
Administrative and general	22.6
Heat, light, and power	7.0
Repairs and maintenance	6.1
Grounds and maintenance—excluding greens	1.6
Total Unapportioned Expenses	46.4%
Net Cost of Operations	57.1%
Membership Dues	71.6
Dues Available for Fixed Charges	14.5%
Rent, Taxes, and Insurance	9.8%
Balance of Dues Available for Debt Service, Capital Improvements, etc.	4.7%

Note: Payroll taxes and employee benefits distributed to each department. Figures are based on a nationwide sample of 250 private country clubs.
Source: Pannell Kerr Forster, *Clubs in Town and Country—1984* (Houston: Pannell Kerr Forster, 1985), p. 7.

Maintenance

By far the largest single expense item for a course—one that constantly challenges developers, club managers, and superintendents—is maintenance. In the last 20 years, maintenance expenses for a typical course have increased more than five times.[59] In the same period, revenues per member at private country clubs have roughly tripled. This gap between revenues and costs can only be expected to rise in the future, unless management efforts are undertaken to control expenses or to increase revenues. Significantly, says Richard McElyea of Economics Research Associates, "resorts can more easily increase green fees and cart fees to cover costs than private clubs can increase dues."[60]

Generalizing about maintenance costs is impossible. A 1984 survey of 2,309 golf courses nationwide conducted by the National Golf Foundation and the Golf Course Superintendents Association of America confirmed as much, stating that "golf course maintenance costs vary dramatically both between and within facility types and regions."[61]

Maintenance costs will depend on a wide variety of factors, including the course's location, length of season, type, market, size, and pur-

Brian Silva

Many real estate–related golf courses will spend upwards of $25,000 per hole for maintenance every year.

pose. The last factor is particularly important. Nearly an unlimited sum of money could theoretically be spent on a regulation course every year. Beyond some point, of course, every additional dollar spent would bring an ever-smaller increase in the course's quality. The challenge for the developer is to determine this point of diminishing returns and to structure a maintenance

program that makes appropriate trade-offs and adjustments. If a course is intended to help sell real estate that carries the imprimatur of cost-is-no-object luxury, it will be likely to be maintained within an inch of its life, at a cost of perhaps three-quarters of a million dollars

---

Figure 3-9
COUNTRY CLUB GOLF COURSE MAINTENANCE COSTS

	Overall Averages	Geographic Divisions			
		East	South	Midwest	Far West
Average Cost per Hole in 1984					
Payroll	$ 9,365	$ 7,667	$ 9,311	$ 8,064	$13,870
Payroll taxes and employee benefits	1,751	1,406	1,502	1,257	3,002
Course supplies and contracts	3,154	2,901	2,790	3,235	3,714
Repairs to equipment, course buildings, water and drainage system, etc.	1,930	1,618	1,833	1,269	2,561
All other expenses	2,324	1,512	1,551	1,893	4,629
Total Golf Course Maintenance	$18,524	$15,104	$16,987	$15,718	$27,776
Add: Golf shop, caddy, and committee expenses	3,857	2,952	7,921	3,819	3,738
Total Golf Expenses	$22,381	$18,056	$24,908	$19,537	$31,514
Less: Income from golf fees, golf carts, driving range, etc.	10,293	7,430	15,125	10,044	13,705
Net Golf Expenses	$12,088	$10,626	$ 9,783	$ 9,493	$17,809

Source: Pannell Kerr Forster, *Clubs in Town and Country—1984*, p. 12.

annually, or about $40,000 per hole. This type of course will probably contain extensive water features, oversized greens and tees, and other items that are costly to maintain. Even at a more typical real estate–oriented course, maintenance costs can run about $20,000 per hole annually. At the other extreme, a simple and straightforward daily fee course might operate on a relatively restrained maintenance budget of $8,000 to $12,000 per hole annually.

Maintenance costs clearly depend on regional location. Numerous surveys have consistently found, for example, that courses in the western states are more expensive to maintain than those in other regions. A good deal of this variation can be linked to a region's amount of natural precipitation and to the length of the season. The most expensive-to-maintain courses are those in the arid West that must purchase their irrigation water. Courses in the South and in the upper Midwest tend to report the lowest average maintenance costs.

Private courses, as might be expected, tend to spend more on maintenance than do comparable municipal or daily fee facilities. Nationwide, the NGF/GCSAA survey found that the average private club's operating costs (which excluded capital expenditures) in 1984 were 14.6 percent higher than municipal courses and nearly 72 percent higher than daily fee courses. Although municipal courses may not always be maintained at the same level as many privately owned clubs, labor costs are significantly higher in the public sector.

The Vintage Club

The Vintage Club's Mountain Course—with the 16th hole shown here—is the site of the annual Vintage Invitational golf tournament, which features several top senior golf professionals.

In addition to operating costs, the NGF/GCSAA survey examined capital expenditures in two categories: projects and equipment. A capital project, for example, might include green reconstruction or installation of new cart paths. The survey found that for private courses, the median annual capital project expenditure was nearly $12,000. In addition, private courses spent about $17,000 every year on equipment. For daily fee courses, the figures were $8,984 and $10,919, respectively.

Recent estimates by Pannell Kerr Forster, an accounting firm known for its work with country clubs, determined the overall average country club golf course maintenance figure to be about $18,500 per hole per year.[62] The net golf expense, which adds pro shop, caddy, and golf committee expenses but deducts income derived from fees and rentals, averages about $12,000 per hole annually. Like the NGF/GCSAA figure of about $12,157 for private clubs, this statistic does not include capital expenditures for equipment.

Based on these data, along with the numbers provided by the case study courses, a reasonable assumption for a developer intent on developing a golf course as part of a real estate project would be that annual maintenance expenditures will range between $15,000 and $25,000 per hole. This estimate puts the yearly budget for 18 holes, not including capital items, at anywhere from $270,000 to $450,000. Many courses spend much more on maintenance. The developers of Gainey Ranch, for example, expect maintenance costs to approach $1.25 million per year, or an astounding $46,000 per hole! (Some western courses may run even higher.) Because it is located in one of the nation's most expensive-to-maintain regions, one would expect a higher-than-average cost for Gainey Ranch. The substantially higher figure, however, is also due to Gainey's status as a premier residential and resort community. Its meticulous attention to course maintenance is an integral part of its image.

Programming

As the recreational and often the social focus of a residential or resort community, a course can fulfill a variety of purposes that extend beyond golf itself. New residents can be introduced to the game and to a new set of friends. Juniors programs can serve important roles. Leagues, club tournaments, and clinics all represent significant elements of a development golf course. Although these individual programs may focus on golf, they also reach outward into other parts of the community, and for many residents they constitute a core of activity that separates their community from any other.

Generally, activity programming is the responsibility of the members, although much of the day-to-day work will fall to the golf professional or the club manager. In a primary-home community intended to appeal to families or to a wide variety of groups, the expected level of activities will be quite high. In a members-only private club at, for example, a retirement community, there may also be numerous activities, but since they will all cater to a similar age group, the programming itself will be simpler.

Some developers are intrigued by the national visibility certain courses achieve by hosting major professional tournaments. While PGA tournaments, especially if nationally televised, can lend a project tremendous exposure and can pay big public relations and marketing dividends, the costs to mount such an event can be extremely high. The developers of Desert Highlands in Carefree, Arizona, estimated their cost to host the nationally televised "Skins Game" in 1984 at about $425,000, for an event that was substantially smaller than a typical PGA Tour stop.[63] Some projects are clearly better suited than others for tournament play, and PGA National in particular retains an interest and an obligation to host such events. But because of the high expense, the additional infrastructure, different course requirements, and the uncertain benefits to the real estate operation, most developers should take a hard look at the economics of competitive professional events before committing their projects' resources.

CHAPTER FOUR

DEVELOPING WITH TENNIS

In the past 20 years, the sport of tennis has enjoyed a period of unprecedented popularity and growth. Although since the end of the 1970s the tennis boom has lost some of its steam, the sport remains one of the most popular outdoor activities in the United States. As a recreational amenity, tennis holds tremendous appeal: land requirements, develop-ment costs, and maintenance needs are all low relative to the facility needs for comparable activities; regulatory and permitting issues are virtually nonexistent; the game can be played almost year-round in many regions and enjoys a strong complementary market with golf; and the court itself is a relatively simple unit, around which a developer can build a host of supporting facilities, from a straightforward clubhouse and locker room to an elaborate, four-season health and fitness facility. In short, tennis is relatively economical and tremendously flexible. In a residential or resort development, tennis can considerably broaden a project's market appeal for a relatively low investment.

Unlike many other recreational amenities, such as golf courses or boat slips, however, tennis courts are not likely in most cases to directly add significant value to real estate. In some strongly tennis-oriented markets or at tennis camps and resorts, of course, condominiums and home lots located close to or overlooking courts are likely to command premium prices or rental rates. Some developers of rental apartment complexes have also realized higher rents from units overlooking tennis courts. If improperly managed, however, a close proximity can mean excessive noise and other negative impacts, most of which can be addressed by restricting playing hours and similar measures.

INTRODUCTION

In most second-home and primary-home communities, the primary incentive for adding tennis will be to create an important marketing tool. In the right market, a credible tennis facility can more than offset its development costs by accelerating sales or by boosting prices or rents—not because people like to look at tennis courts, but because they want to play on them. Tennis is therefore more of a purely recreational, user-oriented activity than many other amenities that are perceived as valuable even by nonusers.

There are, as always, significant exceptions. Several developers have used tennis as the nucleus of a project's image and identity. At Otter Creek, near Little Rock, Arkansas, for example, a seven-court complex plays a role similar to that of a golf course in many other primary-home communities, with a full calendar of activities and events centering around tennis. Arvida's Boca West in Boca Raton, Florida, has put tennis on approximately equal footing with golf in the project's marketing and operations.

Because a tennis facility can be built relatively quickly and at a moderate cost, tennis is frequently a key amenity in the early stages of many projects (often, for example, while the golf course is growing in). And, of course, many tennis camps and resorts across the nation have used innovative teaching techniques, gourmet food, high-end accommodations, and exceptional court availability to take maximum advantage of the relationship between tennis and real estate.

Paul Barton, Pearson McGuire Associates

Boca West Tennis Center, Boca Raton, Florida

An important development trend in the 1970s was the proliferation of standalone commercial tennis centers and racquet clubs. In many areas, these are still being built and continue to be viable enterprises. In other locations, however, this trend has largely been supplanted by health clubs and fitness centers, which sometimes include tennis courts but are today more likely to offer racquetball or squash. These alternative racquet sports offer particular advantages for commercial recreation in certain markets and as supplemental recreational amenities in real estate projects.

This chapter emphasizes tennis as a recreational amenity in residential and resort development projects. While much of the technical information presented here is applicable to commercial tennis projects as well, some of the market and feasibility information may differ for a tennis project that is developed independent of a larger real estate project.

83

Origins

Although various types of racquet sports and tennislike games have been played as far back as the 14th century, modern tennis is just over 100 years old. In 1873, an English cavalryman named Major Walter Clopton Wingfield adapted a game he had seen played by monks in which a ball was batted against a wall. Major Wingfield, an aristocratic sort, introduced his new contest, played with long-handled rackets and hollow rubber balls, at a lawn party for his friends, or so the story goes.

Wingfield promoted and dominated the game for several years, during which time it traveled west via British officers stationed in Bermuda. By 1877, however, the sport had a new benefactor: the All England Croquet and Lawn Tennis Club, located in a London suburb called Wimbledon.

Around the same time, an American visitor to Bermuda returned to the Staten Island Cricket Club with tennis rackets, balls, and nets, thereby introducing tennis to the States. In 1883, the United States Lawn Tennis Association was formed to standardize rules and equipment and to govern U.S. tennis, a role it continues to perform today as the United States Tennis Association (USTA).[1]

For the sport's first 90 years or so, tennis continued to reflect its aristocratic origins. The game, its players' amateur status, and even their dress remained tightly controlled. Tennis was largely a country-club pastime, although as public parks were built in large numbers after World War II, it began to reach a larger audience. Until the 1960s, however, growth in the number of tennis players and courts remained fairly modest. Then, as part of the social and cultural upheavals of the 1960s, the game began to change. The resulting boom, one of the most remarkable growth periods experienced by any sport, democratized tennis and led to unprecedented demand. Suddenly, tennis became a popular addition to a variety of real estate projects.

Today's Tennis Market: After the Boom

Currently, about 20 million Americans play tennis at least occasionally.[2] Although accurate and timely data are limited, in 1982 the sport ranked 12th among the 30 activities surveyed by Nielsen, down from eighth in 1979 at the crest of the boom.

Judging by the available data (and by the lack of data), the tennis boom is clearly over. At its peak, according to the 1979 Nielsen survey, more than 32 million Americans played tennis. The boom really began in the late 1960s, according to most observers, when the sport's big tournaments were opened to professionals. Also during the 1960s, public spending on parks and recreation, including public tennis courts, rose quickly. On the heels of open tennis came extensive television coverage of the major tournaments. The top pros quickly attained celebrity status.

The figures speak for themselves: In 1960, about 5 million enthusiasts played tennis. By the next decade, this figure had doubled to 10 million. In three short years, it doubled again. By 1973, just over 20 million played tennis—a 400 percent gain in 13 years! And by 1979, the number topped 30 million. Between 1973 and 1976 alone, participation increased 45 percent. The next three years saw another 10 percent jump. Retail sales of tennis equipment rose 90 percent from 1974 to 1978.[3]

After a 10-year period of unprecedented growth, the slump in popularity that followed was probably inevitable. In 1982, the triennial Nielsen survey documented a remarkable 21 percent decline in participation. That year, about 25.5 million players were active. The most recent figures, according to the USTA, show about 19.4 million players—or about as many as were active in 1972.

What happened? Why the tennis bust? Undeniably, there was a certain fad aspect to the boom. Unlike many popular activities, tennis is not an easy sport to master. And although one reason for its popularity was that it requires only a small investment in equipment and clothing (unlike skiing, for example), this also made it easy to drop the sport. Players who felt they were not improving fast enough could easily turn to some other activity without feeling they had wasted much. And by the late 1970s and early 1980s, plenty of available substitutes had emerged. Racquetball, a game whose rudiments can be picked up quickly, soared in popularity. And although the fitness boom was in full swing by the early 1980s, the primary beneficiaries were health and fitness clubs, many of which either offered racquetball or dispensed with racquet sports altogether in favor of sophisticated weight machines and aerobic exercise classes.

For a prospective developer, one of the most revealing figures related to tennis participation is the ratio of total players to the total number of tennis courts. In 1979, at the boom's peak, the ratio was just over 200 players for every court. By 1982, with the addition of some 20,000 courts and a 7 million drop in the number of players, the ratio stood at only 141 players per court. Assuming for the moment that no new courts were built between 1982 and 1984, the ratio again dropped to less than 110 players per court.[4] Assuredly, this analysis is relatively simplistic. Thousands of tennis courts during this period were probably taken out of service or were poorly located or otherwise unused, no matter what the demand. Equally true, however, is that many markets now probably are relatively oversupplied with courts.

This is not to say that it makes no sense to incorporate tennis in a development project. Population growth, demographic shifts, and intraregional migration patterns alone will result in strong individual tennis markets through the rest of the century. An important difference is that these markets will not be found nationwide as they were in the 1970s, but will instead be highly localized. In some areas, the market will perceive tennis as an absolute necessity in a planned residential community. Virtually throughout the nation, a strong, balanced amenity package in a recreational primary- or second-home community will include tennis. In a continuing period of uncertain demand, however, shrewd developers will consider tennis in relatively conservative terms. Happily, the game's physical facilities are well suited to a phased approach. Because each court constitutes an identical unit, additional courts can be added over time as demand warrants. A seven-hole golf course makes little sense, but two rather than six tennis courts may be perfectly suitable.

The post-boom tennis player is more likely to take the game seriously and will probably be more active, playing up to four or five times per week. And although tennis players are notorious for spending little money at the pro shop, bar, or restaurant (golfers have a more generous reputation), serious players will demand a high level of quality and service. Thus, maximizing tennis's potential contribution to development requires close attention to maintenance, events programming, and other management issues.

After the tennis boom, markets will vary widely by region.

The tennis-related development oppportunities most apparent in the next several years will be numerous, but much more targeted than before. Courts will continue to be viable as part of a balanced package of amenities. Few recreational communities will be built in Florida, for example, without at least a modest tennis facility. In the Sunshine State, tennis is considered a natural complement to golf and swimming, and together these three amenities form the most popular basic package. And these "balancing" facilities are not always modest: the developers of PGA National near Palm Beach, in an effort to broaden the market appeal of their golf-oriented project, built a 19-court tennis complex that includes the world headquarters of the Women's Tennis Association.

New tennis complexes, built either independently or as part of a larger project, will probably be coupled with a wider variety of health and fitness facilities: weight rooms, whirlpools, tanning centers, aerobics facilities, squash courts, and so on. The average indoor tennis club will probably be more complex and more expensive to develop because of these additions.

A trend likely to continue is the development of these tennis and fitness complexes as part of what have been primarily single-season resorts. In the past, for example, some ski resort developers have turned to tennis to bolster occupancy during their off-season. Recently, developers James Chaffin and James Light built the $11 million Snowmass Club, a luxurious 76-room hotel that includes tennis as part of a comprehensive health and fitness package at this Colorado destination resort.[5]

Tennis will also continue to be a highly attractive and relatively economical amenity for multifamily projects targeted to young buyers or renters. At Players Place, near Fort Lauderdale, Florida, the developers of this 440-unit townhouse community (targeted to the first-time buyer) combined two lighted tennis courts with a swimming pool, spa, and a small pavilion. According to the developers, the amenity package provided the key to reaching the targeted market.

In some established resort locales like Palm Springs, California, and Scottsdale, Arizona, a viable market will continue to exist for relatively small, luxurious resorts that focus exclusively on tennis. Based partly on the success of such pioneering projects as John Gardiner's Tennis Ranch and Lakeway World of Tennis near Austin, Texas, these resorts cater to the affluent tennis nut. As important as high-quality courts at such projects are first-class food and lodging, superb service, highly developed instructional programs, clinics, tournaments, and a low player-to-court ratio.[6]

SITE SELECTION AND DEVELOPMENT FEASIBILITY

Given the nature of today's segmented and localized tennis market, a predevelopment feasibility study assumes added importance. This preliminary look gives a prospective developer the chance to study the dynamics of the local market as it relates to his or her proposed project and to define the most appropriate type of tennis operation—the amenity that will indeed produce benefits that outweigh its costs.

PGA National's tennis and fitness complex effectively broadened the project's market.

A primary-home community developer who is considering including a few scattered, unsupervised tennis courts will probably not spend a great deal of time on a tennis feasibility study. For this type of facility, the main concerns will be that the site's physical characteristics are suitable for tennis courts and that the investment will prove worthwhile to the project's marketing and sales efforts. The tennis facility, in this case, will be considered as part of a much larger feasibility study and preliminary plan developed for the project as a whole.

On the other hand, the feasibility study for a full-service tennis club to be built as part of a resort or recreational community project can require a relatively complex and somewhat independent assessment. In many cases, such a facility will be examined as part of a feasibility study for a whole package of amenities, typically including a golf course and swim club. The point is that the range of types and formats of feasibility studies for tennis facilities is as wide as the spectrum of facilities themselves.

In any case, a prospective developer must consider how a tennis facility will relate to the other project elements, the physical suitability of the site, and the tennis market, both in terms of demand for and the existing supply of facilities similar to those planned. For all but the simplest, non-revenue-producing facilities, the developer must also consider the proposed operation's economics: the sources, distribution, and timing of development; operating costs and revenues; preliminary considerations as to membership options; and the most appropriate combination of services and programs.

Like most feasibility studies, a review of tennis options can proceed from either of two viewpoints. A developer, having defined a preliminary vision of the facility, can study the market, perhaps even considering alternative sites, to determine how best to realize that vision. Alternatively, one can conduct a market analysis and then from the results review what types of facilities will offer the most development potential. In practice, most feasibility studies combine these two approaches. Most developers enter the preliminary planning stage with a fairly firm idea of what they want to build. Then, based on the results of the market study, they alter their plans to fit existing conditions.

Tennis resorts, as here at Laguna Niguel, California, usually offer state-of-the-art teaching facilities. Note the practice alleys to the player's left.

Physical Requirements

Unlike ski areas, marinas, or golf courses, tennis courts and their related facilities can be adapted to a wide variety of site conditions. In fact, because of this flexibility, tennis can be used to reinforce many different elements of a larger real estate venture. For example, the developers of Lochmere, a primary-home community near Raleigh, North Carolina, built a four-court tennis and swim center near the eastern boundary of their 1,039-acre site, even though the first several phases were developed in the project's western and central areas. One of the reasons for building the amenity relatively far away from the completed units was to help reassure prospective homebuyers of the developers' commitment to the entire project and not just to the early phases.

At Lakeridge, in Torrington, Connecticut, the developer chose to build two types of facilities: an indoor tennis club associated with a pool and clubhouse in a large amenity complex, and scattered pairs of outdoor courts that relate to individual clusters of housing. Vail Associates, in developing Beaver Creek, Colorado, located the project's tennis complex away from the base village but close to both the ski slopes and the higher-density real estate. It therefore complements these other elements but remains an identifiable facility in its own right.

The most popular location for tennis within a larger real estate project is in some centralized core of amenities, designed to ease access for all project residents. This arrangement offers considerable savings because of the potential for sharing such facilities as parking, clubhouse, and other commmon areas with those using other amenities. In some cases, however, tennis facilities are particularly suited for those portions of a site that might otherwise be considered "leftovers." At Harbour Ridge in Stuart, Florida, the location of the main roadway created a relatively narrow strip of land not appropriate for housing but well-suited for the project's swim and tennis center. A fortuitous additional result of this location was that the club's nonresident members—important revenue producers in the project's early years—could reach the club without having to go through the main security entrance.

Climate will affect the demand for tennis more than it will affect the physical feasibility of the facilities themselves. By influencing demand, however, climate can have an important effect on the facility's design and planning. In hot desert climates, for example, extensive lighting for night play will make economic sense, because court use would otherwise be too low. The heat may also require such mitigating measures as shade structures, additional landscaping, and so on. Similarly, wet or cold climates with at least 30 weeks of inclement weather per year may make an indoor facility feasible.[7] Climate may carry implications for other planning decisions, such as the selection of a court surface. These concerns are discussed in more detail later in this chapter.

Courtside atmosphere at Harbour Ridge, Stuart, Florida.

Retaining walls and terraces can help adapt a difficult site for tennis courts.

Site constraints for tennis court development are relatively few. Obviously, a prospective site should be large enough and of adequate shape to support the facility desired. Generally, an acre of land can support about three courts, while providing enough room for parking, sitting areas, landscaping, and associated elements. This rule of thumb varies widely. A single court, for example, measures about 60 feet by 120 feet, so theoretically as many as six courts could be crammed into an acre, although on most sites such density would be inappropriate. A developer should consider a site that will permit future expansion of the tennis facility. The most space-efficient sites will be relatively flat and rectangular in shape, with the long axis oriented east and west. Many of the most interesting tennis layouts, however, have been produced on sloping or irregularly shaped sites, although such sites will generally be more expensive to develop. Slopes of greater than about 8 percent, for example, may require costly terracing and retain-

ing walls and special drainage and circulation measures. As for any similar type of paving construction, soils should be well-drained and stable. Close scrutiny of soil borings on the proposed site during the project's early stages can prevent considerable time loss and expense later on.

The best court sites will be sheltered from the wind and free from such distractions as moving vehicles or noise. A dark background helps players see the ball more easily. Trees and other vegetation can often help block wind and, to a lesser extent, noise, and can provide an attractive backdrop. Trees can also, however, increase needed maintenance through leaf litter; in some cases, their roots can damage court surfaces.

The Market

An accurate analysis of demand for tennis and the supply of existing facilities is critically important to a feasibility study, particularly given the range of potential tennis-oriented amenities—from scattered courts to a full-service private club. An analysis of demand may reveal, for example, that although overall demand may be strong, there is little market for lessons, or a shortage of participants for a juniors program. A look at the existing supply may indicate a relative surplus of free public courts but a dearth of high-quality lighted courts for night play.

Two of the best indicators of tennis demand are average household income and climate. Demographically, tennis is similar to golf, except that the average player tends to be younger and is more likely to be female. Tennis participation can be expected to increase with household income, however, and indoor tennis is particularly strongly correlated with income.

In 1982, the Nielsen surveys revealed that about 12 percent of American households included at least one tennis player. Given the recent decline in participation, a reasonable average rate today might be about 10 percent. The proportion of players will be higher in a warmer, drier climate, or where tennis historically has had a strong foothold—in the suburbs of larger cities, for example. Lower median age and larger family size are also indicators of likely higher participation. Many of the qualities that make a location suitable for a residential or resort development, of course, will also lead to stronger than average demand for tennis.

At private clubs, supporting services, programs, and activities can be as important as the physical facilities themselves.

Beyond a basic estimate of the tennis playing population, a developer will want to determine more qualitative aspects of demand. What, for example, is the favored playing surface? Do younger players favor hard courts, while their parents prefer a softer surface? Is the level of play, on average, strictly recreational, or does a strong demand exist for tournament-quality facilities and instruction? Do players prefer a reservation system that enables them to book the same hour each week for an entire season, or are they more interested in flexibil-

ity and convenience? If the prospective project is a destination resort that will attempt to capture distant markets, it may be necessary to consider such questions on a regional or even a national scale.

A prospective developer should also undertake an inventory of the existing and planned supply of tennis facilities in the market area. Each public and private facility should be examined in terms of age, number, and type of tennis courts and associated facilities for racquetball, squash, swimming, pro shops, locker rooms, and restaurants. Beyond the physical plant, the inventory should include the number of members at each club by type (family, individual, junior, and so on), waiting list status, guest policies, age group orientation, and programs. Programmatic aspects will include instruction, leagues, ladders, and tournaments. Public parks and school tennis courts should be included in the survey.

Based on this basic understanding of the tennis-playing population and the places available to play, the prospective developer can then estimate the existing ratio of players to courts. This ratio can be a useful preliminary indicator of a relative glut or shortage of tennis facilities. The general communitywide standards for tennis courts published by the USTA are presented in Figure 4-1. These standards are based

Figure 4-1
COMMUNITY STANDARDS FOR TENNIS COURTS

Population	Number of Recommended Public and Private Courts
15,000	20
25,000	30
50,000	50
100,000	80
250,000	130
500,000	210
750,000	270
1,000,000	320
1,250,000	360
1,500,000	400
over 1,500,000	1 per 3,600 population

Source: United States Tennis Association, *Tennis Courts 1986–1987* (Lynn, Mass.: H.O. Zimman, Inc., 1986), p. 16.

on the gross population, however, and not the number of tennis players per court. Therefore, if the USTA recommends, on average, 25 courts for a population of 20,000 people, the number of players per court is 96, assuming a 12 percent participation rate.

A more useful figure for those considering tennis as an amenity for a real estate project is the number of players included in the project's market. In a semiretirement project where tennis constitutes the only significant amenity, the participation rate may be as high as 40 percent. The same project with two golf courses may yield only 15 or 20 percent tennis participation.

Most private outdoor tennis clubs will accommodate between 30 and 60 players per court. A typical residential amenity club with six courts, a pro shop, and a clubhouse with lockers, for example, could support a project with a player population of about 240. If the participation rate in this hypothetical project was a healthy 20 percent, this club could serve an overall project population of about 1,200, or perhaps 400 units.

Certain physical improvements and management techniques can greatly boost the number of players each court can support. Lights, for example, can increase the available playing time, and thus court capacity, by a third.[8] A reservation system can help accommodate up to 60 players per court. And, according to the USTA, an indoor court can handle 160 to 170 players. Reasonable estimates of average court vacancy rates at private clubs range from 25 to 30 percent.[9]

As another example, consider the reverse process. Let us postulate a project with a planned buildout of 1,200 multifamily units and 300 detached single-family homes. It will include a golf course and an extensive fitness complex as well as tennis courts. Assuming the average number of occupants at 1.45 for the multifamily units and 2.7 for the single-family homes, the respective populations for the two types will

be 1,740 and 810. Because the residents of the single-family houses are more likely to play golf than tennis, but the multifamily dwellers are avid tennis fans, we can assume participation rates of 8 percent and 15 percent, respectively (only 15 percent for the younger, more active condo residents because of the competing interest in the fitness fa-

cilities). These calculations yield an estimated tennis-playing population of about 325. With lights and a reservation system—standard features in our assumed market—the project will probably need five or six tennis courts. If we discover that high-quality, free public school courts are located close by, we might opt for the lower figure.

Hal Millgard

In some regions, platform tennis has strong appeal as a substitute for tennis or as a supplementary recreational amenity.

TENNIS FACILITY PLANNING AND DESIGN

One of tennis's principal advantages is the extraordinary flexibility in facility planning and design. A tennis court is a standardized unit that can be installed individually or as part of a multicourt complex. Similarly, a whole range of alternative surfaces are available, depending on the desired market, maintenance expectations, and a host of other factors. Moreover, the courts themselves can be supplemented by a variety of supporting facilities or by none at all.

Space Requirements

Although most players would probably prefer to play on individually placed courts surrounded by landscaped walkways, in most residential and resort projects it generally makes sense to construct courts in clusters. Some luxury tennis resorts do, however, offer individual courts, usually as part of a patio home or "tennis villa."

The in-bounds dimensions of a standard doubles court are 36 feet by 78 feet.[10] The amount of space required behind and next to the boundaries depends on the level of play, but the recommended standard is 21 feet in the backcourt and 12 feet on each side. A standard court for tournament play therefore measures 60 feet wide and 120 feet long, or 7,200 square feet. In most cases a typical facility's gross density, including parking and a clubhouse, amounts to about three courts per acre. For rooftops and other tight spots, a 54-foot-by-114-foot court can be playable, but in most cases the standard court is recommended.

Figure 4-2
COURT CONFIGURATION OPTIONS

LAYOUT DESCRIPTION	IN-BOUNDS (Sq. Ft.)	OUT-BOUNDS (Sq. Ft.)	TOTAL (Sq. Ft.)	
STANDARD SINGLE UNIT	2808	4392	7200	
2 Courts End-to-End	5616	8784	14,400	
2 Courts In Battery	5616	7344	12,960	
3 Courts In Battery	8424	10,296	18,720	
4 Courts In Battery	11,232	13,248	24,480	
2 Batteries of 2— End-to-End	11,232	14,688	25,920	
2 Batteries of 3— End-to-End	16,848	20,592	37,440	
6 Courts In Battery	16,848	19,152	36,000	

Courts built in batteries of up to eight or 10 use space more efficiently and are easier and cheaper to build than individual courts. When built side by side, courts can be as little as 10 feet apart, although 12 feet is the recommended minimum. Because each additional court in a battery adds 48 feet of width (with a 12-foot separation), the overall area required is smaller and the cost per court lower. A pair of courts will be 108 feet by 120 feet; three courts will be 156 feet by 120 feet; and four courts will be 204 feet by 120 feet.

The best tennis facilities will consist of individual or paired courts with 24 feet between sidelines and a low dividing fence. Whenever possible, courts should not be placed end-to-end, although the impacts of this arrangement can be mitigated somewhat by high-quality fencing and windscreens. Stadium courts, essential at projects that expect to host high-level tournaments, generally measure 70 feet by 130 feet, to accommodate ballboys and officials.

Stucco walls and grassy slopes help a tennis court visually to fit into a hotel complex. While attractive, the walls, causing balls to rebound, may prove annoying to serious players.

Court Orientation

Courts should be oriented to minimize the adverse effects of facing the sun while playing. The location of the sun, of course, varies with the site's latitude, the season, and the time of day. In temperate climates, outdoor play is concentrated into the nine nonwinter months, when the sun rides relatively high. Play is also divided about equally between the morning and afternoon hours. Therefore, in most of the United States, the most suitable orientation will be with the court's long axis aligned to the north and south. In warmer southern latitudes, however, people play tennis year-round and in the winter months tend to play in the later afternoon hours, when the sun is low in the southwest sky. In these warmer climates, a designer should consider turning the court so that the long axis lies 15 to 25 degrees counterclockwise from true north. This northwest-southeast orientation will keep the player on a court's north side from looking directly into the sun.[11]

There may, however, be other important factors to consider in orienting courts. Steep slopes, for example, may require a less-than-optimum east-west orientation. On some sites, this may not matter. A tennis facility at a Rocky Mountain ski resort, for example, will be used mostly in the summer and mostly in the warmer hours around midday, when the sun is highest; orientation is therefore less of a factor. Similarly, those planning a facility that will host a major championship should ensure that its stadium court is oriented for optimum playing conditions during the event's two weeks.

Selecting a Surface

Court surfaces were once fairly simple: the game originated in England on grass courts (hence the name "lawn tennis"); later, clay courts also proved suitable. During the last 30 years, however, the list of alternative surfaces has lengthened considerably. No less than 14 basic types of surfaces, many of them represented by a number of different manufacturers, are available today. Choosing among this array requires a close evaluation of an individual project's needs.[12]

One of the most important variables in choosing a surface is player preference. Although some gross generalizations can be made (eastern players tend to prefer clay or its fast-drying cousins, while westerners like hard courts), a developer must closely evaluate local conditions and preferences. At Naples Bath and Tennis Club on Florida's Gulf coast, the developers found that the club's hard courts were vacant much of the time; the largely retirement-age market found the softer Har-Tru courts more to their liking, and the developers decided to convert the seven hard courts. Many resorts that cater to the tennis aficionado offer several surfaces.

Another important consideration is the amount of supervision under which the courts will be operated. Concrete courts, for example, require little maintenance and are extremely durable. A concrete surface may therefore be a good choice for courts that will be scattered throughout neighborhoods in a residential project, where they may be subject to bicycle riding and roller skating, activities that can seriously damage some court surfaces.

Climate has a major influence on surface suitability. Clay courts are slow to dry after a rain, whereas other clay-like surfaces dry quickly. In hot climates, it may be desirable to select a court that stays relatively cool, unlike concrete, for example. Excessive surface glare is a related concern. Some surfaces are subject to cracking or softening in the heat, or to adverse effects from frost.

As always, cost also constitutes a key concern. Initial capital costs should be weighed against longer-term maintenance costs (both for materials and labor), as well as the expected life of the surface and resurfacing costs. Because many surfaces are sold as proprietary products, a developer may need to be wary of relatively untested products and should certainly investigate the availability of future service from the manufacturer.

Some special situations may dictate a particular surface. Although most surfaces can be used indoors, some may raise additional concerns, such as dust or excessive moisture. For example, fast-drying courts require daily watering; if they are installed indoors, the ventilation system may need to be upgraded considerably to avoid condensation and high humidity. Courts constructed over garages or on other rooftops should be lightweight and relatively easy to maintain.

Court surfaces can be basically classified into two principal categories: porous and nonporous. Within the nonporous category, courts can either be cushioned with a variety of materials or noncushioned. Figure 4-2 summarizes the characteristics of the major types of surfaces within each of these categories.

Figure 4-3
CHARACTERISTICS OF VARIOUS TENNIS COURT SURFACES

Court Type	Repairs May Be Costly	Glare	Initial Cost per Court Including Base[2]	Maintenance	Average Time before Resurfacing	Resurfacing Cost (1984 prices)	Surface Hardness	Ball Skid Length
POROUS								
Fast drying	no	no	17,000–18,000	daily and yearly care	annual	1,000–1,500	soft	short if damp court
Clay	no	generally	6,000–8,000	daily and yearly care	5 years	1,000–1,500	soft	short if damp court
Grass	no	no	14,000–16,000	daily and yearly care	indefinite	varies	soft	moderately long
NONPOROUS NONCUSHIONED								
Post-tensioned concrete	yes	no (if colored)	16,000–18,000	very minor	5 years (if colored)	3,000–3,500	hard	controllable
Concrete	yes	no (if colored)	14,000–18,000	very minor	5 years (if colored)	3,000–3,500	hard	
Asphalt plant mix (colored)	no	no	14,000–16,000	very minor	5 years	2,500–3,000	hard	
Emulsified asphalt mix	no	no	18,000–19,000	very minor	5 years	2,500–3,500	hard	
Combined hot plant & emulsified asphalt mix	no	no	17,000–18,000	very minor	5 years	2,500–3,500	hard	long if glossy finish medium if gritty finish
Asphalt penetration macadam	no	no	11,000–13,000	very minor	5 years	3,000–3,500	hard	
NONPOROUS CUSHIONED								
Asphalt bound system (colored)	no	no	14,500–18,000	very minor	5 years	2,500–3,500	soft	long if glossy finish short if gritty finish
Carpet[1]	no	no	24,000–27,000	very minor	varies	varies	soft	short
Synthetic turf[1]	no	no	12,000–22,000	very minor	varies	varies	soft	varies according to specification
Modular[1]	no	no	19,000–23,000	very minor	varies	varies	soft	medium to short
Removable[1]	no	no	20,000–23,000	very minor	varies	varies	soft	varies shortest to longest

Ball Spin Effective	Colors	Drying Time after Rain	Balls Discolored	Surface OK In & Out	Surface Cool on Hot Day	Slide Surface	Lines Affect Ball Bounce	Cushioned Surface	Durable	Court Speed Adjustable
yes	green red	fast	yes	yes	yes	yes	yes if tapes	no	hard objects can damage	yes
yes	varies	slow	yes	yes	yes	yes	yes if tapes	no	hard objects can damage	yes
yes	green	slow	yes	out only	yes	yes	no	yes	hard objects can damage	no
yes	variety	fast	no	yes	no	no	no	no	yes	yes
	variety	fast	no	yes	no	no	no	no	yes	yes
	variety	fast	no	yes	no	no	no	no	yes	yes
no if glossy finish yes if gritty finish	variety	fast	no	yes	no	no	no	no	yes	yes
	variety	fast	no	yes	no	no	no	no	yes	yes
	variety	fast	no	yes	no	no	no	no	yes	yes
no if glossy finish yes if gritty finish	variety	fast	no	yes	no	no	no	yes	yes	yes
yes	variety	fast	no	in only	N/A	no	no	yes	yes	no
yes	green red	fast	no	yes	yes	yes	no	yes	yes	yes
yes	green red	fast	no	yes	yes	no	no	no	yes	no
yes	variety	fast	no	in only	N/A	no	no	minor	yes	no

[1]Including base construction.
[2]Prices vary regionally, do not include site preparation or fencing, and will be somewhat reduced when building or resurfacing batteries of courts.
Source: United States Tennis Association, *Tennis Courts 1986–1987* (Lynn, Mass.: H.O. Zimman, Inc., 1986), p. 30–31. Reprinted with the permission of the United States Tennis Association Facilities Committee.

Porous Courts. Porous courts permit moisture to drain through the surface material. These traditional materials consist basically of grass, clay, and a variety of fast-drying surfaces that resemble clay in their playing characteristics. All porous courts are relatively soft and are therefore easier on the player's legs, but they are more susceptible to damage through unsupervised use. These softer surfaces, as a rule, also require a much higher degree of maintenance than hard courts, with daily and annual procedures.

The key attraction of grass, the oldest surface, is its luxurious playability. A grass court, if properly maintained, offers a superb playing surface—attractive to the eye, easy on the legs, and free of dust and glare. Unfortunately, grass courts are extremely expensive to build and maintain, are slow to dry after a rain, and can be difficult to play on

Porous courts have wide appeal in projects oriented to active adults.

if not kept in virtually perfect shape. Nevertheless, a grass court or two can lend a particularly distinctive cachet to a development project, expecially in a market saturated with high-quality but ordinary tennis clubs.

Clay courts also offer a soft playing surface, but with a relatively short ball-skid length that tends to make play slower than on grass. Clay courts are relatively inexpensive to build and generally last longer than many surfaces, but clay can be slow to dry and requires moderately high maintenance.

Grass and clay have been largely supplanted by fast-drying surfaces known by their various trade names (including Har-Tru, Rubico, and Fast Dry, among many others). These surfaces are essentially composed of crushed green stone or crushed burnt brick, which is finely ground and then combined with a chemical binder. This special surfacing is laid over a base of crushed stone to provide a durable but well-drained court. Fast-drying courts are quite popular with players across the nation, and are the courts of choice for most private clubs. Many installations include automatic or manual sprinkler systems for the daily watering these courts require. In addition, fast-drying courts must be filled and rolled regularly to keep them in top condition.

One of the most recent innovations in court surfaces attempts to combine the slow bounce of porous courts with the ease of maintenance of hard courts. These porous concrete courts are composed of precast concrete sections, each with many small holes to allow quick drainage to a subsurface drainage system. These durable courts must be carefully installed to ensure a true bounce, but they are virtually maintenance-free.

Nonporous Courts. Nonporous courts are durable, easy to maintain, and quick-drying. They can be either noncushioned, with a concrete or asphalt base and a thin synthetic sealing coat, or cushioned to varying degrees, with the addition of a membranelike or asphalt-bound layer.

Nonporous noncushioned courts have a hard surface that prevents players from sliding, as they do on porous courts. Most hard courts play rather fast, with a long ball-skid length, although with some surfaces the speed can be controlled by adding abrasives to the surface coat. Although noncushioned courts do not discolor balls or shoes, they are harder on players' feet, legs, and backs than soft courts and can be less popular as a result.

Noncushioned concrete courts can be built in various ways. Among the most common are concrete slabs reinforced by steel mesh or rebar, and post-tensioned concrete reinforced by tightened steel cables. These courts are extremely long-lasting if properly built and require almost no maintenance. In some areas, asphalt courts offer virtually the same characteristics as concrete at a lower cost. Both types are commonly surfaced with liquid-applied acrylic materials. These color finishes provide a uniform texture and a durable, attractive surface. Although no official color scheme exists and the finishes are available in a wide variety of hues, green for the in-bounds area and red for out-of-bounds has found wide acceptance.

This straightforward hard-court installation will require little maintenance.

Nonporous cushioned courts offer all the maintenance advantages of nonporous courts without the usual leg-fatiguing hard surface. Like fast-drying courts, cushioned courts are available from a wide variety of manufacturers. Although individual characteristics vary, most work by incorporating a cushion course over the surface course during construction. This cushion can include rubber granules or cork particles in emulsified asphalt or acrylic latex mixtures, or can consist of continuous elastomeric membranes (which are particularly suitable for rooftop courts because the membranes are also waterproof). Whatever the material, the cushion course measures between one quarter inch and one inch thick.

In addition to these basic surface types, a variety of other synthetic surfaces are available. Some, like special carpets, are suitable only indoors. Others, such as synthetic turf, are finding fairly wide applications. In each case, these materials attempt to be both resilient and easy to maintain.

Modular surfacing is essentially a grid of rubber, plastic, or other material that comes in interlocking, one-foot squares. These tiles can be easily placed over an existing deteriorated surface. Because of their light weight, they are especially suitable for rooftop courts.

Synthetic turf consists of polypropylene fibers woven into a backing material and laid over a prepared surface. This surface is then covered with a layer of sand, the thickness of which determines the playing characteristics. The results are maintenance needs somewhere between porous courts and hard courts; a tough but resilient surface; and flexibility in application. According to the USTA's *Tennis Courts,* the sand has a tendency to absorb unpleasant odors. The developers of Sun City in Florida, however, have reported an extremely favorable response to the new surface from a retirement age market playing in a warm climate.[13]

Synthetic turf court at the Wyndham Hotel in Orlando, Florida.

Sportec International

Court Lighting

Lighted outdoor courts can offer about a third more playing capacity than unlighted courts, an advantage that can provide a big boost to a tennis club's occupancy in a climate where evening hours are playable much of the year. In particularly hot climates or in markets where evening demand for tennis is strong, the cost of court lighting systems can be recovered relatively quickly, through higher occupancy and, usually, through higher court fees. Many experts on tennis facility development even claim that, if budget restrictions exist, a developer will be better off building a few lighted courts rather than a larger unlighted facility.[14]

Of course, if courts are not lighted properly, they may as well not be

Older fluorescent lighting (above) and newer high-intensity discharge lighting at Naples Bath & Tennis Club, Florida. (Note sprinkler head mounted near the net post, at left.)

lighted at all. Poor quality lights are extremely frustrating to play under and may, in the long run, prove more trouble than they are worth. The key objective, of course, is to provide uniform illumination of the ball throughout all aspects of play. At the same time, lights should remain unobtrusive both to players and to surrounding residents or other land uses. Finally, the developer needs to ensure that the benefits of lighting courts will be commensurate with the costs.

Lighting experts, who should in any case be consulted in planning such a facility, generally agree that the quality of light is more important than the quantity.[15] Quality is measured primarily by the uniformity of light levels over all court surfaces, by an absence of glare, and by an acceptable color tone. Quantity is measured in footcandles, or their metric equivalent, lux. The amount of footcandles needed depends on the level of play expected. National championships, for example, require so-called Class I illumination of at least 75 footcandles (750 lux). Class IV lighting, acceptable for social and recreational, nontournament play, on the other hand, requires only about 20 footcandles (200 lux).[16]

Light fixtures are best located along the court alleys so that light will be thrown across the playing surface. Lights should never be placed directly behind the baselines or in the corners, where players would look directly into the glare during play.

The acceptable height depends on the type of fixture, but lights are generally mounted between 15 and 35 feet above the court surface. Newer designs have produced high-quality lighting on poles as low as 20 feet, which are less obtrusive and easier to maintain than the traditional 30- or 35-foot steel or aluminum poles.

Fluorescent lighting indoors at Lakeridge in Torrington, Connecticut.

The three basic light sources for court systems are incandescent, fluorescent, and high-intensity discharge (HID), which includes high-pressure sodium, metal halide, and mercury vapor. Each type varies as to efficiency, lamp life expectancy, initial cost, maintenance cost, color, and luminaire characteristics.

Incandescent systems are relatively inexpensive to install, but if operated heavily they can be quite expensive in the long run due to short lamp life and low efficiency. Light from incandescent lamps, which are usually quartz iodine or tungsten, has good color, however, and requires no warm-up time. Incandescent luminaires are relatively small and lightweight, making installation and maintenance easier.

Highly efficient fluorescent systems are usually installed in continuous rows along the court sidelines at a fairly low level. Their lamps are relatively long-lived and offer good color, but if mounted low can produce an unacceptable glare.

HID sources are efficient and long-lived, although each type requires several minutes to warm up to full brightness. Mercury vapor lamps emit about twice the light

per watt as incandescent lamps and endure an exceptionally long life (24,000 hours). Standard mercury vapor lamps, however, produce a bluish-white light unless color-corrected lamps are used. Metal halide lamps can produce the same amount of light with fewer fixtures, although each lamp has a shorter expected life. Metal halide lamps also avoid color problems. High-pressure sodium systems are both more efficient and longer-lasting than other HID types; they produce a distinctive bronze or orange-colored light.

Three-foot sideline fencing.

Court Fencing

Fencing arrangements can range from simple and unobtrusive backstops to extensive individual enclosures for each court. Like many other design criteria, the proper type of fencing will reflect the amount, type, and level of play expected. Public parks will generally require higher backstops and full-length sideline fencing, along with secure gates to discourage improper use (to keep out bicycles, for example, many public court gates do not fully open). A private club, on the other hand, may eschew the standard chain link for more attractive fabric fencing and may limit the use of sideline fences.

Generally, however, tennis fencing is of chain-link fabric on galvanized steel poles. Vinyl-clad fabric is both more attractive and quieter than uncoated galvanized steel fabric. Backstops generally rise between 10 and 12 feet. Sideline fencing can range between 3 and 10 feet. Many private clubs separate courts with fabric netting or use side fencing for only the first 20 or 30 feet from the backstop.[17] Ideally, players should be able to get to any court without crossing any other.

Indoor Tennis Structures

Although most residential and resort tennis facilities will include only outdoor courts, in some climates indoor courts make sense, provided that strong enough demand exists and outdoor conditions are unacceptable for a good portion of the year. According to the USTA, profit-oriented indoor clubs require about 110 to 120 players per court to break even. Assuming a 15-hour operating day, each court can handle about 160 players per court.[18]

At Lakeridge in Torrington, Connecticut, a second-home project developed in 1973 during the middle of the tennis boom, developer George Giguere included three indoor courts as part of a 27,000-square-foot complex that also included an indoor pool. Although indoor tennis at that time was seen as a key amenity for the New York City–area second-home market, it is unlikely that such a facility would make economic sense today. An indoor facility would today be more likely to include racquetball or squash courts, as well as extensive exercise and fitness facilities. But if adequate room exists, an indoor tennis court may be a highly attractive addition to such a complex in a development project.

Most indoor tennis facilities are housed in prefabricated steel structures, with about 30 percent in air-supported fabric "bubbles," masonry block buildings, or other structures. One promising alternative to fully indoor or fully outdoor tennis is to cover the courts with a tension-supported fabric structure with open or closed sides. Air-supported structures, which cost only about half as much as the same size steel building but which are generally shorter-lived, can also be used to cover outdoor courts during the winter season.[19]

The visual impact of fencing can be mitigated through the use of windscreens. These plastic or fabric curtains hung on fences can be effective in reducing the effects of moderate winds as well. In higher winds, however, windscreens will not make a great deal of difference to a player and can result in damage to the fencing. If windscreens are used, fencing should be designed to withstand these stresses, with stronger fabric and closer-set posts. In particularly windy areas, one strategy is to shield the courts with earthen berms or to step the courts into a slope, providing a far more effective wind barrier than windscreens. Perimeter plantings can also be effective windbreaks, although they may increase court maintenance.

Whatever the structure, an indoor tennis facility will require a 120-foot clear span. Generally, courts are built in groups of two or four, side by side. If fabric court dividers are used, courts can be as close as eight feet apart. To avoid interfering with play, the roof over the net should be positioned at least 26 feet high, although 35 feet is recommended for tournament play. At the eaves near the baselines, the overhead clearance should be at least 16 feet.

This overhead structure shades the players at Laver/Emerson Tennis Weeks resort in April Sound, Texas.

Loews Hotels

Fabric baffles at Loews Paradise Valley Resort mitigate lighting glare.

Practice and Support Facilities

Most tennis facilities will offer areas that facilitate clinics and other instructional programs as well as simply individual practice sessions. In the simplest case, this could be a practice backboard. At the other extreme, some resorts offer large and elaborate circular facilities with machines at the center spraying tennis balls at players in pie-shaped practice alleys.

A simple backboard can be made of fiberglass, wood, or concrete. Factors to consider in choosing a material include cost, noise, and durability. Concrete is the most expensive but the quietest, wood is cheap but less durable and noisy, and fiberglass falls in between concrete and wood for both cost and noise. Fiberglass backboards are quite durable, however.

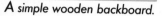

The Tennis Clubhouse

Clubhouses vary tremendously, depending on the specific project and on the type and size of other amenities such as a golf course or swimming pool. Some clubhouses will integrate all users, with common locker rooms and dining facilities for tennis players, golfers, and social members. Others will attempt to orient different users to different parts of the facility. A lounge catering to golfers, for example, may overlook the 18th hole, while tennis players order drinks on a deck overlooking a row of courts.

Generalizing about the compatibility of golfers and tennis players is quite difficult. For every club manager who claims the two groups are vastly different in their outlook and interests, there is an architect or developer who claims no difference exists at all. Each such situation must obviously be considered carefully in view of a specific market and project type.

For clubhouses oriented primarily toward tennis players, the basic elements should include a control counter and pro shop; a lounge and viewing area, perhaps with a snack bar or grill; locker rooms; offices; and storage space. Many clubs will also offer a child care area and rooms for card-playing, meetings, or social events. A few will include large-scale ballrooms or conference facilities. Suggested square footage

A simple and portable alternative to a backboard is a rebound net, a fabric net suspended on a strong frame. Rebound nets are less expensive and quieter than backboards.[20]

Any club that offers instruction will need a host of other equipment, including ball machines. The newest generation of microprocessor-controlled machines even retrieve balls themselves when operated on a specially built practice court. In recent years, video recording and playback equipment has become an important part of instructional programs. Electrical outlets and microphone jacks can therefore be necessary additions to the courts themselves.[21]

At any amenity-oriented development project, and especially at resorts, image and atmosphere are critically important. Unlike a golf course or a ski slope, each with its own individual character, one tennis court, except for surface variations, is not much different from any other tennis court. What makes the difference at any tennis facility, no matter what size or complexity, are the character and quality of the support facilities. Shade structures such as pavilions, pergolas, and gazebos; landscaping and walkways; viewing areas; and drinking fountains, benches, courtside telephones, and other "furniture" all serve to make the activity more pleasant. While most involved in country clubs agree that tennis players prefer simpler support facilities than golfers, it is apparent that projects that carefully consider the needs of the tennis player are likelier to yield long-term dividends.[22]

ranges for these basic program elements are presented in Figure 4-3.

In most clubhouses, the entrance area will be devoted to a reception and control desk. Staff requirements can be minimized if this area offers a clear view of as many of the tennis courts as possible, the pro shop, and the locker room entrances. If the pro shop is expected to produce significant revenue, it may be desirable to channel foot traffic through the pro shop on the way to and from the courts or the control counter.

Most tennis clubs will require from eight to 10 parking spaces per court.

Figure 4-4
PROTOTYPICAL TENNIS CLUBHOUSE PROGRAM

RIVER BRIDGE
COMMUNITY Primary residences, 522 acres, 4,300 dwelling units
LOCATION   Palm Beach County, Florida
AMENITIES   Lagoon system, tennis club

Program Elements

	Square Footage
Reception/Administration	
Lobby & coat storage	250
Club administration	180
Men's toilet	300
Women's toilet	400
Porte cochere[1]	2,300
Food and Beverage Service	
Lounge	1,180
Kitchen	330
Activity Support Space	
Tennis pro shop	460
Lounge	2,570
Indoor Activity	
Exercise room	6,350
Meeting rooms	1,050
Building Support Space	
Mechanical/electrical/elevator	820
Building storage	710
Circulation	140
Maintenance	110
Conditioned Total	**15,030**
Unconditioned Area Total	**2,300**
TOTAL BUILDING AREA	**17,330**
Outdoor Activity	
Tennis courts	6
Auxiliary Facilities	
Parking spaces	110

[1]Unconditioned area.
Source: Diedrich Architects & Associates, Inc. Atlanta, Georgia.

Locker room planning is fairly straightforward. Although some authors have claimed that women's locker rooms need only be one third as large as men's, the addition of exercise rooms and other facilities, as well as changing patterns of recreation, have probably made this rule of thumb obsolete. In most cases, a locker room should provide a shower for every 1.5 to 2 courts, and five to seven lockers per court, depending on whether lockers are used regularly or only when players visit the club.

Generally, full-scale restaurants should be reserved for clubs with large enough memberships to support them or for resort clubs, where quality food is expected. Even a modest club, however, should include at least a pleasant place to get a drink after playing, even if it is merely dispensed from a vending machine.

A typical tennis club should offer enough parking spaces to accommodate eight players per court, plus one for each employee.[23] This ratio will essentially be twice the static court capacity, thus providing for arrivals and departures at the same time as courts change over. Obviously, if some players will reach the club on foot or by other means, or if golfers or swimmers will share parking, this figure should be adjusted accordingly.

TENNIS FACILITY MANAGEMENT

The management issues concerning tennis facilities pertain mostly to tennis clubs: amenities that include some basic supporting features and services, such as a clubhouse, pro shop, restaurant, locker rooms, a reservation system, lessons, clinics, and perhaps club leagues or tournaments. Simpler tennis amenities that consist of courts alone, or courts along with some limited amount of programs, will often be managed simply as one component of a homeowners'

association or as a line item on a developer's budget. Even extensive clubs may be managed as one department or profit center within a larger amenity complex, in conjunction with such other facilities as a golf course, swimming pool, or yacht club.

As with any major recreational amenity, ownership of tennis facilities can vary, and each alternative form of ownership carries broad implications for operations and management. Generally, ownership patterns for tennis clubs are quite similar to those for golf courses associated with development projects. Typically, a developer maintains ownership and operational control until a project matures to some prearranged point (usually based on some percentage toward buildout or of total units sold, or when the club's cash flow is positive), then transfers the facilities to a home-owners' association, nonprofit country club, or other entity. In resort projects, a developer will often either retain ownership after a project is complete or will sell or lease the amenities to a resort operator. Myriad variations on these themes exist.

One clear trend in tennis club management, similar to that displayed by golf courses and marinas, is for a developer to contract with a specialized tennis management firm. At Stuart, Florida's Harbour Ridge, for example, developer John B. Dodge has retained overall management control of the Harbour Ridge Country Club, including the project's golf course. Because of the special operational characteristics of tennis, however, he has signed on with an international tennis management group, Burwash International. The firm provides the project with a resident tennis professional responsible for directing all court scheduling and maintenance, instructional programs, tournaments, and pro shop operations.

In a project with complete in-house club management, the tennis pro is essentially analagous to the golf pro. Each supervises the specialized aspects of their department. Whereas most golf pros or golf directors are assisted by a superintendent who manages course maintenance, tennis pros often are responsible for maintenance as well. In a full-scale club, both a golf pro and a tennis pro, along with a head chef, fitness director, and other department heads, will generally report to a club manager or assistant manager. Smaller-scale facilities, such as at Otter Creek, near Little Rock, Arkansas, may be run by a full-time manager with a staff of part-time tennis pros who essentially are responsible only for instruction and pro shop operations.

Guy Mancuso

Most of the useful data that have been compiled on tennis club management relate to standalone commercial facilities, often with indoor courts. As profit-oriented business ventures, these clubs avoid some of the issues associated with developer's clubs. At a commercial club, for example, all members are more or less equal in the eyes of management. Dues, fees, and court scheduling thus remain relatively straightforward. At a combined residential and resort project, however, a club will be used by both project residents and by resort guests. To meet the slightly differing needs and priorities of these two groups presents a particularly tricky management challenge. Solutions, similar to those devised for golf courses, usually revolve around priority scheduling for homeowners, differential fee structures, and so on. Developer's clubs are also key marketing tools for real estate sales. As such, they may be operated and maintained at a level that is not necessarily profitable from a club manager's point of view but that makes sense for the overall project.

Nevertheless, many of the operating principles and experience gleaned from commercial tennis clubs also apply to amenity clubs. The following discussion emphasizes management issues associated with facilities that are designed and operated to provide high-quality tennis at some reasonable return on investment. Because many tennis-oriented amenities will be complicated by the presence of golf or other facilities and by multiple objectives (some, like marketing, only tangentially related to tennis), management issues may be at once more complex and simpler for a development-oriented club.

Revenues and Expenses

Tennis club operating costs and overhead costs, like those of a golf course, are largely fixed. Therefore, one of the key management objectives is to maximize the revenues from various membership dues and fees, which constitute the largest category of club income. There are nearly as many membership plans and structures as there are clubs. A simple tennis amenity, for example, may build the costs of membership into the price of the real estate and then levy a nominal user fee to cover variable costs. More complex facilities may be open to both residents and outsiders and may rely on a dues and fee structure similar to that of a commercial club. Whatever the arrangement, this revenue category will produce, on average, between 40 and 70 percent of total revenues.[24] Other significant sources of revenue include the pro shop, food and beverage service, equipment rentals, lessons and clinics, and, in some cases, tournaments.

Membership clubs are the most common arrangement in real estate projects, particularly while the real estate products are still being marketed. In the early stages, outside members are often invited to join, both to provide important revenue while the project itself is relatively underpopulated and to help spread the word about the new club. Usually, these nonresident members are phased out as a project matures. In some clubs, the coexistence of residents and outsiders may pose a challenge similar to that experienced by resorts that cater to both residents and guests. Sometimes, the two groups may use the facility during different seasons. Clubs at several Florida projects, for example, offer low-priced, off-season memberships to nonresidents.

The three basic types of member revenue are initiation or membership fees, monthly or annual dues, and a variety of user fees. The relative importance of each type depends on the nature of the club, the market, and to some degree the regional norms. Traditionally, amenity clubs, like standard country clubs, charge a relatively high initiation fee and monthly dues, plus nominal fees for the use of the courts. Commercial indoor clubs, on the other hand, tend to charge a low initiation fee, modest seasonal dues, and a relatively steep hourly user fee. Many indoor clubs sell one hour each week for a 30-week season at a special seasonal rate. User fees will often vary by membership type. A full member might play an unlimited number of hours at no extra charge, for example, while a social or golf member might be assessed an hourly fee.

The aim of any dues and fee structure, of course, is to maximize the use of the courts by setting up appropriate incentives gauged to demand. A prospective club developer must examine the market's characteristics to establish a membership structure: What are the established patterns of play in the area? Does strong demand exist for evening, midday, or morning play? What time of day is demand weakest (when hourly rates should be

Figure 4-5

INCOME AND EXPENSE DISTRIBUTION PER MEMBER, 1984
(Based on a Sample of 73 Clubs)

Source of Income per Member				Disposition of Income per Member			
Membership Dues	Food and Beverage Sales	All Other Sales and Income	Total Revenue	Payroll and Related Costs	All Other Operating Expenses	Total Costs and Expenses	Available for Debt Service, Capital Improvements, etc.
$560	$792	$290	$1,642	$791	$796	$1,587	$55

Source: Pannell Kerr Forster, *Clubs in Town and Country—1984* (Houston: Pannell Kerr Forster, 1985), p. 15.

dropped)? Is the market predominantly novice players, who may respond to organized leagues and clinics rather than straight hourly play, or experts, who simply want to book a twice-weekly, two-hour slot?

Perhaps most important at an amenity club, a developer should relate the way members pay to the club's overall intended ambience and character. A club whose financial aspects resemble a straightforward commercial club (low initiation fee and dues, high hourly charge, few services) may not be appropriate for a luxury residential community. An important aspect of a club in a residential project is its social atmosphere, its "clubbiness," which usually connotes exclusivity and a sense that the club is a key part of a community or even an extension of the members' homes. For many developers, this kind of amenity will be operated much like a private country club.

A club owner who retains control of the pro shop, rather than leasing it to the tennis pro, can expect the shop to produce between 15 and 30 percent of total revenues, the second largest single income category. Clubs with substantial food and beverage operations, however, will see this category account for up to 50 percent of total revenues.[25]

For a relatively modest facility, the key advantage of placing a shop in the pro's control is that a pro will come to know the individual needs of each member, and will therefore be likely to provide better service. In many lease operations, the pro keeps all revenues from the shop and pays a negotiated rent, sometimes based on sales. Many tennis consultants point out, however, that most pros are relatively inexperienced at merchandising, often weak in selection and display of goods, and generally slow to take advantage of the nearly captive market at the typical club.[26] They suggest limiting a pro's involvement in the shop, allowing him or her to concentrate on instruction. Pro shops at resort clubs will usually be managed by an experienced retailer because of the higher volume of clothing sales.

The largest single expense category for a tennis club will be for salaries and related costs, which tend to account for about half of all expenses. Heat, light, and power requirements vary widely by the type of club and the climate, but in most cases will average between 10 and 20 percent of total expenses. Facility maintenance and repairs will also vary; a typical figure lies between 10 and 15 percent of total expenses. Maintenance costs for porous courts will be higher. A variety of other operating expenses will account for 10 to 15 percent of all expenses, leaving about 5 percent available for debt service and capital improvements.

Compensating club personnel can be problematic, depending on the relationship with the tennis pro. If a pro receives a nominal salary plus a hefty commission on lessons and pro shop revenues, it may be appropriate for the pro, or his or her staff, to handle many routine maintenance tasks. If the pro is paid hourly, it may make sense to hire a variety of other, cheaper personnel to perform these duties. Other jobs may also be suited to nonprofessionals. For example, Paul Pastoor, manager of John Gardiner's Tennis Ranch in Scottsdale, employs a number of competent but lower-priced "counselors" to direct the resort's children's program.[27]

Facility Maintenance

As discussed above, courts vary in their maintenance requirements. Generally, porous courts will require daily attention and annual resurfacing. Nonporous courts need little routine maintenance and should be resurfaced only when considerably worn. Proper installation of all types of courts will significantly reduce maintenance needs. In many cases, poor preparation of the sub-base, for example, can result in a variety of short-term problems and a long-term need for complete court reconstruction.[28]

Grass constitutes the most fragile and finicky of all court surfaces. Grass courts are quite similar to golf course greens in their construction and materials. Greens, however, are usually treated with unusual respect by golfers, whereas tennis players tend not to modify their game because of a delicate surface. Grass courts should be maintained by a trained turf expert, well-versed in the fine points of fertilization, fungus and insect control, soils, and drainage. Although a properly maintained grass court can last for decades, the playable surface will need to be relocated periodically to avoid excessive wear and soil compaction.

On a daily basis, clay courts must be brushed to remove any loose material and rolled to compact and even the surface. Lines on clay courts, which are usually tapes fastened with nails, should also be checked daily. Clay courts require watering only during prolonged dry spells and should be periodically top-dressed with a layer of new material, either clay or the fast-drying variety. Although a well-built clay court can last up to five years without resurfacing, many leading clubs resurface their clay courts annually. Existing clay courts are sometimes resurfaced with fast-drying material, provided the underlying layers are in good condition. Usually this reconditioning takes place in the spring, at the beginning of the outdoor season.

Maintenance for fast-drying surfaces is similar to that for clay, except that becuse the top material is looser, the courts must be more carefully checked for evenness and watered daily. Sprinkler systems for fast-drying courts can either be manually or automatically controlled, with impact-type heads or smaller spray heads. Sprinkler heads are usually mounted about 18 inches above the court surface. Courts should be watered just enough to saturate them, without washing away any of the surface material. In choosing a sprinkler system, a developer should look for convenient operation, an adequate spray pattern to guarantee proper coverage, and a safe location of sprinkler heads for players. In cold climates, sprinkler lines should be protected from freezing, either by being buried below the frost line or by permitting complete emptying of the lines. Fast-drying courts can also be protected from surface damage during cold months by covering them with plastic sheeting or

a deep layer of mulch. The surface should be top-dressed at each season's beginning, with the addition of about one to two tons of material per court. A reasonable life span for a fast-drying court is about five years. Beyond that time, it will be difficult to maintain a level playing surface without constant attention.

Nonporous courts virtually dispense with such daily care and feeding. Beyond a daily sweeping and an occasional washing, their maintenance needs are minimal. Most manufacturers of color sealants warrant their products against discoloration or oxidation for some period, but eventually nonporous courts will need resurfacing about every five years. At John Gardiner's Tennis Ranch in Scottsdale, fully half the courts are resurfaced annually, at a cost in 1985 of about $15,000. In most cases, resurfacing simply involves a new colored surface coat, with minor filling or patching as required. Most manufacturers offer a variety of surface treatments to counteract minor cracking and spalling. Badly worn courts, however, usually need a full asphalt layer as well. Major cracking and heaving of the subgrade typically call for major reconstruction. Synthetic surfaces generally require less maintenance than porous courts but more attention than concrete or asphalt courts.

Beyond maintenance of the courts themselves, a pro or club manager should maintain daily, weekly, and semiannual inspection schedules for such items as nets and posts, fencing, gates, windscreens, and other supporting equipment.

Marketing and Promotion

In a national market that currently has, to some arguable degree, an oversupply of tennis clubs, effective marketing and promotion efforts are crucial for any club. With a residential or resort tennis facility, proper promotion and appropriate programs can help a project's overall marketing efforts by creating a sense of activity and community. Tennis players are generally not as loyal to their current clubs as golfers; they are more easily persuaded to change clubs. To entice established local tennis players to a fledgling club, however, a developer must establish the facility's credibility early on. One valuable technique may be to establish a tennis advisory board or committee, composed of key members of the local tennis establishment and perhaps a well-known touring professional.

An increasingly popular method of establishing credibility is to host a tournament. Men's and women's professional circuit tournaments can be expensive to host, but they can greatly boost a project's image. Sea Pines Plantation's Family Circle Cup and Mission Viejo, California's Virginia Slims tournament are widely known and attract thousands of potential real estate buyers to these projects.

Some experts caution, however, that the costs of a major tournament may not equal the benefits. For example, pro tournaments will require costly stadium courts and seating areas, accessory parking, and a whole range of temporary support facilities. In addition, the courts and all attendant facilities—lights, fencing, and so on—must meet tournament-level specifications. Usually, the tour will specify the type of surface required, which may or may not correspond with the needs of those who play on the courts the rest of the year. Hard tournament courts may therefore

need to be converted later to soft courts, at a cost of up to $10,000 per court.

Worthwhile alternatives to the major pro tournaments exist, however. Florida's Naples Bath and Tennis Club, for example, has established itself as the "Official Home of the Grand Masters," where a group of well-known former professional champions play several tournaments each year. Not only are these tournaments far less costly than a major tour stop, they also reflect the project's older but tennis-hungry market. In a similar manner, John Gardiner's tennis ranches reap a great deal of publicity by sponsoring celebrity pro/amateur tournaments. These popular events are especially suitable at resort clubs.

For more localized promotions among the membership, clubs can pursue a variety of tournaments, leagues, competitive ladders, and other events, usually under the direction of the tennis pro. One of the most important management issues is adequate access to courts and an ability to match players by ability level. Although some 70 percent of a typical club's memberships are family memberships, most players play without another family member, and so are in need of appropriate partners.

This courtside slope at Naples Bath & Tennis Club is used by spectators at the club's Grand Masters tournament series.

CHAPTER FIVE

SKI AREA DEVELOPMENT

Although the development of nearly every type of major recreational amenity is limited by site constraints, this limitation assumes perhaps greatest significance for ski area development. Advances in snowmaking technology and wider participation in cross-country skiing have broadened the range of potential ski area projects, but one indisputable fact remains: Alpine skiing—still the heart of the industry—requires hilly terrain and cold, snowy weather. For this reason, any ski facility beyond a rudimentary backyard layout or a simple trail network inherently differs from other types of amenities in its relationship to real estate development.

INTRODUCTION

Compared to other major amenities, ski areas are much likelier to be profitable business ventures that may, as a logical adjunct, also engage in real estate development. For most other amenities, the relationship is the mirror image: the recreational facilities exist to support the real estate. At ski areas, real estate is more likely to play a subordinate role. There are, of course, some notable exceptions, and in recent years skiing has been nearly inseparable from development, especially at larger areas. In 1983, however, only 32 percent of North American ski areas engaged in land development.[1] And, surprisingly, eastern and midwestern areas were more likely to be involved in development, although the western areas are more often considered the epitome of American skiing.

This relationship may again be shifting. Increasingly, ski area owners are turning to development as a means of revitalizing their operations. At Hidden Valley near Pittsburgh, a small day ski area has been transformed into a multi-season second-home community and conference center, replete with a rounded-out amenity package that will include golf and tennis. This type of retrofitting has become more prevalent, in fact, than the development of new ski areas.

Skiing, then, carries with it a somewhat different set of development parameters than the other facilities discussed in this text. Marinas, perhaps the next most restrictive amenity from a site standpoint, can nevertheless be built at a fairly wide range of locations in many different regions. Golf, and especially tennis, are quite flexible. But a developer considering a ski area will be entering a fairly limited field, one with a relatively short but rich history and an optimistic if less than certain outlook.

The Skiing Economy

A 1982–83 survey conducted by the National Ski Areas Association (NSAA) estimated North American ski industry gross revenues of $1.04 billion and payrolls of $241 million.[2] In 1983–84, some 19 million skiers spent more than $1 billion on consumer goods related to the sport. Indeed, by any yardstick, skiing is a multibillion-dollar industry in the United States.

Estimates of the number of active skiers in the United States range between 14 and 22 million, depending on how the category is defined. In 1982, the triennial A. C. Nielsen surveys pegged skiing as the 14th most popular sport of the 30 surveyed, claiming more than 19 million participants in both Alpine and Nordic, or cross-country, skiing.

In the 1984–85 season, Alpine skiers set a record, visiting the nation's approximately 700 downhill ski areas a total of 51.4 million times. In recent years, total annual skier visits have fluctuated around the 50 million mark, depending on weather conditions and a variety of economic factors. In addition, cross-country skiers took advantage of nearly 600 touring centers (80 percent of which were built between 1970 and 1980, according to Ski Industries America). Based on data from the NSAA's annual *Economic Analysis of North American Ski Areas* (perhaps the most reliable and comprehensive review of any recreational industry and a model for other national associations), in 1983 the Alpine component of this physical plant represented gross fixed assets of more than $5 billion on nearly 400,000 acres.

A Demographic Profile

Over the years, many in the skiing industry have decried the sport's image as the domain of only the rich, young, and beautiful. Certainly, this popular image has in some cases impeded efforts to broaden the base of active skiers, but to some degree it is accurate.

Team Russell Photography

Wintergreen, Virginia.

Skiers, on average, are indeed more affluent and younger than the U.S. population as a whole. As for beauty, so far this variable has escaped measurement.

Nearly 70 percent of America's 20 million or so skiers are under the age of 30, and just over 56 percent are male. Cross-country skiers tend to be slightly older, with a median age of 32.6 years, and are equally represented by men and women.[3] The ski industry depends heavily on the teenage and young adult markets. In the age brackets from 12 to 17 years and 18 to 34 years, the rate of participation is nearly twice that of the next most active age group, those from 35 to 54.

Like most sports activities, skiing participation is strongly related to income and education. In 1980, skiers were twice as likely as the average American to report incomes of more than $25,000. About one in four skiers has had some graduate education, compared to less than 10 percent of the overall population. Partly due to the strong participation by young people, half of all skiers are single; about 80 percent of U.S. adults are married.

Figure 5-1
SKIING PARTICIPATION

	1976	1979	1982
Incidence of Participation (Total Population)	5.0%	6.8%	8.4%
Number of skiing participants	10.5 million	14.6 million	19.1 million
Downhill only	n.a.	10.5 million	13.6 million
Cross-country only	n.a.	2.7 million	3.6 million
Downhill and cross-country	n.a.	1.4 million	1.9 million
Incidence of Participation (Total Population)			
Male	5.9%	7.7%	9.8%
Female	4.6	6.6	7.5
Under 12	6.2	5.2	7.8
12–17	16.7	21.4	27.5
18–34	19.6	26.7	29.0
35–54	7.3	11.0	15.8
55 or over	1.0	2.8	2.7
Participant Profile			
Male	55.0%	53.2%	56.3%
Female	45.0	46.7	43.7

n.a. = not available.
Source: A.C. Nielsen Surveys and Economics Research Associates.

According to the 1982 Nielsen survey, the average Alpine skier had been actively pursuing the sport for 6.9 years. Nordic skiers averaged four years of experience. Many skiers, of course, are fairly inactive. Just under half of all skiers participate fewer then five times per year. At the other end of the scale, most studies agree that about one quarter of all skiers account for nearly 75 percent of all skier visits.[4] One of the most visible—and telling—trends in the past few years, however, has been the declining frequency of participation: In 1976, the average skier reportedly skied 12 days per year. By 1979, the average frequency had declined to 11.5 days, and in 1982, according to surveys, the rate was down to nine days per year.[5] Frequency of participation is about the same for cross-country skiers. During the same five-year period, the overall incidence of participation had grown from 5 percent of the total population to nearly 8.5 percent. The trend is clear: the number of skiers is larger than ever, but they are skiing less often. So far, the number of total skier visits is still rising (depending on weather conditions in a given year), but the declining frequency is troubling to those in the industry.

Skiing participation also varies by region. On a per capita basis, the sport ranks as most popular in the West, where more than 22 percent of all residents ski. Northeasterners are nearly as active, with a participation rate of nearly 20 percent.

Mountain sites can pose severe development constraints.

Southern states and midwestern states have rates of 6.8 percent and 13.5 percent, respectively. Recent interregional migration patterns, however, have created shifting markets, and many analysts now predict a bright future in the southern skiing market.[6] Regional participation rates also reflect historical supply patterns, with a relative dearth of ski facilities in the South. With improvements in snowmaking and grooming technology, an expanded supply is likely to accommodate some latent demand for southern skiing.

Traditionally, cross-country skiing has been heavily based in the Northeast and Midwest, which together accounted for better than seven out of 10 Nordic skiers in 1980. Since then, however, the popularity of cross-country has grown considerably in the West.[7]

The North American Ski Area

When the seminal Sun Valley area opened in Idaho 50 years ago, organized ski facilities were a true novelty on the American scene. Although the sport itself was popular in some regions, the primary technology that makes the modern ski area possible—the ski lift—was still in its infancy. By some estimates, as few as four ski areas existed in the early 1930s.[8] The numbers grew exponentially, however, during the next three decades. By 1947, there were about 90 areas, and 10 years later more than 200 existed. Between 1960 and 1968, ski area development exploded, rising to a total of 600 areas. Yet by 1978, only an additional 100 had been added to the inventory. Since then, the number of ski areas in the United States has stabilized at around 700.[9] The comprehensive listing in *The White Book of Ski Areas* in 1984 placed the total figure at 689.[10]

Most studies acknowledge, however, that the actual total, including a number of smaller areas that operate on weekends only and may close from year to year depending on snow conditions, may be around 1,000.

Somewhat surprisingly, during the heyday of ski area development in the 1960s, the East assumed dominance over the West in its share of total ski sites. In 1960, western states had acccounted for nearly half of all U.S. areas, and about 38 percent of ski facilities were located in the East. By 1968, this relationship had flipped; eastern states boasted half the total inventory, with only about one in three facilities in the West. In 1978, this relationship still held true, with the Midwest and South accounting for about 20 percent of all areas.

Figure 5-2
AVERAGE SKI AREA CHARACTERISTICS

	1982–83	1981–82	USFS Permittees 1982–83
Size			
VTF/hour (000)	6,207	6,159	7,575
Gross fixed assets (000)	$7,706	$6,740	$9,174
Location			
Within 50 miles of SMSA	32%	32%	22%
With 6+ areas in 1 hour	29	34	24
New England	15	17	7
East	16	13	0
Midwest	13	10	2
Rockies	30	33	52
West	26	27	39
Site Characteristics			
Number of beds at base	1,203	1,170	1,849
Number of beds (10 miles)	3,860	4,032	4,571
With snowmaking	68%	63%	51%
With a night operation	38	38	20
Terrain: Beginner	26	26	23
Intermediate	49	49	48
Expert	25	25	29
Business Characteristics			
Operating with USFS permit	50%	53%	100%
Engaged in land development	32	37	29
Operational Characteristics			
Average days/nights of operation	117	130	139
Average peak day crowd	4,166	4,291	4,713
Average skier visits (000)	194	207	253
Average age of ski areas	24 years	23 years	25 years
Average revenue/skier visit	$15.24	$14.40	$15.49
Average lift ticket revenue/skier visit	$12.90	$12.46	$13.24
Average adult lift ticket price			
Weekend	$16.43	$15.60	$16.48
Weekday	$14.89	$14.29	$15.82
Average night ticket price			
Weekend	$ 9.01	$ 8.42	$ 8.54
Weekday	$ 8.47	–	$ 8.42
Average adult season ticket price	$ 325	$ 327	$ 353
Average utilization	38%	40%	39%
Average profit (loss) before tax (000)	$ 143	$ 679	$ 368
Ratio: Revenue/GFA	42%	53%	46%
No. of areas reporting	118	115	59

Source: C. R. Goeldner et al., *Economic Analysis of North American Ski Areas, 1982–83 Season*, pp. 6–7.

But while the East may still have the greater number of facilities, the West holds a clear advantage in capacity.[11] Western areas tend to be substantially larger than their eastern cousins, and in the 1984–85 season accounted for more than 62 percent of total skier visits.[12] Nationwide, about 200 ski areas accommodate nearly 75 percent of all skier visits.

Average ski area size can be, and has been, measured in various ways. The 1982–83 NSAA *Economic Analysis of North American Ski Areas* was based on a national sample of 118 areas that represented 49 percent of the nation's skier visits. Because the areas sampled made up less than 20 percent of the total number of areas, yet accounted for nearly half the nation's skiing, the data clearly represented the larger areas. Nonetheless, because these areas are perhaps more likely to be engaged in real estate development than the smaller facilities, the NSAA data are useful.

The average ski area characteristics based on the NSAA survey are presented in Figure 5-2. Size is measured in terms of gross fixed assets (GFA) and by vertical transport feet per hour (VTFH). Gross fixed assets represent "the total of the original undepreciated costs of the improvements and fixtures plus the cost of equipment necessary to generate sales and other income."[13] The 1982–83 average GFA figure of $7.706 million represents a 14 percent gain over 1981–82.

Perhaps a more revealing measure of ski area size is provided by VTFH, which is the product of the manufacturer's rated hourly lift capacity times the number of vertical feet transported. Thus a double chairlift with a rated capacity of 1,000 skiers per hour that carries skiers up 500 feet of vertical rise would have a VTFH of 500,000. The total of all VTFH figures for all lifts at an area provides the VTFH for that particular area. Based on the NSAA sample of 118 ski areas, the average VTFH in 1982–83 was over 6 million. Further, U.S. Forest Service permit holders—which tend

Figure 5-3

CHANGE IN AVERAGE VERTICAL TRANSPORT FEET PER HOUR (VTFH) PER SKI AREA BETWEEN 1983–84 AND 1984–85, BY REGIONS

Region	No. Reporting[1]	NSAA Survey Respondent Data Average per Ski Area		Percent Change
		VTFH (000) Per Ski Area 1983–84	VTFH (000) Per Ski Area 1984–85	
Northeast	51	4,365	4,755	8.9%
Southeast	25	2,281	2,370	3.9
Midwest	33	1,748	1,761	.7
Rocky Mountain	51	6,440	7,025	9.1
Far West	28	6,102	6,465	5.9
Pacific Northwest	13	5,266	5,434	3.2
Alaska	4	2,937	2,969	1.1
Total United States	205	4,472	4,789	7.1%
Canada	19	6,451	6,663	3.3%

[1]Number reporting an answer for both years.
Source: Marvin W. Kottke and NSAA, *National End of Season Business Survey 1984–1985*, p. 10.

to dominate the large end of the scale—had a VTFH average of 7.575 million.

The 1984–85 NSAA *End of Season National Business Survey* presented a slightly different picture, based on a larger sample of 205 areas. These figures, shown in Figure 5-3, show a U.S. average of 4.472 million VTFH. As might be expected, midwestern areas were the smallest on average and ski areas in the Rockies were the largest. The annual growth rate of average VTFH since 1982 has remained constant at about 7 percent.

One interesting conclusion drawn by the 1983–84 *End of Season Survey* concerns the relationship between size, as measured by VTFH, and volume of skier visits. Clearly, the larger the ski area, the more visits occur. But when measured as the number of skier visits per 1,000 VTFH, the survey data suggest that larger areas enjoy a clear advantage. Except for areas with less than 1 million VTFH, as VTFH rises the number of skier visits grows at an increasing rate.

For example, mid-size areas with between 2.5 and 4.9 million VTFH experienced about 26.6 skier visits

per 1,000 VTFH. The largest areas, however, with total VTFH of 10 million and over, hosted 32.4 skier visits per 1,000 VTFH. Based on these data, beyond a certain threshold a unit increase in lift capacity will yield an increasing boost in skier visits.

With this pattern in mind, it is perhaps not surprising that the big ski areas are getting bigger. In 1980–81, only about 4 percent of the respondents to the NSAA survey reported a VTFH of 10 million or more. In 1982–83, these large areas constituted nearly 18 percent of the sample. During the same period, the number of small areas of less than 2.5 million VTFH stayed roughly the same, while the number of mid-size areas represented in the sample dropped significantly.

In the 1982–83 survey, the average ski area offered 557 acres of skiable terrain that supported a crowd of 3,841 skiers, or an average density of 6.9 skiers per acre. Densities were significantly higher in the Midwest and Northeast.

As will be discussed in the following section on physical development issues, VTFH is still somewhat limited as a measure of a ski area's size. After all, a ski area is more than just lifts and vertical feet. These elements must be balanced by the slope acreage and by the capacity of such ancillary facilities as food and beverage service and parking areas. A more definitive measure, often referred to as Comfortable Carrying Capacity, can be used both to evaluate the performance of existing areas and as a valuable tool in the planning of new developments.[14]

About 70 percent of all ski areas lie within 75 miles of a major metropolitan area. For day ski areas, this figure jumps to nearly 85 percent. Nearly half of all destination resorts are located further than 100 miles from a metropolitan area.[16] Ski areas also tend to be clustered, due both to the nature of the required terrain and to more typical patterns of consumer behavior. In the 1982–83 NSAA survey, nearly 29 percent of the sampled ski areas reported six or more competitive areas within an hour's drive.[17] About 40 percent of the ski areas surveyed offered night skiing and nearly 75 percent reported some snowmaking capability.

Skiing and Real Estate

Skiing has been intertwined with real estate development ever since the first remote resorts opened, thus creating an instant market for lodging, accommodations, entertainment, and shopping. Many of today's major ski areas very nearly qualify as communities unto themselves, with all types of real estate products, from hotels and high-density attached residential products to retail shops, single-family homes, lot sales, and so on. While most major ski-related developments are closely related to the ski area operator or developer, many other development entities may become involved. Sometimes, as is the case at Loon Mountain in Lincoln, New Hampshire, several developers will work closely with each other to meet complementary segments of the residential, recreational, and retail markets.

Today, resorts are including a much wider variety of products in

In the 1982–83 NSAA study, the authors present average calculated capacities for ski areas by region, based on the assumption that demand varies by region and that skiers of differing ability levels demand different amounts of vertical feet per hour of skiing.[15] These calculated capacities were then compared to operator's estimates of both a "comfortable" crowd and a peak-day crowd. The authors found that nationwide, the estimated peak crowds and comfortable crowds measured 108 percent and 107 percent of calculated capacity, respectively. At eastern areas, peak crowds exceeded the calculated capacity by 43 percent, while areas in California and Nevada maintained a small amount of excess capacity, even in the face of a peak crowd.

Landownership at ski areas is also related to regional location. In the East, nearly 90 percent of ski areas occupy wholly private land. Rocky Mountain and western facilities, on the other hand, are found on public land about 80 percent of the time. In the East, state land leases are relatively common, while western sites most often are permitted by the U.S. Forest Service.

their development plans. In the late 1960s and 1970s, whole-unit condominiums were by far the predominant form of ski area development. Now, whole units are complemented by timeshare projects and, increasingly, by quartershares and other forms of segmented ownership. In 1982, for example, Purgatory, a major ski area in southwest Colorado, embarked on an ambitious expansion program, expected to cost $250 million over 10 years.[18] One key objective that emerged four years later was to increase product flexibility. Early on, condominiums near the ski lifts sold well, even though the lowest-priced product was about $100,000. Soon, however, that market was exhausted. In the search for alternatives, the developers, the Durango Ski Corporation, turned to quartershares (13-week segments) and to standard one-week timeshares. Similarly, the developers of the Mountain Club at Loon in Lincoln, New Hampshire, sold quartershares of individual units in a 114-unit hotel at the foot of the slopes. Nearby are whole-unit condominiums and standard timeshare projects.[19] In this type of real estate development, the product may differ little from the familiar ski area condominium, but the form of ownership and the nature of the use can vary widely. The popularity of condominiums, timeshares, and variations in ski-oriented development stems partly from the nature of ski areas as traditional resort destinations, well suited to short-term accommodations and investor-oriented real estate. The ski area itself is a heavily capitalized facility, dependent on a fairly high seasonal volume of resort guests.

Ski area planner Jim Branch of Sno-engineering, Inc., has outlined a typology of ski areas that is useful when considering ski area real estate development issues. According to Branch, this relatively simple classification extends beyond the "day-weekend-destination" breakdown in "an attempt to segment the perceived market appeal of resort areas into their respective consumer classifications."[20]

In Branch's scheme, a Type I resort is a true international destination facility. It contains a superb natural ski mountain or series of mountains, a wide range of lodging, accommodations, and real estate operations, and usually is located in a larger, more complex town or village. Snowmass, Aspen, Vail, Deer Valley, and Sun Valley all fall into this rarefied category. Type I resorts appeal to a wide range of potential real estate investors, often attracting significant amounts of foreign capital and corporate investment.

Type II resorts are where a great deal of real estate development is occurring today. These areas are similar in scope to a Type I resort, but offer fewer social and cultural opportunities, are less diverse, or are not as well established in the marketplace. The difference is one of degree, rather than substance. Typically, Type II areas will appeal to a more limited market, will tend to cater more to ski clubs and other groups, and will be more likely to offer various discounted package plans. Telluride and Breckenridge in Colorado, Sugarloaf Mountain in Maine, and West Virginia's Snowshoe illustrate this category.

Type III areas feature high-quality skiing, but offer little in the way of on-site real estate development, for a variety of reasons but often because of a lack of space. They may operate only on weekends or will otherwise not cater to destination or overnight skiers. Colorado's Loveland Basin and Massachusetts's Wachusett Mountain fit this profile. Significantly, many Type III areas may aspire to Type II status. The missing link is real estate development. Many relatively small areas, particularly those near urban areas, are turning toward some type of real estate planning to help revitalize their operations. These areas, particularly if they are well located, can offer substantial development possibilities.

Rounding out this typology are the numerous very small ski operations that, while providing an important local recreation resource, are often operationally marginal. These areas are usually open only on weekends and often only offer surface lifts. As such, they are extremely vulnerable to weather conditions. As areas that help to cultivate new skiers, however, these small areas can be very important to the ski industry.

Branch goes on to note that Type I and Type II areas, where the bulk of real estate development occurs, often cater to slightly different market segments. The major destination resorts usually offer real estate products that are more expensive, larger, and oriented more toward the user and less toward the investor. Real estate buyers in these Type I resorts tend to be older, more loyal to the area, more family-oriented, and less inclined to rent their units. The probable buyers in the Type II resort are more likely to be interested in the investment potential of a condominium or second home, but because they are generally younger and more likely to be single or divorced, they usually ski more often and at more areas than the Type I buyers.

Clearly, there are ski areas and ski-related real estate ventures that belie these hypothetical profiles. In the discussion and case studies that follow, however, such classifications will be useful.

The History and Development of Skiing

In one form or another, skiing has played an important part in people's lives in snowy regions for several thousand years, a fact attested to by Stone Age cave drawings in Norway. First used for basic transportation and subsequently employed for important military purposes, skis were not used widely for recreation until the mid-1800s. Then, one Sondre Norheim of Telemark, Norway, created a stiff, toe-and-heel binding that enabled him to carve long, gliding turns—later dubbed the Telemark turn. Norheim's innovation was the first in a long line of advances that gradually converted skiing technique from what we know as Nordic (cross-country) skiing to the beginnings of today's Alpine techniques.[21]

The true revolution, however, was still about 60 years away. By the late 19th century, skiing had caught on in the United States, where the first ski club sprang up in California shortly after Norheim's exploits in Norway. It was left to the Austrians, during the first 30 years of this century, when Europe witnessed a surge in the sport's popularity, to develop the basic principles and techniques of modern Alpine skiing. In 1930, Alpine skiing received its biggest boost when its two key competitive events—the downhill and the slalom—were recognized by the sport's ruling body, the International Ski Federation.

Shortly after the Alpine world received this sanction, the first world championships were held, followed the next year by the 1932 Olympics, the first to be held at Lake Placid, New York. Although the Lake Placid games showcased only Nordic events, they were nevertheless responsible for a surge of American interest in the young sport. By 1932, skiing was poised for the first of a rapid-fire succession of innovations that have helped to make it one of America's most popular recreational activities.

The advent of modern American skiing is perhaps best dated from 1934, when Gilbert's Hill near Woodstock, Vermont, was the site of a pioneering experiment: the first ski lift in the nation, consisting chiefly of a rope and a model T engine, dragged Vermonters up the hill for a dollar a day. In the following five decades, the hallmark of skiing has remained innovation, not only in technology and equipment, but also in instruction, clothing and fashion, real estate development, and political effectiveness. Each period of innovation has boosted the sport's popularity. Over the years skiing has not only become more fashionable; it has also become safer, easier to learn, and far more accessible. The sport has also benefited from the same postwar demographic and economic patterns that have helped create strong markets for golf, boating, and a number of other recreational activities.

Many of the first notable strides in the 1930s and 1940s occurred in the design of basic ski equipment. The first modern bindings, coupled with new steel edges, gave the skier a much greater degree of control, which in turn led to new turning techniques and to refined methods of instruction. Although skiing remained still very much an activity for the hardy, the appearance of first the J-bar and then the chairlift eliminated one of the sport's major drawbacks: the tedious trudge back up the hill.

The first chairlift appeared at the nation's pioneering ski resort, Sun Valley near Ketchum, Idaho. This venture by the Union Pacific Railroad still stands as the nation's seminal winter destination resort.[22]

Deer Valley Resort

Snow Park lodge at Deer Valley, Utah. Deer Valley is one of the largest western resorts built wholly on privately owned land.

With the development of a remote site like Sun Valley came the idea of housing skiers at the mountain itself, thereby planting the seed for the connection between skiing and real estate that continues today. By 1938, lifts were beginning to appear around the nation—not only chairlifts, but also T-bars and aerial trams.

During the Second World War, although ski area development came to a standstill, two events occurred that would produce a major impact on the sport. First, the most decorated American division of the war, the Tenth Mountain Division, was hailed for its Alpine exploits. After the war, many Tenth Division veterans would join the skiing industry, among them one of the founders of the Aspen Skiing Corporation. Also as a result of the war, dozens of Europe's most famous skiers and instructors came to the United States, forming an important pool of talent for the infant industry that had the unintended effect of lending the sport a distinctly European flair and style, an image still much in evidence.

In the 1950s, technological advances continued apace: easier-turning metal skis, buckle ski boots, and step-in bindings all made their debuts. Ski areas also began to pay more attention to the quality of their trails. Early grooming machines appeared on Colorado slopes and the first commercially used artificial snow fell at Grossinger's in New York. The link between skiing and fashion was forged for good in 1955 with the first appearance of stretch pants. Seemingly unrelated events also had influence. The federal interstate highway system, for example, made formerly distant areas much more accessible and helped fuel the rapid pace of ski area development.

One of the most important ski areas opened in 1954 in southern Vermont. Mount Snow, near West Dover, pioneered the mass marketing of the sport to neophytes. With wide trails over relatively gentle terrain, Mount Snow could be skied by

Slopeside development at Wintergreen, Virginia.

practically anybody, and innovative lift designs moved skiers up the mountain at the unprecedented rate of 1,200 every hour. The developers of Mount Snow recognized that ski areas, to tap the growing demand, had to stop catering solely to expert skiers. As a result they were able to attract up to 10,000 skiers per day at a time when most operators would have been happy with 2,000.

Skiing in the 1950s grew steadily as a result of these innovations, but the real boom began in 1960. That year, the Winter Olympics were again held in the United States, this time at Squaw Valley in California. And for the first time, the games received broad television coverage, thus exposing many Americans to the sport.

The connection between real estate and skiing, forged 30 years earlier in Idaho, took off in the 1960s. One key factor was the steadily increasing popularity of the condominium form of ownership, which was formally recognized in this country in 1962. Tailor-made for ski areas, condos could be built at higher densities than traditional single-family second homes, thereby conserving scarce land at a mountain's base. Attractive to both users and investors, they could be easily

rented for short-term intervals during the ski season, thus ensuring a steady supply of customers to the slopes and to the attendant restaurants, bars, and shops.

Coupled with the condo phenomenon emerged today's concept of the destination resort. Although many such ventures preceded it, perhaps the most notable archetype of the destination ski resort is Vail, Colorado, which opened in 1962 with 870 acres of skiing served by two chairlifts and a gondola. Vail set the standard for later resorts, with its pedestrian core, variety of accommodations, emphasis on quality food and entertainment, and carefully controlled planning and design. It was also one of the first ski areas to establish itself initially as a destination resort, unlike most other areas that evolved from a local or regional resort.

The history of skiing in the 1970s—the environmental decade—is paradoxical. On one hand, continuing advances in equipment and clothing made skiing safer, easier, and more comfortable than ever. On the other, the pace of ski area development slowed precipitously. Hamstrung by high land prices, spiraling capital costs and interest rates, and an increasingly arduous development approval process, many prospective ski area developers abandoned the scene.

Between 1968 and 1978, the rate of ski area development slackened by about 75 percent. Demand, however, still rose at a healthy 12 to 15 percent every year.[23] The major difference from the earlier decade was that instead of new areas coming on line, the larger, more established areas proved able to add to their existing capacity.

All was not gloom, however. Cross-country skiing, energized by the development of waxless skis and benefiting from a broader environmental consciousness, reached new heights of popularity. Major advances in instruction techniques were developed and a new citizens' racing program (NASTAR) introduced to skiing a concept not unlike the golfer's notions of par and handicap. The net effect of the 1970s, though, through increased regulation and changing economic conditions, was to dramatically politicize and retard the process of ski area development.

The Current Outlook

Most ski area developers and operators agree that in the 1980s the bloom is off the real estate rose. Even at Vail, the pacesetting resort of the 1960s and 1970s, the local economy, according to former Vail Associates president Harry Frampton, is "changing from a real estate orientation to a service orientation."[24] The Snowmass Company's James Chaffin echoes that sentiment, commenting that ski-oriented real estate is "turning from the investor market to the user market."[25]

One of the reasons for the shifting focus has been a weak condo and resort real estate market, especially at many large western resorts, during the early 1980s. Although capital for ski area development has remained relatively available due to favorable tax policy shifts, the market has suffered for a myriad of reasons, including the slower growth in demand for skiing, higher fuel costs, and the early 1980s recession. In addition, skyrocketing land values have helped to drive real estate prices to formidable, and for many, unaffordable, levels. The importance of public policy to ski-oriented real estate was reemphasized in 1984 and 1985, years that saw a potential recovery frustrated by the uncertain status of the second-home mortgage-interest tax deduction.

Demographic shifts through the remainder of the century will send mixed signals to the ski industry. On one hand, the number of teenagers, historically a crucial skiing market, is declining precipitously, although the teen population will again begin to grow in the late 1990s. On the other hand, the population as a whole is aging. Although today's and tomorrow's elderly are more active than previous generations, this group has traditionally accounted for very few skiers. And ski areas have historically not geared a large proportion of real estate development toward the retirement market.

At the turn of the century, the middle adult age groups from ages 35 to 55 will be occupied by the baby boomers, those born between 1946 and 1964. They will then represent about the same proportion of the population as they do currently. Although people of these ages will be the most likely to be part of the second-home and resort real estate market, and household income will generally rise, it does not necessarily follow that the market for skiing will be strong. With a greater proportion of two-income families, and with childbearing years delayed, competition for affluent adults' available leisure time will be intense.

For this reason, one of the most promising ski-related development opportunities may be in relatively small areas located close to metropolitan areas. These areas could both serve as a convenient local alternative to destination areas and could act as feeders for the major resorts, potentially broadening the base of active skiers.[26] The increasing value of time should also reemphasize the growing popularity of cross-country skiing, thus presenting another major development opportunity.

For those who do take up skiing in the next several years, continuing advances in equipment and clothing promise to make the sport more comfortable and more convenient. Recently introduced synthetic fabrics such as Gore-tex and polypropylene keep today's skiers warmer. Also, the first major advance in chairlift design in 30 years made its debut at several American mountains during the 1985 season. The new high-speed, detachable quad chairlifts offer capacities of up to 3,000 skiers per hour and can greatly extend a lift's potential range. This advance should give the large areas with the acreage, the capital, and the excess demand an even greater advantage. As service and quality become the industry's watchwords, advances in both snowmaking and grooming technology will help extend the length of the ski season and will help ensure prime skiing conditions.

The prospective ski area developer still faces a variety of hurdles. Perhaps chief among these, especially for those considering a large project, is the significant cost involved. In 1985, speaking of a mid-sized resort project, Jim Branch cautioned that, "if you can't handle at least a $20 million investment, you shouldn't be in the ball game."[27] High capital costs are exacerbated by the long lead time and sizable soft costs for planning, engineering, and securing the necessary approvals. Branch has noted that the planning stages alone for a typical western resort could easily entail costs of $1 million or more and take up to seven years.

Development on public lands involves mean lengthy public reviews to secure the necessary operating permits. According to many observers, the approval process has become more rational, focused, and reasonable since the 1970s.[28] Still, the paucity of suitable sites coupled with diverse political demands make the approval process a significant barrier to ski area development.

Once developed, ski areas face a number of operational constraints. Business, and therefore labor, is highly seasonal. In remote locations with high local housing costs, employee housing often becomes a significant part of a resort development program. Marketing costs are also high, and new areas can face tough competition from established facilities. Most recently, ski area operators have been frustrated by rising costs and decreasing availability of liability insurance coverage.

Over the next several years, then, the major development opportunities related to skiing will lie predominantly in one of two major categories. First, smaller locations near urban areas will offer the most potential for success, especially if associated real estate development is carefully conceived for an increasingly segmented local market.

Wachusett Mountain Ski Area

Wachusett Mountain Ski Area in Massachusetts represents one of the most promising development alternatives: a medium capacity area close to a large market.

Cross-country facilities, either in conjunction with these Alpine areas or as amenities to residential development, will also grow in popularity. Much of the prospective real estate activity, however, will occur within the sphere of influence of major, established areas, which by virtue of their history, size, and marketing advantage will continue to capture the majority of skier visits in the foreseeable future.

SITE SELECTION AND DEVELOPMENT FEASIBILITY

Two primary factors distinguish the early stages of planning and developing a ski area from those of most other recreational facilities. First, few sites meet the basic physical criteria for a first-class ski area; fewer still can also boast of a strong local skiing market with convenient access. For these reasons, and because of the high capital costs involved, the preliminary planning for a ski area will be longer, more costly, and more complicated than for any other recreational facility. Even a rudimentary feasibility analysis will probably require a bevy of specialized consultants. A detailed review for a public agency will call for a virtual battalion of experts, from wildlife biologists to avalanche trackers.

In much of the nation, the only suitable sites for a downhill facility will be located on public land. Fortunately for prospective ski area developers, the U.S. Forest Service, part of the U.S. Department of Agriculture, recognizes the need for public recreational use of these lands. Under the terms of the 1960 Multiple Use Sustained Yield Act, the Forest Service permits concession-operated private ski areas on National Forest lands. Many states also permit similar operations on state-owned land. The base areas of these facilities are often developed on private lands. Virtually all the ski areas with substantial real estate development are built on a combination of public and private lands.

For the developer, the necessary trade-off in building on public lands is that the primacy of recreational use, as opposed to the many other potentially competing interests in public lands, must be established to receive a permit. A project's feasibility, of course, hinges on the issuance of a permit. Thus, the preliminary planning and feasibility analysis for a public lands project must make the case for a ski area's development from a public-benefit standpoint, as well as meeting the developer's private objectives. The Forest Service itself makes its position clear: "Although private land values are affected by the location of resort areas, maximizing the value of individual tracts of private land must be a secondary consideration of the Forest Service."[29]

The public review and permitting process is discussed in detail later. It will suffice at this juncture to point out that the process can be formidable indeed.

Basic Feasibility Criteria

Because of the importance of physical issues to ski area feasibility, the early planning process should begin with an examination of such basic physical criteria as terrain, climate, and other factors as necessary to develop a conceptual plan. From this preliminary physical inventory, a developer can estimate a propsoed facility's potential capacity and then generate the expected capital cost per skier or, more precisely, the cost per unit of capacity. According to planner Jim Branch, in late 1985 a developer could expect this figure, which includes all capital costs but not land costs, to range between $4,000 and $5,000 per skier, depending on location. Labor costs tend to raise costs in urbanized areas.

Based on this rough analysis, plans can be refined or modified as necessary to produce the detail needed for a break-even analysis. This projection of revenues over time, based on assumptions of the average revenue per skier visit, will indicate the level of demand (in skier visits) needed to cover fixed and variable costs. In the 1982–83 season, average revenue per skier visit was $15.24.[30] By factoring in an analysis of local supply and demand, a developer can estimate the chances of receiving at least a break-even demand. With further refinements in the physical and operating plan, detailed financial pro formas can then be prepared by department and category, including both ski operations and real estate development.[31]

This thumbnail sketch of the feasibility process simplifies an extremely complex procedure, which varies tremendously according to individual conditions. Because the basic initial criteria are predominantly physical characteristics, these are discussed in greater detail below.

Site Suitability

The relative desirability of a prospective ski area site is clearly related to the proposed facility's type. Destination resorts ever since Sun Valley have been developed in remote locations, which is undoubtedly part of their appeal. Today, however, accessibility is critically important to a resort's economic viability. In recent years, Utah's major ski areas have made much of the fact that they are clustered in a region they say is less than an hour's drive from Salt Lake City's airport. Similarly, Beaver Creek is minutes from Colorado's Interstate 70. Adam's Rib, a proposed resort in Colorado, has been stalled for years, principally over a county requirement that the developer build a $14 million state highway to its site.[32]

Destination resorts lying beyond a three-hour drive will find it difficult to tap a local and regional market in the early years of operation. Without this business, reaching operating capacity can take many years. According to former Vail Associates vice president Robert Parker, about 80 percent of the skiers at Vail during the resort's first season were from the region. Today, however, the local share stands only at about 30 percent. Parker says that with the exception of Aspen and Steamboat, all the major destination areas in Colorado have experienced more or less the same pattern.[33]

Smaller areas that cater to a local market will be optimally located within about an hour's drive from an urban center. Jim Branch frequently cites the success of Wachusett Mountain, a 450-acre day ski area 52 miles outside Boston. According to Branch, Wachusett generated approximately 200,000 skier visits and more than $4 million in gross revenues during its first year of operation. Central to this success was its location, with more than 5 million people living within 50 miles of the base lodge.

Beyond location, the most fundamental site criteria are size, terrain, and potential snowfall ("potential" because snowfall depends both on what falls naturally and on what the operator can create, given the proper temperature and humidity conditions). What constitutes a large enough site clearly depends on a project's market and overall concept. In the United States, ski areas range from less than 100 acres to several thousand acres. Many potential sites are constrained, however, by inadequate room at the base area to provide all the necessary support facilities, especially parking. Sometimes, this requirement can be alleviated by developing these facilities nearby, but the most successful areas will offer well-developed base facilities. Similarly, the best mountains will disperse skiers throughout the area via a lift system that radiates from one or more central points at the base. A site, therefore, should be wide enough to permit this type of lift pattern.

A typical Type I or Type II ski area—one with extensive real estate development playing an integral part—will exhibit planning principles similar to any planned community. The base area, the principal activity focus, typically will be surrounded by high-density, expensive real estate products—usually hotels or other accommodations, whose occupants stay a relatively short length of time. Often located farther away from this core area will be medium-density vacation condominiums or timeshare products of a similar design. Real estate having direct ski access to the slopes will command premium prices, either through hotel room rates or through real estate prices. Single-family homesites will generally be set away from the actvity core, but perhaps on surrounding slopes with desirable views.

Retail development is usually arranged to serve these various groups, with specialty shops, restaurants, and ski shops and services located close in; convenience retail space located in a middle zone; and various services and larger stores set farther out. Satellite developments—which may involve lower-priced hotels or condominium developments built by developers independent of (or sometimes in cooperation with) the ski area operator—will often spring up still farther from the ski area. Many such projects will offer transportation service to the mountain.

Terrain is more than just vertical drop or average slope. Experienced trail planners look for a wide variety of gradients as a mark of a potential Alpine or Nordic ski area. As they begin to lay out potential trails, designers will attempt to match the various grades with the prospective market. A mountain with a predominance of expert terrain—gradients between 45 and 75 percent—will not be financially viable in most markets.

Instead, the best areas will match the distribution of terrain types with the distribution of the market's ability levels. For example, as a national average, beginning and novice skiers constitute between 10 and 15 percent of all skiers. They require an average slope gradient of about 8 to 25 percent (see Figure 5-4). Assuming that the local market profile reflects the national average, a developer should look for a mountain with a proportionate amount of novice terrain. The appropriate percentage of novice slopes may not necessarily equal 10 to 15 percent of the total, however, because more novices can be accommodated by an acre of slope than can experts. Each case must be examined individually.

Overall vertical drop provides one relatively simple way of measuring a ski area. Although Aspen Mountain in Colorado offers about 3,000 feet of vertical drop, an adequate ski hill can have far less. A small, one-lift hill built as a residential amenity or an in-city public facility, for example, could be built with as little as 150 feet of drop. (The nation's smallest ski area, Iowa's Winter World, features an even 100 vertical feet.) Most areas in the East contain between 500 and 1,500 vertical feet.

Nearly as important as a site's snowfall is its ability to retain snow. Slopes should face predominantly north or northeast to avoid long exposure to the sun. But, in some cases, modern snowmaking and grooming technology can make sites with other orientations viable. Wind can be even more destructive, stripping exposed slopes bare in hours. For obvious reasons, wind is also unpopular with skiers.

In previous years, a prospective ski area site needed at least 100 annual inches of natural snowfall to be considered viable for development. More recently, however, successful facilities have been built in relatively snow-barren locations where, without snowmaking, the ski season would last less than a week.[34] In most regions, a ski area will need a combination of natural and artificial snow to permit about 80 to 100 days (or equivalent days, if night skiing is offered) of skiing. For snowmaking, this requirement translates to about 800 to 1,000 hours of temperatures below 28 degrees Fahrenheit. Such climatological data are available from local U.S. Weather Service offices.

In areas of heavy snowfall, avalanche hazard areas may be an important concern. Protecting skiers' safety may require special patrols to identify and eliminate potential slides, or may restrict a site's ski-able area.

Heavy snow loads often require special construction techniques.

Snowmaking, as well as a host of other ski area functions, requires a dependable, high-quality water supply and adequate room for a reservoir. Similarly, a developer should ensure access to other utilities. In remote areas, extending public utility services or building decentralized facilities can pose considerable development costs. For the first seven years of its existence, Vail operated on a central propane system, installed after the developers discovered that the nearest natural gas service was 30 miles away. A related concern is that some services, such as telephone, may be substandard at remote sites.

Soil types, which are usually correlated with slope, constitute another critical factor. Soil erosion is one of the most pernicious environmental impacts of ski area construction, and it usually requires carefully designed mitigation measures. Erosion problems can be particularly severe with certain soil types. If wastewater disposal systems are unavailable, soils must meet rigorous standards for septic suitability. A shallow depth to bedrock or the presence of ledge rock may require costly blasting and removal.

Similarly, groundwater patterns can be problematic. Water from subsurface springs can quickly melt snow on the slopes, or can cause icy conditions. Preventing such runoff may require expensive tile systems, culverts, and piping.

As the element that defines the edge of the ski trail, frames vistas, and shelters skiers from harsh winds, vegetation is an important part of the skiing experience. Ski areas tend to be built on predominantly north-facing slopes. In the West, because of greater soil moisture retention, there tends to be a greater variety and density of vegetation on these slopes. Most slopes will therefore require clearing. A significant concern on public lands is the visual impact of ski area development, which depends in large measure on the diversity of existing vegetation. Among other elements, the Forest Service evaluates the ability of a prospective site to visually "absorb" the ski area development.

Market Characteristics

A perfectly suitable candidate site will be of little use to a developer without a strong existing or potential market. Like any feasibility decision, an accurate review of a ski area's potential depends upon a clear understanding of the local, regional, and national supply-and-demand characteristics and trends. The scope and detail of this investigation should reflect the overall project concept. A large destination resort will obviously require a clear understanding of national trends, while a weekend ski area near a city will have a much more discrete, easily defined market.

A logical first step is to construct a demographic profile of the expected market area. Estimates of the number of active or potentially active skiers can be based on the information presented earlier in this chapter and from similar demographic descriptions of the skiing market. The most relevant variables include household income, education, and age. Equally useful is a distribution of the local or regional market by skiing ability levels. Nationwide, a breakdown of the skiing population by ability level is illustrated in Figure 5-4. Some regions, for example in the South, will mirror this national profile. Others may vary considerably. The West, for example, contains a larger proportion of advanced and expert skiers. To obtain the most meaningful data, this skiing ability assessment may need to be based on an analysis of skiers at existing facilities in the targeted market area.

The primary market area for a facility can change significantly over time. Most destination resorts become established in their early years by catering primarily to a local and regional market. As the base facilities are developed and as skiing capacity expands or management and marketing efforts mature, a day ski area can often blossom into a regional or destination resort. With this pattern in mind, a market analysis should include a review of the dynamics of each prospective market over time.

An examination of supply factors should also reflect multiple markets. The developers of Deer Valley, a destination resort near Salt Lake City, decided in the initial planning stages that a gap existed in the national supply. They have since filled it with an easily accessible, expensive resort that focuses on extremely high-quality lodging, food, and skiing. Many large Type I resorts in the United States compete with European resorts. As a result,

their market studies must also consider the competition abroad.

An inventory of the existing supply should include a comprehensive description of the region's ski facilities, support services, price structure, and lodging or real estate offered. In addition to gathering basic descriptive information such as vertical drop, daily capacity, and number and type of lifts, a prospective developer should evaluate several qualitative aspects of the competition. Are lift lines excessively long? Are the slopes adequately groomed? Are skiers distributed throughout the mountain or concentrated on only a few slopes? Do the areas cater to the expert, the beginner, or to a wide range of abilities?

Support services may include mid-mountain and base lodges, parking, food and beverage operations (both associated with the ski area and available nearby), equipment rentals, ski school and ski patrol facilities and programs, and retail shops. If a competing area is more than a day ski area, are there a variety of lodging options: condominiums, hotels and lodges, hostels, and so on? Such an evaluation may highlight significant development opportunities in conjunction with existing facilities.

The Public Policy Context

For the ensuing 30 years after the Union Pacific Railroad descended upon Ketchum, Idaho, to build Sun Valley, most communities welcomed winter sports development as a key boost to their remote, sometimes struggling economies. In the 1970s, however, attitudes toward ski area development began to change as the environmental, social, and economic impacts of such development became clearer. This shift in public perception was perhaps best symbolized by Colorado's ballot-box rejection of the 1976 Olympics.[35]

Today, as a result of much closer scrutiny by government authorities and watchful citizens, developers are held to a strict standard of quality. From a developer's perspective, the time and expense involved in documenting a proposed project's environmental performance—a requirement for most ski area developments, under federal or state law—can dramatically affect the project's feasibility.

Figure 5-4

MARKET DISTRIBUTION AND DESIGN CRITERIA BY SKIER ABILITY LEVEL

Ability Level	Market Proportion	Acceptable Terrain Gradients (Low–High)	Skiing Demand[1]
Beginner	1–4%	8–25%	1,500–2,500
Novice	10–15%		2,500–5,000
Low Intermediate	15–25%	15–40%	5,000–7,500
Intermediate	30–50%		7,500–10,000
Advanced Intermediate	15–30%	25–75%	10,000–18,000
Expert	10–25%		18,000–25,000

[1]In vertical feet of skiing per day.
Source: James Branch, "Developing an Urban Ski Facility," *Ski Area Management*, January 1986, p. 102.

Water quality management will be a key concern for the ski area developer.

The key factor that determines to what extent public policy will affect development feasibility is ownership: developers intent on developing on public land will face considerably larger upfront expense and delay than those with privately owned sites. Early discussions with public officials, beginning with the highest applicable agency (usually the Forest Service), can help a developer plan for this difficult but necessary stage.

Prospective developers must also deal with a wide variety of state and local requirements. Often, especially in remote areas, local controls are rudimentary at best. State agencies, however, may possess broad powers, including wildlife management, public health standards, transportation requirements, and mandated periodic inspections of ski lift components. At the same time, local or state departments of recreation or economic development may offer certain incentives, such as cost-sharing or tax-exempt financing for infrastructure or other facilities.

In addition to public review, ski area development plans will often encounter opposition from a plethora of private groups, both ad hoc and formalized. Sensitive mountain environments may appear primitive, but they often belie the presence of dedicated and politically savvy interest groups, ready to defend values they perceive as threatened by development. In the 1970s, the Sierra Club and others successfully denied the development of Walt Disney's proposed Mineral King resort high in California's Sierra Nevada mountains.[36]

SKI AREA PLANNING AND DESIGN

Many of the assumptions and analyses made in the feasibility stage will guide the more detailed subsequent planning and design decisions. One of the most important of these early analyses is an estimation of a potential ski area's capacity. Branch and others have defined "comfortable carrying capacity" as "the maximum number of participants who can utilize the facility at any one time without excessive crowding and without damaging the quality of the environment."[37] Because of the large number of potential variables that can affect this number (highly erodible soils on the site may, for example, reduce the number of potential lifts), capacity calculations cannot be reduced to a standard set of formulas or equations. Rather, capacity is determined based on a number of factors, and seasoned by the analyst's experience.

Basic factors in calculating capacity include vertical drop and trail acreage, uphill or lift capacity, and the characteristics of the expected skiing market. Such factors as trail acreage and lift capacity assume at least some preliminary design specifications. Capacity is therefore a figure that will evolve along with the planning process. Frequently, a developer determines a target capacity, based on some minimum level of financial performance, and then makes planning decisions to attempt to achieve this target. For example, a prospective developer may, assuming some predetermined capital and operating budget, require a capacity of 4,000 skiers to break even over a 100-day season. Lift capacity decisions, trail size determinations, and similar design decisions will in turn reflect this broad performance parameter.

A thorough understanding of the skiing market is critical to accurately estimating capacity. The most efficient mountain plan should offer the correct amount of trail acreage to support the expected number of skiers at each ability level. Figure 5-4 presents basic design criteria for each type of skier, from beginners to experts. One of the most important implications of these data is that, ignoring slope gradients, a given area of ski slope can support fewer skiers as their ability increases. In addition, experienced skiers will demand many more vertical feet of skiing per day than will novices.

For the planner, the upshot is that optimal capacity will be attained by a mixture of skiable terrain that best reflects the market's distribution of ability levels. And for the developer, the conclusion should be that less accomplished skiers are far less expensive to accommodate than experts. Experts, after all, tend to ski the top of a mountain, where construction and maintenance are more expensive. Fewer of them can be accommodated on a trail, because they ski faster. And because they demand more vertical drop per day, they ride the lifts more often. Add to these observations the fact that novice and intermediate skiers tend to generate the most revenues per skier visit, and it becomes clear that, in most markets, a ski area cannot be financially viable by catering only to advanced skiers.

Trail Planning

Designing the heart of the ski area—the trails themselves—is an art that requires a great sensitivity both to a mountain's natural features and to skiers' perceptions. Although trail design can be compared to roadway and golf hole design, it is substantially different from both activities. Skiing is, after all, much more than mere transportation between two points. And unlike a long, watery par 5, more than a golf ball is at risk. Indeed, poorly designed ski trails can be irritating at best and a threat to life and limb at worst. Like golf holes and roads, however, ski trails are sequences of spaces through which a person travels, expecting to be challenged, rewarded, and exhilarated.[38]

The best trails capitalize on the features inherent in a site. Planners begin the task by identifying all the fall lines, or gravity slopes, and then looking for logical lift locations. Because of the limitations of contour maps and the vital importance of accurate routing, many of these initial decisions must be reconfirmed or modified on the site.

Major cut-and-fill can be minimized by tucking trails into natural hollows and depressions. Following the fall line as much as possible will produce the most efficient and highest-quality trails. Natural clearings can be incorporated into proposed trails to lessen the need for disruptive clearing. When trails are cleared, edges should be feathered and uneven, with trees left at varying heights and distances from the trail's centerline. These edges will not only look better but will also help to reduce wind turbulence. Similarly, islands of trees can be useful to help channel traffic, separate skiers by ability level, and create visual interest.

Of special concern in managing existing vegetation on the mountain is the degree to which clearing operations expose weaker or shallow-rooted trees to damaging winds. Islands of conifers left after clearing, for example, may be blown down quite easily without the protection of a surrounding forest.

Trails should be oriented primarily north-northeast to reduce the erosive effects of the sun and prevailing westerly winds. Staging areas at the top of lifts should likewise be sheltered from the wind. Knobs and ridges should generally be avoided.

As a mountain plan evolves, designers must balance the uphill capacity of the lifts with the downhill capacity of the trails. Otherwise, during peak periods the top and bottom of the trails would become unacceptably crowded. Trails should also be wider at the top and bottom to help ease congestion.

Perhaps the most fundamental guideline is to conceive of a ski trail as a series of experiences that adds up to some unified, memorable whole. The designer should strive for a wide variety of speeds, views, and perceptions. Skiers entering the trail at the top should be able to see enough of the trail to determine its general character, but should also face some surprises and discoveries on the way down. Trails should generally widen as they get steeper, increasing from a minimum of about 80 feet to up to 250 feet.

The lower trails at Beaver Creek show the use of careful clearing techniques.

WACHUSETT MOUNTAIN SKI AREA: AN EMERGING PROTOTYPE

Wachusett Mountain Ski Area—a four-season, privately owned and operated recreational facility—occupies 450 acres in a central Massachusetts state-owned reservation near the towns of Princeton and Westminster. The facility has been expanded significantly and now includes 17 trails with three chairlifts and a new base lodge on Wachusett Mountain. Designed to serve skiers who have traditionally traveled longer distances to out-of-state resorts, the project has trails with an elevation of 1,000 feet—downhill slopes plus 12 miles of cross-country trails.

Wachusett Mountain Ski Area lies 52 miles from Boston (to the west), 86 miles from Hartford, Connecticut, and 61 miles from Providence, Rhode Island. Wachusett Mountain itself is the highest mountain in central Massachusetts, with an elevation of 2,006 feet. Its peak affords the most scenic views in the central and eastern portion of the state, and the 1,955-acre Wachusett Mountain State Reservation has become a favorite destination for motorists in search of fall foliage.

Wachusett Mountain has operated as a ski area since 1933, when skiers drove to the top then skied down. In 1961, the

state installed two T-bars and, six years later, voted to move Wachusett and other reservations to state control, to be administered under the Massachusetts Department of Natural Resources. The

state operated the ski area during the 1967–1968 ski season but did so unsuccessfully; for this reason, Wachusett Mountain Associates was established and has managed the facility privately ever since that season.

In June 1981, Wachusett Mountain Associates made plans for an expansion of the existing facility. A limited partnership was formed to finance the expansion, and by July 1982, the partnership had leased additional reserve land and begun construction. Because Wachusett Mountain Associates wanted to reopen for the 1982–1983 ski season, it implemented a rapid development schedule during which five new ski trails were cut, three new lifts were installed, the new lodge was built, and snowmaking operations were put in place before December 1982. The whole project was phased over two years, although most of the development, including 60 percent of the additional trails, was completed before the first season.

By managing all of the lodge concessions with the exception of the retail ski shop, Wachusett Mountain Associates produces additional revenue for the partnership. The state of Massachusetts receives 2 percent of the area's gross revenue.

ARCHITECTURAL DESIGN

The lodge was designed to provide easily for the logical route taken by skiers from the parking lot to the slopes. Skiers enter to buy tickets, after which they may change to boots and go directly to the slopes; visit the restrooms and then go out; or purchase food or beverage and then exit through the rear of the building. The entire building is at grade level and is thus both easily accessible for the handicapped and more easily entered by heavy-booted skiers. Taking advantage of skiers' warm dress, major skier circulation was also provided outside the building. This arrangement saved 20 percent of the floor area that would usually be dedicated to internal circulation, while decreasing the lodge's overall maintenance and heating requirements. Throughout its design, the lodge was oriented to the outdoors. To accomplish this, the architects created for it

multiple access points by which skiers could enter the lodge for one activity only, or for several activities, with little inconvenience.

Throughout, the design's family-centered emphasis comes across in several special features. An area within the lodge that serves as a nursery in the winter converts to an art gallery in the summer. Through the use of a raised platform, the bar is visually separated from the dining room. The lodge also offers a teen center, with an ice cream parlor and video games. And bus service provides access to the area for children below driving age.

Adequate air circulation and natural lighting come partly through primarily glass chimneys that protrude 10 to 15 feet from the building's roof. These chimneys were designed to exhaust hot summer air from the building and to allow fresh air circulation, while their glass allows natural light to enter.

The lodge also has a unique energy-saving element: waste heat from snowmaking heats the building. A small pond constructed next to the lodge supplies water for the snowmaking process, and the lodge was designed to take advantage of the aesthetic qualities of the pond. The snowmaking equipment, built into the side of the lodge, stands enclosed in matching exterior wall materials that blend into the overall design. The heat produced travels through ducts that release it directly into the lodge; unneeded heat flows to the outdoors. The snowmaking process, which produces about five times the heat needed for the lodge, operates constantly during the winter season, when temperatures fall below 30° Fahrenheit. Other energy-saving features include solar orientation for the lodge, and windows that allow summer air to circulate from the building's base through the chimneys, thereby reducing dependence on air conditioning.

MARKET

Wachusett Mountain Ski Area's primary market comprises a population of 5 million people and extends for a radius of about 50 miles. The secondary market covers a 90-mile radius from the resort. Wachusett Mountain emphasizes its appeal to the day-trip or after-work skier because of its convenient location in a region with few high-quality ski facilities. With its expanded runs and new lodge, the ski area can attract customers who would normally have to travel to Vermont or western Massachusetts to enjoy features of equal quality. The location is a positive selling point, for Wachusett Mountain is the largest ski resort in southern New England east of the Connecticut River.

The ski area management employs a wide variety of marketing strategies. The primary strategy uses discounted group rates for corporate workers and for college and university students. A coordinator organizes a ski group, for whom the resort offers a package of six ski sessions—with lessons and rentals optional—for a discount to the skier of more than 50 percent. These group rates are popular in neighboring communities and in the Boston area: up to 1,000 tickets are presold per day. This figure compares well with the ski area's capacity for 1,900 day skiers and 1,900 evening skiers. The ski area also transports groups by bus, a service especially attractive to local customers.

Much of Wachusett's growing reputation derives from word-of-mouth advertising. The area's several salable ameni-ties help to market it: the day-and-night skiing on slopes improved by 24-hour snowmaking, the high-quality ski school, the economic prices for the level of facilities offered, the handsome lodge design, and the slopes that are balanced in their degree of difficulty and of quality and that, thus, rarely have long lines building on one or two lifts.

PROJECT DATA

LAND USE INFORMATION:

Site Area: 450 acres
Base Lodge: 23,885 square feet
Other Buildings:[1] 9,550 square feet
Ski Trails: 99.9 acres
Base Area: 22 acres
Parking: 660 car spaces, 9 bus spaces
(7.5 acres)[2]

ECONOMIC INFORMATION

Site Acquisition Cost N/A[3]
Site Improvement Cost

Excavation	$ 235,134
Grading	134,000
Sewer/water	1,012,000
Paving	23,000
Other	12,000
Total	$1,415,135[4]

Construction Cost: $2,203,949[5]
Amenities Cost: $5,484,324[6]
Total Project Cost: $9,103,408[7]

Operating Expenses

Taxes	24,000
Insurance	161,000
Services, maintenance, janitorial	84,812
Utilities	279,144
Legal	141,000
Management	343,184
Miscellaneous	267,140
Total	$1,300,280[8]

BUILDING INFORMATION:

Gross Building Area (GBA) of Base Lodge (Square Feet)

Ticket sales	100
Administration	1,818
Dining area	6,210
Lounge	1,620
Cafeteria serving	1,566
Hearth room (changing area)	2,036
Retail	3,516
Kitchen	1,503
Restrooms	922
Ski school offices	564
Snowmaking	2,356
Electrical	60
Circulation	1,614
Total	23,885

GBA of Other Buildings (Square Feet):

Ski equipment rental building	2,575
Maintenance building	5,000
Ski patrol building	1,975
Total	9,550

SKIING INFORMATION:

Lift System	Length (Feet)	Vertical (Feet)	Capacity (Persons/Hour)	Acreage	Lighted Acreage
A	3,800	600	1,200	37.5	26.5
B	4,550	940	1,200	44.2	25.4
C	2,390	290	800	18.2	18.2
Total				99.9	70.1

Estimated Daily Skier Capacity: 1,900
Total Vertical Transport Feet per Hour: 2,080,000

Trail Ability Level	Acres	Percent
Beginner	9.9	10
Novice	15.1	15
Low intermediate	30.7	31
Intermediate	35.5	35
Advanced intermediate	8.7	9
Total	99.9	100

PROJECT CREDITS

Developer:
Wachusett Mountain Associates
Princeton, Massachusetts

Architect:
Lindsay Shives & Associates
Boston, Massachusetts

Mountain Planner:
Sno-engineering, Inc.
Lyme, New Hampshire

Notes:
[1]Excluding base lodge.
[2]Formula used: three skiers per car, plus 5 percent of total space (30 spaces) for employee parking.
[3]Site leased from Commonwealth of Massachusetts for 2 percent of gross revenue from ski area operation.
[4]Site improvement cost for base area.
[5]Construction cost for base lodge. Includes $600,000 for snowmaking equipment.
[6]Cost for ski lifts, trails, snowmaking distribution system, and trail lighting.
[7]Cost for base lodge and ski area improvements.
[8]Expenses for fiscal year ending April 30, 1984.

High-capacity double-triple chairlift at Hidden Valley, Pennsylvania.

Novice and intermediate trails should offer strategically placed bail-out positions and stopping points at more challenging sections. Intersections with other trails or with service roads should be "announced" in advance.[39]

Ski Lifts

Next to the obvious—the mountain and the snow—the most important element in a ski area is the system of lifts. Improvements in ski lift technology through the years have accounted for a large proportion of the sport's growth, and recent advances should continue this trend. Four basic types of lifts are employed today: tows, surface cable lifts, chairlifts, and gondolas or tramways.[40]

The first lifts were the familiar, and formerly quite popular, rope tows, which essentially dragged skiers uphill. Although rope tows were relatively cheap and simple, they were also uncomfortable and dangerous over longer distances or up moderately steep hills. Today, a modified version with handles affixed to a moving cable suspended a short distance above the ground offers a promising alternative for some applications. These lifts, called handle tows or cable tows, are effective replacements for rope tows for distances of up to 1,000 feet.

The second generation of lifts also uses moving cables, but in this case the cable stretches overhead while the skier stays on the surface. T-bars, J-bars, and platter lifts (also called Poma lifts, after one of the major manufacturers) are popular, mechanically simple alternatives to chairlifts over moderate distances. Like tows, however, these surface lifts act as boundaries that skier traffic is unable to cross. They therefore restrict skier circulation.

Chairlifts, in the words of Jim Branch, have become the "work-horses" of the industry.[41] The vast majority of lift capacity added to the nation's ski areas every year takes the form of some type of chairlift. Originally adapted from machines that loaded bananas onto boats, chairlifts have proved equally adept at transporting skiers. One of the greatest advantages of chairlifts is that they enable the skier to rest on the journey uphill. Another benefit is that they do not interrupt ski traffic across the lift line.

Chairlifts have evolved from single to double, triple, and quadruple arrangements, each offering a big boost in uphill capacity at some lesser proportional increase in capital costs. Most recently, some large resorts have installed high-speed, detachable quad chairlifts. These advanced systems run on a high-speed, continuously moving cable. For loading and unloading, however, the chair unit detaches from the cable and remains virtually still. The operation is therefore much safer. Because of the speed, these lifts can cover much greater distances than ordinary chairlifts: journeys of over a mile were formerly reserved for enclosed gondolas. A further advantage is that these lifts need not be routed in a straight line. By angling their way up the mountain, detachable quads can transport skiers over extremely difficult terrain. One concern, notes James Chaffin of the Snowmass Company, is that the high-capacity lifts, by moving more people up the mountain faster, can lead to overcrowding on the slopes themselves, especially at the top of the mountain.[42] For long rides, or where wind and temperatures make riding a chairlift uncomfortable, gondolas and trams offer an effective but expensive and relatively slow alternative.

Although tunnels and mountain railways are not likely to appear soon in the United States, such exotic skier transport systems have been constructed in Europe, where public funds often subsidize such schemes as part of an economic development strategy. In Zermatt, Switzerland, an underground funicular is said to offer a staggering capacity of 5,000 skiers per hour.[43]

Most lifts are powered electrically, although diesel engines are sometimes used in remote areas. State agencies often regulate both the installation and operation of ski lifts, usually requiring periodic inspections.[44]

Base Area Relationships

Base area planning should be approached as largely a function of what will happen on the mountain. Most of the basic planning and design criteria related to base facilities, from the number of ski storage racks to the size of remote parking lots, will depend on the number and type of skiers accommodated on the slopes. There may be elements that are not, strictly speaking, dependent on skiing, however. Retail development, lodging, and second-home development, for example, may be planned independently of a ski facility. In most cases, though, the immediate base area development program will reflect the skiing market.

From a purely physical standpoint, the most problematic part of base area planning is mitigating the potential conflicts between vehicles, pedestrians, and skiers. In recent years, many large ski areas, such as Beaver Creek, Park Creek in Utah, and New Hampshire's Loon Mountain, have opted to partially place parking underground and to develop the surface real estate. Such a solution, though expensive, helps to create a safer, more pleasant pedes-

Maintenance buildings at Beaver Creek are functional and attractive.

trian environment and a more cohesive resort village core.

Most base lodges, depending on the nature of the resort complex, are designed with between 10 and 14 net square feet per unit of skier capacity. Like golf clubhouses, ski lodges can vary tremendously in their design and in the facilities and services they offer.[45]

Lodges need not be located only at the base. Mid-mountain lodges, although they can pose tricky operational problems because of their limited vehicular access, can provide a highly attractive, away-from-it-all atmosphere.

Even the most basic facility will offer space for equipment rental, a ski shop, a first-aid station and ski patrol office, a ski school with adequate gathering room outside, and food and beverage service areas with areas for eating and warming up. In the past, most ski areas paid but scant attention to food and beverage service, usually offering only a snack bar or cafeteria. In recent years, however, a renewed emphasis on quality and service has resulted in a vast spectrum of eating and drinking arrangements. The cost of the lodges at Utah's Deer Valley resort reportedly exceeded that of all the resort's skiing facilities, resulting in higher-than-average food and beverage revenues.[46]

Many successful lodges are designed to accommodate warm weather uses as well as skiing. Wachusett Mountain, for example, reports a greater number of visitors in summer than in winter, partly due to the area's award-winning lodge and quality food service.[47]

The Silver Lake day lodge at Deer Valley.

visitors. If vehicles will be stored indoors, the size range should be adjusted upward accordingly.

Grooming vehicles are the most expensive and most useful maintenance tools at today's ski areas. Depending on snow conditions and the frequency of grooming expected, one vehicle for every 25 acres of skiable terrain in the East and for every 50 to 75 acres in the West is an approximate standard. In 1985, these vehicles ranged in cost between $60,000 and $150,000, depending on type of transmission, size, and attachments. Most ski areas will also need a utility vehicle and one or more four-wheel-drive support vehicles. Rounded out by a range of miscellaneous tools and equipment, a typical budget for grooming and maintenance equipment for a ski area of about 3,000 capacity will total between $500,000 and $700,000.[48]

Snowmaking

Within the last decade, snowmaking systems have become one of the most crucial elements in managing ski areas. In 1983, nearly seven out of 10 facilities in a nationwide sample reported some snowmaking capability (see Figure 5-5). According to the same study, more than 90 percent of the areas in the East, New England, and the Midwest offered snowmaking.[49] Not surpris-

An area's maintenance headquarters, sometimes combined with the snowmaking facilities, should also be located near the base area. Like their golf course counterparts, ski maintenance buildings can run the gamut from prefabricated metal structures to the attractive wood buildings at Beaver Creek. A maintenance shop and garage of 3,000 to 5,000 square feet will accommodate an area serving about 1,500 daily

Figure 5-5
SNOWMAKING ACREAGE, COVERAGE, AND CAPACITY OF SKI AREAS WITH SNOWMAKING

	New England	East and Midwest	Rockies and West	All
Average skiable acres	193	108	780	387
Average snowmade acres Proportion	112 58.0%	93 86.1%	84 10.8%	94 24.3%
Average skier capacity/snowmade	2,438	2,008	521	898
Average skier density/snowmade	22/acre	22/acre	6/acre	10/acre
No. of areas reporting	17	32	31	80

Source: C. R. Goeldner et al., *Economic Analysis of North American Ski Areas, 1982–83 Season,* p. 112.

ingly, the percentage of total acreage covered by snowmaking was highest in the East and Midwest and lowest in the Rocky Mountain and western regions.

Snowmaking technology has evolved into one of the best ways to reduce the risk inherent in operating a ski area. These systems have also come to represent one of the ski industry's largest expense items and one of its most important design elements.

A snowmaking system is not unlike a golf course irrigation system. The basic components include a water reservoir, a distribution network of piping and pumps, and a series of nozzles or guns to distribute the snow on the slopes.

The physical phenomenon of snowmaking is quite simple. At appropriate temperature and humidity conditions, water can be atomized, or broken into small droplets, and forced into the atmosphere under pressure to create snow. In its composition and skiability, there is little "artificial" about this snow; it exhibits the same characteristics as natural snow, although it is denser, composed on average of more water and less air. For the ski area operator, the principal concern is generating sufficient quantities and then distributing it adequately on the slopes to approximate the real thing.

Since the basic process was patented in the early 1950s, the dominant technology has been based on compressed air. These systems use air compressors to force large amounts of water through the small nozzles of guns. Such air-water systems are relatively easy to operate, and can produce snow under a wide range of subfreezing conditions. As energy costs began to rise in the late 1970s, these air-water systems

Wendy Roth

Snow-cats on parade at Vail, Colorado.

were supplemented by compressorless systems that use large fans to mix the water and air. Many of today's most sophisticated snowmaking systems take advantage of both technologies.

Wendy Roth

Air-water guns perform well under a wide range of temperatures, but are generally noisier than newer compressorless snowmaking systems.

One of the key advantages of compressorless systems is that they require far less energy and therefore are generally more economical to run. The conventional systems, on the other hand, are less demanding of maintenance and can be expected to last longer. Air-water systems are also easier to operate; the large fan units of compressorless systems require special equipment to move them around the slopes.

The basic plant for conventional systems, with its compressors and pumps, can cost more initially, but the components, including the spray guns themselves, tend to be less expensive than those for compressorless systems. For a ski area with real estate development near the slopes, compressorless systems offer another key advantage: the fans are much quieter than the air-water guns. For this reason, compressorless units tend to be a better choice around base areas.[50]

The suitability of each type of system depends most, however, on the expected range of temperature and humidity and on the amount of snowmaking required. Conventional air-water systems offer the greatest flexibility, performing well in a wide range of subfreezing temperatures and operating relatively efficiently at higher temperatures. Airless systems, on the other hand, perform best at colder temperatures and optimally at around zero degrees Fahrenheit.

One of the most important parts of a snowmaking system is the reservoir. Even the smallest systems will use up to 500 gallons of water per minute (gpm), and the most ex-tensive systems can demand up to 10,000 gpm. Operating at capacity, most top-quality guns will use from 60 to 100 gpm to produce about 24 cubic feet of snow per minute.[51] Efficiency will increase as both temperature and relative humidity fall. Under marginal conditions, however, snow production may fall to as low as eight cubic feet per minute.

Some ski areas have turned their reservoirs into a key amenity. Others, like Wachusett Mountain, have integrated snowmaking into the design of the base lodge. At Wachusett, waste heat from the snowmaking process is recovered and used to warm the lodge.

In 1985, ski area planner Jim Branch estimated the capital cost for a snowmaking system at $20,000 to $25,000 per acre of coverage. Significantly, however, efficiencies of scale can greatly reduce this figure. As coverage increases, the cost per acre declines. Vertical rise can also affect cost. Accommodating a vertical rise of greater than about 1,300 feet requires costly booster pumps. New, high-pressure systems, though promising, are relatively untested.

Over the years a number of products have been developed or proposed to replace snow. Mostly variations of plastic bristles, these artificial surfaces have not proven widely successful, although they may offer a useful supplement to natural snow in high-traffic areas such as a lift terminus.

Night Skiing

Lighting the slopes for use after dark can be an effective way to boost revenues at ski areas, provided the area is located close enough to a market with a strong night skiing demand. For only a slight increase in capital and operating costs, the percentage of capacity used can increase as much as 60 percent through a well-marketed night skiing program.[52]

In the 1984–85 season, about 46 percent of the ski areas in the United States and Canada offered

The snowmaking reservoir at Hidden Valley, Pennsylvania, is a key amenity in itself.

night skiing. Lighted slopes were most popular in the Southeast, where ski areas are more accessible. Lights were reported least often in the more remote western areas. Nationally, however, night lift tickets accounted for more than a quarter of all tickets sold. In the Midwest, more than a third of all lift tickets were sold after dark.[53]

From a design standpoint, one of the most important issues of night skiing is deciding which terrain to illuminate. Because of the enhanced illusion of speed experienced by the skier at night, gentle slopes can challenge better skiers than they would in the daylight. An intermediate slope, for example, will more likely satisfy an expert skier at night, because of the changes in perception caused by shadow patterns and the darkness. (Some ski area operators claim, however, that artificial light actually enhances contrast, enabling skiers to ski faster at night.)

Proper slope illumination is thus a key criterion in choosing a lighting system. Most modern systems use high-pressure sodium vapor or metal halide lighting. The best sports lighting also illuminates in an irregular "batwing" pattern that promises more uniform brightness on the slope.

Cross-Country Skiing

One of the brightest spots in the skiing industry is the growth of cross-country's skiing's popularity as a recreational activity. Traditionally, Nordic skiing enthusiasts have practiced their sport much in the same way as hikers: on trails, often informally maintained, located on public lands or privately owned lands open to public use. Relatively few organized cross-country ski areas exist. Many observers, however, believe that the future of cross-country skiing will include a demand for well-developed and carefully maintained areas specifically designed to serve the cross-country skier. Although in many cases new Alpine areas are recognizing the complementary cross-

Base-area lighting at Hidden Valley.

country market, an ever-increasing number of Nordic facilities are being developed independent of Alpine areas. And according to advocates, the potential relationship between real estate and cross-country as an amenity is promising.

Nordic facilities are following a path similar to Alpine areas. A growing number of cross-country areas now charge a trail fee in exchange for improved trail design and management, snowmaking, night lighting, and a host of Alpine-like amenities, from restaurants and bars to instruction and lodging. As the cross-country market expands, skiers will demand a much higher level of quality and service.

For the consumer, the principal advantage of Nordic skiing is its accessibility. Since a much broader range of terrain is suitable for cross-country, facilities can be located closer to the market. For the developer, Nordic facilities involve much lower capital and operating costs, since lifts are unnecessary

and trails are relatively narrow. A much greater number of potential sites are suitable for cross-country skiing than for Alpine: little natural snow is needed, only consistent temperatures below 29 degrees Fahrenheit for snowmaking. And cross-country areas, because they are much less disruptive to the environment, are unlikely to face substantial regulatory hurdles. Further, because of the lower fixed and variable costs, a developer can break even on a cross-country facility with a season of only 40 to 80 days.

Most industry experts view cross-country as a complement, rather than a substitute, for Alpine skiing in most markets. Cross-country's potential for helping to increase Alpine participation is unclear. Advocates have claimed up to a 50 percent crossover rate from Nordic to Alpine at several major resorts that offer both types of skiing.[54] According to others, however, the potential overlap between the two markets is slight. By any measure, however, demographic and lifestyle shifts point to a potential boom in cross-country skiing.

In an attempt to document cross-country development potential, Ski Industries America, in conjunction with Sno-Engineering, Inc., has published a useful manual describing the special requirements of a cross-country ski area. The manual presents four prototypical facilities, each intended for development in urban areas. All, however, are adaptable as guidelines for development as part of a larger Alpine facility. The characteristics of the prototype are summarized in Figure 5-6.

SKI AREA PERMITTING: THE NATIONAL FOREST SYSTEM PLANNING PROCESS

Although ski areas may be located on privately owned land (Deer Valley, Utah), on state-owned land (Wachusett Mountain, Massachusetts), or even on municipally owned land, most of the most visible and largest ski areas in the United States are built at least partially on federal land. Leasing public lands for ski area operations, whether owned by a state or by the federal government, can form the basis for a successful business venture, one that offers a reward commensurate to the risk assumed by the private investors. At the same time, the public can enjoy the developed ski area, at reduced financial risk to the taxpayers.

The process of building a ski area on public land is much more complicated than on privately held land. States may vary widely in their approaches to leasing lands for ski area operations. Colorado, for example, is continually involved with corresponding federal agencies through a so-called joint review process. Other states tend to take a more passive approach, allowing the federal agencies to review most aspects of a developer's proposal. The following description summarizes the planning process as described by the U.S. Forest Service.[55] Each situation, however, will vary by location and circumstance.

Figure 5-6

PROTOTYPE CROSS-COUNTRY SKI AREA CHARACTERISTICS

| | | Area Type | | |
	Pilot	Small	Medium	Large
Total track length (kilometers)	4–9	8–15	14–24	20–26
Snowmaking/lighting	none	1 km	3 km	5 km
Lodge size (sq. ft.)	1,000	3,000	6,500	10,000
Total area capacity (no. of skiers at one time)	150	300	500	800
Season length (days)	40	70	70	80
Season capacity[1]	12,000	42,000	70,000	128,000
Revenue per skier visit	$6.50	$8.50	$10.50	$12.00
Total capital cost	$30,000	$190,000	$225,000	$315,000
Cost per unit capacity	$200	$633	$510	$394
Cash break-even				
Skier visits	3,900	11,250	17,000	23,400
Gross revenue	$25,350	$84,375	$178,500	$280,800
% Seasonal utilization	32.5%	26.8%	24.3%	18.3%
Economic break-even				
Skier visits	4,600	16,000	22,000	29,600
Gross revenue	$29,900	$136,000	$231,000	$355,200
% Seasonal utilization	38.3%	38.1%	31.4%	23.1%

[1]Season capacity is twice the skier-at-one-time capacity times the season length. This reflects the fact that there are several skiing periods per day.
Note: This analysis indicates that cross-country ski areas can achieve cash break-even (cash in = cash out) at utilization rates from 18.3% for large areas to 32.5% for pilot areas. Economic break-even (including reserve for replacement) is achieved at utilizations of from 23.1% to 38.3%. These utilization levels appear to be realistically achievable under normal weather circumstances and with the expressed strength of markets.
Source: Ski Industries Association, "Executive Summary for Urban Cross-Country Ski Areas."

The Forest Service and the various state departments of natural resources or outdoor recreation do not merely react to private proposals as they come along. Rather, these agencies generally conduct ongoing studies to identify opportunities for private recreational development, as well as to plan for the appropriate public improvements required for such development. One of the critical first steps, therefore, for an interested private developer is to work with the Forest Service to identify a potential site. The developer will then become integrated into the larger recreation planning process.

Upon nomination and selection of a potential site, the prospective developer is issued a study permit by the Forest Service, to allow the kind of close examination of physical site characteristics required in the early planning stages. At this point, the developer's consultants will likely be gathering the reams of data necessary to document both the project's feasibility and its potential environmental impact. The typical result of this early study phase will be a fairly comprehensive preliminary plan.

Significantly, however, a developer who has conducted this preliminary work (which probably will take more than a year to complete) is not necessarily guaranteed the development rights for the project. Based on the preliminary analysis, the Forest Service may opt to issue a development prospectus, thereby opening the right to development to bid. A number of prospective developers may then bid for the rights by submitting to the Forest Service conceptual physical development plans, management and business plans, and documentation of their financial capabilities. The awarded developer may then get on with the master planning process.

An environmental assessment is usually prepared concurrently with the master plan. As a "major federal action," the issuance of a special use permit for a ski area is subject to the documentation requirements of the National Environmental Policy Act (NEPA). If the action is likely to result in significant adverse environmental impacts, as is virtually any sizable ski area, NEPA requires an environmental impact statement (EIS). The specific requirements of the assessment and, if required, the EIS will vary among the different Forest Service regions. All regions, however, will require a close consideration of alternative development scenarios to the proposed master plan, the impacts of each alternative, and proposed plans to mitigate the impacts. The scope of this review is not limited to impacts on natural systems; it will also include such elements as the project's potential effects on local police and fire protection, sewage treatment plant capacity, employment patterns, and so on.

One of the Forest Service's principal concerns is the visual impact of a proposed ski area, or the relationship between the "development components and the existing visual character of the area."[56] To help evaluate this somewhat subjective performance criterion, the Forest Service has developed a Visual Resource Management system. In a nutshell, the system evaluates the existing landscape in terms of visual quality, then considers the appropriate level of management (for example, "retention," "partial retention," "modification") and the ability of the landscape to "absorb" the proposed changes that would result from development. This analysis then becomes one of the major criteria by which the resulting master plan is evaluated.

U.S. Forest Service

The U.S. Forest Service planning process often includes the use of computer simulations of the visual impact a project would have on a proposed area.

This policy focus on visual quality aims to ensure the compatibility of a proposed development with a fragile and politically sensitive environment. As a result, a prospective developer can expect a great deal of attention from the public agencies to such details as building color and massing, lift tower location and color, and landscaping. Like any public review of a development project, this process will also consider transportation and parking issues, impacts on public utilities (especially water supplies in the arid West), air quality, and historic and cultural resources.

Once the Forest Service is assured of a master plan's viability and soundness, it will issue the required special use permit, which constitutes the legal contract and operating agreement between the agency and the concessionaire. Permits are issued either for a specific term, usually 20 or 30 years, or on an annual basis.

The term permit is issued for areas of up to 80 acres, usually those areas at a mountain's base where capital investment will be concentrated. Annual permits cover the rest of a development—ski trails, roads, and other areas away from the base. Permits issued at a project's outset will typically contain detailed provisions governing the rate and character of all future development, provisions that are often the subject of major negotiations between the permittee and the Forest Service. All future development is also subject to agency review, to ensure compliance with the agreed-upon master plan and to monitor changing conditions.

This two-tier permit structure can pose certain problems for developers on some sites. The 30-year term of the special use permit, according to the Public Lands Committee of the National Ski Areas Association, can complicate long-term financing for capital improvements. Some base area developments can also be constrained by the 80-acre limitation.[57] Proposed federal legislation would allow longer-term leases for base area developments and could even provide for transfer of lands to the ski area operator as part of a land exchange program with state agencies.

In exchange for the right to use public land, the Forest Service charges a fee based on the extent of physical improvements and the amount of revenue derived by the permittee. A "graduated rate fee system" is used to calculate the fee based on a variable percentage of gross sales. This percentage is based on the ratio between revenues and gross fixed assets: as the revenues increase relative to the physical improvements, the percentage charged against those revenues also rises.[58] Nationwide, the land use fee ranges from 1 percent to 4.5 percent of gross revenues. In 1982–83, the average Forest Service permittee paid about $105,000, or about 2.5 percent of gross revenues, in fees for the use of public land.[59]

SKI AREA MANAGEMENT ISSUES

In a ski area, the management issues typically associated with any recreational amenity—catering to both residents and outsiders, maintaining design and appearance standards, controlling costs, and so on—are compounded by a number of other factors. Remote locations, for example, often require limited affordable housing for seasonal employees. Similarly, ski area managers experience difficulty predicting accurate expenses and revenues in the face of uncertain weather conditions. The risks inherent in the sport also pose a management challenge in the form of liability insurance issues. For the developer, these and many other characteristics make an expedienced team of ski area managers essential.

Retail shops at Wachusett Mountain Ski Area.

From the standpoint of organization and management, the relationship between real estate development and ski area operations varies widely, depending on a project's type, location, complexity, and experience of those involved. Because skiing has evolved primarily as a standalone commercial enterprise, real estate operations are frequently later additions or adjuncts to the central business entity. In other cases, however, real estate and ski operations, though different lines on an organization chart, constitute highly interdependent parts of a single enterprise.

Today, according to resort analyst Bill Shanahan of Sno-Engineering, Inc., some ski areas effectively function like many golf courses: they add value to the real estate but may only break even themselves. Over the long run, however, says Shanahan, any ski area worth developing should make a significant financial contribution on its own. The best chance for this occurs when the mountain plan and the management plan evolve concurrently.[60]

Revenues and Expenses

By a large margin, the biggest revenue source at the typical ski area is the sale of lift tickets. Most ski areas offer a variety of lift ticket prices for weekdays versus weekends, adults or juniors, and so on. On average in the 1982–83 season, each skier visit generated $12.90 in lift ticket revenue. That season, the average adult day weekend ticket cost $16.43, and lift ticket revenue accounted for 57 percent of gross revenues.[61]

Food service and bar operations produce the next largest amount of revenue at the average area—about 10 percent of the gross. Both real estate operations and summertime services and activities, on average, contribute about 8 percent of revenues. Revenues from ski lessons, retail sales, and equipment rentals round out the revenue picture, each accounting for 3 to 5 percent of gross revenues.

On the cost side, direct labor and payroll taxes constitute about 26 percent of the average ski area's expenses. Utilities, supplies, and maintenance costs account for about 18 percent of all costs. Figure 5-7 presents an income statement showing revenues and expenses for the average ski area in 1982–83.

Figure 5-7
AVERAGE SKI AREA FINANCIAL DATA: INCOME STATEMENT

	1982–83 Total (000)	USFS Permittees
Gross fixed assets	$7,706	$9,174
Revenue:		
Ski lift gross—winter	$2,502	$3,349
Ski lift gross—summer	22	34
Supporting margin—winter	456	507
Supporting margin—summer	40	21
Year-round margin	236	330
TOTAL REVENUE	$3,256	$4,241
Less:		
Ski lift direct expense	$ 708	$ 958
Payroll taxes	111	127
Property operation	218	216
OPERATIONS MARGIN	$2,219	$2,940
Less:		
General & administrative	$ 595	$ 795
Marketing (advertising, public relations, promotion, etc.)	203	224
Insurance (property, liability)	112	145
Land use fees (public)	64	105
Land use fees (private)	20	16
Property taxes	62	80
Other taxes (except income)	56	80
Snowmaking	114	75
Snow removal	12	17
Miscellaneous	27	35
Depreciation & amortization	511	662
OPERATING PROFIT (LOSS)	$ 443	$ 706
Less: Interest	300	338
PROFIT (LOSS) BEFORE TAX	$ 143	$ 368
No. of areas reporting	118	59

Source: C. R. Goeldner et al., *Economic Analysis of North American Ski Areas, 1982–83 Season*, p. 27.

Deer Valley's restaurants play a prominent role in the marketing of the resort.

Goeldner, in his annual economic analysis, has devised a rule-of-thumb measure to evaluate a ski area's economic performance. He compares total revenue to gross fixed assets, then divides by percent utilization (total skier visits divided by total capacity) to produce a performance factor. For example, in the 1982–83 season, total revenues equaled 42 percent of gross fixed assets at the average ski area. This figure, divided by the average capacity utilized at ski areas that season, 38 percent, yields a factor of 1.11. According to Goeldner, this factor "summarizes all of the critical economic variables (capacity, utilization, length of season, revenue per skier visit) and relates them to investment." As long as the percentage of GFA represented by revenues is greater than the percentage utilization, these factors remain roughly in balance. Therefore, a fig-

ure of greater than 1 is a sign of a healthy facility, while a figure of less than 1 suggests that "one or more factors are impairing a ski area's ability to make profits commensurate with the risks."[62]

Departmental Operations

Most ski areas are fiscally organized into a variety of departments or profit/cost centers. At the typical facility, about 80 percent of gross revenues are produced by seven major departments: lift, ski school, food service, bar, retail sales, rentals, and accommodations. Other departments may include real estate, conference center, utilities and snowmaking, and summer or year-round sports (tennis, Alpine slide, health club, and so forth). Figure 5-8 summarizes data from the 1982–83 NSAA survey on the revenues per skier visit, costs, average

Figure 5-8

AVERAGE SKI AREA FINANCIAL DATA: DEPARTMENTAL MARGIN TOTAL SKI AREAS, 1982–83

| | Gross Sales | | Less: | | | | No. | No. |
	Per Skier Visit	%	Cost of Goods Sold	Direct Labor	Direct Other	Gross Margin	Areas Reporting	Employees per Average Day
WINTER SEASON								
Ski lift department	$12.90	100.0%	—	18.9%	8.6%	72.5%	118	45
Ski school	1.54	100.0	—	59.1	6.6	34.3	104	31
Food service	2.53	100.0	35.0%	28.9	9.5	26.6	88	24
Bar	0.79	100.0	27.8	16.9	8.1	47.2	64	4
Retail	1.43	100.0	56.5	11.7	2.7	29.1	62	3
Rental	1.02	100.0	15.8[1]	21.7	6.8	55.7	89	7
Accommodations	—	100.0	—	30.6	37.8	31.6	29	8
Other	.45	100.0	4.3	47.4	20.6	27.7	98	35
Total	$20.66							157
YEAR-ROUND								
Real estate		100.0	35.2	7.4	10.0	47.4	22	
Utility		100.0	—	35.3	96.1	(31.4)	16	
Miscellaneous		100.0	10.3	16.0	10.7	63.0	73	
SUMMER SEASON								
Lift department		100.0	—	51.9	40.4	7.7	21	
Food service		100.0	39.2	39.8	15.7	5.3	40	
Retail		100.0	59.9	21.2	3.5	15.4	22	
Sports		100.0	—	48.4	43.3	8.3	22	
Accommodations		100.0	—	37.0	39.6	23.4	21	
Slide		100.0	—	21.7	9.8	68.5	11	

[1]Represents retirement and replacement of rental equipment.
Source: C. R. Goeldner et al., *Economic Analysis of North American Ski Areas, 1982–83 Season*, pp. 53 and 61.

number of employees, and gross margins by department.

From these data, one can ascertain the importance of lift revenue to a ski area's bottom line. Lift department labor costs as a percentage of gross sales are fairly reasonable, producing a healthy average margin of more than 72 percent. Lift personnel constituted about 29 percent of the total number of employees at the average area in 1982–83. Usually, slope maintenance and grooming and ski patrol operations are also part of the lift department. Maintenance and repair costs over the last several years have run about 4 percent of total lift revenue for the average ski area.[63]

Insurance and Risk Management

In the 1982–83 season, according to the NSAA's economic study, the average North American ski area paid about $70,000 for liability insurance coverage. This figure represents a cost of about 36 cents per skier visit. By 1985, according to a detailed survey of NSAA's member areas, this cost had jumped to a nationwide average of 96 cents per skier visit. If the same visitation figures that were used in the 1982–83 study are applied to the 1985 cost, the average liability premium in 1985–86 reached about $186,000— a jump of 165 percent. The 1985 survey revealed an increase in premiums of more than 100 percent in the last year alone. And while in 1983 liability insurance costs represented about 2.2 percent of total revenues, in 1985 Bill Shanahan estimated its proportion of total revenues at about 5 percent.

The ski industry's insurance problem extends beyond rising premiums. Ski area operators are also facing higher deductibles and reduced coverage, and in some cases a dearth of willing underwriters.[64] Part of the problem, according to the NSAA's 1985 insurance liaison's report, is that only two or three insurance agencies write coverage for virtually the entire U.S. ski industry.

David Lokey

A *mid-mountain lodge at Beaver Creek.*

One proposed solution would create an industry-owned "captive" agency to insure its members.

The current insurance crisis, no matter how it is ultimately resolved, usefully highlights the importance of risk management in ski area operations. Skiing today is not an especially risky sport. In 1985, every 1,000 skier days resulted in, on average, three accidents serious enough to report. About 85 percent of these were incurred while skiing.[65]

Most ski areas today maintain fairly comprehensive programs designed to mitigate the risks inherent both in the sport itself and in the operation of the facility. Many elements of these programs are features that well-managed ski areas may take for granted: suitable training for lift operators and ski patrol members; timely and thorough maintenance and repairs, with suitable markings and warnings on nonskiable areas; ongoing safety

programs with strict enforcement of rules and regulations; and careful monitoring of hazardous snow conditions, ice, avalanche potential, and so on. The NSAA and other organizations have issued a variety of publications, films, and other materials that are useful in organizing a risk management program.

The nature of the sport dictates that risks cannot be eliminated. Given the institutional pressures on the industry, however, ski area operators should assign a high priority to reducing risk.

CHAPTER SIX

MARINA DEVELOPMENT

In a real estate context, the term "marina" can apply to a tremendously wide range of facilities, from a small community pier with a handful of boat slips to a 2,000-slip municipally owned marina that helps to support dozens of associated businesses and development projects. Since 1928, when the National Association of Engine and Boat Manufacturers (now the National Marine Manufacturers Association, or NMMA) adopted the Italian word for "small harbor" to describe a modern, service-oriented facility for recreational boats, its meaning has expanded in common usage to include any collection of slips for pleasure boats. Today marinas can be found on virtually all types of coastal and inland sites, either as independent entities or associated with residential, resort, retail, or office development. Some offer nearly every conceivable service to the boat owner, from boat sales and lodging to major repairs and yacht brokerage. Others, often those small facilities associated with residential development, will offer few genuine services (and although not "marinas" in the technical sense, docking facilities with no associated services are included throughout the following discussion).

Bohicket Marina Village, Diedrich Architects and Associates

According to the A. C. Nielsen reports, in 1982 boating was the fifth most popular recreational activity in the nation with nearly 41 million participants.[1] In real terms, this figure represents a 6 percent jump from 1979. Sailing, a separate reporting category in the Nielsen reports, adds another 11 million participants. NMMA figures put the total number of recreational boaters at over 67 million. Since 1950, retail expenditures on recreational boating have shot upward, from $680 million to over $12 billion in 1984.[2] By a large margin, the most popular type of boat is the outboard-powered fiberglass boat 15 to 30 feet long. Some 317,000 of these craft were launched in 1984, and figures from a year earlier indicate that outboard boats accounted for almost 78 percent of boats registered in the United States.

Patterns of boating activity vary widely by region, based on climatic differences as well as the influence (or the absence) of boating traditions. Donald Adie, author of a well-known marina reference work, notes that in the northern half of both American coastlines, boaters favor sailing over power boating. Northern climes also display a greater variety of boats, with a noticeably higher number of wooden

GROWTH AND DEVELOPMENT

For years after boat owners became convinced that safer and more convenient alternatives to open anchorages in a naturally protected harbor were available, marinas were relatively industrial affairs, long on boatyard ambience and short on creature comforts. Of course, many yacht owners preferred (and still prefer) it that way. In the last 25 years, however, the common image of a marina has evolved from the disheveled boatyard into an attractive, lively, and often luxurious waterfront activity that can serve as a key recreational amenity in residential development, a catalyst for large-scale urban redevelopment, or the principal organizing element for entire resort areas.

A Boom in Recreational Boating

Like many recreational activities in the United States, the post–World War II growth in recreational boating was driven by an accelerating prosperity that, in turn, led to increases in income, leisure time, and mobility. Consequently, a much larger share of the population could afford to participate in what, like tennis and golf, had been considered a pastime for the upper crust. Technological advances also helped spur boating's popularity. Polyester resins and fiberglass made boats nearly maintenance-free and led to the design and development of popular new kinds of small sailboats and outboard-powered runabouts.

Racing and cruising sailboats at Chandlers Landing, Rockwall, Texas.

boats. In the southern states, especially in Florida and South Carolina, fiberglass power boats predominate. With the development of water-supply and flood-control projects in landlocked states, boating has evolved from a novelty to a mainstream activity. In 1983, for example, Oklahoma, a state with a fairly limited maritime heritage, ranked 17th among all states in the number of boats registered—just ahead of Maryland and Massachusetts.

Even with this tremendous growth in the number of boats and boaters, however, the actual number of marinas, according to the NMMA, has remained relatively stable since 1950. In the last 35 years, the total number of marinas has ranged from 5,000 to 6,000. Since 1982, the number has remained fairly constant at about 5,700. From 1983 to 1984, the last year for which data are available, only 70 new marinas opened or reopened.

A survey conducted by the U.S. Army Corps of Engineers in the mid-1970s found that the average marina contained about 255 slips, although the 394 marinas surveyed ranged in number of slips from six to 6,000. Just over a third of these facilities were located on bays or estuaries, with 22 percent sited on rivers. About 15 percent of those surveyed were found on lakes, with about the same percentage on the seacoast. The remainder were located on canals, reservoirs, and other waterways. Sailboats were prevalent in larger waters and in areas with long boating seasons. Power boats dominated on river sites and in noted fishing areas.[3]

Marinas and Real Estate Development

As noted, many of the early marina facilities were small, relatively ramshackle affairs that often evolved from an existing boatyard or as part of a commercial harbor. Marinas were perceived, and were operated, as industrial activities, relatively incompatible with residential or resort land uses. Around the same time, however, some far-sighted developers in rapidly growing areas were envisioning entirely new communities organized around boating and water. Fort Lauderdale, Florida, laced by a network of canals, and Huntington Harbor, California, were early examples of such communities. In the 1960s, Kaiser-Aetna's 6,000-acre Hawaii Kai development on Oahu advanced the same concept.[4]

Over the last two decades, hundreds of existing marinas have been redeveloped to include single-family or multifamily housing, hotels, office buildings, and retail shops. Marinas have also become the central feature of some well-known resorts, such as Sea Pines Plantation's Harbor Town on Hilton Head Island, South Carolina. In each case, developers who were able to create a marina with a greater resemblance to a fishing village than to a boatyard, with a close relationship between real estate, boats, and

Less formal boat access at New Seabury on Cape Cod.

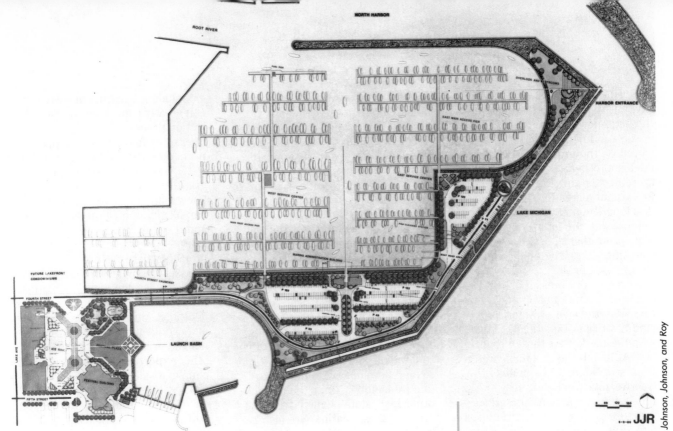

Johnson, Johnson, and Roy

water, greatly improved the value of their property. Developers of residential subdivisions, especially in Florida, often dug intricate canal systems to guarantee all buyers a waterfront lot, where they could park their boats "out back" in much the same way as they parked their cars "out front." Marinas as residential amenities are not limited to single-family subdivisions, of course. At Marina City in Chicago, a lakefront luxury high-rise apartment building includes a basement marina, where boats are launched into the Chicago River by a forklift.

At a much larger scale, marina ventures have helped generate substantial real estate investment through complex, long-term, public/private ventures. One of the best-known examples is Marina Del Rey in Los Angeles County. The project, which began with federal assistance in the late 1950s, opened in 1965 with 5,600 boat slips on 780 acres. By the mid-1970s, the $36 million public contribution had generated well over $100 million in private development.[5] More recently, many American cities have used public investment in marinas and other facil-

ities to help spur redevelopment of deteriorated and underused waterfronts.[6] Some European ventures are even more ambitious. In the Languedoc-Roussillon region of southwest France, for example, an $800 million public/private venture includes 20 new harbors berthing 40,000 boats along 120 miles of Mediterranean coastline.[7]

Marina Development Issues and Trends

Undoubtedly, the most important influence on marina development in the last 20 years has been the environmental movement and its impact on public policy regarding coastal development. Environmental regulations have lengthened the marina approval process, required costly environmental impact mitigation measures, and greatly reduced the number of potential marina

Racine, Wisconsin, after witnessing a gradual economic decline through the 1980s, has turned to its waterfront as a means to help spark a dramatic reinvestment downtown by private developers. A key element of the plan, developed by the firm of Johnson, Johnson, and Roy, is a $9.4 million, 1,000-slip marina, along with some $11 million in harbor improvements and a nearby festival park, all scheduled to open in 1987. According to a University of Wisconsin study, the marina will pump nearly $29 million annually into the local economy and will create upwards of 400 jobs. Like most such projects, funding comes from an array of sources, including the city and county, the federal government, the state of Wisconsin, and numerous business and community organizations.

sites. However, the same regulations have vastly improved the quality of the nation's waters, reduced coastal erosion and flooding hazards, and increased the productivity of fisheries and other wildlife habitats, thereby enlarging the opportunities for coastal recreation. Nevertheless, developers contemplating a marina in most states must now convincingly prove that their proposal is compatible with the public's environmental goals.

As regulatory pressures have reduced the number of potential marina sites, the cost of waterfront land has risen dramatically, along with the market for these properties. Although this can make waterfront real estate development attractive, high land costs may preclude development of marinas for more profitable waterfront uses. Operating costs, especially for fuel and labor, have also risen steeply.

The annual boat sales statistics compiled by the NMMA trace a relatively erratic line that corresponds closely with larger economic conditions. Demand for boating supplies, hence marinas, is highly price-elastic. After the oil shock of 1974, when fuel scarcity increased the cost of fiberglass products, for example, boat sales dropped by 40 percent in two years.[8]

Established marinas, however, if well managed, can be quite successful. In fact, the Corps of Engineers' survey in the mid-1970s found that one of the marina owners' biggest concerns was that they had inadequate room for expanding their businesses. The survey results also clearly show that the upfront costs of marina development can be formidable. Two other critical issues cited were undercapitalization of marinas in their early stages and inadequate upfront attention to fundamental infrastructure.[9]

Many of these obstacles to marina development are being addressed through new types of products. The popularity of small fiberglass boats, for example, coupled with site development hurdles, has led to a boom in stack storage marinas, where boats are housed in warehouse-like buildings and launched on demand. Some developers are selling slips as fee-interest condominiums, with individual ownership of the airspace between finger piers and common ownership of all other facilities.[10] Another means to address the site shortage is to reuse existing sites. Established marinas, as well as deteriorated waterfronts, will continue to be redeveloped into more productive facilities, often including other real estate elements. Developers of these marinas are also becoming more creative with management and ownership options to create self-supporting, even profitable, amenities.

SITE SELECTION AND DEVELOPMENT FEASIBILITY

At first glance, the process of finding a suitable marina site does not seem much different from any other site selection process. The prospective developer must identify a place where physical characteristics and social and economic patterns combine to support the vision of the project. Rarely, of course, does a potential site perfectly dovetail with a preconceived development program. Instead, the developer makes trade-offs and adjustments, modifying programs, shifting economic projections, even changing a site's physical characteristics, until eventually either the project gets built or the idea is abandoned.

Including a marina in a project can greatly complicate the site selection process. After all, the developer must find a location that supports both the land uses *and* the water uses envisioned in the program. And while most developers know a good deal about land, the complexity of offshore conditions and the special needs of a marina can pose formidable challenges. In projects where the marina functions as an amenity for a residential or resort development, a great many factors are involved in site selection decisions. Most often, the suitability of a candidate site for a marina is not the principal criterion. The other expected uses—a hotel, a golf course, residential neighborhoods—will obviously exert strong influences on site selection. Rather than covering every such case, the following discussion concentrates on the special site requirements of marinas, while recognizing that other needs may change the profile of the ideal site for many projects.

The site requirements for a marina should be considered in view of the basic reasons that marinas exist: convenience, safety, and security. Any site must satisfy these criteria, recognizing, of course, that engineering and programmatic measures can make a potential site safer or more accessible. Roads can improve landward access; breakwaters can make berthing safer; effective management can improve convenience. A potential marina site, however, must allow such measures at a reasonable cost.

Money spent on solid analysis of alternative sites will probably prevent crippling problems later in the development process. A poorly sited facility, on the other hand, will make it more difficult to obtain needed permits, will be more costly and difficult to develop and maintain, and will ultimately prove unpopular with boaters.

Figure 6-1
WATER ACCESS REQUIREMENTS FOR TYPICAL BOAT USES

Deep Sea Fishing (includes fishing on the American Great Lakes and similar bodies of water)
- Access to open water within no more than 15 miles and access to the fishing waters (such as the Gulf Stream off the east coast of the United States) within 15 to 50 miles.
- No restrictions on speed or wake except within the immediate vicinity of the marina.
- Safe access to a port of refuge at all times but especially during unfavorable weather or at night.
- Easy navigation to and from the marina, with many aids to navigation.
- Minimum channel depths of 5 feet.

Estuarine and Fresh Water Fishing (includes typical inland lake fishing)
- Access to suitable fishing waters within no more than 5 miles.
- Easy navigation with readily identifiable landmarks and many aids to navigation.
- Minimum channel depths of 4 feet.

Water Skiing and Similar Aquatic Sports
- Access to suitable open water within 10 to 15 minutes.
- Little or no restriction on speed or boat utilization except in the immediate vicinity of the marina.
- Minimum channel depths of 4 feet.

Casual Cruising—Powerboats
- Access within 30 miles to interesting waters containing many inlets, islands, small beaches, and safe and quiet anchorages.
- Minimum channel depths of 5 feet.
- Easy navigation to and from the marina, especially at night.

Casual Cruising—Sailboats
- Access within 15 miles to interesting waters, containing many inlets, islands, small beaches and safe and quiet anchorages.
- Located so that the course to and from the interesting waters is essentially at right angles to prevailing winds.
- Minimum channel depths of 7 feet.
- Easy navigation to and from the marina, especially at night.

Long Distance Cruising
- Easy access to the ocean or major lake on a course compatible with prevailing winds, easy access to an inland waterway, etc.
- Easy access to the marina at night or during fog or storm conditions.
- Minimum access channel of 7 feet.

Small Sailboats
- Access channel very short or wide enough to permit easy tacking (small sailboats will not usually have auxiliary power).
- Access channel oriented essentially at right angles to prevailing winds.
- Minimum channel depths of 5 feet.
- Relatively protected waters within one mile of the marina.
- Open waters of at least one mile in diameter within one mile of the marina, with few shoreside obstructions which would cause variations in wind velocity and direction. (This requirement is dictated primarily by sailboat racing activity. Racing with large sailboats has the same requirement for open waters but the dimensions are greater, and the distance to the starting line may comfortably be two to five miles.)

Source: Clinton J. Chamberlain, *Marinas: Recommendations for Design, Construction, and Management* (Chicago: National Marine Manufacturers Association, 1983), p. 3.

The single site requirement that most clearly separates a marina from other uses is that it must offer safe access to a usable body of water. What constitutes "usable water," of course, depends on the anticipated market characteristics and local use patterns. The water access requirements for deep-sea fishing, for example, are quite different from those for small sailboats. Figure 6-1 identifies the typical requirements for a variety of boating uses. A single site may, however, accommodate apparently conflicting demands. At Harbour Ridge in Stuart, Florida, for example, the open ocean lies about an hour away under power, well within range for cruising and deep-sea fishing. At the project site, the St. Lucie River is about a mile wide, providing plenty of room for small sailboats and freshwater fishing. An appropriate marina site, in other words, can accommodate a number of different uses.

Any detailed site selection and feasibility process grows directly out of a developer's initial evaluation of the market and the preliminary program requirements. After a relatively informal and largely intuitive process of identifying development opportunities and scouting potential locations, the prospective developer should enter a more detailed period of investigation. This process, in which site selection often blurs with feasibility analysis, generally probes four broad (and somewhat overlapping) categories of information: the legal and policy context, the physical environment, the marina market, and financial conditions. The goal of the process, of course, is to select the best physical location for the project in light of other constraints, and as accurately as possible to test the proposed marina's technical feasibility and financial viability.

The process is iterative, repeated for each hypothetical project situation or potential site. In each case, the development team gathers data in each of the four categories mentioned above and evaluates the results according to some analytic criteria—often return on investment or other financial measures, although in real estate projects a marina may not be expected to be profitable and may have an altogether different purpose. The product of such an analysis should be a concise and complete profile of a successful marina for a chosen site. A full-scale feasibility analysis will describe the basic objectives for the facility; list and justify any necessary assumptions; identify the design, construction, and operation of the marina, including the solutions to any outstanding technical problems; and forecast the financial performance of the marina through pro forma statements of income, expenses, and cash flow.

The Legal and Policy Context

The degree to which the public interest—as expressed in policies, regulations, and plans—affects the feasibility of a proposed marina largely depends on the potential project's location. In some areas, a project may be subject to few regulations, required permits, or applications for approval. In other areas, usually where high growth is pressuring sensitive or scarce resources, the potential marina developer must overcome a long line of hurdles presented by local governments, state and federal agencies, regional coastal commissions, community organizations, environmental groups, and a host of others.

All these groups may be hostile or hospitable to a proposed marina, depending on the particular circumstances. An early reconnaissance by the developer of a potential location's legal and policy context is therefore a key compo-

nent of site analysis. This context may be broken down into issues of site ownership, local plans and policies, existing public services and programs, and regulatory requirements.

Ownership Issues. If the marina under consideration is part of a larger, more complex project, site ownership will probably be examined in view of the total project needs. Several special ownership considerations are germane to marinas, however, because of the almost inevitable link between private and public ownership. Most marinas offer some link to public waters. Many are located on or next to publicly owned land or submerged lands. Because dredge-and-fill restrictions have made fully dredged marinas on private land the exception rather than the rule, many new marinas are developed on or over land leased from the state or federal government.

The terms of such lease arrangements may pose formidable obstacles to a marina proposal. Requirements for public access or for "public benefit" may conflict with marketing objectives, for example. Some marinas, built as part of public/private ventures and open to the public, may carry restrictions on rates charged for slips or services.

Garden apartments overlooking Chandlers Landing Marina on Lake Ray Hubbard, an Army Corps of Engineers reservoir near Dallas.

In other cases, regulations governing the lease of state lands may determine the marina's size. At Harbour Ridge, for example, the state issued new regulations near the end of the developer's planning process. The rules based leasable area on the site's river frontage. Based on the more stringent new formula, the developer was forced to cut the number of slips by 20 percent and to reduce the number of walkways. Similar restrictions may constrain noncoastal marinas as well. At Lake Ray Hubbard, an Army Corps of Engineers reservoir near Dallas, land within 60 feet of the mean high-water line is subject to Corps control. In California and Hawaii, regulations mandate public access and space set aside for public use.

Even when a marina basin is located on privately owned land, an entrance channel may be leased. Under such an arrangement, the responsibility for developing and maintaining these waterways should be carefully spelled out. A decision as to what submerged land is private and what is public may be beneficial to a developer. At Sarasota, Florida's Longboat Key Club, a state official made a fortuitous decision that lands dredged and submerged years earlier were private, not public, and could thus be developed without further restrictions.

Community Plans, Policies, and Politics. Local acceptance of a marina proposal will depend on how well the facility fits the community's overall land use objectives. Sometimes, these desires (and fears) are stated more or less explicitly in state and local policies, plans, and other documents. More often, however, these plans are only part of the picture. A complex network of economic conditions, local attitudes, and political traditions— often unstated or implicit—can also work to streamline or block a proposed marina. Shrewd developers will not only review the explicit planning and policy documents, but will also survey these "hidden" factors as well.

Shipyard Quarters Marina, part of the redevelopment of the Charlestown Navy Yard near Boston.

Although federal agencies may strongly affect the marina development process (their role is discussed in detail below), the most important policy influence lies at the state and local levels. Two overriding goals expressed by nearly all these governments are to provide adequate recreational opportunities for their residents and to protect sensitive or scarce environmental resources. The dilemma inherent in reconciling these two broad state and local policies is nothing new, of course. Balancing development and conservation is at the heart of many land use disputes, and the importance of both goals is the reason for the plethora of state and local planning and regulatory programs.

Governments differ widely in their approaches, either favoring development, favoring preservation, or aiming to balance the two. Official statements of policy toward development can be found in local comprehensive plans, which often include a section devoted to recreation and a section on natural resources. Zoning ordinances also implicitly express official land use policy. Zoning and other ordinances may in fact deal extensively with marina development, and may include detailed site planning and development standards for particular locations. Other elements of local government plans may offer clues to marina feasibility. General development policies may, for example, aim to revitalize an urban waterfront, potentially recognizing a marina as an attractive catalyst for other development. Local plans may also clue a developer in to the principal public concerns regarding specific aspects of coastal development. The concern may focus on maintaining water quality, for example, or on the desirability of views to the water from certain areas. Some public plans, such as those of the California Coastal Commission, severely limit land uses that are not strictly water-dependent; while a marina may be allowed, for instance, adjacent residential development may be prohibited.

A potential marina must often satisfy a wide range of such criteria at the regional or the state level as well. Most marinas will require state-level permits. Although most states do not produce comprehensive plans in the same way as do local governments, various agencies often produce similar documents that should be researched and reviewed in advance by a potential developer.

Under the provisions of the federal Coastal Zone Management Act, 28 states have prepared coastal management plans. These plans and the resultant programs attempt to balance coastal development, resource management, public access, and many other concerns. Nearly all these state programs deal prominently with recreational development and marinas. Usually, the state policies are implemented at the local level. Local governments, of course, may adopt more restrictive attitudes. Statewide comprehensive recreation plans (SCORPs) also reflect statewide attitudes toward marina development.

State and local plans can be particularly useful for evaluating a potential marina site after a specific parcel is identified. They can identify adjacent land uses, current and planned, and they often outline important capital investment plans for parks, roads, or other infrastructure that would affect a marina. Similarly, future investment in waterway development or maintenance can be critically important.

An early review of the planning and policy context tends to yield other useful information. Such public documents are usually replete with demographic projections, economic statistics, and other data that will prove helpful in evaluating a marina market.

At some point official plans and other public policy statements become less useful to a prospective developer. Although the official line on marina development may be favorable, there remain potentially a host of other obstacles, from neighborhood groups angry at a potentially lost water view to poor relationships among federal agencies. Although all the ramifications of these situations can never be predicted, a developer who undertakes a thorough preliminary investigation of this "unofficial" policy context stands a better chance of ultimately prevailing. Intelligent strategies and countermeasures, after all, must be based on knowledge of the potential opposition.

Government agencies, for example, may have agendas only partly related to marinas. One prominent coastal engineer in Florida argues that state permitting agencies routinely deny marina permits as a general means of controlling growth and development, not because of an evaluation of each marina proposal itself. Interagency battles over jurisdictional "turf" may also stymie a marina proposal, regardless of its merits.

Perhaps the most important unofficial policy context can be found within the proposed site's immediate neighborhood or community. A variety of groups, formally organized or ad hoc, can arise to oppose a marina project. Few, outside of boating organizations, perhaps, can be expected to support it. Common objections to marinas are that they will inevitably lower water quality, destroy wildlife or marine habitats, aggravate erosion or sedimentation problems, and cause traffic congestion on land and water. In some areas, residents may fear that marinas and related development will displace cheaper moorings or water-dependent industrial uses. It is incumbent upon the developer to seek out these groups or individuals, identify their concerns, and honestly and openly work with them toward a resolution.

Clearly, potential opposition can play a major role in site selection, assuming other variables remain relatively equal. The very qualities that attract a developer to a project site—a pleasant view, easy water access, a strong boating market—are often the same qualities that invite fervent opposition.

Public Services and Programs. In addition to the public sector's general development plans and policies, existing or proposed public services and programs may have some impact on marina feasibility. As with such landside infrastructure and services as fire protection and trash removal, waterways are often managed and maintained by a variety of agencies. Relevant activities might include, for example, mosquito control, boat traffic restrictions such as age limitations or speed zones, Coast Guard or local marine patrols, and ferry or water taxi services. Other broad categories of activity might be conducted at higher levels of government, such as state or federal fish and wildlife agencies, beach nourishment, or other resource management programs.

Permits and Regulatory Requirements. Ultimately, the most important single criterion in evaluating a potential marina site is whether or not the site can legally be developed as planned. Of course, like many variables in a feasibility study, regulatory and permitting requirements are rarely absolutely fixed and wholly predictable.

The philosophy and evolution of the major regulations and permit programs are discussed in detail below. As part of the initial site screening and feasibility evaluation, it is important for a developer to identify as completely as possible the requirements for development approval. Depending on the site's physical characteristics, the plan, and the location, an approval process can be extremely rigorous, lengthy, and often frustrating. Clearly, a plan that conforms to the spirit and the letter of the regulations will have the best chance of success, although conformance by itself does not necessarily guarantee approval.

A prospective developer must determine at this stage what approvals are needed, from which agencies, and in what sequence. Generally, approvals move upward from local development approvals such as zoning or planned unit development to state offices, and then to federal agencies, if applicable. Many states have established coordinated permit programs, wherein a developer submits an application to one agency that oversees distribution and review to other agencies. Similarly, the Army Corps of Engineers coordinates the federal response.

Based on his experience in marina permitting, coastal engineer Fred Klancnik says, "It's important to break down the anonymity of the agencies by focusing on key individuals." Once the basic program and objectives are set, he says, a developer is likelier to persuade the agencies to agree on a site's potential opportunities and constraints.

The next step is to identify, given the constraints of a particular site, what additional consultant studies or reports will be necessary, their format and content, and their likely cost. From the developer's perspective, the most costly item related to the approval process is not additional information; rather, it is the cost of delay in the development process. By reckoning the expected time required for approval early in the process, the developer can save a good deal of frustration, and probably some money as well, later on. These time estimates may figure prominently in the later preparation of such financial pro formas as cash-flow projections.

The Physical Environment

Physical site selection variables for a marina can be conveniently divided into two categories: onshore characteristics and offshore characteristics. The most basic onshore requirement for a marina is adequate space. Although one author recommends a minimum of 10 acres of usable land and an equal amount of water area for a full-service marina, many boating facilities that are developed as part of real estate ventures will be smaller.[11] The land area should, however, be roughly equal to the water area, no matter what the facility size. While every marina will vary in the total area needed, an acre of water area can generally be expected to handle from 25 to 65 boats, depending on the facility layout and boat size.[12]

Many onshore factors will probably be considered only as part of the site selection process for the entire project, and not simply for the marina. It may be assumed, for example, that the marina market will be largely provided by other project elements, such as a hotel, residential products, or other uses. If, however, the marina will depend on outside markets, it should be readily accessible to those users.

Existing (or formerly existing) uses may also affect site feasibility. Many older marinas have been redeveloped to support other uses at a higher level of service. Urban waterfronts that once berthed travelers and warehoused goods now berth yachts alongside luxury condominiums. In each instance, a developer must consider the potential for renovation, adaptive use, or demolition.

A prospective developer should also consider future expansion needs, especially where a marina is a supporting amenity to a phased, master-planned project. The landward requirements of a marina will expand as slips are added: more land will be needed for parking, boat and marina maintenance, and storage. One option, of course, is to plan the onshore facilities to support the ultimate capacity, and then to add slips as necessary.

The land on which these facilities will be built should lie above the floodplain and should have adequate bearing capacity to support construction. Soil characteristics should be examined carefully in areas of recent fill; where fill operations are proposed, the qualities of the source material must be checked. A developer should pay careful attention to shoreline conditions, since erosion or sedimentation potential may be exacerbated by marina development unless the shoreline is stabilized with bulkheads, revetments, or other measures.

Onshore factors for marina site suitability do not differ much from any development activity: appropriate access, enough space, adequate soil properties, and so on. Offshore factors, however, are complex and unfamiliar to most developers. Once a developer selects a candidate site, there is no substitute for the advice of an experienced coastal engineer. In fact, a wise developer will have consulted such experts early in the site selection process.

At Port Louis, tall steel piles and floating piers can accommodate a sizable storm surge on Lake Ponchartrain.

In evaluating offshore conditions, it is important to first consider water-depth and water-level fluctuation patterns. An ideal minimum depth is eight feet below low-water datum. Many sites can be dredged to create a deep enough basin, The possibility and cost of dredging depend mainly on the bottom material's physical and chemical makeup. Shallow sites, if dredging is precluded, will restrict the sizes and types of craft that can be accommodated. A very deep basin, on the other hand, may not provide adequate protection from wave action or may inhibit proper water circulation, and will limit pier design alternatives.

Water-level fluctuation constitutes a critical factor in site selection. Water-level changes occur as a result of tides, storm surges, wind and wave action, precipitation patterns, and, in reservoirs, by periodic drawdowns. While in the latter case, extremely low levels will be a concern, a more severe limitation is usually extremely high water levels. High water levels clearly pose a threat to marina facilities and equipment, and, if berths are over public waters, fluctuations may raise questions of landownership as well.[13] Since water-level fluctuation is such an important criterion, and is also highly variable, it is wise to supplement official data, such as the Geodetic Survey Charts or Corps of Engineers records, with local history and observation at the site.

Without an adequate flow of water through the site, a marina will likely face a number of water-quality problems, including stagnation, pollution from runoff or fueling operations, and floating debris collection. At the same time, however, excessive tidal action or stream currents can make a potential marina site infeasible.

In all cases, a marina needs to be protected from wave and wind action. Data on wind velocity and direction, like water-level information, should be supplemented by local knowledge and experience. Developers should examine wind patterns over different seasons, paying particular attention to seasonal extremes.

Wind patterns affect wave patterns, which in turn can pose substantial challenges to the marina designer. A variety of engineering measures may be undertaken to protect a marina from waves, but their effectiveness depends on careful analysis of existing conditions. The site feasibility study should consider at least basic data on storm wave direction, size, period, and frequency over the course of several years.

Waves, currents, and other water action can also change shoreline or bottom conditions. Patterns of erosion and sedimentation should be analyzed first, based on existing conditions. The developer should also, however, consider postconstruction impacts on these phenomena. Bulkheading to stabilize a vanishing shoreline or periodic dredging to clear an entry channel are not only expensive, but also can aggravate the marina's impact on its environment.

In cold climates, ice can severely damage a poorly sited or inadequately protected marina. Choosing a site should include a review of the ice's seasonality and thickness, its horizontal movement due to wind, currents, and thermal expansion, and its rise and fall with water level. Often, marinas in severe climates are designed so that virtually everything can be removed from the water. Other strategies such as aeration systems to prevent ice formation can also be employed, although at significant capital and operating costs.

Depending on the particular location, other more peculiar characteristics may be important to review. A developer should check with other local marinas to assess such factors as insects (which can be a nuisance to equipment or to people), algae growth, underwater weeds, and so on.

A potential marina developer must consider each of these onshore and offshore factors in view of the design and engineering measures available to overcome or modify them. In each case, the purpose of evaluating the candidate site's physical conditions is to obtain an early sense of whether the costs of marina development will justify its benefits to the overall venture. A preliminary review of these conditions can enable the developer to make such basic determinations as whether or not dredging will be required and to what extent the shoreline will be bulkheaded or otherwise stabilized. Analysis should also reveal whether floating or fixed piers will be favored, and what types of piles should be used. Physical factors alone, of course, will not indicate whether a marina is feasible, although they may indicate that development is impossible. A developer can only determine feasibility after considering the potential marina market.

The Marina Market

In larger or more complex projects, where a marina is a supporting amenity and not a freestanding, independent business venture, the marina's market will usually coincide with the market for other project elements: a hotel, houses and condominiums, or office space. This observation is not, however, always true. Nonresidential yacht club members or transient visitors to a marina can be a significant part of its market. This is especially the case in projects in which a marina is built early, in a long, phased development process.

In any case, the formal or informal market analysis for a project containing a marina should include a review of two basic areas of information: the demand characteristics of the local, regional, or other targeted boating markets; and the existing supply of marina facilities' capacity and quality. As with any market evaluation, one might start with local demographic and economic data.

As might be expected, personal income constitutes one of the most important demographic variables. Depending on the nature of the project, age distribution and projections also may be important. Valuable economic information will include local expenditures on boating supplies and services, as well as tourism patterns and potential.

Beyond these typical demand factors, a potential marina developer needs to understand the local boating environment. A first step would be to determine the number of boats registered in the expected market area, and the per capita rate of boat ownership. Nearly as important as the number of boat owners is the types of boats they own, and how they use them.

Marina markets vary widely in their values and lifestyles. Local and regional boating promotions, regattas, and other activities of sailing clubs and boating associations can provide a general indication of these values.

Existing public and private marinas, yacht clubs, and other moorings should be carefully studied to evaluate whether the proposed facility would be competitive or complementary. Besides the obvious characteristics—size, number, and types of crafts and berths—a developer should also check the kinds and levels of services and programs offered, and supporting facilities such as restaurants or other recreational amenities. Finally, a developer should inventory the rate and fee structure for existing facilities, including slip rentals, initiation fees and dues, haul-out charges, and other service rates, along with terms of slip lease, yacht club memberships, and other agreements. The analysis should include a review of occupancy levels and absorption rates, as well as plans for expansion. Information on existing marina waiting lists will also prove valuable; in fact, creating a waiting list for slips in a prospective marina can be an effective marketing device. This survey should be complemented by an assessment of other local boating services that may not be affiliated with an existing marina, such as boat dealerships and brokers, instrument and equipment dealers, sail lofts, dry storage facilities, and others.

Figure 6-2
COMPARISON OF PAYBACK PERIODS: 26' V. 40' SLIPS

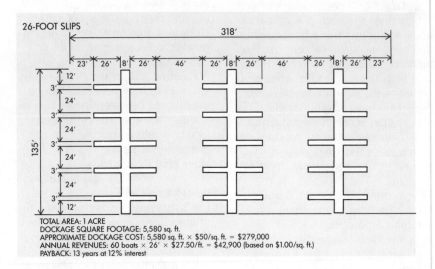

26-FOOT SLIPS

TOTAL AREA: 1 ACRE
DOCKAGE SQUARE FOOTAGE: 5,580 sq. ft.
APPROXIMATE DOCKAGE COST: 5,580 sq. ft. × $50/sq. ft. = $279,000
ANNUAL REVENUES: 60 boats × 26' × $27.50/ft. = $42,900 (based on $1.00/sq. ft.)
PAYBACK: 13 years at 12% interest

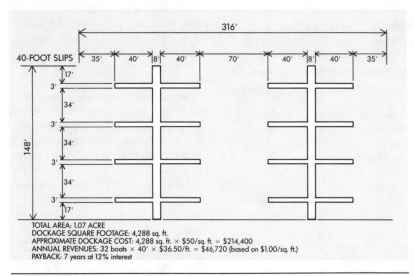

40-FOOT SLIPS

TOTAL AREA: 1.07 ACRE
DOCKAGE SQUARE FOOTAGE: 4,288 sq. ft.
APPROXIMATE DOCKAGE COST: 4,288 sq. ft. × $50/sq. ft. = $214,400
ANNUAL REVENUES: 32 boats × 40' × $36.50/ft. = $46,720 (based on $1.00/sq. ft.)
PAYBACK: 7 years at 12% interest

Source: Warzyn Engineering, Inc., Madison, Wisconsin.

The object of this market analysis is to place the physical, legal, and policy characteristics of the proposed site into some programmatic context to obtain an initial sense of development feasibility. A more rigorous test of whether a marina is indeed workable is provided by a detailed financial analysis.

Financial Conditions. A financial analysis of a proposed real estate venture must necessarily rely heavily on assumptions. This only poses a problem, of course, if the assumptions are false. Because they are generally based on reliable empirical data and reasonable experience, however, the assumptions in most financial analyses will directly reflect the attention already paid to the planning context, the physical environment, and the marina market. This data base forms the foundation for a financial analysis. In addition, the developer must now begin to attach monetary figures to each physical and program element, and to schedule these costs and revenues over time.

Estimating certain costs such as land is relatively straightforward and not much different from any development proposal. Other costs, however, can be highly variable and difficult to estimate without a well-developed physical plan. Planning, design, and engineering services are relatively expensive, especially for a difficult site, but a fairly detailed plan will enable much more precise costing. Besides land and construction costs, the developer must ascertain a variety of operating costs, which will clearly vary with the proposed level of services. Revenue estimates are based on the earlier assessment of local slip rental and service rates. The expected length of season can have an important impact on revenues, as can local absorption rates. Taxes, insurance, and other overhead items may need careful attention. At the feder-

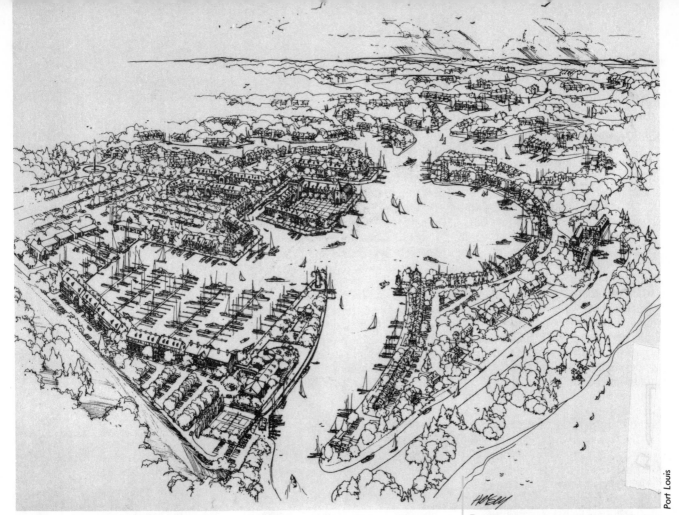

al level, for example, floating piers are considered equipment, not real property. They have therefore been eligible for certain tax credits and special depreciation provisions. Insuring a marina, because of the nature of its activities and operations, is complex and requires the specialized knowledge of an agent with marina experience.

Modeling a proposed marina's financial flows over time may be subject to factors not related to business considerations, although these are hard to predict. At Sarasota, Florida's Longboat Key Club, for instance, the developers stalled off work on their marina, since the local absorption rate was too low to support a major infusion of slips. Nevertheless, after three extensions, their marina permits were about to expire. Since the developers knew that the Corps of Engineers was unlikely to expand the permits further, they were forced to build the entire 277-slip facility. The gamble paid off: the absorption rate has not declined, while the permit process is now much more difficult.

MARINA PLANNING AND DESIGN

For many people, images of nautical communities are quite clear and distinct, and are often based on the forms and patterns of European and northeast American traditional fishing villages. In these archetypes, a small, clearly defined harbor filled with a variety of boats is closely surrounded by shops, houses, boatyards, and other buildings. Together, the ensemble is harmonious, a good fit of land uses to geography with a pleasing balance of variety and unity. Nantucket harbor (Massachusetts) and Block Island (Rhode Island) and countless European fishing villages convey this image. The primary source of this form in these examples is the pro-

Port Louis, on the north shore of Lake Ponchartrain in Louisiana, is French architect Francois Spoerry's American encore to his earlier Port Grimaud project, begun near St. Tropez in 1966. The Port Louis plan, developed by Spoerry with American architect Charles Legler, calls for a multiuse waterfront village including some 1,200 housing units and a 256-slip marina. In addition, waterfront townhouses will include 55 feet of fee-simple private mooring space alongside individual floating piers.

tected natural harbor itself, which over many decades supported a local maritime economy and thus became the community's central focus. Boats became inseparable from the harbor, which became inseparable from the village.

In many contemporary marinas, the design is a result of a quite different set of circumstances. Marinas are often sited on reclaimed or barren land, harbors are shaped according to engineering criteria rather than natural forces, and land uses are usually segregated rather than closely integrated. The results are often sterile, albeit functional, places that fail to capitalize on the tremendously attractive potential of mixing people, water, and boats. There are some notable exceptions. Harbor Town on Hilton Head Island, South Carolina, and Port Grimaud on the French Riviera (and its new American cousin, Port Louis in Madisonville, Louisiana) are two contemporary resorts that take as their chief design cue the patterns of the older villages. They do not merely mimic, however; their designers have carefully analyzed the relationships between land and water activities, local forms and materials, circulation and views, and, most important, the needs of the boaters.

Any successful marina development must carefully mesh water- and land-based program elements. Design criteria should reflect the program's demands and the site's capabilities. The program, based on an analysis of the market, will include preliminary determinations of:

- Expected boat size (length, beam, and draft);
- Percentage of sail and power boats;
- Transient slip demand;
- Required services;
- Cruising versus racing orientation;
- Shoreside amenities; and
- Seasonal variation in use.

A detailed assessment of the site's physical status and capabilities should be coupled with these program criteria. A basic property survey may need to be supplemented by a detailed description of bottom conditions. In addition, the developer must have a clear sense of offshore conditions during changing seasons and in different weather conditions. If a marina already exists on the site, a comprehensive description of its physical facilities and an assessment of its operations are required. As already noted, another important step prior to detailed plan preparation is to identify the permits and approvals required, their sequence, and the data needed to support applications.

Basic Marina Types

The heart of the marina design problem lies at the land-water edge. Although a marina's basic configuration is usually a function of the site's geography, some sites offer numerous alternative plans. As already mentioned, a basic rule of thumb for marina planning is that the land and water area should be approximately equal. Using this guideline, Adie has classified the essential types of marina configurations can be classified as offshore, recessed, built-in, and land-locked. Each type has certain advantages and disadvantages.[14]

The *offshore marina* can be the least costly type, since it minimizes both dredging and bulkhead construction, two of the most expensive marina features. Many offshore marinas, however, will require expensive breakwaters, and in deep water the cost of pilings or other pier anchorage systems can more than offset any savings. This type of marina will usually have the least environmental impact. Since the offshore marina is not protected by land, boats and marina structures are more subject to weather, wave, and current action than in other marina types. On rivers and estuaries, they may also pose a navigation hazard. Littoral drift, the

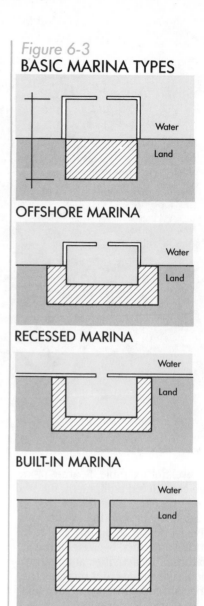

Source: Donald W. Adie, *Marinas: A Working Guide to Their Development and Design*, 3rd ed. (New York: Nichols Publishing Company, 1984), p. 98.

longshore movement of sand by wave action, may also cause shoaling in shallow waters. The offshore marina also creates the fewest opportunities to locate land uses directly adjacent to boats.

The principal advantage of the *recessed marina* is that, where bottom conditions are unsuitable for the offshore type, it allows for an economical balance of dredge and fill. Material inland of the original shoreline is dredged and deposited offshore to raise the bottom to a suitable level. Alternatively, material dredged beyond the bulkhead line is used to fill and stabilize the upland area for building sites, parking, and other uses. A potential disadvantage of this popular configuration is that, like the offshore type, the marina can encroach upon existing waterways and create a navigation hazard. The feasibility of this configuration also depends highly on the composition of the dredge material.

Built-in marinas offer a developer more opportunities to locate housing, retail, or other land uses close to boat moorings and, at the same time, to maintain open views to the larger water body. Since the shoreline is uninterrupted, it creates no navigation hazard, and the near-total enclosure, if the marina is properly sited, makes for extremely safe conditions. Because the entire site must be dredged, however, and the shoreline must be stabilized on three sides, built-in marinas are more expensive, all other factors being equal, than the protruding types. The high cost of waterfront land in many instances can make converting usable land to a boat parking lot difficult to justify economically. An additional concern in built-in marinas is the quality of the water, which may be prone to stagnation.

Land-locked marinas, wholly dredged out of existing upland and connected to open water by a channel, are generally both the safest and the costliest of marina types. The safety results from the entirely enclosed basin, protected from the action of waves and currents. The expense stems partly from the dredging and bulkheading required to create the basin and channel. In addition, unless mechanical means are used for water circulation, land-locked marinas can encounter severe water-quality problems. The configuration may be less popular with boaters because of the distance from open water. For creating real estate value, however, the land-locked marina may be the best choice, since this configuration maximizes the potential amount of desirable frontage on boat slips.

Other factors besides these considerations and the site's geography may influence which marina type is appropriate. At Chandlers Landing in Rockwall, Texas, a project fronting on an Army Corps of Engineers reservoir, the Corps jurisdiction extends inland 60 feet, precluding any shoreline changes and dictating an offshore marina with a breakwater. The difficulty of the permit process in most jurisdictions will usually increase proportional to the amount of dredging and filling involved, depending on the site. And in many areas, such as Chandlers Landing and at Harbor Ridge, Florida, dredging may simply not be an option.

Spatial Requirements

One of the most basic reasons that marinas exist is that they offer a more efficient and convenient way to store boats than individual piers or offshore moorings. Boats stored at freely swinging moorings can occupy as much as 100 times the space of a similar craft in a marina berth. Equally attractive to the boater is that a marina offers safety, an attractive environment, and valuable services.

The dictum that marina-related land acreage should be roughly equivalent to the usable water area may not hold true, of course, for all types of projects. The bounds of the "marina-related" land may be hard to judge if, for example, a hotel or dockside townhouses are included. Nevertheless, in most projects the basic equivalency assumption will apply.

Figure 6-4

SPATIAL REQUIREMENTS FOR BOAT STORAGE

Boat Storage Method	Boats/Acre	Density
Parked	Clearance on two sides, 29′ × 12′	150/acre
Parked with car	Clearance on two sides, 49′ × 12′	50/acre
Stacked	Two levels	300/acre
	Three levels	450/acre
Anchored	Varies, depends on depth; @15′ depth	1.5/acre
Berthed	30′ × 12′ ships, allowing for clearance and finger piers	50/acre

Source: Donald W. Adie, *Marinas: A Working Guide to Their Development and Design*, 3rd. ed. (New York: Nichols Publishing Company, 1984), pp. 100–101.

Depending on a host of variables, including average boat size, pier type and layout, and maneuvering room allowances, most marina sites can accommodate between 25 and 60 boats per acre of water. Fuel docks, transient piers, locks, and other "wet" facilities will, of course, reduce the feasible density. These facilities aside, about 50 to 60 percent of the water area will be occupied by slips and piers. The remaining 40 to 50 percent will serve as fairways, turning basins, and other maneuvering room.[15]

Just as boat storage is the largest user of water area, car storage eats up the most land in the typical marina. Parking can be expected to occupy about 40 percent of the land area, assuming an equal amount of land and water. The ratio of cars to boats is highly variable, and may be prescribed in local zoning codes or as a condition of development approval. In most areas, however, marinas usually offer between one-half and two parking spaces per boat slip, with a ratio of .5 to .75 the recommended minimum. Assuming this minimum ratio, and a parking density of 90 cars per acre, each acre of parking could thus support about three acres of water area.

To illustrate these spatial requirements, assume a 10-acre marina site, half water and half land. On the five acres of land, about 40 percent, or two acres, is devoted to parking. These two acres hold about 180 cars. At a ratio of .75 parking spaces for every boat, the two acres can support 240 boats. Since the water area totals five acres, the feasible density is about 48 boats per acre, a reasonable figure for boats up to about 35 feet long.

Functional Relationships

Like many other recreational facilities, marinas have operational characteristics that can potentially conflict. On one hand, marinas can be supremely luxurious "yacht clubs," designed with every comfort for people and their boats. Even in more modest marinas, the recreational aspect conjures images of quiet, relaxing surroundings in a fresh, invigorating outdoor environ-

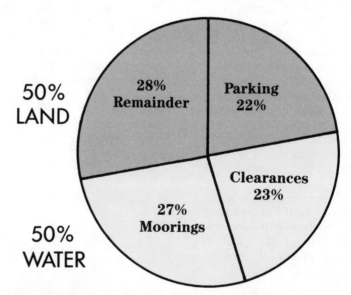

Figure 6-5

PRINCIPAL SPACE ALLOCATIONS AS PERCENTAGES[1]

50% LAND

50% WATER

28% Remainder

Parking 22%

Clearances 23%

27% Moorings

[1]Data based on averages from 10 American marinas; assuming 9 × 20 ft. parking bays.
Source: Donald W. Adie, *Marinas: A Working Guide to Their Development and Design*, 3rd. ed. (New York: Nichols Publishing Company, 1984), p. 111.

Figure 6-6

RECOMMENDED SLIP WIDTHS FOR VARIOUS SLIP LENGTHS

(Does not include widths of fingers. All dimensions are in feet.)

Slip length	25	30	35	40	45	50	55	60	65+
Width, floating slips	10	11	12	14	15	17	18	18	19
Width, fixed slips	11	12	14	16	18	19	19	20	22

Source: Clinton J. Chamberlain, *Marinas: Recommendations for Design, Construction, and Management* (Chicago: National Association of Marine Manufacturers, 1983), p. 21.

ment. On the other hand, marinas usually contain elements that might be found in any industrial setting: heavy equipment, paint shops, and noisy service yards that may use a variety of flammable, toxic, or foul-smelling materials.

The marina designer must carefully consider the physical and functional relationships between uses with these opposing characteristics. This is not to say, however, that the recreational function and the industrial function are necessarily incompatible. Longtime observers of marinas note that sailors make fairly simple demands on shoreside facilities. Like tennis players, boaters are less likely to expect a luxurious setting and a high standard of personal service in their recreational facilities. Moreover, most sailors are keenly interested in boat maintenance and repair. They not only do not mind the grittier aspects of marinas, but often truly enjoy this side of boat ownership.

Nevertheless, marinas that operate as amenities to residential or resort projects will often include supporting facilities that are not necessarily targeted to boaters, such as restaurants, a beach, or shops. The marina, in addition to serving boaters' needs, provides an attractive backdrop to other project elements. The closer the relationship between these real estate products and a marina, and the greater the diversity of other land uses, the more attention must be paid to the potential conflicts between the recreational and industrial aspects.

Mooring Layout and Water Circulation

When a site lends itself to several different harbor shapes and configurations, decisions regarding mooring layout and circulation are best made at the same time that the marina engineers determine a basic harbor shape. Usually, however, a mooring and circulation plan aims to fit an existing basin. Marina author Donald Adie likens this sequence to an architect considering a floor plan only after a building's exterior walls are half-finished. The greatest efficiencies and best relationships will more likely result from a plan where the mooring layout is considered early in the process.

Mooring layout is clearly a function not only of the site's constraints and opportunities, but also of the expected market. A marina developer will need to predict the expected size distribution of boats using a facility along with the number of permanent, seasonal, and transient slips needed. The more accurate the planners can make these predictions, the more time and money the developer will save in short-term planning and engineering costs and, potentially, in longer-term expansion or retrofitting costs. Since smaller boats can be berthed in shallower water, dredging costs can be greatly affected by mooring layout decisions, if the number of such craft can be accurately predicted.

A site protected from weather, tides, storm waves, and currents will generally present more layout and design options. The economics of any marina will depend upon its capacity, or more specifically, its density. Specific density will depend upon boat size and type, site limitations, services and facilities included, and legal and regulatory restrictions.

Within these parameters, a number of criteria will govern layout decisions. At first blush, laying out mooring space is similar to designing a parking lot or subdividing land into building lots. So it may seem that maximum efficiency is the most important criterion for designing pier, slip, and circulation space. In many instances, especially for small or relatively simple marinas, efficiency will in fact govern most design decisions for the water area. But as in parking lot design and subdivision planning, efficiency must often be coupled with other considerations. Endless rows of boats, except for perhaps the saltiest of us, are only marginally more attractive than unrelieved rows of parked cars or identical tract houses.

Depending on a marina's size and the characteristics of its patrons, for example, mooring layout can have an effect on boat security. Just as smaller neighborhoods can be more cohesive and secure, well-planned subareas of a large marina can help create a much more pleasant atmosphere for users. While subdivisions with generous open space, socially coherent neighborhood units, and logical, safe circulation systems may be less efficient users of land in a narrow sense, they clearly make better places to live. The same lesson often applies to marina design.

Basic Elements. The primary problem in marina design is the layout and sizing of slips, which are simply the spaces in which boats are stored. Slips, also called berths, are the safest and most efficient method by which to store boats. In many marinas, slips are supplemented by a limited number of moorings located within or outside the main boat basin. In the most basic marina form, slips are reached by piers or walkways that extend out from the shore or bulkhead line. Piers may be fixed in place over the water or may float on the water's surface.

In the case of floating piers, a ramp or gangway will connect the pier to a fixed structure or to land. Fixed piers are supported by piles driven deep into the harbor bottom. Floating piers are most often attached to piles by guides in a manner that allows the piers to rise and fall with the water level. Sometimes floating piers are anchored to the marina bottom or attached by cables to a riverbank or shoreline.

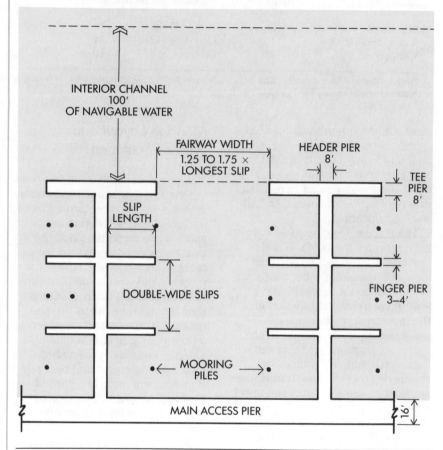

Figure 6–7
PROTOTYPICAL SLIP LAYOUT

INTERIOR CHANNEL
100'
OF NAVIGABLE WATER

FAIRWAY WIDTH
1.25 TO 1.75 ×
LONGEST SLIP

HEADER PIER
8'

SLIP
LENGTH

TEE
PIER
8'

DOUBLE-WIDE SLIPS

FINGER PIER
3–4'

MOORING
PILES

MAIN ACCESS PIER

16'

Source: Warzyn Engineering, Inc.

Slips are generally located perpendicular to a main pier or header pier. Smaller piers extending alongside slips are called finger piers and permit access to boats. A more substantial tee pier at the end of a main pier can improve the stability of the entire structure and can provide additional tie-up space. Slips may be arranged singly, separated on both sides by a finger pier, or in pairs (called double-wide slips) with a finger pier on one side of each slip. In the absence of finger piers, additional piles, called mooring piles and spring piles, are often used to secure the boats. The water area between main piers is referred to as a fairway.

The ambiguous term "dock," which to some means "pier" and to others means "slip" (as those terms are used above), will be used in the following discussion as a verb, meaning "to bring a boat into a slip."

Floating versus Fixed Piers. One of the most important decisions in marina planning is the choice between floating or fixed piers, a choice that will have important implications for mooring layout, use patterns, cost, and maintenance. Which type of pier is most suitable depends primarily on the expected water-level fluctuation at the marina site, the marina budget, and concerns about safety and convenience—which largely depend on the users' characteristics. Some marinas effectively use a combination of floating and fixed piers.

Fixed piers are usually preferable for marina sites with regular water-level fluctuations of up to five feet. They are generally easier and less costly to maintain than floating systems, and are stronger and more stable. In extremely deep marinas, or in marinas with unsatisfactory bottom conditions, piling may be difficult and a floating system the only feasible alternative. If properly designed, fixed and floating systems should be comparable in cost.

Floating piers maintain a constant level between the pier deck and the water surface, allowing easier and safer boat docking and boarding. In tidal conditions, or in any situation with a sizable water-level fluctuation, floating systems are less likely to result in boat damage. Floating piers are also the choice when winter conditions can damage fixed structures, because the piers can be removed from the water during extreme conditions. As marina needs change, a floating system permits easier expansion or modification than fixed piers. Floating piers demand greater maintenance, however, and usually have a shorter life span.

Fixed piers are relatively straightforward structures, usually made of treated wood, supported by steel or wood piles. Tubular and pressed steel frameworks with wood decking are also used, most often for small installations. Reinforced concrete is also suitable for pier structures and piles, sometimes combined with timber superstructure or decking. Myriad variations of materials can be used.

Floating piers, single-wide slips.

In the mid-1970s, a U.S. Army Corps of Engineers survey of American marinas showed that 65 percent of the responding marinas used floating piers. Most of these systems, the survey also revealed, were self-manufactured, using a wide variety of materials including old oil drums.[16] Anyone developing a new marina is well-advised to turn instead to one of the many satisfactory proprietary systems developed in the last several years. The best of these products combine a rugged and effective floatation system with a rigid structure and attractive and safe decking.

Solid flotation finger pier, double-wide slips.

The floats on these systems are generally either hollow, box-type structures of steel, plastic, or concrete, or solid blocks of styrofoam or similar material. The hollow structures each have their advantages and drawbacks, but ultimately all hollow types are sinkable. Non-sinkable floats are made of several types of expanded foam, usually coated to prevent unsightly marine growth. The best and most expensive of these are also coated for oil resistance. A marina designer considering a floating pier system should seek a balance of structural strength and buoyancy, low installation costs, simple and infrequent maintenance requirements, and a strong manufacturer's warranty. Many suppliers will also install these systems, and will usually offer such additional items as ramps, stairs, and mooring hardware.

Basin Shape. Basin shape can have dramatic effects on a marina's layout options, water quality, and cost. Rectangular basins will usually yield the greatest density, because the layout will be the most efficient. Rectangular basins also make boat maneuvering easier. Curving bulkhead walls, though they may be desirable for other reasons, make docking and boarding difficult. The basin plan should minimize the amount of vertical bulkheading, which is not only expensive but can also impede water circulation and reflect waves. Bulkhead corners should be rounded to avoid collecting floating debris. If dredged, the basin bottom should slope gradually toward the entrance and the main waterway to encourage the greatest amount of natural flushing action.

Entrances and Channels. The optimum size and orientation of entrances to a marina basin will depend upon the local wave and weather conditions, as well as on the marina's use patterns. Entrances, if possible, should be turned away from the predominant wave direction. Other options for protection include breakwaters, peninsulas, or artificial islands to shelter the entrance. Generally, the entrance should measure at least four times the beam of the marina's widest boat. A reasonable minimum entry width is about 60 to 100 feet. An excessively narrow entrance will be trickier to negotiate for sailors, and in periods of heavy use it can create traffic bottlenecks. If a marina will be heavily used by small sailboats, an entrance channel is best oriented perpendicular to the prevailing winds. A key factor in entrance design is the possibility of sedimentation or littoral drift closing the harbor entrance and requiring expensive dredging.

Turning Areas. Turning basins are needed when a marina contains such facilities as fueling docks and transient piers. These facilities are usually located between the end of an entrance channel and the main slip area. The size of turning basins depends on the type of boats expected to use the marina and on the skill level of the users. Inexperienced sailors need more maneuvering room. Shoal draft and single-propeller power boats require more room than two-propeller power boats or fin-keel sailboats. Generally, the narrowest dimension of a turning basin should be about 2.25 times the length of the marina's longest boat. If the marina is heavily

Box-type floating piers being installed in a double-wide slip configuration.

Curving bulkhead walls can encourage free water circulation, but can also signal an inefficient mooring layout.

used by sailboats and experiences frequent onshore winds, the basin should be larger. Conversely, a marina with a preponderance of twin-screw power boats in calm water and genial weather conditions will not need as much room. With long main piers, slips sited so that shorter boats can dock closer to shore will maximize the amount of turning room in fairways.

Slip Sizing and Placement. The safest slip arrangement is when the slip's long axis lies parallel to the current or to the prevailing winds. The safest mooring arrangement within each slip is when a boat is secured on all four corners with adequate clearances on all sides. The most convenient slip for boaters has finger piers extending the full length of the boat on both sides. Countless variations in slip design exist: cluster moorings, star-shaped piers, gunwale-to-bulkhead mooring, and so on. Each alternative should respect local conditions and practice while optimizing safety, security, convenience, and efficiency.

The distribution of slip lengths should reflect the anticipated mix of boats. Finger piers, if used, should be at least two-thirds as long as the boat occupying the slip. Otherwise, the placement of mooring piles will determine the slip length. Slip widths should be balanced as much as possible on either side of a main walkway in order to reduce stress differentials on the main structure. Thus, a 12-foot-wide slip should be located opposite another 12-foot-wide slip. If finger piers are used, the number of intersections between the fingers and the main pier should be minimized, making the installation of utilities easier and the walkways safer. Boats in slips adjacent to fixed piers in tidal waters need at least 1.5 feet of clearance on each side. In nontidal waters, or with floating piers, as little as a foot of lateral clearance is satisfactory.

A double-wide slip arrangement will save money and space and will offer the marina manager the most flexibility. Boats not separated by piles or piers, however, remain more subject to damage from other boats and from wave action. Fixed piers in tidal waters will require mooring piles or spring piles if finger piers are not provided. With the additional stability of mooring and spring piles, double-wide slips can accommodate boats as large as 50 feet.

Tee walkways or piers at the end of main piers are desirable whenever possible. The tee pier should measure at least as long as the longest slip extending from the main pier. These structures make the entire pier more stable, provide accommodations for transients (visitors), and in floating systems help protect other slips from wave action.

The flotation system alongside this finger pier allows out-of-water storage for this racing sailboat.

Dockside services and utilities at Harbourside Moorings, Longboat Key Club, Florida.

The major structural elements of a marina—bulkheads, breakwaters, and piles—form the basic framework for piers, slips, and other service facilities. Along with dredging and sometimes locks, these features also account for the major costs in marina construction. Although the design and engineering of structural items is best left to experienced marina engineers, a developer considering a marina as an amenity should have a grasp of the basic issues associated with these critically important elements. The placement of breakwaters, channel entrances, bulkheads, and other marina structures can have significant impacts on existing natural patterns of siltation and erosion. By modifying the existing bottom profile and hydraulic regime, dredging, for example, often exacerbates siltation problems. Excessive siltation can prevent needed marina expansion. Maintenance dredging and disposal to alleviate siltation problems is expensive and inconvenient. Erosion can pose a threat to piles, bulkheads, and other marina structures. Thorough analysis of the natural hydraulic patterns can help avoid these pitfalls, and will be money well spent.

Dredging

Dredging is both a common and a costly element of marina construction. Basically, dredging modifies the bottom profile of the boat basin to permit dockage of deeper draft boats, to facilitate construction of piers and other structures, and to encourage flushing action. Dredged material is also often used as fill to raise or stabilize the land next to the basin. Sites where dredging is precluded will be limited in the number of marina design alternatives available, or in the craft that can be berthed.

Main walkways should measure a minimum of six feet wide. Piers that berth boats larger than about 40 feet or that are expected to carry light maintenance vehicles on their surface should run eight to 10 feet wide. Finger piers can be as narrow as two feet in single slip arrangements. A wider finger pier is safer for double-wide slips. At many European marinas, a hinged pipe or truss with a float attached to the end is used for a mooring aid in lieu of a finger pier. Since the deck level of fixed piers in tidal waters will sometimes be a considerable distance above the water surface, these walkways may need to be wider than those on floating piers or at inland sites.

Fairways, the water area between rows of slips (analogous to lanes in a parking lot), should be from 1.25 to 1.75 times the longest boat length. Like turning basin and channel dimensions, generous fairways will make boat handling easier. Wider fairways should be used to compensate for a strong current or prevailing winds in a direction parallel to the slips.

The range and level of dockside services will vary with the type of marina and the demands of the market. Water is universally provided, and most marinas also provide electrical power to each slip (either 120 or 240 volts AC). Pier lighting, public address systems, and centralized telephones are also popular. In some areas, boaters will expect individual telephone service and cable television hookups. These utilities are usually run in conduits built into the pier structure, often with access panels for ease of maintenance.

The wholly dredged marina basin at Port Louis.

The expense of marina dredging depends on the size of the area, the bottom profile and material, the existing and required depth, the equipment used, and the method used to dispose of the dredged material. The minimum depth for a marina should accommodate the draft of the largest vessel expected, allow for an extremely low tide (or drawdown condition in the case of a reservoir), provide adequate clearance, and include some extra measure to allow for siltation. Keel sailboats have the deepest draft. Inboard power boats generally have deeper drafts than outboards. Draft generally increases with boat size.

To economize on dredging costs, a marina can opt for a stepped or graduated bottom profile, although this means that deeper-draft boats will need to be restricted from certain areas of the marina. Often, the bottom will slope away from the lower edge of vertical bulkhead walls. This strategy saves money and materials both in dredging and in bulkhead construction but will restrict close-in berths to smaller, shallower draft boats.

In some cases, such as when maintenance dredging to remove siltation is problematic, dredging to a uniform depth greater than the immediate need may be cost-effective. Although dredging costs will be higher, subsequent maintenance dredging will be greatly reduced. Permit provisions sometimes restrict subsequent dredging operations. Extremely deep marinas, especially if fully enclosed, however, can have serious water quality problems, especially low dissolved oxygen levels. This may require the developer to install costly aeration systems as a mitigation measure.

Depending on the bearing capacity of dredged material, it can be used on site to level and stabilize areas behind bulkheads or for building sites. Just as in cut-and-fill for grading, the most economical marina construction method is to balance the dredging and filling requirements. If not useful on site, the dredged material can be sold in some rare cases. The developers of Florida's South Seas Plantation on Captiva Island, for example, recovered the $250,000 cost of extending their marina basin by selling the dredged material as fill. Typically, however, disposal is quite expensive. Offshore disposal can be extremely difficult in today's regulatory climate, and disposal in wetlands, for obvious reasons, is no longer an acceptable alternative.

Land-based dredging equipment constitutes the most economical and suitable choice for small marina sites. Draglines are most often used at small marinas. Portable floating dredges also offer a relatively economical alternative. Large, water-based mechanical equipment is quite expensive to use and is less efficient than similar hydraulic methods. Under the right conditions, large hydraulic dredges are the most economical alternative, but unless the job is extremely large the costs of setting up a floating plant can be prohibitive.[17]

Aeration system enhances water quality in this marina basin.

Breakwaters

As their name suggests, the purpose of breakwaters is to protect a marina from wave action. These structures are common but not always necessary, especially on naturally protected inland sites. Wave analysis is a complex procedure that considers the length, period, or distance between waves; wave direction; and size. Engineers model the impact of a proposed marina on existing wave patterns and determine the appropriate breakwater design in view of the project's budget and program.

The most important consideration in breakwater design is location. A poorly positioned breakwater will not only be ineffective for its basic protective purpose; it can also inhibit flushing action, aggravate erosion and siltation problems, and foster dangerous currents at

channel entrances. In addition, a breakwater with a high profile above the water level or made of inappropriate materials can block desirable views.

The most common breakwater is constructed of riprap or rubble piled in a long narrow mound, although materials can range from precast concrete units to old car bodies. Alternatives include a single

Attractive decking atop breakwater at Chandlers Landing Marina.

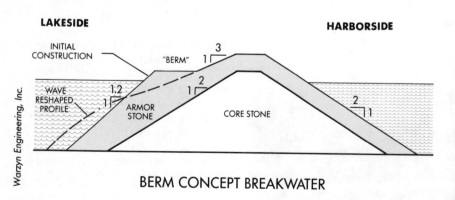

Warzyn Engineering, Inc.

A conventional rubble mound breakwater, in cross section, top, is made up of three stone layers: a core of relatively small stones (weighing up to 50 pounds); an intermediate layer to prevent the core stone from washing away; and a protective armor stone layer, sized so that the outer stones will not be displaced by wave action. Because of their large size, armor stone materials are often not available locally, and are therefore relatively expensive. Recently revised design standards call for even larger armor stones, thus raising the cost even further. An alternative breakwater concept, termed the "berm breakwater" by its designers, uses locally available armor stone to cut construction costs. The berm breakwater, with a wider horizontal cross section, employs a permeable armor layer made up of much smaller stones. After construction, the armor layer is reshaped by wave action to produce a stable, protective layer. The lighter weight stone, in addition to being more readily available, allows use of less expensive, land-based construction equipment. According to the engineers who developed the alternative design, in several successful applications it has produced cost savings of up to 50 percent.

Concrete bulkhead at Port Louis.

or double row of piles, which will not interfere as much with water circulation, or a vertical-face structure of steel or concrete, most often used for large breakwaters in deep water. Sometimes, the harbor design can make breakwaters unnecessary, such as at Longboat Key Club in Sarasota, where a long, narrow spit of dredged material serves as a breakwater.

Breakwaters can also float on the water's surface. The key advantage of floating breakwaters is that they do not alter the hydraulic regime. The bottom is modified only by the placement of the breakwater anchors, and water flow is not impeded. In addition, the capital cost is lower than for a fixed breakwater. Floating systems may require more maintenance, however, and are generally not suitable for areas with severe weather and long-period waves—which includes most Great Lakes and ocean sites. Like floating piers, some floating breakwaters are prefabricated proprietary systems.

Piles

Piles serve a number of structural purposes. They support other structures such as fixed piers and bulkheads, and can anchor floating piers. Piles are often made of timber, although concrete, steel, and combinations of materials are also used. One such combination is PVC-jacketed concrete piles. Whatever the material, piles should be durable, stable, and straight. Floating pier systems may hang up on misaligned piles, and ice can potentially uproot inadequate seated piles. In colder climates, clusters of piles are commonly used to break up ice floes before they can damage individual piles. Piles can be installed in a number of ways, either when the marina basin is dry or full of water. A wet basin generally requires a floating rig to drive piles.

Bulkheads

Bulkheads provide one means of stabilizing the edge of a marina basin. In some situations, the banks of the shoreline can be left unprotected or can be stabilized by vegetation. The principal purpose of bulkheading is to prevent erosion of the shoreline and to provide safe and convenient access to the waterborne parts of the marina.

Besides the cost, another reason to avoid bulkheading except where necessary is that it precludes development of a beach area. Beaches, even if quite small, are extremely popular marina amenities.

Bulkheads are of two main types. Sheet bulkheads, similar to retaining walls, use sheeting of steel, concrete, or wood anchored by piles and stabilized by tiebacks or deadmen. Gravity bulkheads, usually made of precast concrete, retain the shoreline by their weight and shape. The vertical edge permits easy access to boats, but it also can reflect waves, causing greater water turbulence at the shoreline.

Revetments at Longboat Key Club mean shoreline protection at a far lower cost than bulkheading. Note mangrove swamp in background.

167

Revetments serve the same basic function as bulkheads but are not vertical and are much less expensive. Revetments lie at the shoreline's natural angle of repose. The bank is usually covered by concrete or riprap. Wire baskets filled with stones, or gabions, are also used. Revetments' advantages include superior wave attenuation and a more congenial environment for fish habitat.

In a completely dredged marina, the basin will usually be dug dry, with a coffer dam erected to keep the water out. The bulkheads act as retaining walls. After piles and other structures are installed, the dam is broken and the basin is flooded.

Locks

Locked marinas, while not common in the United States, can be the only development alternative for some difficult sites. Locks overcome the constraints posed by an excessively high tidal range (greater than 12 feet) or a major change in elevation between the marina basin and open water. Though expensive, a lock system can make an otherwise infeasible site work. A decision to build a locked marina should be approached cautiously, however. Locks interrupt free passage of boats, and since locks are rarely economical in marinas of less than 500 slips, peak periods may produce long waiting lines to get in or out of the marina. Locks require careful design of channel approaches and turning basins to ensure safe entry and exit. Locks will also necessarily create additional management and maintenance concerns.

Fueling Facilities

Fueling piers can provide a valuable service to boat owners and can be a profit center for the marina owner. However, as a potential safety hazard and, if poorly designed or improperly used, a threat to water quality, marina fueling facilities are often subject to close scrutiny by regulatory agencies. In many cases, they are simply not permitted. A primary concern is that fuel or oil, if released into the water, must be confined to the marina basin itself to avoid polluting the larger water body. Marina users are likewise concerned about spills entering the marina from outside. Floating, absorbent oil and gas containment booms are often installed to check this threat.

From a functional standpoint, fuel piers should be located as near as possible to the marina entrance to reduce conflicts with other boats. Peak fuel demand periods can generate heavy traffic and wakes around the facility. Adequate maneuvering room and unobstructed tie-up space along a fuel pier are required. An appropriate potential location for a fuel pier is at the tee walkway on the pier closest to the marina office, where fuel transactions will be recorded. Some busy marinas have manned fuel stations during peak hours. Large marinas may have fuel facilities centralized at a bulkhead location to serve both motor vehicles and boats.

Access and Circulation

The potential conflict between the social and the industrial aspects of the typical marina also affects the layout of roadways, parking areas, and pedestrian circulation ways. Marinas, especially those with a wide range of service and repair facilities, must be able to accommodate a wide range of vehicles. For circulation planning, the basic breakdown between social and service traffic might be further classified by destination. Cars and trucks with boats will head to a launching area or service yard. Other cars will head directly to a moored craft. Visitors and owners alike may be destined for the clubhouse. The distance between a parked car and an owner's boat should be minimized, although if drop-off areas are provided, the distance can be longer. Locating a marina parking lot highlights the trade-off between convenience and real estate economics. Car storage may not be the best use for valuable waterfront land.

Parking can serve other functions in the off-season, including storage of boats in cold climates. Cars with trailers clearly have special parking needs. Lots catering to day users in marinas with launching facilities should have pull-through bays of not less than 10 feet by 40 feet with generous maneuvering room. For maneuvering sailboats on land, vertical clearances are crucial. All areas should be accessible to heavy trucks and equipment.

Other Facilities

A marina clubhouse will often be combined with a number of marina-specific facilities. Clubhouses often include a chandlery, or marina store. In smaller marinas, the harbor master's office will likely be part of the clubhouse. Marina clubhouse design is not unlike clubhouse design for other amenities such as golf or tennis, although coastal environments may require special considerations for building materials. Lightweight metal roofing and large expanses of glass, for example, prove in many cases unsuitable for seaside structures. A general rule is that 10,000 to 15,000 square feet of clubhouse floor space are required to support 500 slips, depending on the number and extent of clubhouse facilities.[18]

Pump-out facilities to remove wastes from boats are sometimes expected by the market, especially at large marinas, and can be required by the terms of marina permits. The use of these facilities, as well as policies regarding the discharge of wastes from boats, require close management attention.

Boat Handling Equipment and Storage Options

A large, full-service marina will generally include facilities to launch, haul out, and store boats. Even in mild climates, owners will still periodically need to inspect, repair, or service their boats. Colder areas require winter storage. Depending on the type of project, however, these facilities may not be necessary or even desirable. The economic feasibility of hauling, launching, and storage operations depends mainly on the length of the season. Many marinas associated with real estate projects will use all the valuable waterfront land for more profitable uses. Some marinas will offer off-site winter storage areas. In markets with many nearby commercial marinas and boatyards, little incentive exists to sink substantial sums into boat handling equipment or to devote large land areas to storage.

In some areas, however, secure storage and quick launching facilities can greatly extend the boating season, especially for owners of shoal draft power boats up to 25 feet long. Stack storage marinas have appeared in recent years to serve this fairly large segment of the boating market. At a smaller scale, most marinas provide for land storage of small sailboats, dinghies, and, increasingly, sailboards. An intermediate scale solution in temperate climates is to use parking areas for winter storage of smaller boats.

Stack storage systems developed largely as a result of technological changes in small boat manufacture and of innovations in boat handling equipment. Small fiberglass boats, unlike wooden craft, can be regularly hauled out of the water with no ill effects. In the 1950s, improvements in forklift capacity coupled with the popularity of the small boats made stack storage an alternative to in-water marinas. Today, these facilities essentially use forklifts, stacker cranes, and other equipment to "warehouse" small boats. A well-planned system can launch up to 25 boats per hour. Owners can expect to have their boats in the water, fueled, and ready to go with just a few minutes' notice. Besides the convenience and security, the stack storage operation usually means lower insurance premiums for the boat owner. For the marina developer, this type of operation can satisfy a particular market's demand for boating facilities even on a difficult or marginal site. The appearance and operating characteristics of these facilities, however, may not be compatible with a project's other real estate elements. To date, boat storage buildings have not proved much more attractive than any other type of small warehouse operation.

A simple boat-launching facility, with ramp, fuel, and tie-up space.

Marinas with service operations or limited seasonal storage will often require some sort of boat handling equipment. One popular option is the mobile straddle hoist, or Travelift. Essentially, a Travelift is a self-propelled hoist that is driven over a hoist-well where a boat is docked. The Travelift offers a much more flexible alternative to the somewhat outmoded marine railway systems that were once common. Smaller hydraulic lifts can be used in conjunction with pickup trucks to tow boats to distant storage or maintenance yards.

Smaller boats are often launched by fixed, bulkhead-mounted cranes operated on a do-it-yourself basis. The most popular alternative is a launching ramp, which can range from a sandy, packed beach to sophisticated systems with rollers and winches.

LEGAL AND REGULATORY ISSUES

The process of obtaining government approval for marina development in the United States obliges a developer to demonstrate that a proposed facility will serve the public interest, which entails lengthy review by a number of federal, state, and local authorities. A complex web of both specialized and overlapping agencies at all levels of government exists to ensure that a marina proposal accommodates many particular interests. For the prospective marina developer, the task of shepherding a proposal through the permit application and review process can be daunting. Although federal government permits can be obtained in as little as six months, in many states a more realistic time frame, especially if appeals are required, is at least two years. At South Seas Plantation on Florida's Gulf Coast, the permit to dredge the entry channel took three-and-a-half years to obtain. (The dredging itself took about three-and-a-half days.) To these delays the applicant must add the cost of detailed studies to document permit applications, as well as increasing uncertainty about the ultimate fate of the marina amenity and its program, usually while other project elements are proceeding.

This arduous process results from the expansion, principally over the last 30 years, of the scope of the major federal regulatory programs. And though the impetus has originated at the federal level, state and local governments have also expanded their regulatory interests in coastal development. State and local actions often respond to wider concerns about growth management, rather than questions related specifically to marinas. The justification for marina development regulation, long established at the federal level, has helped make state and local marina regulations popular as tools to manage more general growth and development.

Figure 6-8
THE U.S. ARMY CORPS OF ENGINEERS PERMITTING PROCESS

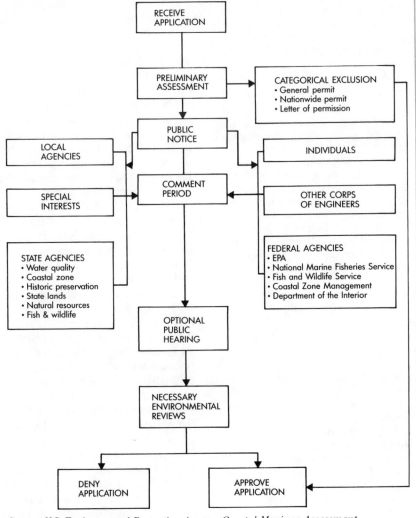

Source: U.S. Environmental Protection Agency, *Coastal Marinas Assessment Handbook*, pp. 6–24.

Federal Regulatory Programs

The federal programs that regulate marina development are administered by the U.S. Department of the Army, acting through the U.S. Army Corps of Engineers. Most construction or fill activities in U.S. waters, including wetlands, require a Corps of Engineers permit. The Corps's jurisdiction usually exceeds that of state and local regulation. The Corps's approval is also usually contingent upon state and local approval.

The 1899 River and Harbor Act initiated the Corps of Engineers regulation of public waterways. One key concern of this program, under Sections 9 and 10 of the act, is to protect navigation in the nation's waterways. In 1968, the scope of the River and Harbor Act permit program was greatly expanded to include fish and wildlife conservation, water pollution, ecological values, and other public concerns.

In 1972, the Corps of Engineers was authorized by Section 404 of the Federal Water Pollution Control Act (the Clean Water Act) to initiate a second permit program. Section 404 permits govern the discharge of dredged or other fill material. The program's jurisdiction was initially limited to "navigable waters of the United States," as established by the River and Harbor Act. In 1975, however, a court decision broadened the scope of coverage to "all waters of the United States," including wetlands. By 1977, this definition encompassed not only coastal wetlands but also isolated wetlands and lakes, intermittent streams, and other nonnavigable waters.

All this points up the importance of an overall permit strategy. By contacting the appropriate agencies at each governmental level early in the planning process, a developer can economize on data gathering efforts and technical studies, foster interagency support for the project, and help ensure complete and timely applications.

According to the Corps, Section 10 permits apply to the smallest recreational pier as well as to large commercial port projects. Bulkheads, revetments, and other bank stabilization efforts are also covered if proposed in navigable waters. The Corps defines "navigable waters" as follows:

"Navigable waters of the United States" are those "waters of the United States" that are subject to the ebb and flow of the tide shoreward to the mean high water mark and/or are presently used, or have been used in the past, or may be susceptible for use to transport interstate or foreign commerce. A determination of navigability, once made, applies laterally over the entire surface of the waterbody, and is not extinguished by later actions or events which impeded or destroy navigable capacity. The term includes coastal and inland waters, lakes, rivers, and streams that are navigable and the oceans.[19]

For Section 404 permits, the Corps adds the following:

"Wetlands," including those adjacent to "waters of the United States," are those areas that are inundated or saturated by surface or ground water at a frequency and duration sufficient to support, and that under normal circumstances do support, a prevalence of vegetation typically adapted for life in saturated soil conditions. The term "adjacent wetlands" includes:

- Those areas that are separated from other "waters of the United States" by man-made dikes or barriers, natural river berms, beach dunes, and the like;
- Tributaries to navigable waters of the United States including adjacent wetlands;
- Interstate waters and their tributaries including adjacent wetlands; and

- All other waters of the United States not identified above, such as isolated wetlands and lakes, intermittent streams, and other waters that are not part of tributary systems to interstate waters or to navigable waters of the United States.

This expanded definition broadens the Corps's permit authority to cover virtually all feasible marina sites in the United States. Developers should pay special attention to the above phrase that defines wetlands as areas that "support a prevalence of vegetation typically adapted for life in saturated soil conditions." In some instances, this definition could mean that a dry site may be classified as a "wetland" if the appropriate plant species grow on the site. A site does not necessarily have to be wet to be a wetland under the Corps's interpretation.

The Corps evaluates Section 404 permit applications under guidelines developed by the U.S. Environmental Protection Agency (EPA). To ensure compliance with a variety of other federal laws, the Corps coordinates application review by a host of other federal agencies, including the U.S. Fish and Wildlife Service, the Coast Guard, the Department of Commerce, and others. Each agency issues advisory comments to the Corps, which retains the ultimate permitting authority. In recent years, the principal snag for marina permit applicants has been the Section 404(c) guidelines, wherein the EPA examines a proposed project's impact on water quality and supply, shellfish beds, fisheries, wildlife, and recreation.[20]

U.S. FISH AND WILDLIFE SERVICE MARINA SITING EVALUATION CRITERIA

- Deep-water access is best gained by piers that extend out from the shoreline far enough to obviate the need for dredging. Breakwaters should be floating types or should allow for adequate circulation in other ways, such as openings in the breakwater or gaps between the breakwater and the shoreline.
- Where long pier extensions into deep water are not feasible, excavation of upland basins is the preferred alternative.
- Dredging of access channels should be minimized. Channels should not be dredged through submerged grass or shellfish beds. All channels should be clearly marked to avoid boat traffic impacts on grass beds or siltation impacts.
- Stack storage, elevator lifts, and other alternatives to dredged basins should be considered wherever feasible.
- Entrances should be located at least 1,000 feet from shellfish harvesting areas to reduce pollution and siltation impacts.
- Turning basins and channels should be designed to avoid a sump effect that could degrade water quality. The basin depth, for example, should not exceed the depth of the receiving body of water.
- The basin depth should be less than the depth that light penetrates the water column.
- The marina should not disrupt currents or tidal flows. Flushing channels, with more than one entrance for tidal waters, should be considered in the marina design.

- Shorelines should be stabilized through revetments, gabions, or vegetation rather than vertical bulkheads. Where unavoidable, bulkheads should be designed with a shallow zone maintained at least 10 feet from the toe of the bulkhead.
- Sharp angles and turns in the basin perimeter should be avoided to reduce potential debris collection, shoaling, and flushing problems.
- Marinas in upland sites should be dredged and the shoreline stabilized before the basin is flooded and connected to open water. Turbidity and siltation produced during excavation can also be avoided by using silt curtains, weirs, and other protective measures.
- Permanent spoil disposal areas should be established in nonwetland areas for use in initial construction and subsequent maintenance dredging.
- Proposals must provide for proper handling of petroleum products, wastewater, and solid waste.
- Land areas of the proposed marina should drain away from the basin to avoid contamination.
- All nearby development should be hooked to a public sewage system or a central wastewater treatment facility. Septic systems, which can leach polluted groundwater into the basin, should be avoided.

Source: U.S. Environmental Protection Agency, Region IV, *Coastal Marinas Assessment Handbook* (Atlanta: U.S. Environmental Protection Agency, 1985).

State Regulation

A variety of state agencies get involved in marina permitting and regulation. These usually include departments of natural resources or environmental protection, public health, water quality, and fish and wildlife. At the state level, the primary substantive issue is environmental protection. Several states, in an effort to streamline the permitting process, have designated a central agency to coordinate permit application review among the many agencies charged with review. In Florida, for example, a developer submits an application for marina approval to both the Army Corps of Engineers and the state Department of Environmental Regulation (DER), which coordinates statewide review among several agencies, including the Department of Natural Resources. The Corps of Engineers permit is issued contingent on approval by the DER.

State-level permits often contain detailed conditions that can have a major impact on a proposed marina's design and program. A permit, for example, may specify the bottom configuration allowed by dredging, require revetments rather than bulkheads, or require a detailed revegetation plan for a shoreline. State agencies may also require detailed monitoring of water quality, wildlife populations, and marina use. Other conditions may affect construction schedules and project phasing. At Harbour Ridge in Stuart, Florida, the DER permit required the developer to periodically submit harbor master's logs. According to the permit, the second marina phase could not be initiated until phase one was fully occupied.

Harbormaster's building and chandlery at Harbourside Moorings, Longboat Key Club.

Local Government Regulation

Some states perform an additional function that can affect the marina development approval process. States with federally approved Coastal Zone Management plans are eligible for federal assistance to help local governments develop standards, criteria, and regulations for coastal developments. Although they are implemented at the local level, these state-determined criteria can dramatically alter the marina development process.

In Maryland, for example, the Chesapeake Bay Critical Areas Commission has identified criteria for local coastal programs. The criteria, to be incorporated in local master plans, zoning ordinances, subdivision regulations, and other development controls, will effectively make marina development much more difficult outside already developed areas.

Most local regulation of marinas occurs through zoning, subdivision regulations, and building codes. Often, these basic ordinances will not specifically include marinas as an allowable land use (they may require a special permit, a variance, or a zoning amendment). Building codes may not adequately cover such items as bulkheads and piers, making the permit approval process less than certain. In some coastal areas, however, marinas may be specifically included in local codes.

Although most local regulations will aim for compatibility with state and federal criteria, particularized local concerns may pose additional demands for a marina developer. Local conditions, for example, may dictate special erosion control, landscaping, or hurricane protection measures. Marinas in built-up areas may be subject to the provisions of local sign codes or historic preservation ordinances.

MARINA MANAGEMENT AND OPERATIONS

As with most aspects of marinas, operations and management present a range of options and alternatives. Clearly, the most basic requirement is that the management structure and level of service be congruent with both the physical facilities and a marina's overall purpose. An overcapitalized but undermanaged facility can quickly become a serious cost burden; maintenance costs will mount as customer satisfaction and slip occupancy rents fall. Conversely, a relatively simple facility can be inefficiently overmanaged. This can be particularly true with marinas intended to function primarily as "loss leaders" for real estate operations. As long as real estate sales remain strong, wasteful expenditures on operating costs and overhead will not be matters of deep concern. However, such a facility will ultimately become a drain on its owner's resources, and retrenchment measures will be more traumatic than if the problem had been addressed earlier. Ultimately, the facility may become less attractive to patrons.

Facilities Management

Besides a marina's physical plant, one of the greatest influences on facilities management will be the range and level of services offered to patrons. A full-service facility will generally offer comprehensive boat services, including boat and engine sales; engine service; hull cleaning, repair, and painting; rigging repair; sailmaking and repair; storage; and yacht brokerage. Rarely will all these services be performed inhouse by marina personnel. Usually, a set of local operations will perform these tasks on a contract basis, although a marina may handle all the administrative work.

Marina services need not be limited to boat service and repair, of course. Many marinas also maintain a fleet of boats for rental or lessons. Special party boats or ski boats complete with a driver are also popular. Again, independent contractors often handle these services.

In deciding what services are appropriate for a given marina, Donald Adie suggests the following questions: First, "What is possible?" given the marina's physical and environmental characteristics, the local labor market, and the facility's overall purpose. It makes little sense to plan for extensive out-of-water services on a small site, or in a marina adjacent to a resort hotel, for example. The second question,

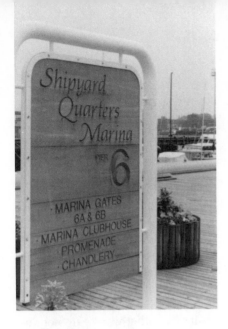

"What is popular?" requires a sense of the local market, to identify both unmet demands and development opportunities and those services already adequately provided by nearby marinas. Finally, the marina owner must consider "What is profitable?" Even in projects where the marina is not intended to make a profit per se, each potential service activity, since it may have a large impact on the marina's organizational structure and budget, should be carefully analyzed in terms of its profitability.[21]

The array of services offered will of course greatly affect a marina's personnel requirements. Skilled service staff can be difficult to find, and they may require high salaries, but in areas of strong market demand, they will be worth it. Such service staff will usually work on a year-round basis, unlike many seasonal club employees.

It is axiomatic that a marina "offering only berths and moorings will fail."[22] In many marinas, however, the greatest management challenge is keeping slip occupancy levels high. Slip rentals, usually handled through a dock master's or harbor master's department, provide the greatest single source of marina revenues. A well-managed marina will not only set slip rental rates carefully, based on an analysis of comparable nearby facilities, but will also maintain clearly defined procedures for filling slip vacancies. These procedures may include waiting lists, slip "inheritance" rules that apply when a boat is sold, or other measures.

If a marina owner is not lucky enough to be facing unlimited demand for slips—as will often be the case in a new facility—slip management can also serve an important marketing role. Transient slips can be valuable ways to introduce newcomers to a marina, for example. An added benefit for marinas with lodging, restaurants, fuel docks, or other amenities is that visitors tend to spend more money than full-time slip occupants; transient slips can thus provide significant revenue for other marina operations.

Customer satisfaction and profitability will depend largely on the quality of marina maintenance. Adequate levels of property and equipment maintenance are essential to smooth operations. Marina structures and equipment, because of their location, use, and materials, can deteriorate at a rate that accelerates with time.[23] And the consequences of key equipment failure can be severe. Even relatively minor maintenance items, if deferred, can make a marina unpleasant or dangerous.

For these reasons, even the most modest marina should implement a formal maintenance program that, based on regular inspections, identifies and ensures completion of regular maintenance items, repairs, and overhauls. Chamberlain suggests that such a program might consist of regular inspection and maintenance items for each component (decking, piers, piles, bulkheads, and so on) broken down by frequency (daily, monthly, annually). Each inspection report would then be tied to a work order and performance record. Ultimately, each operation would be costed and charged to the appropriate expense account. In some areas, nonroutine maintenance may be highly seasonal, with slack periods in the off-season providing the best opportunities to perform major maintenance.

Because they are located in the water, piers and piles will demand the greatest attention. Marina personnel should perform a routine inspection at least weekly and a thorough, below-deck inspection once or twice a year. Generally, floating piers are difficult to inspect thoroughly without taking them out of the water or removing the decking.

Marina services can be highly profitable, but require specialized expertise and close management.

Wooden structures, especially if untreated, can be plagued by a number of culprits, including fungal rot, insects and mollusks, and ice. Inspections should pay particular attention to the tops of wooden piles (if uncapped) and to the intertidal zone, which is subject to alternate wetting and drying. Steel structures, if submerged, remain relatively corrosion-resistant. Corrosion can be severe in areas that are alternately wet and dry. The most common damage to concrete is corrosion of the reinforcing steel, causing spalling and cracking.

Bulkheads should be inspected for signs of tilting, changes in linear alignment, or sinking areas behind the bulkhead line. Bulkhead failures can be extremely costly, and can only be ultimately repaired by building a new structure outboard of the old one, a measure that, if it involves fill, may require a new permit.

Along with the maintenance of a marina's physical plant, the marina operator must also monitor the quality of the marina environment. This necessity includes such mundane elements as trash collection and disposal, as well as more complex issues of water pollution control and impact of operations on plants and wildlife.

Sedimentation and erosion patterns should be carefully monitored. If left unattended, excessive sedimentation can interfere with boat traffic, clog entrances, and require expensive corrective dredging. Erosion can help unseat piles or cause structural failures of bulkheads. Bottom conditions should be checked closely after major storms or spring floods.

The quality of stormwater draining into a marina basin can also have severe impacts on operations. Oil and gas from parking lots or roads, for example, can foul boats at the waterline. Runoff high in nutrient levels from fertilizers or organic materials can cause algae blooms and promote weed growth. Marinas, especially if poorly planned or inadequately operated, can clearly affect levels of environmental pollution. A corollary, of course, is that levels of pollution clearly affect marinas. Patrons who are there to escape pollution can end up causing it. Many potential environmental problems, however, can be avoided by careful design and planning and by conscientious management.

Administrative Management

Developers have traditionally used waterfront amenities to enhance land values and add marketing appeal to their projects. Yet, according to Bruce Blomgren of the Brandy Group, a leading marina management firm, "the profit potential in waterfront property has been viewed only in light of the value given to the land by the presence of water. Few developers pursue the profitability inherent in the usage of the water amenity itself."[24] Many marinas, in other words, are not designed, built, or operated to produce profit. Blomgren, however, represents one of the forces—the rise of specialized, professional amenity management firms—that are influencing developers to reconsider the traditional relationship between marinas and real estate. A profitable marina, like any business, is based upon clear articulation of goals and objectives, along with the systems and tools to measure performance.

Budgets. One of the most important management tools is the marina budget—or budgets, since systems for cash flow, capital outlays, and debt may be organized separately. Budgets serve as benchmarks for evaluating an operation's expected versus actual performance. They enable managers to make adjustments as necessary to narrow any gaps between objectives and actual performance. In real estate projects, a marina budget will usually be subordinate to the overall project budget, phasing, and capital investment plans.

Budgets are based on historical data on the various expected costs and revenues associated with operating a marina. New operations generally use data from comparable operations to generate budgets. An integrated marina budget should be organized on a monthly basis to respond to seasonal fluctuations in revenues and expenses, staffing levels, and inventory. The key products of the budgeting process include projections of monthly cash flow, a comprehensive array of all revenue and cost categories, and income and expense reports.

To both develop and implement a budget requires a well-developed system of tracking the sources and flows of costs and revenues. Because of the wide range of potential costs in marina operations, it is essential that they be matched as closely as possible to corresponding revenues. The way in which these elements flow directly should reflect the marina's organization.

Organization. A marina that offers a full range of services will generally be organized around portions of the operation that generate an identifiable category of revenues and that can be specifically assigned corresponding costs. These "profit centers" are typically isolated by function: marina management, dock master or harbor master, service, boat sales, retail sales, and food and beverage.

The dock master department is generally responsible for all day-to-day activities related to boat storage, including slip rental operations and, if offered, such services as boat rentals, chartering, and fuel sales. In addition, this department will usually be responsible for marina maintenance. The service department can be highly profitable, with a reasonable net profit on sales of about 12 to 16 percent.[25] It will

Yacht club member programs can greatly enhance a marina. Shown here, the training fleet at Chandlers Landing Yacht Club.

often depend on the retail sales operation for parts, rather than maintaining its own extensive inventory. Such an arrangement highlights the need for procedures to accurately charge costs to the responsible department. In this instance, one potential solution is to sell parts and supplies from the retail sales department to the service department at wholesale cost. Boat and engine sales are often distinct from retail sales because of the large but infrequent cash flows and the high sales costs.

Marina management is the department responsible for such indirect overhead costs as insurance, accounting, and administration. Insurance is usually the single largest overhead expense, with workmen's compensation and liability insurance premiums running approximately 5 percent of gross revenues.

FINANCIAL CASE STUDY: WALDEN MARINA

Walden Marina is located on a 1,200-acre Texas peninsula that extends from the western shore of Lake Conroe, 56 miles north of Houston. A full-service resort with condominiums for sale and rent, Walden offers tennis, golf, and other amenities to complement the marina. Conroe, with a full range of shopping and medical facilities, lies 18 miles away, and Montgomery, a rural community with municipal services and schools, is just five miles away. Growth in the immediate area is still being fueled by lakeshore development.

Lake Conroe is a 22,000-acre impoundment with 8½ miles of shoreline. Formed by a dam that was closed in 1973, the lake features a wooded shoreline and a gently sloping bottom. Boating is a year-round sport, although participation falls off sharply between late October and March when the water temperature is too low to permit comfortable swimming and waterskiing.

THE MARINA

Walden Marina was constructed and maintained in keeping with the quality image of a resort complex. Its piers float on styrofoam blocks with enclosed frames of galvanized steel. The dock surfaces are concrete and polyurethane, specially treated to resist the effects of sunlight. Currently, there are 520 slips, of which 388 are covered and 142 are open.

Walden Marina serves a private clientele from the resort and is not open to the public. About one-half the boats are power, generally in the 20-foot range, while the others are sailboats of similar size. To cater to guests who do not own their own boats, the marina rents fishing boats, sailboats, and ski and pontoon boats (with a driver) and owns a 55-foot party cruiser named Reflections II. The rates for these services are outlined in Figure 1.

SERVICES

Walden Marina maintains a service facility for the repair and maintenance needs of its customers. It is an authorized dealer for Mercury, Outboard Marina Corporation, and Volvo Penta. Two certified mechanics work year-round and are supported by a $50,000 parts inventory. The marina charges $32.50 per hour for all labor on boats and motors.

A well-received aspect of service at the marine has been the winter maintenance program. For a $200 fee, the marina assures that a boat will be kept in good running condition, as well as protected against freezing.

FINANCIAL PERFORMANCE

As shown in Figure 2, the financial performance of Walden Marina has improved steadily through the years. In its latest documented year, 1981, it produced a healthy return on assets of 20 percent and a remarkable net profit as a percentage of sales of 25 percent.

In the early stages of Walden's development, the marina served as an integral part of the marketing package offered by the resort. As such, it was not expected to show a profit per se. Some of the financial history in the formative years is also distorted due to learning experiences. For example, boat sales were discontinued in 1977 after they proved infeasible. Similarly, salary expenses have fluctuated through the years as management improved the fit between personnel and positions. In evaluating the financial data, one must keep in mind that profits generated by the marina do not necessarily show up in the marina's financial statement, but may accrue to other parts of the organization. For example, if visitors from another resort came over to join a Walden resident for a day's visit, left their boat at the marina, and spent $100 in the bar and restaurant, the marina would show no increase in sales, but the bar and restaurant would show $100 more in

Figure 1
WALDEN MARINA, PRICES CHARGED FOR SLIPS

Covered slips	
10 × 10	$ 75.00/month
12 × 24	85.00/month
Open slips	
10 × 10	60.00/month
16 × 40 (Houseboat)	100.00/month
Board boat lockers	22.50/month

Figure 2
FINANCIAL PERFORMANCE OF WALDEN MARINA

Year	Gross Sales	Cost of Sales	Gross Profit	Indirect Costs[1]	Net Profit	Gross Profit/Sales	Net Profit/Sales	Return on Assets[2]
1976	$394,273	$377,106	$ 17,167	—	—	.04	—	—
1977	476,799	440,685	36,114	—	—	.08	—	—
1978	556,568	441,639	114,929	60,476	54,453	.21	.10	.07
1979	711,864	590,447	121,417	58,356	63,061	.17	.09	.05
1980	825,816	606,711	219,105	72,008	147,097	.27	.18	.12
1981	962,449	627,028	335,826	85,826	249,595	.35	.26	.20

[1]Does not include depreciation or land costs.
[2]Total assets were as follows:
    1976—$595,192
    1977—$716,158
    1978—$765,658
    1979—$1,235,658

revenues for that day. Hence, the revenues generated by the marina tend to be understated.

On the other hand, the revenues shown in the financial statements have elements that tend to overstate the profits. Walden's financial management system is largely based on cash flow in the current year of operation. For example, the financial statement includes no allowances for land costs, nor for depreciation of plant and equipment. Hence, the profits are overstated. However, all in all, the Walden Marina must be considered an extremely successful project.

This case study is adapted from the 1984 National Marine Manufacturer's Association publication, Financial Profiles of Five Marinas, *by Douglass G. Norvell, Don Rickwalt, James R. Hall, and Thomas Beckering. Reprinted with permission.*

Figure 3

WALDEN MARINA INCOME STATEMENT—1981

Item	Amount		Item	Amount
I. Sales			**V. Other Expenses**	
1. Food	$ 30,246		1. Auto & Travel	$ 3,873
2. Beer	4,843		2. Cash Short & Over	842
3. Accessories	68,841		3. Contract Labor	25,336
4. Hydro-Hoists	40,121		4. Credit Card Discounts	507
5. Gas	216,155		5. Dues & Subscriptions	382
6. Oil	8,078		6. Employee Benefits	1,652
7. Vending	10,078		7. Insurance—General	2,416
8. Parts	53,447		8. Insurance—Group	43,653
Total Sales	431,809		9. Insurance—W/C	1,973
			10. Interest Expense	828
II. Cost of Sales			11. Linen & Laundry	477
1. Cost of Sales—Food	$ 22,036		12. Licenses, Fees, & Permits	1,220
2. Cost of Sales—Beer	1,428		13. Maintenance & Repair—Building	23,850
3. Cost of Sales—Accessories	45,748		14. Maintenance & Repair—Equipment	3,163
4. Cost of Sales—Hydro-Hoists	31,226		15. Maintenance & Repair—Docks	8,792
5. Cost of Sales—Gas	186,009		16. Maintenance & Repairs—Boats & Motors	8,791
6. Cost of Sales—Oil	4,046		17. Maintenance & Repairs—Reflections II	3,641
7. Cost of Sales—Vending	5,472		18. Miscellaneous Service Charges	1,139
8. Cost of Sales—Parts	34,266		19. Supplies—Office	1,931
Total Cost of Sales	330,249		20. Postage & Freight	3,956
GROSS PROFIT—SALES	101,560		21. Promotions	1,510
			22. Remodel—Ships Store	2,162
III. Other Income			23. Tools	793
1. Electrical Income	$ 1,326		24. Supplies—General	3,113
2. Dock Rental	383,896		25. Taxes—Payroll	8,846
3. Reflections	19,270		26. Taxes—Property	4,080
4. Boat Rentals	33,425		27. Taxes—Liquor	483
5. Ancillary Labor	5,628		28. Telephone	6,325
6. Shop Labor	62,793		29. Training & Seminars	147
7. Other Sales	24,296		30. Utilities—Electrical	9,325
Total Other Income	530,637		31. Utilities—Water	1,708
OVERALL GROSS PROFIT	$632,195		32. Utilities—Waste Removal	1,070
			Total Other Expenses	177,994
			Total Expenses	296,765
IV. Salaries			NET INCOME BEFORE ALLOCATION	335,930
1. General & Administrative	$ 47,862			
2. Shop	42,993		**VI. Intercompany Allocations**	
3. Store	7,025		1. Accounting Service	$ 33,600
4. Other	20,890		2. Administrative Service	28,800
Total Salaries	118,771		3. Facility & Grounds Maintenance	21,402
			4. Depreciation	2,023
			Total Intercompany Allocations	85,826
			NET INCOME	$250,104

CHAPTER SEVEN
CASE STUDIES

The case studies that follow illustrate how the general principles discussed in previous chapters are actually put into practice on real sites, with real markets, under differing economic circumstances, and with widely varying overall strategies. Each example presents an overview of the project as it exists, summarizes the development strategy, and discusses specific issues related to project design and planning, the role of amenities, and operations and management.

With the guidance of the Executive Group of ULI's Recreational Development Council, case studies were selected to represent as wide as possible an array of geographic locations, site characteristics, project sizes and types, intended markets, and amenity combinations. Ultimately, the location of the case study projects depended largely on where the bulk of recreational development had taken place over the last decade. Because of this, southern climates tend to be represented more heavily.

Most of the projects highlighted include many different recreational facilities. In most instances, the case study focuses on the dominant facility, with a brief summary of other amenities. Several case studies, considered prototypical of most recreation-oriented development, contain more comprehensive descriptions of these facilities.

Equally as important as these criteria in selecting projects was a willingness on the part of the developers and their consultants to share with readers a variety of data, including basic economic information. Wherever possible, these data support the discussion in the text. Because of widely varying accounting methods, regional costs, site conditions, and other factors, readers should use caution when interpreting and using these cost data outside the context of the specific project.

For each project, a questionnaire was sent to the developers and, in some cases, their consultants. After basic descriptive information on the project and its recreational facilities was documented, visits were made to each site, where those responsible for the project's development, planning, and management were interviewed. Most site visits were made in 1985, with follow-up interviews in mid-1986 on those projects still under development. Sources for data, except where noted, were the developers themselves. In each case, the developer had the opportunity to review the case study before publication.

LONGBOAT KEY CLUB
Sarasota, Florida

From its initial conception by Charles Fraser in 1957 through its development in the 1960s and 1970s, Sea Pines Plantation on Hilton Head Island, South Carolina, set a new standard for coastal resort development. Sea Pines demonstrated the value of combining a destination resort with a mixed-density recreational community, and established new design and planning principles for relating amenities and housing units to a sensitive environment. These lessons have since been replicated at projects throughout the nation.

This "second generation" of recreation development responded to changing real estate economics and market characteristics by including more uses at a wider range of densities—from single-family detached to high-rise condominium—and a spectrum of recreational amenities, usually coupling a major natural attraction, such as a beach, with a golf course, a tennis club, or a marina. These projects usually offered a host of sophisticated services and programs to resort guests and club members, and often used sophisticated marketing and promotional techniques to help create a memorable public image.

Since the mid-1970s, the difficulty and expense of assembling large coastal sites and the severe regulatory constraints on most coastal development have made such projects even more time-consuming and costly. The experience at Longboat Key Club, a 1,100-acre resort and recreational community on a barrier island just off Sarasota, Florida, illustrates both the earlier transition in coastal development and, as it approaches its projected buildout in 1995, today's challenging development climate.

Arvida Corporation solved the site acquisition problem through the forward-thinking purchase in 1959 of 2,000 acres of 10-mile-long Longboat Key by the company's founder, Arthur Vining Davis. In 1968, Arvida began building relatively small beachfront condominium projects, each with a separate identity. The company also added the first of two golf courses on the key, just upland of the beachfront projects.

After about 10 years of planning, Arvida secured planned unit development (PUD) approvals for the two distinct neighborhoods that together comprise Longboat Key Club. The earlier beachfront condominiums have since been incorporated into the overall project as part of the 380-acre Islandside PUD, located at the key's southern tip on the Gulf of Mexico. Islandside currently contains 1,141 dwelling units in five mid- to high-rise condominium villages, one of which includes Longboat Key Club's resort accommodations, the 221-unit Inn on the Beach. Islandside also offers 18 holes of golf, a 14-court tennis center, and a clubhouse.

Harbourside, the more recent and lower-density PUD, borders Sarasota Bay and currently contains 503 dwelling units on 732 acres. Harbourside includes Town Plaza, the town center for Longboat Key. Master-planned by Arvida, it contains the town hall, a post office, banks, a library, and a shopping

Mid-rise development at Harbourside, showing perimeter channel and mangrove swamps.

Arvida Corporation

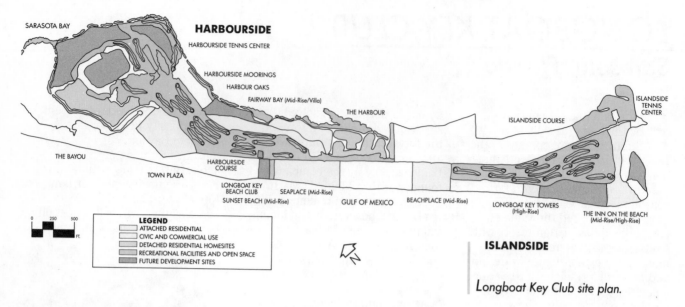

SARASOTA BAY

HARBOURSIDE TENNIS CENTER

HARBOURSIDE MOORINGS

HARBOUR OAKS

FAIRWAY BAY (Mid-Rise/Villa)

THE HARBOUR

ISLANDSIDE COURSE

ISLANDSIDE TENNIS CENTER

THE BAYOU

HARBOURSIDE COURSE

TOWN PLAZA

LONGBOAT KEY BEACH CLUB

SEAPLACE (Mid-Rise)

SUNSET BEACH (Mid-Rise)

GULF OF MEXICO

BEACHPLACE (Mid-Rise)

LONGBOAT KEY TOWERS (High-Rise)

THE INN ON THE BEACH (Mid-Rise/High-Rise)

LEGEND
ATTACHED RESIDENTIAL
CIVIC AND COMMERCIAL USE
DETACHED RESIDENTIAL HOMESITES
RECREATIONAL FACILITIES AND OPEN SPACE
FUTURE DEVELOPMENT SITES

0 250 500 FT.

ISLANDSIDE

Longboat Key Club site plan.

plaza. Major amenities include a 277-slip marina, a second 18-hole golf course, 10 tennis courts, and a clubhouse. Harbourside residential units include 189 single-family detached homesites in two neighborhoods. Other projects contain a mix of townhouses and mid-rise condominiums. Many of the privately owned units in both PUDs are also available for monthly and seasonal rentals.

Arvida's work on Longboat Key is about 50 percent complete. Major planned additions include 650 gulf-front mid-rise and high-rise units in Islandside and another 1,200 villas, townhouses, and mid-rise and high-rise units in Harbourside. At expected buildout in 1995, Longboat Key Club will contain 3,494 dwelling units.

DEVELOPMENT STRATEGY

The history of Arvida's involvement on Longboat Key shows a resilient corporation willing to make tactical adjustments in response to shifting economic, marketing, and regulatory factors. The project's present form stems largely from the company's initial strategic decision to build a first-class resort hotel on a portion of the gulf-front property. This hotel, along with the existing condominium projects and the attendant recreational amenities at Islandside, would in turn support the long-term community development at Harbourside, the larger PUD on the bay.

This combination of resort and residential development was intended to encourage resort guests to eventually purchase real estate. The two uses would therefore need to coexist, but each would serve slightly different groups: the short-term resort guest and the seasonal or year-round resident. The strategy was to orient each PUD to a respective group.

At Islandside, the higher-density condominium projects are available for monthly and seasonal rentals. The hotel, the Inn on the Beach, offers nightly accommodations, a full resort package including two restaurants, and the principal access to the beach. Harbourside supports these resort guests as well, but it also geared toward the more community-minded resident—hence the inclusion of the Town Plaza, churches, and other community facilities. Harbourside also offers products in a wider price range and a more diverse amenity package.

This relationship is also illustrated by the Harbourside location of the single-family homesites. These selected land sales projects were intended to set an appropriately high standard of quality early in the project's overall development. Arvida set density standards and retained strict architectural review over construction on these sites.

THE ROLE OF AMENITIES

The various recreational amenities at Longboat Key Club play an integral part in the overall plan. The plan's fundamental objective, according to Arvida, has been to enhance land values by emphasizing the physical relationships between the various residential projects and the site's natural and created amenities. Thus, high-density residential clusters focus on the golf courses, beaches, and waterfronts. By far the most popular amenity at the project is the beach, with golf a distant second. Still, in 1984, some 122,000 rounds of golf were played on Longboat Key Club's two courses.

The project's recreational facilities are structured as membership clubs, owned and operated by Arvida, except for the Harbourside Landings marina, which is managed by The Brandy Group, a Florida-based marina services company. The resort hotel also remains under Arvida's control. In the view of the company, their strong resort and club management experience—Arvida developed and operates several other major planned recreational and resort communities—is essential to operating the amenities at the high standard necessary to maintain the project's overall image and credibility. Golf club memberships are restricted to owners of Arvida products and resort guests. A small proportion of social and tennis memberships are held by non-residents, as are marina slip leases.

The central amenity strategy has been to build enough amenities to convince the market of Arvida's commitment to the project, to protect the residents' and future owners' use rights, and to expand the facilities as neighborhoods within the PUDs are completed.

Ultimately, the Harbourside facilities will likely be sold to the members through a phased-in equity program, according to Arvida officials. The planned offering will likely encompass a four- to five-year sellout period, with early buyers receiving reduced prices. Arvida intends to continue managing the facilities after the transfer. As the project nears buildout, the Islandside hotel and club will be sold to a resort operator, according to current plans.

THE SITE

When Arvida acquired the Longboat Key Club site in 1959, the island had been only partly cleared and was laced with mosquito control ditches dug by the county. Mangrove swamps ringed the perimeter of what became the Harbourside community. The ruins of circus impresario John Ringling's unfinished resort hotel stood on the site of what is now the Inn on the Beach.

Major dredge and fill operations began in 1973, creating buildable land on the island's bay side. Arvida dug a perimeter channel around Harbourside; the submerged land and mangrove swamps were deeded to the state in return for permission to dredge and fill.

North of the Town Plaza the island features a mixture of hotel and resort projects, small multifamily and detached residences, and scattered commercial properties. The islands south of Longboat Key (Lido Key, Bird Key, and St. Armands Key) include resort developments and an extremely exclusive shopping area at St. Armands Circle. All the keys are connected to the mainland by a causeway.

The view to the north from the Inn on the Beach.

HARBOURSIDE MOORINGS

Longboat Key Club's 277-slip marina, Harbourside Moorings, ranks as one of the largest private marinas on Florida's Gulf Coast. According to its principal engineer, William Bishop, it will probably not be matched in the foreseeable future, at least in Florida. Because much of the Harbourside PUD required dredging, plans for the marina were greatly advanced by Arvida's acquisition of the necessary dredge and fill permits early in the project's life, when the approval process was much easier. The early dredging of the boat basin, plus some fortuitous decisions by state agencies, enabled Arvida to open this major facility in 1983, at a cost of about $4.7 million.

The marina occupies a 37-acre rectangular site in the Harbourside PUD on Sarasota Bay. Its 18 fixed piers can accommodate up to 277 boats in slips from 28 feet to 60 feet long. Craft enter from the bay though a short dredged channel, passing the state-owned mangrove swamps and Harbourside's perimeter channel. The basin itself is buffered from the bay by a 50-foot-wide breakwater peninsula along its eastern edge. Because the developers needed fill for Harbourside's building sites, the basin depth averages a remarkable 18 feet. The basin's inside edge is lined with concrete seawall on three sides. The fourth side, which will form the edge of a future hole of the Harbourside golf course's third nine, is stabilized with riprap. Both support piles, which measure up to 40 feet long because of the deep basin, and pier structures are made of concrete

with wood decking; mooring piles are of treated timber. To mitigate against low dissolved oxygen levels in the deep water, Arvida installed a bubble-type aeration system at the basin's mouth. Nearby sits the fuel pier and, on shore, the 1,500-square-foot harbor master's building. Besides the harbor master's office and control desk, the structure contains a chandlery, restrooms and showers, laundry facilities, and vending and ice machines. Dockside services include water, electricity, telephone, and cable television.

Distributed along the basin's perimeter are 105 parking spaces, for a low parking ratio of about .38 spaces per boat. To a great extent, this low density reflects the marina's role as part of a destination resort and a recreational community. A freestanding commercial marina in a moderately remote location might require up to two spaces per boat.

The marina operates on a slip lease basis and in some ways is intended to support Arvida's real estate activities in the same manner as the Inn on the Beach: by providing short-term accommodations to well-heeled sales prospects. The marina offers nightly, 30-day, and annual leases to both project residents and nonresidents.

Although no live-aboards are permitted under the terms of an agreement with the town of Longboat Key, visitors can stay up to two weeks on their boats. Short-term visitors have access to the social, golf, and tennis facilities at the Harbourside club and, of course, to nightly or monthly accommodations at the Inn on the Beach or any of the rental projects.

MARINA PERMITTING

In 1968, as Arvida was opening its beachfront condominium tower and golf club at what would later become the Islandside PUD, the firm was already in the earliest planning stages for the larger bayside community, including the marina. Its first application for dredge and fill permits was filed with the U.S. Army Corps of Engineers in July of that year. After 61 months of negotiations with state and federal agencies, the Corps issued the critical permit. Significantly, Arvida's application preceded the state's rigorous Development of Regional Impact review process. For the marina development, the key bargain struck in the negotiations between Arvida and the state was that in exchange for permission to dredge the boat basin, the developers

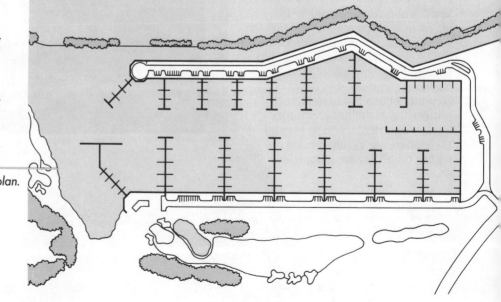

Harbourside Moorings site plan.

ceded to the public the submerged lands and mangrove swamps at the island's edge.

Arvida took three years to complete the dredging for Harbourside, and in 1976 it installed the aeration equipment in the boat basin as a condition imposed by the state for extending the permits. Three years later, the developers received the critical state approvals from the Departments of Natural Resources and Environmental Regulation to proceed with marina construction. One major factor in the state's decision was that, in the DER's judgment, because the basin lay inside the breakwater line as established by the earlier dredging, its land was outside the public's jurisdiction. Arvida's decision back in 1973 to dig the hole for the marina thus proved essential to the 1979 approval.

Even with the permits finally in hand, however, all was not smooth sailing. The problem was that a facility this size would drastically increase the supply of leasable slips in a market absorbing less than 50 slips per year. Certainly, the presence of the marina itself would boost the image of Harbourside and Longboat Key Club, but the impact would be even stronger if it could be filled with boats and surrounded by activity. But from 1979 to 1982, the marina market remained too soft to proceed with construction.

Arvida was able to negotiate several extensions of its permits. In 1982, however, with demand for slips still only moderate but with the other Harbourside neighborhoods and amenities taking shape, the state refused to again extend the permits. Arvida had little choice but to swallow hard and proceed. It dredged the entrance channel in August 1982 and completed the over-water construction in May 1983. By summer 1985, although in full operation, the marina was only about 50 percent leased. Absorption remains steady, however, and Arvida vice president Thomas Hale expects little difficulty leasing up by the 1987 winter season. The slow demand for slips, he suggests, was exacerbated at Longboat Key

The marina represents an important element in the overall project's marketing plan.

Club by a lack of dining facilities (which will be remedied by the 1987 opening of the new Harbourside clubhouse), inadequate ground transportation to other parts of the resort, and, in the early months, by a lack of a good chandlery.

Arvida now plans to construct an 80-slip facility at Islandside, adjacent to the Inn on the Beach. Although the site is already dredged, the submerged land is owned by the state. The new facility would be ideally situated, close to the resort, but the permitting process may require the developer to make substantial concessions in size or to provide additional impact mitigation measures.

Although it is highly experienced in golf and tennis club operations and management, Arvida admits that the specialized nature of marinas led it to contract with a separate firm to manage Harbourside Landings. Since the relationship was agreed to a year prior to construction, the operators were involved early in the marina's planning and design. According to Arvida, they made several important recommendations regarding the harbor master's building design, dockside service requirements, and the marinawide communication system. The developers also report that they are pleased with the marina's operating performance over the past two years.

EVALUATING THE EXPERIENCE

Undoubtedly, Longboat Key Club would be a difficult project to replicate given today's regulatory, political, and economic attitudes toward barrier island development. There are, however, valuable lessons to be learned from Arvida's experience on the key.

One of the most problematic tasks in large-scale recreational development is combining a destination resort, residential communities, and an amenity package shared between the two groups. At Longboat Key Club, Arvida has employed two basic strategies for dealing with this delicate relationship.

The first strategy is reflected in the master plan, with its two PUDs, one on the beach and one on the bay, each oriented principally to one of the two groups. The specific recreational amenities, access to commercial areas, and other more detailed elements of the neighborhood site plans also support this dichotomy. The support relationship is perhaps weakest between the marina and the Inn on the Beach, which are located at opposite ends of the project. Individually, however, the marina and the hotel each enjoy outstanding locations. Although resort guests and residents are by no means restricted in moving about the project, there is nonetheless a degree of physical separation intended in the project's design, simply because of the differing needs of the two groups.

The second strategy is operational and programmatic. Arvida has retained strong control over the resort operations, including the hotel, all the amenities, and the rental program. The 30-day minimum stay required in the rental units (other than at the Inn on the Beach) is one way the company has tried to reduce the impact of resort guests on residents. Developer-owned membership clubs rather than member-owned facilities also fit the scheme. For a large developer, who does not require the cash flow advantages of an equity club and who is facing a long period to buildout, membership clubs permit maximum control over club management and operations. For the more specialized marina operations, however, Arvida recognized the necessity to trade off a modest amount of control for the advantages of experienced management.

Approvals obtained early in the project's life from the State Departments of Environmental Regulation and Natural Resources, and from the U.S. Army Corps of Engineers (which dealt with the marina and the surface water management system) were extremely important assurances for Arvida. These general approvals allowed development to proceed in an orderly fashion and gave the company the confidence to make major commitments to infrastructure on a barrier island, where environmental issues are extremely sensitive.

Based on its experience at Longboat Key, Arvida believes it is extremely important for a developer to maintain a high level of community relations, as well as buyer confidence and a commitment to quality. For some time, Arvida has been the principal developer on Longboat Key, having built 80 to 90 percent of the units from 1975 on. The company has aimed to be a responsible corporate citizen by participating in community activities such as the Chamber of Commerce and Beach Preservation Association. Arvida has demonstrated that it is committed not only to its specific project, but to the Sarasota community in general. Such responsiveness is particularly important when dealing with local regulatory bodies over a 10- to 20-year period to buildout.

PROJECT DATA:
LONGBOAT KEY CLUB

MEMBERSHIP INFORMATION[1]

Membership Category	Number of Members	Initiation Fee/Dues
Annual family golf	405	$2,500/2,000
Annual single golf	386	$1,500/1,500
8-month family golf	97	$ 900/1,200
8-month single golf	111	$ 700/900
Total golf members	999	
Annual family tennis	280	$1,500/1,000
Annual single tennis	183	$1,250/750
Total tennis members	463	
Social members	555	$ 500 (dues)
Beach club members	179	$ 180 ($125 for members in other categories)
Total members	2,196	

User Fees
Golf[2]: $20–30 (winter) $15 summer
    (cart fee $17 for 18 holes and $12 for 9 holes)
Tennis: $8–12

GOLF COURSE INFORMATION

Islandside Course
Length: 6,158 yards (middle tees)
Acres: 136
Annual rounds (1985): 63,800
Daily average: 175
Development and construction costs (1960): $1,435,000
1986 operating/maintenance costs total budget: $445,000
    Per hole budget: $24,700
Pro shop size: 1,444 square feet

Harbourside Course
Length: 6,223 yards (middle tees)
Acreage: 140
Annual rounds: 58,400
Daily average: 160
Development and construction cost (1982): $2,500,000
1986 operating/maintenance costs total budget: $452,000
    Per hole budget: $25,100
Pro shop size: 1,536 square feet

TENNIS FACILITY INFORMATION

	Harbourside	*Islandside*
Number of courts	10	14
Lighted courts	6	none
Surface	all courts Har-Tru (synthetic clay)	
Court hours used annually (1985)	4,110	11,480
Annual usage per court	411 hours	820 hours
Development and construction cost	$169,000 (1984)	$228,000 (1975–80)
Per court cost	$ 16,900	$ 16,300
1986 operating/maintenance costs		
total budget (24 courts)	$110,000	
Per court cost	$ 4,600	

[1] As of September 1985.
[2] Green fees required December 15 through April 15.
Source: Arvida Corporation.

PROJECT CREDITS

Developer:
Arvida Corporation
Sarasota Division
Longboat Key, Florida

Architects:
Edward J. Siebert, AIA
Sarasota, Florida

Fisher-Friedman Associates
San Francisco, California

Planners:
SWA Group
Sausalito, California

Willard Byrd
Atlanta, Georgia

Engineers:
Bennett and Bishop, Inc.
Sarasota, Florida

Landscape Architect:
David Johnston Associates
Sarasota, Florida

Marina Management:
Brandy Marine of Sarasota, Inc.
Longboat Key, Florida

BEAVER CREEK
Avon, Colorado

In 1980, when Vail Associates unveiled Beaver Creek, its second major resort project in the Colorado Rockies, many heralded the venture as "the last resort." Observers felt that the project's scale and complexity would be difficult to replicate.

Indeed, Beaver Creek's development has proved a tremendously complicated process, involving myriad consultants, government agencies, codevelopers, and investors. Not only have the developers had to oversee the operations of numerous private business aspects, they have also had to form and direct a group of organizations to provide municipal services and facilities, from transportation to public safety. The time frame is similarly daunting. Vail Associates began planning

Beaver Creek in 1971; by 1985, the project was only about 20 percent complete. By the time Beaver Creek is fully built out—around the turn of the century—it should, like its neighbor Vail, function as a year-round resort community, with a full range of real estate products, a diverse social structure, and a mature economy.

Beaver Creek is located 110 miles west of Denver, just south of the town of Avon. Vail lies 10 miles away via Interstate 70. Vail Associates owns about 2,200 acres of the valley, which runs north and south. At the southern end, the mountain rises to an elevation of 11,500 feet. Ski facilities are operated primarily on 2,775 acres of public land under U.S. Forest Service permits. Under the terms of a county-approved

planned unit development resolution, the project will ultimately contain 3,223 dwelling units at gross densities ranging from one to 26 dwelling units per acre. Only about 275 single-family homesites are planned. Beaver Creek will also offer 380,000 square feet of commercial space, of which all but 50,000 will be concentrated in a resort core at the mountain's base, which will also feature about 70 percent of the dwelling units. Of the 2,132 acres in the PUD, more than 80 percent are reserved for open space, including about one-third of the ski area and an 18-hole golf course.

DEVELOPMENT STRATEGY

With the completion of Interstate 70 through Vail Pass and beyond, and with the later opening of the Eisenhower Tunnel, greatly improving access from Denver, the Forest Service had targeted the Beaver Creek site as a potential ski area development as early as 1968. The site's advantages were clear: a nearly perfect location, size, and orientation for a first-class ski area, with broad, north-facing slopes dropping 3,350 feet to the mountain's base, then flattening into a gentle stream valley, with ridges affording spectacular views.

The Forest Service had pegged the site early on as a prime candidate for ski area development.

David Lokey

European archetypes and the local vernacular inspired Beaver Creek's architecture.

David Lokey

Vail Associates, attracted by the same qualities, purchased the site from its former owner, a sheep rancher, for $4.4 million in 1973, after starting preliminary planning two years earlier. Working closely with the Forest Service, the developers obtained their ski area permit in 1976 (the same year the site was to have been used for the Winter Olympics, before Colorado voters rejected the games). The next year, the Forest Service approved the mountain plan, and in 1978 Vail Associates started to build.

The company, by virtue of its pacesetting development at Vail, had accumulated considerable experience in large-scale resort development. Its success at Vail also provided important capital to sustain Beaver Creek during the venture's early years. The developers aimed to preserve Beaver Creek's assets—land and buildings—by relying on long-term, recurring income generated by operating revenues and lease payments.

Typically, large resorts sell land to generate funds to keep developing. A changing national outlook for resort development, along with Vail Associates' reputation, led to a boom in land values at Beaver Creek, and in the past several years the developers have turned to land sales to offset the project's early operating losses.

ORGANIZATIONAL STRUCTURE

Vail Associates and its subsidiaries own and operate all of Beaver Creek's ski-related services except ski rental. Off the ski mountain itself, individual businesses offer lodging, restaurants, and retail shops. Through various quasi-municipal organizations, however, and through the company's role in design review and other development approvals, Vail Associates exerts a strong influence on development and operations within the overall project.

Because Beaver Creek is an unincorporated community, Vail Associates essentially had to create a group of organizations to provide the required level of public services that would otherwise have been delivered by a local government. The most important of these organizations are the Beaver Creek Metropolitan District and the Beaver Creek Resort Company. The Metropolitan District, funded by a 40-mill property-tax levy plus tap and user fees as appropriate, provides roads,

domestic water, cable television, fire protection, and storm drainage. Considered a branch of state government and administered through the county, the district is also structured to provide recreational services, although it does not currently do so.

The Beaver Creek Resort Company, a private, nonprofit corporation, is composed of all property owners and commercial tenants in the resort, who pay an assessment of 20 mills on the value of their property. The company is also funded by a fee based on taxable sales, a portion of lift ticket revenues (paid by Vail Associates), a real estate transfer assessment (1 percent of the sale value, usually paid by the buyer), and fees for use of recreational facilities, including golf and tennis.

PLANNING AND DESIGN

A principal bulwark of Vail Associates' strategy at Beaver Creek is a carefully conceived overall design theme, spelled out in remarkable detail in the 75-page design regulations. The overriding design philosophy, as stated in these regulations, is to "establish a remote village with its own identity . . . complementing rather than competing with the landscape." The guidelines aim to encourage architecture and outdoor spaces that, from a distance, will appear as a unified, almost indigenous, mountain village, with simple, strong, and understated forms. The regulations present detailed prototypes and guidance on architecture, including roof forms, exterior wall materials and colors, fenestration, walls and fences, and so on. Site planning and landscape design are treated in similar detail.

Beaver Creek's spatial organization, circulation, and land use pattern help reinforce this theme. Visitors enter the project at the mouth of the valley. Day visitors park in surface lots near the entrance and are shuttled to the ski area about two miles up the valley. With the valley floor devoted to the golf course (with limited housing development along the fairways and on overlooking slopes), the high-density resort core nestles between prominent open spaces. This contrast between the village cluster and surrounding space is highlighted by the absence of large surface parking lots. Under the ski school area at the mountain's base are an 18-foot truck service corridor and a 375-space parking garage. Most buildings in the resort core are multiuse structures with ground-floor retail and accommodations above.

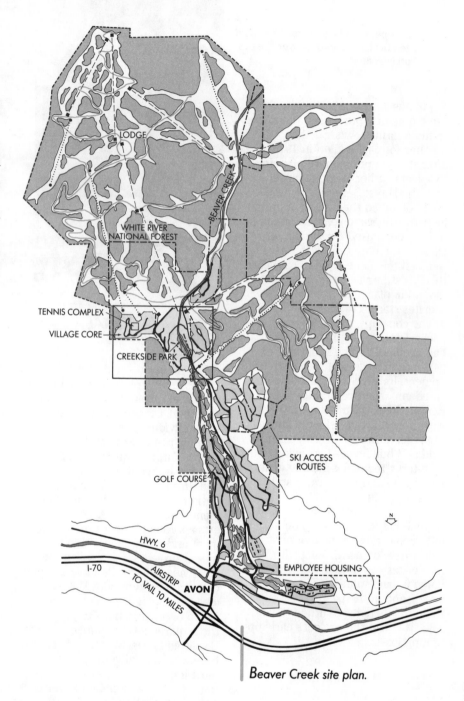

Beaver Creek site plan.

TARGETED MARKETS

Like many similar projects, Beaver Creek's markets for skiing, conferences, hotel accommodations, and real estate are expected to evolve and shift as it matures. Former Vail Associates vice president Robert Parker has noted that in virtually all cases, Colorado's large resorts have depended heavily in their early years on the regional day and weekend skiing markets. Gradually, he notes, they grow into destination resort status.

In situations where an established resort already exists close by, this process may be slowed somewhat. Such was the experience, for example, at Snowmass, because of its proximity to Aspen. With Vail nearby, Beaver Creek has had to develop a critical mass of restaurants, shops, and other off-mountain attractions to hold the attention of destination resort guests. In 1981, company officials estimated this critical mass to be 600 to 800 guest beds and 75,000 square feet of retail space. Four years later, former Vail Associates president Harry Frampton acknowledged that in its early years, the project's development had not been tightly clustered enough. He stressed the importance of adhering to the project's fundamental planning concept—emphasizing the core area of the resort village.

The developers have targeted the high-end business executive and professional markets for their real estate products. A hallmark of Beaver Creek is that each type of product, whether timeshare, fractional interest, hotel, or single-family home, is of premium quality. To date, Vail Associates and other developers at the project have sold to buyers at the highest income levels. Because of the generally soft regional market for recreational real estate in the past several years, however, the developers have broadened the range of products for the upper-middle markets, including

The golf course, hidden under a mantle of snow, runs along the valley floor.

timeshares and fractional interests. These new, relatively more affordable products are primarily oriented toward users, not investors.

Beaver Creek is marketed mainly through on-site efforts by Beaver Creek Properties, a subsidiary of Vail Associates. A targeted direct-mail effort is also used. The basic advertising strategy aims to use resort media rather than real estate media to generate traffic to both Vail and Beaver Creek. As such, Beaver Creek's public image tends to downplay the project's real estate side and to emphasize the skiing and resort experience.

BEAVER CREEK SKIING

By the end of the 1985 season, Beaver Creek's ski facilities were about 55 percent complete, with 670 acres of trails completed. Ultimately, 1,200 acres of trails will spread throughout the area's approximately 2,800 total acres, serving a daily capacity of about 9,000 skiers. Trails have been designed to serve the beginner, intermediate, and expert skier about equally in overall acreage. About 150 acres are served by a compressed-air-and-water snowmaking system.

Prime homesites hug the shoulders of the valley and face the village core below.

Eight chairlifts are currently in place, ranging from 1,200 to 6,850 linear feet. Seven more are planned. In 1986, the developers installed a high-speed, detachable-quad chairlift, replacing the former number 6 lift. The new lift, with an hourly capacity of 2,800 skiers, has cut the ride time from the village to mid-mountain by more than half. The older lift will be relocated on the mountain, opening a new zone of ski terrain in the process. In addition to the extensive ticketing, ski school, and restaurant facilities at the mountain's base, a mid-mountain lodge offers food and drink, storage lockers, a picnic area, and a ski school. Two additional mid-mountain lodges are planned. Ski patrol headquarters are at the mountain's summit, at an elevation of 11,440 feet.

In a broad valley at about 9,840 feet, Beaver Creek offers 20 kilometers of groomed cross-country ski track. Nordic skiers can get to this area, called McCoy Park, via a chairlift from the base area, where beginning cross-country instruction is offered. A track access fee of $10 allows one ride up the lift and one ride down. The trails are diverse enough to appeal to a wide range of ability levels, and because the area is located high on the mountain, advanced cross-country skiers can telemark their way down to the resort village.

GOLF AND TENNIS

To round out the recreational amenities at Beaver Creek, Vail Associates has built a regulation 18-hole golf course and a 15-court tennis complex. Designing a golf course in a narrow mountain valley posed some problems. Course architect Robert Trent Jones, Jr., opted to site the clubhouse near the resort core and to string the holes down the valley in a parallel-fairway, continuous layout. Golfers play out nine holes and back nine holes. In the process, they descend and climb about 450 vertical feet. Because this layout could have created an undesirable alley effect with housing lining the fairways, Vail Associates has limited adjacent development. On the east, a small area of large-lot, single-family homes shares the edge of the fairway with a heavily vegetated creek bed, making the houses even less visually obtrusive.

In its first year of operation, 1984, the course was open to the public. Vail Associates planned in 1985 to convert the facility to a private membership club, with use privileges for resort guests. The clubhouse, designed in a style compatible with the overall project theme, offers a complete pro shop, restaurant and bar, and locker rooms. A driving range is located above the clubhouse and a practice green lies adjacent to the first tee. Golf carts are required on the course. One unusual strategy the developers have used to help mitigate the drawbacks of the continuous layout is to offer food and beverage service on the course via beverage carts, which have proved quite popular. In the winter, golf club members have access to the Mountain Club, a log-built lodge of about 5,000 square feet located on the ski mountain.

Beaver Creek's tennis club is owned and managed by Vail Associates, which operates the facilities for access by resort guests within Beaver Creek. In 1985, four courts were complete. Eleven more are planned in a complex that steps down the sloping terrain in a series of terraces. (In the winter, these terraces can provide beginner terrain for the ski school.) The court surfaces, due to the limited season and severe conditions, are nonporous. Cool night temperatures obviate the need for lights. Clubhouse facilities are planned to grow with the overall development of adjacent real estate. They currently contain only a check-in facility with limited food, beverage, and pro shop operations. Ultimately, the developers plan an extensive sports club facility.

Additional amenities include a creekside park and an equestrian center operated by a third party. In the summer, Beaver Creek operates two chairlifts to serve the mountain restaurant and day hiking trails. Various additional activities, from Jeep tours to raft trips, are available off site.

EVALUATING THE EXPERIENCE

Undeniably, Beaver Creek exists because of its mountain. If not for Vail Associates' ability to create a world-class ski area, there would be little justification for the project. Many of the key lessons to be derived from Beaver Creek therefore focus on skiing, from obtaining permits to grooming the trails.

The Forest Service's positive relationship with Beaver Creek is evident in its recent publication on ski areas in the National Forest Landscape Management series, issued in 1984. Beaver Creek is featured throughout the document, consistently cited as a state-of-the-art development. Indeed, reports Harry Frampton, "they refer to the project as 'our resort'—meaning Vail Associates *and* the Forest Service."

Eagle County has shown a similar support for the project. In the early 1970s, it enacted a planned unit development ordinance to enable quality large-scale development. Tax-exempt industrial revenue bonds also played an important role in the project's financing. As an example of the developer's expanded social role in such a complex public/private venture, Vail Associates plans to build as many as 600 units of employee housing within the project, according to need.

Maintaining an elusive balance between controlling front-end expenditures and creating a full-service amenity package with a marketable identity is the critical issue in projects like Beaver Creek. One of Vail Associates' mistakes, Frampton says, was opening the mountain before it was sufficiently complete. Although the area constituted a serviceable facility, the mountain did not then live up to experienced skiers' expectations. This damaged Beaver Creek's reputation among good skiers—an important market—and the perception has taken some time to overcome. Similarly, the golf clubhouse opened well after the course was open for play; until then, the course was serviced from a trailer.

Frampton points to a trend in ski resort development that emphasizes consumer service and quality over physical facilities themselves. Deer Valley, Utah, perhaps best exemplifies this trend. According to Frampton, "resorts that work—that make money—downplay the importance of real estate. Instead, they focus on the service and management aspects of operating a resort." He also perceives a corollary trend: the "quality-conscious skier" who demands adequate lift capacity, well-groomed slopes, and such conveniences as mid-mountain lodges and self-service ticketing.

In its land use management and design regulations, Beaver Creek has expanded on the lessons of Sea Pines Plantation and other major destination resorts. In providing for public services and overall community management, the developers have relied mostly on their own experience at Vail. While difficult to replicate today, Beaver Creek has provided useful techniques for more recent projects, including Deer Valley, Purgatory in Colorado, and others. Notwithstanding the perceptions when it finally opened after so many years of planning, Beaver Creek is probably *not* "the last resort."

PROJECT DATA: BEAVER CREEK

LAND USE ALLOCATION

Zone	Tract	Area	Dwelling Units	Gross Density[1]	Commercial Space	Tract Name
RC/OSR	A	82.478	2,164	26.213	329,574	Village core
RHD	B	26.900	410	15.242	0	Employee housing/Tarnes
RMD	C	2.665	16	6.003	0	Lower Creek townhouses
RMD	D	9.236	86	9.311	0	Ridgepoint townhouses
RMD	E	2.553	30	11.751	0	Scott Hill townhouses
RLD	F	24.326	42	1.727	0	Elk Track
RLD	G	13.610	30	2.204	0	Scott Hill
RLD	H	77.926	132	1.694	0	Borders Place
RLD	I	48.470	130	2.682	0	South Fairway Drive/Beaver Creek Drive
RLD	J	74.953	144	1.948	0	Wayne Creek/Holden Road
RLD	K	4.010	4	1.000	0	Nottingham parcel
RLD	L	9.954	30	3.014	0	Bachelor Gulch
RS	M	6.192	1	0.161	0	Mountain service center/fire station
RS/RC	N	16.090	2	.124	10,426	Real estate sales and information/Mirabelle
RS	O	1.700	0	0	20,000	Commercial corner
RS	P	7.200	0	0	20,000	Resort service area
RS	Q	7.920	0	0	0	West parking area
RS	R	1.410	2	1.418	0	Resort service area
OSR	S	1,714.822	0	0	0	Golf course/unplatted land
TOTALS		2,132.415	3,223	1.511	380,000	

RC—Resort Commercial
RS—Resort Services
RLD—Residential Low Density
RMD—Residential Medium Density
RHD—Residential High Density
OSR—Open Space/Recreation
[1]Dwelling units per acre.
Source: *Beaver Creek Quarterly Report,* December 31, 1984, amended February 12, 1985, p. 1.

ECONOMIC INFORMATION[1]

Site Acquisition Cost	$9.1 million
Site Improvement Costs	
Water	$5.6 million
Roads/storm sewer	7.5 million
Communications	1.8 million
Fire station/equipment	.8 million
Total	$15.7 million
Construction Costs	
Incurred by Vail Associates	$67.5 million
Incurred by others (estimated)	206.0 million
Ski Area Development Costs	
Trail, lifts, snowmaking	$25 million
Lodge (for skiers only)	6 million
Total	$31 million
Ski Area Annual Operating Costs (estimated)	$10.9 million
Golf Course Development Costs	
Course construction and irrigation	$2.5 million
Clubhouse	2.3 million
Total	$4.8 million
Golf Course Annual Operating Costs	
Maintenance	$275,000
Other operating costs	177,000
Total	$452,000
Annual Maintenance Costs per Hole	$ 22,917

[1]All costs to date.
Source: Vail Associates, Inc.

PGA NATIONAL
Palm Beach Gardens, Florida

Among other attributes, southeast Florida can boast of a real estate market that includes virtually every type of recreational real estate. Almost every development archetype can be found here, from grand resort hotels to large-scale speculative subdivisions, timesharing resorts, and premier-quality planned resort/recreational communities. Many influential innovations in recreational real estate were spawned and refined in southeast Florida, a pattern that shows no signs of abating. As a result, the markets for amenity-oriented real estate in this area remain among the nation's most sophisticated and complex.

Large development projects in the region reflect this complexity, with an array of amenities, real estate products, and management strategies designed to capture what developers perceive as an increasingly segmented market. PGA National, a 2,340-acre planned resort/recreational community in Palm Beach Gardens, is a project of such magnitude. Considered broadly, the project highlights the importance of carefully considering the relationships, physical and otherwise, between various community components. Specifically, PGA National offers a textbook example of the various possible relationships between a golf course and real estate.

Located in northern Palm Beach County, one of the nation's most active golfing markets, the project contains a resort hotel and conference center and a variety of residential products: single-family detached homes, zero-lot-line and patio homes, townhouses, and midrise condominiums. PGA National is aimed at the active and semiretired upper-middle-income market. While many buyers have come from the immediate area, the project has also attracted residents from the Midwest and Northeast. About 30 percent of these buyers treat their purchase as a second home, another 60 percent as their primary residence, and 10 percent buy primarily as an investment.

In mid-1985, about 1,800 homes were completed. Some 3,200 more are planned, along with several retail, office, and light industrial projects. PGA National should be finished, according to its developers, by about 1992, when it will represent a total investment of approximately $500 million.

The principal amenities at PGA National are four golf courses, one of which was designed specifically for tournament play. In addition, the community, which serves as the headquarters for the Women's Tennis Association (WTA), offers a 19-court tennis center and a large indoor sports complex. The WTA headquarters complements the administrative headquarters of the Professional Golfers' Association of America (PGA). The PGA's presence, report the developers—PGA National Venture, Ltd., formed by the National Investment Company in partnership with Kemper Realty Corporation—constitutes a key factor in the project's overall development concept and market image.

The PGA owns 625 acres, or about a quarter of the site, and has leased all but five acres back to the developers for the construction of the four golf courses. It has built its

The Professional Golfers' Association of America is fundamental to the overall development concept.

$2.6 million, 36,000-square-foot administrative offices on the remaining five-acre site, located near the project's main entrance. The golf courses, along with the tennis complex and indoor sports center, are owned by the developers and operated as membership clubs, with use privileges by resort guests. The Sheraton Corporation operates the resort hotel.

Construction started at PGA National in February 1979. At the time, the flat, sandy site was covered with a variety of pines, cypress, willows, and marsh grasses. Low areas contained standing water for much of the year. It was an inland site in a resort region oriented toward the beach, and the developers recognized that compelling amenities would have to be created. They had on their side the site's superb access, with a location one-quarter mile west of Florida's Turnpike, within two miles of Interstate 95, and only seven miles from the Atlantic.

DEVELOPMENT STRATEGY

PGA National was conceived as a unified, planned resort community that would offer a variety of product types within a coherent overall framework. The PGA's presence, as well as the tremendous influence of the courses on the land plan, make golf the community's clear and central focus. An important aspect of the development strategy was to use golf in a variety of ways to complement each segment of the overall project. About 80 percent of the single-family lots and 60 percent of the attached units feature golf course frontage, which, combined with water views, has created additional real estate value. At the same time, the tournament-quality course with little direct frontage plays prominently in PGA National's public image. As a means of introducing the public to PGA National, the developers have created a resort core

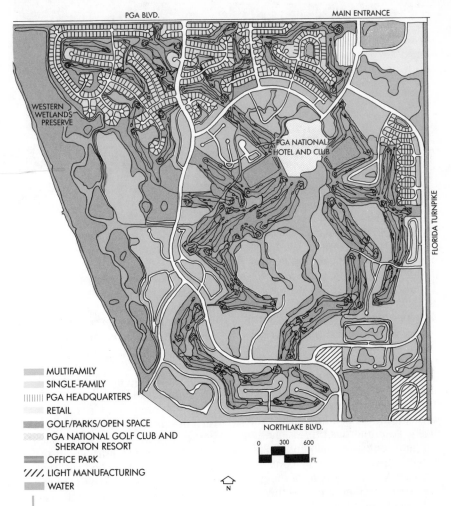

MULTIFAMILY
SINGLE-FAMILY
PGA HEADQUARTERS
RETAIL
GOLF/PARKS/OPEN SPACE
PGA NATIONAL GOLF CLUB AND SHERATON RESORT
OFFICE PARK
LIGHT MANUFACTURING
WATER

PGA National site plan.

to satisfy the need for short-term accommodations. They estimate that as many as half of all buyers have previously stayed in the resort complex.

Individual neighborhoods within PGA National are devoted to a specific housing type and architectural style. While there is diversity throughout the project, each neighborhood is distinctive and unified. Sites on the edges of the project, less suitable for residential development, are devoted to parks, open space, offices, or light industrial uses.

The mix of residential types aims to serve a variety of lifestyles. Products do not compete with each other directly, but do overlap in some of the price ranges. The developers have employed market research heavily, including surveys in target market communities, to determine the housing features and recreational amenities the market finds attractive. In most cases, the amenities were built as early as possible to, say the developers, "establish immediately visible benefits of choosing a home in PGA National."

The Sheraton resort hotel.

The project established itself from the outset as a golf community. Later, to complement the focus on golf and to appeal to a broader and younger market, the Women's Tennis Association was invited to affiliate with PGA National, and the developers added the tennis and fitness complex to the resort core.

Along with the presence of these nationally known organizations, the developers have also used professional sports events and the resulting publicity as cornerstones of their promotional efforts. The project hosts numerous professional golf and tennis tournaments that receive substantial media coverage. Another key component of the project's marketing emphasizes the PGA Sheraton resort.

PLANNING

Guiding the growth and development of a project of this scale requires careful preparation of and adherence to a master plan. In the case of PGA National, one central planning issue was how to best integrate the project's resort elements with the wide variety of residential neighborhoods. A second question was how to balance the demands of the golf courses: creating real estate values on the one hand and maintaining quality play on the other.

PGA National's master plan treats the resort complex as the community's focus, analagous to a high-intensity city core in textbook planning models. The resort, the tennis and indoor sports complex, and the golf clubhouse lie clustered in about 38 acres near the project's main entrance. This location is complemented by a circulation pattern designed so that resort guests enjoy direct access to resort facilities and need not infringe on residents' privacy. Attached residential neighborhoods are located in the site's interior, adjacent to the resort core. Lower-density detached residential homesites are grouped around the perimeter. Generally, the intensity of land use decreases as one moves outward from the resort core.

In theory, at least, residency also relates to location, in a series of roughly concentric zones. Short-term visitors are concentrated in the hotel and the attached residential projects close by. Many attached units in the middle areas will be used as second homes, and most of the highest-quality, primary-residential sites lie toward the edges.

GOLF AT PGA NATIONAL

The four golf courses at PGA National, opened over a five-year period from March 1980 to February 1985, reflect a wide variety of development criteria. Each course has been designed to help stitch the overall project together both by acting as a buffer and spatial organizer for neighborhoods and by providing fine competitive experiences for a range of ability levels.

At the heart of the project lies the Champion course, opened in January 1981, about a year before the Sheraton resort hosted its first guests and only weeks before the PGA headquarters opened. Just three months prior, the developers had opened their sales center and had announced project plans. Although the Haig course on the project's east side had opened a year earlier in February 1980, the Champion was intended to cement PGA National's golfing reputation.

The Champion course covers just over 7,000 yards and boasts 19 water hazards. It was designed by George and Tom Fazio as a true championship course, predominantly in a core configuration with returning nines. Although some development frontage on its fairways exists, the course's design was dictated by the needs of tournament golf. To this end, the course is exceptionally roomy, with special "gallery mounds" and other areas for spectator viewing and media coverage. The course has hosted, among other events, the 1982 Grand Slam of Golf, the PGA Seniors Championship, and the Ryder Cup matches. In 1987, the PGA Championship will be held there.

PGA National

The earlier course, the Haig, relates more strongly to the residential products that line its fairways and to the average golfer. This par 72 course, though long at about 6,900 yards, is the most forgiving course at the project, with generous landing areas and no cross hazards. On the front nine, the course follows mostly a single-fairway configuration, with adjacent single-family homesites averaging about 15,000 square feet. The back nine, which also starts from the clubhouse, has detached and attached housing fronting on parallel fairways.

In October 1981, only 10 months after the Champion opened for play, PGA National debuted the third course, the Squire. This continuous course of 6,550 yards winds through detached single-family neighborhoods on the project's northern portion, with a small amount of attached residential frontage. Virtually all the holes lie in a single-fairway arrangement, with only four holes parallel to another hole. The sixth hole on the Squire course serves as the backdrop for the PGA offices and the PGA Hall of Fame.

The youngest course at PGA National, the General, was designed by Arnold Palmer and opened in early 1985. Also a continuous course, this 6,900-yard layout has mostly parallel fairways lined with attached residential projects. Water comes into play on nine holes.

All four courses are supported by facilities at the Sheraton resort hotel, which contains a pro shop, a private members' lounge, and locker rooms. Practice facilities include two full-size driving ranges and a pitching and chipping area with practice bunkers and target greens, as well as three practice putting greens.

THE TENNIS AND INDOOR SPORTS COMPLEX

Rather than focus exclusively on golf, the developers of PGA National have invested a considerable amount to round out the amenity package in the resort core. This effort has resulted in the PGA National Health and Racquet Club, a 19,000-square-foot structure surrounded by 19 tennis courts. Ten courts are lighted for night play, and one court can be converted to a 4,500-seat stadium court.

The developers selected Har-Tru, a popular synthetic clay surface, based on local preferences and on the projected profile of club players. Seven hard courts are also available, sprinkled throughout the project in individual neighborhoods.

Inside, the racquet and health club contains a pro shop, a restaurant serving light meals and drinks, a Nautilus fitness room, six racquetball courts, a dance and exercise room, and locker rooms with saunas and whirlpools. Together with the WTA, PGA National sponsors youth instructional programs, leagues at all levels of play, and periodic camps and clinics. The facility is also a stop on the women's professional tennis tour.

The tennis facilities at PGA National have proven so popular that in 1985 the developers were considering adding a second tennis center. They also report that demand for night play is considerably stronger than expected. The fitness facilities, especially the Nautilus room and the aerobics classes, have also had wide appeal.

These high-profile resort amenities are complemented throughout the project by ten community pools, the seven additional tennis courts, four additional outdoor racquetball courts, a twenty-station exercise course, and a network of bicycle and jogging trails. Although not recreational amenities, the project's gatehouse and roving security patrol are also attractive to the market.

BALANCING RESORT AND RESIDENTIAL ASPECTS

In projects as large and complex as PGA National, a key challenge is managing the potential conflicts between the two principal markets: short-term resort visitors, and residents who live at the project full-time or seasonally. On the one hand, developers need guests to help market their projects. The resort facilities bring in fresh sales prospects and help to spread the word about the project. However, developers must also protect the residential areas' image and credibility. And with a long period to buildout, they must attempt to mesh these two objectives.

Part of this challenge means making sure that buyers are satisfied with their purchases and are settling into the community. At PGA National, for example, about 65 percent of the golfers from November through April are resort guests. From May through October, this percentage drops to only 20 percent. It is clearly in the developers' interest to satisfy both groups. Too often, however, a succesful resort comes at the cost of exclusivity, and an image as an exclusive private community can be a telling marketing advantage. The prospect of conflicts with short-term guests may deter some buyers.

PGA National has addressed this dilemma in various ways. One key strategy lies in the project's physical plan. The resort core is relatively self-contained, and physical conflicts—traffic, for example—are minimized by its circulation pattern. Other physical patterns, however, tend to exacerbate the potential conflict. By locating the pro shop and the golf clubhouse in the resort hotel, for example, the developers avoided unnecessary and expensive duplication of facilities, but may have overly concentrated the two user groups in one area. This risk is partly mitigated, however, by the members-only lounge and other private areas.

Other strategies focus on management techniques, rules, and regulations to minimize conflict. At PGA National, golf managers attempt to concentrate each group on certain courses. The four courses, two with returning nines, offer exceptional flexibility for the starter. In a similar vein, starting times can be allocated differently to each group. PGA National's policy is to allow members to book a slot up to four days in advance, limiting guests to one- or two-day advance notice. Resort play tends to be concentrated in the morning hours, which also allows the managers to plan for the two user groups, although they acknowledge that groups from the resort's conference center can pose scheduling problems. PGA National has also priced its memberships accordingly, based on the presence of the resort hotel. Although the club may not be as exclusive as some in the area, the lower rates and premier facilities strike many as a relative bargain.

EVALUATING THE EXPERIENCE

PGA National is clearly a product of its unusual market. Its mix of residential types, its premier amenities, its resort hotel and vacation condominiums, its promotion through major tournaments, and its affiliation with national sports organizations all point to resourceful developers operating in a sophisticated, affluent market. The project is notable not only for its prodigious scope, but also for its tightly organized plan that directly reflects the overall development concept. Each golf course, for example, relates to a slightly different set of objectives—tournament play, resort play, member play, real estate values, open-space buffers, and so on. Together, they offer the developer, the club manager, and the member remarkable flexibility.

In its first several years, the developers of PGA National recognized that, even, in the strong Palm Beach market, they could not rely exclusively on golf. Because of their successful arrangement with the PGA, it made sense to take a similar approach to tennis with the WTA. The resulting tennis center was also well timed to take advantage of growing interest in health and fitness, and has been highly successful.

The developers now believe that the total amenity package at PGA National coincides well with the targeted markets for the residential components. Two key advantages PGA National displays are a carefully defined master plan still guiding the project's growth, and a proven flexibility in dealing with short-term market fluctuations and new opportunities.

Champion course, sixth hole.

PGA National

PROJECT DATA:
PGA NATIONAL

LAND USE INFORMATION

Site Area	2,341 acres
Total Dwelling Units	5,000
Gross Density	2.14 dwelling units per acre

ECONOMIC INFORMATION

Site Acquisition Cost (1978)	$10.5 million
Site Improvement Cost	$26.6 million
Construction Cost	$38–$60 per sq. ft. (hard costs)

GOLF COURSE INFORMATION

Total Acreage	600
Length/Par	
Champion	7,137 yards/par 72
Haig	6,973 yards/par 72
Squire	6,550 yards/par 71
General	6,900 yards/par 72
Total Development and Construction Cost	$6 million

Estimated Annual Operating Costs (1985)	
Maintenance	$1.6 million ($22,000 per hole)
Pro shop	$750,000
Management and administration	$350,000

Member Dues	$2,000 per year
Guest Green Fees	$35 to $50

RACQUET AND HEALTH CLUB INFORMATION

Number of Tennis Courts	19
Lighted Courts	10
Surface	Har-Tru (synthetic porous)

Development and Construction Costs	
Court construction and equipment	$250,000 ($13,157 per court)
Court lighting	$70,000
Clubhouse and related facilities	$1 million

Estimated Operating Costs (1985)	
Maintenance	$ 70,000
Utilities	36,000
Pro shop	45,000
Food and beverage	20,000
Management and administration	60,000
Total	$231,000 ($12,158 per court)

Source: PGA National.

PROJECT CREDITS

Developer:
PGA National Venture, Ltd.
E. Llwyd Ecclestone, Jr., Chairman
West Palm Beach, Florida

Architect:
Schwab and Twitty, Inc.
Palm Beach, Florida

Planner:
Edward D. Stone, Jr., and Associates, Inc.
Fort Lauderdale, Florida

Landscape Architect:
Urban Design, Inc.
West Palm Beach, Florida

Golf Course Architects:
George Fazio and Tom Fazio
Palmer Course Design

CHANDLERS LANDING
Rockwall, Texas

Capitalizing on an unusual development opportunity frequently involves yielding some control over the process to others. One example is the requirement in many situations that a marina developer ensure adequate public access to the water. Although public access requirements are most common in coastal areas, they can apply to inland development projects as well. Such a requirement can drastically alter the way in which a developer builds and operates a marina. Yet if the market conditions are right, what some may view as an onerous requirement may actually enhance a project's prospects.

Chandlers Landing is a 285-acre planned unit development in Rockwall, Texas, a small suburban community about 30 minutes from downtown Dallas. The primary reason for the project's location—six-mile-long Lake Ray Hubbard—did not exist until the early 1970s, when the U.S. Army Corps of Engineers built the reservoir for flood control, water supply, and recreation purposes. Since then, Rockwall has blossomed into a fast-growing small city, attractive to Dallas commuters. According to local officials, Rockwall County ranks second in the state in both per capita income and median housing value.

DEVELOPMENT STRATEGY

Initiated in 1972 by Realvest, Inc. (formerly Fracorp), a Tulsa-based real estate development and investment firm, Chandlers Landing offers custom home lots, townhouses, condominiums, and patio homes on a rolling site along the banks of Lake Ray Hubbard. In 1985, the project was about 65 percent complete, with 425 units built. According to Realvest senior vice president James Robertson, the original plan, with lakeside townhouses predominant, was not well received by the market. Under a revised master plan, however, with just under half the units comprised of detached homes, the project has fared well. Nearly all these detached homes are used as primary residences, while about 35 percent of the attached units are used as second homes or for investment purposes.

The project's recreational centerpiece is the Chandlers Landing Yacht Club, a 1,100-member club that supports a 22,000-square-foot clubhouse, a nine-court tennis center, and a 550-slip marina. Roughly 35 percent of the project's real estate buyers have joined the club. In addition to this private facility, Realvest built the Chandlers Landing Marina, a public facility on land leased from the city of Rockwall. This full-service marina offers public launching, boat storage, and boat sales and services, thereby providing the required public use of the reservoir.

Realvest built these amenities early to help establish the project's image and to tap the heavy latent demand for boat slips in the Dallas area. After gradual growth through the late 1970s, Chandlers Landing took off in 1983, just after a slump in the early 1980s' recession. Also in the early 1980s, heavy publicity accompanied the exposure of a fraudulent development scheme involving land sales in the Lake Ray Hubbard area. Chandlers Landing was not involved, but sales at many projects in the area suffered temporarily.

In 1980, Realvest sold the club and marina to a separate, tax-shelter-oriented limited partnership. The new owners retained Realvest to manage the facilities. After several years of generating significant tax losses, the club is now approaching a break-even point. With its management fee, Realvest makes a profit, according to Robertson.

Viewing the marina and Lake Ray Hubbard from the townhouse complex at Chandlers Landing.

Considering Chandlers Landing's large and diverse club membership, this expertise is invaluable. Fewer than half of the 1,100 yacht club members live at the project. Moreover, about a third of the marina slips are leased to nonmembers, and the marina is used on a daily basis by the general public.

One key advantage for Realvest in managing these potentially problematic relationships is the sheer size of the facility. Adequate space exists, for example, to allow separate entrances for club members and public users. Similarly, the clubhouse, pool, and beach are located relatively far from the launching ramp, ship's store, and storage yard.

A second advantage is the marina's quality. Recognized by the Dallas boating market as one of the area's premier facilities, Chandlers has always enjoyed strong demand for memberships and slips. In 1986, the waiting list for a slip numbered 175. In a sense, the marina and yacht club have grown faster than the real estate development. New residents are therefore less likely to resist the presence of outside members. In fact, reports operations director Danny McCoy, the extensive member activity and involvement in the club is nearly as much of an amenity as the physical facilities themselves.

Nevertheless, project officials acknowledge that relations betweeen residents, outside members, and the public can be delicate, especially at high occupancy levels. They expect that gradually the proportion of the total membership represented by project residents will increase, although they have no specific goals or timetables.

THE MARINA AND YACHT CLUB

Developing a marina on a publicly built and owned body of water involves several unusual constraints. First, many of the landside facilities are built on leased land. Within a 60-foot ribbon of land above the mean high-water level (the so-called "take line"), development is severely limited. Maintaining adequate public access is a condition of development.

Secondly, the lake's water level is subject to relatively severe fluctuations. In fact, local agencies have warned that every 50 years or so, for various reasons, the reservoir could run dry. Even every 10 years, the water level could drop up to 10 feet. Already, due to a severe drought and a slackened water supply into the lake, the developers have been forced to dredge the basin several feet deeper. More recently, however, annual fluctuations have run about four feet. The reservoir's average depth is about 35 feet.

The nine-acre marina is basically an offshore type, with 550 slips arranged along 11 large piers, three of which are covered to accommodate power boats. Due to a prevailing southwest wind, the marina designers had to shield the boats from a six-mile wave fetch (the total distance over which waves travel before reaching the harbor). A curving, 1,400-foot breakwater of concrete and timber protects the harbor. A vertical steel bulkhead stabilizes the shoreline. Floating piers are of concrete and wood. In addition, the public end of the marina offers 325 parking spaces and dry storage space for another 125 boats.

The pool from the clubhouse terrace. Note covered slips in background.

Initially, Realvest had assumed a marina market of 70 percent power boaters and 30 percent sailors. In fact, it has proved nearly the opposite. The developers attribute this anomaly to the influence of an extremely active group of sailboat racers who have led the club membership since the early years. Another key factor is a well-organized and well-equipped sailing school for both juniors and adults. The developers estimate that some 65 percent of club members learned to sail through the club's programs, which annually serve about 360 adults and 120 juniors with four full-time and three part-time instructors. Besides the Chandlers Landing Yacht Club, the marina also supports a smaller, lower-cost club organized around dinghy sailing. This group, the Harbor Lights Boat Club, is intended to act, according to McCoy, as a "farm club" for the larger organization.

These relatively active boat owners demand a high level of service. At the juncture between the harbor and the public parking lot is the ship's store and repair shop. Services include complete mechanical, fiberglass, rigging, and paint work. To move boats, the marina has two jib cranes, two concrete launching ramps, and four rail dollies.

Realvest thus far seems to have successfully balanced the competing interests in the recreational amenities at Chandlers Landing. When asked to name the single most important factor in this success, operations director Danny McCoy points to the high level of member involvement in club programs, services, and management. This involvement is actively encouraged by Realvest's management practices. For example, about 8 percent of revenues from member dues goes into a discretionary fund, in effect generating about $50,000 annually to be used however the member board wishes. So far, the funds have gone to subsidize special events, programs, or projects. Access to the discretionary fund helps the board express its own desires without potentially fractious battles over funding, thereby smoothing relations for all.

The full-service marina, mandated by market demand as well as by the public access requirement, has meant a significant investment for the developers. After struggling for several years, its operation appears extremely successful. The key, according to the developers, has been finding the right person to run the operation. The personal reputation and credibility of the marina manager, they note, are critical factors in the success of Chandlers Landing Marina. As Danny McCoy points out, however, the most financially viable marinas will offer "either full service or no service."

Similar to many ski areas, Chandlers Landing illustrates how different parts of a project can appeal to different markets. The marina, one of the largest in the Southwest, attracts a regional market—making a large membership viable. The tennis and social members, however, generally come from a much smaller area.

The marina at Chandlers Landing is one of the largest in the Southwest.

The amenity mix at Chandlers Landing has also worked well. The developers stress the need to emphasize a "menu" of amenity options for residents and members. The lower-cost boat club provides perhaps the best example of this flexibility, and one that in the long run helps ensure the success of the larger, capital-intensive yacht club. The project's extensive recreational facilities, coupled with the moderate pace of development and the public access requirement, have precluded conversion to an equity club. Given Realvest's management expertise, the membership club has already shown the potential to be self-supporting. In addition, say the developers, an equity arrangement is more difficult to sustain in a project whose homeowners are still relatively mobile. Unlike many equity club projects, Chandlers Landing is composed mostly of primary residences, and most residents are not of retirement age. By relinquishing ownership but retaining management control of the amenities, the developers can reduce their financial burden while ensuring compatibility with further real estate development at the project.

PROJECT DATA:
CHANDLERS LANDING YACHT CLUB

MARINA INFORMATION

Number of Slips	550
Covered	192
Open	358
Dry Storage Capacity	125
Parking Spaces	325

ECONOMIC INFORMATION

Marina Construction Costs

Dredging, shoreline stabilization, landscaping	$3,500,000
Piers and moorings	1,200,000
Buildings[1]	150,000
Total	$4,850,000

Capital Cost per Slip	$8,818

Annual Operating Costs

Maintenance	$ 75,000
Utilities	35,000
Services	60,000
Management and administration	50,000
Total	$220,000

Monthly Lease Rates

Open slips	$ 92–175
Covered slips	$110–365
Average Annual Revenue per Slip	$ 1,382

[1]Cost data do not include the 22,000-square-foot main clubhouse. Estimated construction costs for the clubhouse and tennis complex total $3,450,000, with annual operating costs of $895,000.

Source: Realvest, Inc.

OTTER CREEK
Little Rock, Arkansas

The Otter Creek community, located 15 miles from downtown Little Rock, Arkansas, was launched in 1974. A planned community encompassing 548 acres, today the project houses more than 2,000 residents. Otter Creek provides a mixture of housing types ranging from single-family detached and cluster units to townhouses and garden apartments. It includes commercial, educational, religious, and recreational facilities. Otter Creek Mall, located near the community's entrance, is scheduled for completion in 1988 and will be Arkansas's largest regional mall. The recently completed Otter Creek Elementary School serves to enhance the focus on families, while a community-supported racquet club offers recreational activities.

The project site was purchased in 1972. Planning began in 1973, and site improvements were started in January 1974. The first occupancy occurred in summer 1975. Today, Otter Creek has become one of Little Rock's prime development areas.

The existing development contains approximately 500 homes priced between $80,000 and $150,000, with the possibility of constructing 300 more. Of the 316 acres devoted to single-family residences, only 100 acres (32 percent) remain for development.

The clubhouse at Otter Creek.

DEVELOPMENT STRATEGY

Amenities provide a key ingredient in Otter Creek's development strategy. The racquet's club's tennis and swimming facilities were built at a substantial front-end cost, but they proved a critical ingredient in attracting buyers to the single-family homes that were first built.

The club, consisting of tennis courts, a swimming pool, and a clubhouse, was designed to take advantage of the intense local demand for tennis facilities during the boom of the mid-1970s. In fact, much of the entire state's demand for tennis is largely concentrated in the Little Rock metropolitan area, according to the Little Rock office of the U.S. Tennis Association.

In order to incorporate these facilities in a desirable wooded setting, another key element of the development strategy was to find 300 to 500 acres of relatively low-cost land within easy access from downtown Little Rock. The developer intended to offer quality homesites in a rural, low-density setting that would allow for commuting to urban employment opportunities. A suitable tract was found southwest of the city near the interchange of Interstates 430 and 30, an important junction in the region's transportation network. Sites large enough for the project in northwestern Little Rock, the area to which the target market was most

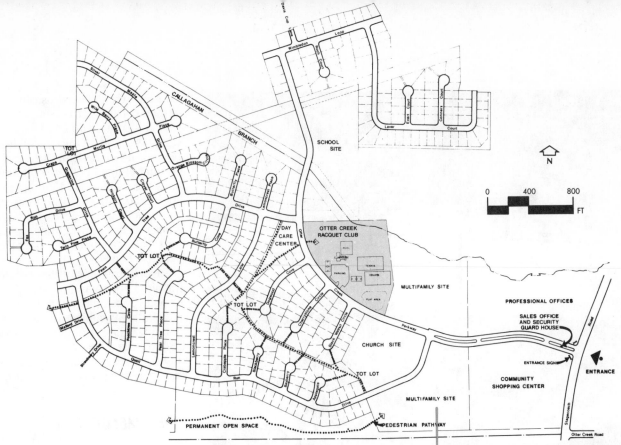

Site plan of the southern portion of the Otter Creek community, showing the centrally located racquet club.

interested in moving, were either few and costly or unavailable. The project's location in a sparsely developed and insulated southwest area provided the acreage at much lower cost: $1,900 per acre in 1972. In addition, the site was strategically located, with the interstate highways serving as a buffer between the project and existing industrial development.

The project's marketing strategy has been based on current housing trends in the Little Rock metropolitan area. Starting with single-family detached units to establish a quality image, the project offers a mix of housing types at costs comparable to other area sales. Approximately two-thirds of Otter Creek's buyers have been residents of the Little Rock area and have moved because they wanted larger houses.

As the project's image has become established and prices have escalated, more buyers over 40 years old have been attracted. The typical household now has one or two children and an average income more than $35,000. The sales program, delivered by an independent company on direct commission, relies mostly on advertisements in local newspapers, but it also sponsors

a spring radio campaign and special events to attract buyers. The current absorption rate is approximately 80 lots per year after nearly flat sales in the early 1980s.

In an effort to achieve effective communications with the home-buyers and early identification of potential problems, the developer has held monthly meetings with the residents. The developer has also published a monthly newspaper with board meeting reports and an activities calendar to keep residents informed. This approach has minimized problems and avoided the adversarial relationship that can arise between developer and residents. Project residents have generally supported the project at county commission, school board, and annexation meetings.

In general, the development strategy has paid off. Although in 1972 the site was not in a mainstream development corridor, its focus on amenities, access to downtown, and reasonable purchase prices, plus the growth of metropolitan Little Rock itself, have resulted in a successful project. To complete a 550-acre community, however, a developer must maintain the financial resources to carry costs for a long period. A more manageable size for most developers would be 40 to 100 acres; amenities could then be provided more easily, and the project could be sold out within two or three years without the risk of a longer, less predictable period.

Otter Creek's eight courts have an easily maintained, nonporous surface.

Otter Creek's layout uses a series of loop collector streets and has collector-street and cul-de-sac lots. Commercial and multifamily development lie at the fringes, with the racquet club and other community uses centrally located. An open-space and pathway system runs throughout the project and follows a natural stormwater drainage pattern. Tot lots are located near the neighborhoods.

Parts of the stream that crosses the site have been directed into a sloped, grass-lined channelway to reclaim areas subject to minor flooding. The main power line has 25-foot easements on each side for any construction; like the channelway, it serves as part of the pathway system.

THE AMENITY PLAN

The Otter Creek Racquet Club, built at the project's outset, was designed to provide a focal point around which the community would develop. It is located on Otter Creek Parkway, the project's main road, bordering the elementary school and multifamily section yet easily accessible from the primary single-family area. In addition, the club is connected with the majority of the single-family sites by the open-space and pathway system.

The club consists of eight tennis courts and a 6,024-square-foot clubhouse with bathroom, bar, office, dressing rooms, and pro shop. The clubhouse was expanded in 1985 from its former 4,100 square feet by the construction of an adult lounge area for social functions. In addition, the clubhouse includes two swimming pools. One is a 25-meter, L-shaped pool with a diving section and children's wading pool, and the other is a 36-by-82-foot regulation-size pool. This second pool, built in 1985 at a cost of

THE SITE

Although formerly farmed and grazed, as some neighboring tracts still are, the Otter Creek site is mostly wooded, with a mixture of pine and hardwoods along a flat-to-rolling terrain of slopes no greater than 20 percent. A high-voltage power line and stream bisect the site.

Development on an adjacent 800 acres is proceeding under the aegis of another developer following a similar locational strategy; these plans include light industry east of Interstate 30, a motel park and regional shopping center on the west side of the interstate exchange, and an office park adjacent to Otter Creek.

$80,000, was required for the project to be eligible for FHA financing. The developer originally built the club in 1975 at a cost of $250,000 ($120,000 for the 4,100-square-foot clubhouse, $50,000 for the 25-meter pool, and $80,000 for the eight tennis courts).

OPERATIONS AND MAINTENANCE

The racquet club is owned and maintained by the Otter Creek Homeowners' Association. All homeowners must join the association; in doing so, they automatically become members of the racquet club.

The club is administered by a full-time general manager. The complement of employees varies according to season. In the summer, the club maintains 15 to 19 employees, including eight lifeguards, two part-time maintenance personnel, four concession station personnel, three to four part-time tennis pros, a full-time manager, and an assistant manager. In the winter, the staff reduces to the manager, the assistant, and two part-time maintenance employees.

Activities at the club are generally at a high level, with events planned for adults as well as children. An active tennis committee annually coordinates five club tournaments, six team tennis tournaments, three sanctioned tournaments, and a number of tennis socials. Entry fees for the tournaments are $15 for singles and $20 for doubles. There are currently 487 families in the club, with some 200 active tennis players.

Swimming is popular as well. The pool is used more frequently by the children and younger residents. A swim team for active competition is sponsored by the local Optimist Club.

In order to offer homebuyers a wide range of financing options, the developer sought qualification for FHA financing. The regional office of the U.S. Department of Housing and Urban Development initially indicated that its definition of a new community did not include situations in which each homeowner was required to join a homeowners' association. To qualify Otter Creek for FHA financing, the HUD office therefore required the developer to relinquish control over and financial support for the Otter Creek Homeowners' Association. In addition, it required that the second swimming pool be constructed. Other aspects of the project that HUD reviewed were the amenity plan, the developer's continuing relationship with the homeowners' association, and the number of homes and residents in the project to date.

The developer was granted FHA financing in 1983. This came after the project was well underway, and the racquet club was able to realize a profit. Initially, dues were $20 per month; they are now $30.50, with daily guest fees at $1.50. There are no additional fees for court time. This monthly membership rate ranks well below the monthly fees charged for comparable facilities. For example, a nearby racquet club in Little Rock with nearly identical facilities charges an $800 initiation fee and a $72 monthly membership fee. Other clubs with various combinations of tennis, swimming, and general fitness facilities charge initiation fees averaging $200 and monthly membership fees averaging $42.

Although the racquet club's operating and capital improvement costs are covered by member dues, the community recently installed tennis court lights—a $12,000 expense—through donation of time and services as well as funds raised by special projects. This approach was taken to avoid a special assessment from the homeowners' association.

In general, operation and maintenance of the club's tennis courts remain relatively inexpensive. In 1985, four nets were purchased for $400. Electricity for court lights was $1,800. A capital improvement fund is maintained for court resurfacing, which is needed every six to eight years at a cost of about $1,600 per court.

EVALUATING THE EXPERIENCE

Otter Creek's amenity plan has proved successful for a number of reasons. One of the principal reasons was the early construction of a substantial, well-designed facility at the height of the nationwide tennis boom. This initial benefit provided the facility and the community with a fast start. The community focus and careful programming have carried through to the present even though the tennis boom has peaked.

A second critical factor in the club's success has been the high energy level and carefully planned schedule of tennis tournaments and social events. Working with a minimal budget and maintaining homeowner's association dues at a low level, the club has nevertheless been able to maximize its impact on the community.

Another factor of special importance has been the choice of a superior resident manager. The manager has been instrumental in organizing activities and tournaments, keeping dues low through a close check on expenditures, and overseeing maintenance of the facilities in general. In addition, the manager has been careful to hire tennis pros and other employees who are personable and work well with club members.

Last and by no means least is the carefully maintained image of Otter Creek in general. The ambience and quality of life created through review of architectural styles, site location and design, and use of pathways and open space have attracted buyers who are interested in supporting the racquet club and the community's other amenities.

PROJECT DATA: OTTER CREEK

LAND USE INFORMATION

Site Acquisition Cost (1972):	$1,148,700
Site Improvement Cost (estimated):	$6,084,875

Amenity Costs[1]

Clubhouse	$212,043
Pool and deck[2]	105,350
Tennis courts	96,000
Parking area	26,640
Landscaping	20,000
Land	183,000
Total	$643,053

OTTER CREEK HOMEOWNERS' ASSOCIATION BUDGET (1985)

Income		*Expenses*	
Dues	$162,288	Salaries	$ 75,000
Food and beverage	28,300	Administration	18,585
Guest fees	900	Taxes	11,548
Entertainment	3,500	Food and beverage	17,100
Rent	3,300	Maintenance	18,500
Tennis leagues/events	5,300	Tennis leagues/events	5,500
Miscellaneous	4,050	Utilities	14,512
Total	$207,638	Insurance	5,500
		Miscellaneous	12,700
		Depreciation	17,525
		Total	$196,470

Excess of Income over Expenses: $11,167

[1]Undepreciated cost, based on value estimates by Appraisal Consultants, Inc., March 1985.
[2]A second pool was added in summer 1985.
Source: Otter Creek Homeowners' Association.

PROJECT CREDITS

Developer:
Rock Venture/Greenbelt Companies
Little Rock, Arkansas

Planner/Engineer:
Hodges, Vines, Fox, Castin & Associates
Little Rock, Arkansas

Landscape Architect:
Wylie Jones
Memphis, Tennessee

NAPLES BATH & TENNIS CLUB
Naples, Florida

In 1968, after the tennis establishment recognized the inevitability of professional playing in major tournaments, the game began a decade of unparalleled growth. By 1978, some 20 million Americans were playing a game once considered a pastime for the elite. Hundreds of newly developed tennis clubs around the nation capitalized on the boom. While dozens of the new clubs foundered when demand slackened in the early 1980s, those that had captured their markets with high-quality, well-maintained facilities and superior programs and services are still going strong.

In Naples, Florida—an established, affluent retirement community on the Gulf Coast—a development project two miles from the beach and without a golf course needs a compelling attraction with which to compete. In 1973, tennis was clearly the ticket. That year, Frates Enterprises, a development company from Tulsa, joined with Denver-based Associated Inns and Restaurants of America (AIRCOA) to create a 160-acre resort and residential community focused on a major tennis club in northern Naples. The development team had substantial experience in residential land development, resort community develoment, and club management.

Naples Bath & Tennis Club, which in 1985 was about 90 percent complete, will ultimately contain about 430 condominium units and 93 single-family detached houses on lakefront lots. The project's centerpiece is a 30,000-square-foot clubhouse overlooking a 32-court tennis complex. The project operates as a destination resort and second-home community, as well as home to many Naples residents.

The slightly elevated clubhouse looks down on the project's 32 tennis courts.

The developers started construction in 1975, two years after they purchased the site. With basic site improvements and infrastructure complete, they began selling homesites in 1976. The last of the 10 development phases, consisting of 86 units, should be completed by mid-1987.

The project is located in northeast Naples, about 20 miles south of Ft. Myers. The older part of the city, with shopping areas, large homes, and small, elegant resort hotels along the beach, lies about 10 minutes away. The more recent development in the city's northeast section is predominantly large planned developments, most of which contain golf courses and other recreational facilities. Westinghouse's 2,000-acre Pelican Bay project lies to the west along the Gulf.

Before development, the site was relatively barren, with low scrub vegetation, rocky soils, and poor drainage. It did, however, offer good access and a visible location within a rapidly developing growth corridor.

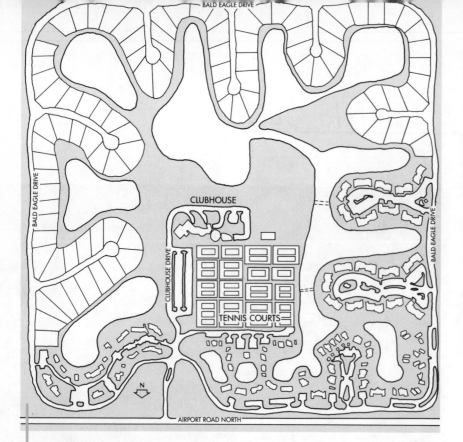

Naples Bath & Tennis Club site plan.

DEVELOPMENT STRATEGY

As in most amenity-oriented projects, the developers of Naples Bath & Tennis Club were concerned in the early stages about balancing the upfront expenditures needed to attract the market with the sales revenues required to drive the development. As a resort, the project needed an identifiable image and a well-structured amenity package, including dining facilities and resort accommodations. At the same time, to attract homesite buyers, the developers needed to create an image of a desirable residential community. Their basic strategy was to install the club facilities, then sell improved lots to finance further site improvements. These improvements would in turn attract subdevelopers whose multifamily projects would serve the second-home market.

Recreational facilities and resort accommodations were expanded as the project grew. Adequate room for additional amenities existed in the site's central portion, around the clubhouse. Tennis courts were easily expanded in modules.

Recognizing the difficulty of accurately projecting market conditions over a 10- to 12-year period to buildout, the developers remained relatively flexible regarding the particular products they would build. Early multifamily projects, basically garden apartments, have given way to a more spacious, less dense configuration in response to market demand. The last two phases of the project, consisting of three-story buildings clustered around a small swimming pool complex, have proved both popular and cost-effective. In 1985, most two-bedroom condominiums in the final phase were priced from $121,900 to $149,900.

Custom homesites were sold relatively early in the development process.

Since the outset, the developers have operated the amenities as a membership club. Gradually, the proportion of total members represented by owners of project real estate has risen and the number of outside members has shrunk. When the project is built out, according to company officials, a cap on outside members is likely to be imposed. Until 1982, the original partnership owned the entire interest in the club. That year, however, a 50 percent share was sold to an outside investment group. AIRCOA retained full management control of the club.

TENNIS FACILITIES

The 32-court tennis complex occupies the heart of Naples Bath & Tennis Club. The courts are configured in batteries of up to three courts, although most are arranged singly or in pairs. Single-family residential areas are separated from the courts by lakes and by the 30,000-square-foot clubhouse. Multifamily buildings are separated on two sides of the tennis complex by roadways or parking. The north side of the courts connects via walkways and bridges over ponds to the newer project phases. Generally, the phases developed early are located closest to the courts. Because these units are older, most are less valuable than units in the newer phases farther away. Proximity to the courts apparently is not a major factor in determining the value of a particular unit.

Because of the region's older tennis resort and real estate markets, the developers chose a fast-drying synthetic clay surface for 25 of the courts. The remaining seven courts have a nonporous surface. These harder courts are far less popular than the claylike courts, and in 1985 the club managers were considering converting them to the more comfortable surface. Fourteen of the courts are lighted for night play. Nearby, two racquetball courts double as practice walls for tennis.

Courtside pavilion and telephone.

Near the clubhouse are two courts that take advantage of a change in grade from the clubhouse patio to the court surface. This embankment is used for seating during the club's many tournaments, including the popular Grand Masters tournaments held every year at the club. Adjacent to the clubhouse are a swimming pool and snack bar. The clubhouse, which also functions as a conference center, includes a variety of meeting rooms, a dining room and lounge, a pro shop, and locker rooms.

During construction of the courts, poor drainage posed significant problems. These were eventually corrected by linking the court drainage system to a series of interconnected ponds to quickly channel water away from the courts.

As the "official home of the tennis Grand Masters," Naples Bath & Tennis Club annually hosts a series of tournaments for a group of senior professional players that includes Rod Laver, Ken Rosewall, and Roy Emerson. These tournaments, which are relatively economical for the club to host, are quite popular with the community and go far in promoting the project's image. In addition, the club hosts a special Davis Cup tournament and several charity events each year. Ten tennis events, including tournaments and clinics, are regularly scheduled each week. A director of tennis runs the pro shop and, with a staff of three pros, also coordinates all instruction and court maintenance.

In 1985, the club had 900 members. Of these, 500 were tennis members. The remaining members use the club socially and are able to use the tennis courts on a user-fee basis. For real estate owners participating in the resort rental program, club membership is required. A portion of each nightly rental fee also goes to the club. According to Bill Beverly, the club's tennis director, about one-fourth of the club members are quite active players, on the courts up to five times per week when the weather is suitable. He estimates that most members play about three times weekly.

EVALUATING THE EXPERIENCE

Naples Bath & Tennis Club's success has been based on careful club management that maintains a high level of activity and offers resort guests fine tennis facilities, dining, and accommodations. The developers note, however, that the activity level is difficult to sustain year-round in a seasonal market. They also report that mixing resort guests with local club members can be difficult. As residents increase and spend more time at the project, this situation becomes even more problematic. The private membership sometimes resists, for example, active promotion of the project as a resort.

Many similar resorts built today design much more modest clubhouse facilities. When Naples Bath & Tennis Club was launched, the clubhouse was seen as the key element in establishing the project's credibility with builders and potential buyers of single-family homes. Ten years later, however, the developers say that, while the dining room and card rooms are popular with the social members, the core tennis membership actually would prefer a more casual facility. A logical addition, they note, would be a health club and a network of jogging paths.

The project has established itself as one of the nation's leading tennis resorts through a careful balance of attention to both real estate and hospitality. One measure of the quality of a tennis resort or club is court availability and the ease with which a member or visitor can line up a game with a suitable partner. Naples Bath & Tennis Club, at buildout, will contain one tennis court for every 16.5 housing units. If single-family homes are excluded, the ratio drops to 13.6 units per court. In a seasonal market, this low unit-to-court ratio means good court availability. Combined with an active tennis director who takes pains to determine the playing level and availability of each guest and member, Naples Bath & Tennis Club scores well in this particular category. And by expanding their tennis facilities as needed, and building in clusters to lower per-court capital costs, the developers have wisely balanced the supply of courts with the demand.

PROJECT DATA:
NAPLES BATH & TENNIS CLUB

LAND USE INFORMATION
Site Area: 160 acres

Number of Housing Units

Condominiums: 436
Single-family homesites: 93
Gross density: 3.3 dwelling units per acre

MEMBERSHIP INFORMATION:

Membership	Number of Members	Initiation Fee	Annual Dues
Social members	400	$1,500	$ 480
Tennis members	500	3,000	1,000

ESTIMATED CONSTRUCTION COST PER COURT: $10,000

PROJECT CREDITS

Developer:
Naples Bath & Tennis Club, Ltd.
Naples, Florida

Planner:
Wilson, Miller, Barton, Soll, Peek, Inc.
Naples, Florida

Architects:
Walter L. Keller & Associates
Naples, Florida

Davies and Poe Associates
Tulsa, Oklahoma

Landscape Architect:
Renfroe Landscape, Inc.
Naples, Florida

Management:
AIRCOA
Englewood, Colorado

214

HIDDEN VALLEY
Somerset, Pennsylvania

Many of today's ski resort development opportunities are emerging out of existing but underused resources and potential but untapped markets. Smaller, older ski areas that find it ever more difficult to compete with the large resorts are turning to real estate development to maintain their financial viability and to reach new markets for skiing, resort lodging, and conferences.

Such spin-off opportunities can make a great deal of sense. For the prospective developer, one major difficulty is the paucity of suitable sites and the extremely high cost of entry into the skiing business. At the same time, existing areas find themselves out on a financial limb by relying on skiing, a seasonal and highly variable source, for the bulk of their revenues. Many existing areas—particularly in the East, where the land is more likely to be privately owned—may have enough additional acreage to support the transition from a ski area to a year-round resort and residential community.

After several smaller experiments with real estate development, Hidden Valley Resort Community and Conference Center, formerly a small ski area open primarily on weekends, has embarked on a major transformation. This 1,700-acre project in Pennsylvania's Laurel Highlands is becoming a year-round second-home and resort community with a $5 million conference center, a doubling of its skiing capacity, an 18-hole golf course, and numerous other recreational facilities, all of which will support nearly 2,500 housing units. Hidden Valley is located about an hour southeast of Pittsburgh and about three-and-a-half hours from Washington, D.C.

The developer's aim is to create a resort for all seasons, only an hour's drive from Pittsburgh.

At the helm of this transformation is the Washington, D.C.–based development company, Kettler Brothers, Inc. (KBI). The firm first became involved at Hidden Valley in the early 1970s, when a KBI executive built a vacation home there. At the time, real estate development at Hidden Valley amounted only to a few homesites on land surrounding the slopes. Since the early 1950s, a small country inn had existed on the site. A few years later, intrigued by the growing popularity of downhill skiing, the innkeepers had opened the first ski slopes. A small subdivision followed. Then, in 1977, the first vacation townhouse project opened, due to the efforts of the KBI executive. At that time, the ski area was drawing about 1,500 skiers a day on a good winter weekend.

By 1983, when it acquired the site, KBI had conceived of a full-fledged resort community, where skiing would be augmented by a range of year-round recreational amenities, including golf and tennis. Additionally, a conference center would help ensure demand for resort rentals and for recreational facilities, especially in the nonwinter months.

By late summer 1985, the project was about 15 percent complete. KBI had built an additional 200 housing units, with eventual plans for some 2,500 single-family houses, townhouses, and condominiums. KBI had also begun construction of an 18-hole golf course, a facility expected to prove instrumental in realizing Hidden Valley's shift in personality. The developers expect to open the first nine holes in 1987 and to open the full 18 holes in the spring of 1988. Additional recreational facilities are scattered throughout the project. A multi-court tennis facility is planned adjacent to the golf clubhouse, supplementing an existing eight courts.

DEVELOPMENT STRATEGY

Since the 1960s, KBI had been involved in the development of Montgomery Village, a 2,500-acre new town 25 miles outside Washington in Montgomery County, Maryland. Although the company believed it unlikely that it would again be involved in a project of such a scale, it had gained valuable experience in large-scale community development and in the role of recreational amenities in such projects. Montgomery Village includes facilities for golf, tennis, boating, bicycling, and many other activities.

The developers realized that Hidden Valley, as it existed in 1983, was an important recreational resource for its local constituency. They also realized that the market was increasingly competitive, with nearby Seven Springs considered to be the area's premier ski mountain. The company could hardly turn its back on Hidden Valley's skiing facilities, however. The area was particularly popular with families and groups, and in the 1983–84 season it counted approximately 90,000 skier-days and gross skiing receipts of just over $1.2 million. Significantly, the ski facilities also accounted for a great deal of the project's name recognition, particularly in the Pittsburgh market.

The centerpiece of KBI's strategy at Hidden Valley has been to transform the place from a single-season recreational facility with limited real estate operations to a four-season resort and conference center with a wide variety of real estate products and recreational amenities. At the same time, Hidden Valley's traditional strength, skiing, is being expanded and improved to help support the surrounding changes. Eventually, the developers hope, golf will be on an equal footing with skiing as a marketing draw at Hidden Valley.

KBI has focused its marketing efforts on the Pittsburgh area, which so far has generated about 70 percent of real estate sales over the past few years. The developers see the project's second-home market as extending south to Washington and Baltimore and west to Cleveland. In addition, conference demand comes from as far away as New York City. Based on its successful experience at Montgomery Village, KBI stresses how satisfied visitors and customers can help generate additional sales.

Based on this market, Hidden Valley's real estate products are priced from $70,000 to more than $200,000, with a median price in 1985 of about $92,000. The primary product thus far is a townhouse of about 1,425 square feet, which can be purchased fully furnished and placed in a rental program managed by KBI. Garden apartment condominiums and zero-lot-line, single-family homes are also offered.

Hidden Valley's dual-triple chairlift.

The spaciousness of the site, the desires of the market, and the relatively low land costs have enabled KBI to keep Hidden Valley's gross density quite low, at about two dwelling units per acre. Along with the 25,000 acres of adjacent public lands, the resort's feeling is remarkably isolated, considering its proximity to Pittsburgh.

The recreational amenities are structured as a mix of community facilities and commercial facilities available for a user fee. Homeowners participate in the Hidden Valley Club, entitling them to free use of the project's tennis courts and pool, and to discounts on dining and skiing, among other benefits.

SKIING AT HIDDEN VALLEY

Since 1956, Hidden Valley has offered reasonably priced skiing in an unpretentious family atmosphere. Although downhill skiing is dominant, cross-country is growing in popularity and will become even more important as the resort is developed. (Already, according to KBI officials, several homes have been sold to families who only ski cross-country, not downhill.)

The 11 slopes at Hidden Valley support an estimated daily capacity of 5,000 skiers. Lift capacity, given the relatively modest area of skiable terrain, is fairly high. Four chairlifts, including a high-capacity dual-triple lift, move skiers up the mountain quickly. The total vertical drop, 511

Many residential sites offer direct access to downhill or cross-country skiing.

feet, is typical for the region. Night skiing and snowmaking are provided on about 90 percent of the slopes. About half the skiable terrain serves the intermediate skier, 30 percent suits the beginner, and about one-fifth is aimed at the expert.

According to a study of the skier market in the Middle Atlantic region undertaken by local business interests, downhill skiers tend to be young and relatively experienced. Most are male, with an average age of 27 years and about nine years of skiing experience. Like most similar studies, this one found that cross-country skiers had taken up the sport within the last three years.

Skiers are relatively active, taking an average of 11 ski trips per year. At Hidden Valley, the average season runs from December 15 to April 1.

In the past, many skiers at the area have come from the immediate vicinity. Somerset County residents in 1984 purchased just under half of all season passes at Hidden Valley. As the real estate development progresses, this percentage should decline somewhat. KBI's plans include an expansion of the downhill area that will nearly double the amount of skiable terrain and add two more chairlifts. A second, smaller base facility to be built adjacent to existing resort condominiums will serve this new area.

The resort also offers about 40 kilometers of cross-country trails, both on the site itself and in adjacent public lands. All trails are maintained by Hidden Valley. In the off-season, this responsibility involves clearing and trimming, bridge repair, and so on. In the winter, special snowmobiles set two cross-country tracks. The trails are supported by a touring center that offers ski rentals, lessons, and various special programs such as moonlight tours.

Hidden Valley's main ski lodge, which is complemented by the resort's conference center facilities.

Part of the planned expansion includes almost doubling the area's skiable terrain.

GOLF: ROUNDING OUT THE PACKAGE

Given enough room on a prospective site, golf can be a natural adjunct to skiing. At Hidden Valley, golf will provide the focus of warm-weather activity and will be marketed as the primary diversion for conference attendees. Hidden Valley's conference center, built in 1983 and slated for expansion in 1987, can currently handle groups of up to 200. By 1988, according to the developers, the resort could be hosting as many as 725 conferences annually, generating nearly 42,000 guest-nights in the resort accommodations. The developers expect that in the middle of the week, up to half the golfers on the course will be attending a conference at the resort. Golf course pro formas are based on about 27,000 rounds per year.

Besides serving the conference center market, the golf course is planned to generate significant real estate values. The 7,000-yard layout, routed in a single-fairway, returning-nine configuration, will create about 800 housing units fronting on the golf course. The course, designed by Russell Roberts of Gaithersburg, Maryland, is targeted to fill a gap between the relatively low-quality public courses nearby and a few extremely exclusive private clubs in the area. Unlike most of the nonskiing recreational facilities, at this point the golf course is not projected to be turned over to the homeowners' association. A key consideration in planning for the course's disposition is the fact that a homeowners' association existed at Hidden Valley prior to KBI's expansion of the resort. These existing homeowners form an important constituency that to some extent limits the developer's disposition options.

Because of the importance of the conference center connection to the golf course, a likely disposition plan is to transfer the course to the conference center owner (which may continue to be KBI). In such a case, the developers would reserve adequate access to the course for real estate buyers. A second option would be to sell the course to a private golf course operator, while reserving appropriate access for residents. For now, however, the facility will be operated as a daily fee course, open to the public but with annual memberships available.

Only a modest clubhouse will support the course, because the conference center and other resort facilities will serve the bulk of residents' and guests' social needs. It will concentrate on golf, offering a small pro shop, locker rooms, and a patio or outdoor dining area served by a snack bar or perhaps simply a vending operation. In the winter, the clubhouse area will be used as a warming stop and trailhead by cross-country skiers. Cross-country trails will be integrated with the golf course along several fairways.

THE IMPORTANCE OF THE PROCESS

Making a transition from a small, family-owned ski area to a major regional resort is fraught with potential pitfalls, but it frequently offers unusual development potential. An important requirement is sensitivity to local needs. In such cases, developers should attempt to capitalize on a place's existing attributes. At the same time, they should ensure that its transformation does not destroy those attractive qualities. And in relatively remote areas, such a conversion may engender political opposition based on perceptions of adverse environmental or social impacts.

At Hidden Valley, KBI has recognized certain limitations on its ability to control all the variables in the development process. Existing residents, for example, maintain an interest in the disposition plan for the golf course. Similarly, the region's residents reasonably expect an economic benefit from the new investment. One strategy KBI has employed in response is to use local resources—attorneys, engineers, banks, and subcontractors—whenever possible. It is important, say KBI officials, that the new Hidden Valley be as much a part of the local environment and economy as it always has been—only more so.

PROJECT DATA:
HIDDEN VALLEY

PROJECT CREDITS

Developer:
Kettler Brothers, Inc.
Gaithersburg, Maryland

Planners:
Greenhorne and O'Mara, Inc.
Fairfax, Virginia

Golf Course Architect:
Russell Roberts
Gaithersburg, Maryland

LAND USE INFORMATION

	Acres	Percent of Site
Housing	350	24.9%
Golf course	117	8.3
Ski slopes, lodge, and parking	111	7.9
Other recreational facilities[1]	20	1.4
Conference center	4.5	.05
Administration/office	5	.05
Infrastructure[2]	51.8	3.6
Open space	742.7	52.9
Total	1,402.0	100.00

SKI AREA INFORMATION

Total Area: 150 acres
Skiable Terrain: 50 acres
Vertical Drop: 511 feet
Daily Capacity: 5,000
Night Skiing: 90% of slopes
Snowmaking: 90% of slopes

Lift Ticket Prices	Weekend	Weekday
Adult	$22	$18
Junior	$12	$10

Ski Area Nondepreciated Assets[3]	
Lifts and tows	$1,600,000
Lighting	83,000
Snowmaking	351,000
Buildings	926,000
Furniture and fixtures	35,000
Equipment	270,000
Total	$3,265,000

Estimated Annual Operating Costs $1,200,000[4]

GOLF COURSE INFORMATION
Golf Course Development and Construction Costs[5]

Course construction	$1,659,000
Irrigation system	140,000
Pro shop building & equipment	125,000
Golf carts	168,000
Maintenance equipment	75,000
Total	$2,267,000

Estimated Annual Golf Course Operating Costs	$290,000
Operating costs per hole	$ 16,111

[1]Includes lake, tennis courts, community pools, beach, playgrounds, and racquet club.
[2]Includes roadways, sewage treatment system, and water system.
[3]As of January 1, 1985.
[4]Excluding depreciation, interest, insurance, and taxes.
[5]Based on pro forma estimates, not including land costs ($345,000) or interest costs during construction.
Source: Kettler Brothers, Inc.

PLAYERS PLACE
North Lauderdale, Florida

Developers frequently emphasize recreation and leisure as means to reach a particular market—retirees, families, childless professionals, and so on. In competitive areas, where many other projects also offer recreational amenities, developers may feel compelled to include them, even if the benefits to the project are unclear. In emerging or undersupplied markets, however, the benefits can be direct and obvious.

Southeast Florida is one market experiencing such shifts. Over the past decade, the economy in Broward and Palm Beach counties has steadily diversified, in turn creating thousands of new jobs in the professional, management, and service sectors. Residential real estate markets, formerly dominated by the retiree and second-home segments, have also diversified and segmented. Notably, strong demand emerged in the early 1980s for affordable, for-sale housing oriented to active, young, white-collar workers. While recreational amenities would fit most projects targeted to this market, developers have had to balance the cost of providing such facilities with the aim of keeping housing units affordable for the first-time buyer.

At Players Place, a 440-unit townhouse community just west of Fort Lauderdale, the recreation orientation extends to the project's name. The developers, Fairfield Communities, Inc., of Boca Raton, Florida, began planning the 44-acre site's development in early 1983. Sales started in March 1984, and the final phase was completed in 1986. The project features a mix of unit types, ranging from one to three bedrooms and from 864 to 1,400 square feet. In 1985, prices ranged from $48,900 to $74,000.

The first five phases consisted of eightplex buildings clustered around parking courts. The final phase introduced 176 townhouses of a slightly different design, planned both to boost the project's overall density and to relate more strongly to a three-acre lake.

The project's recreational focus, and the centerpiece of Fairfield's marketing efforts, is a recreational complex with a swimming pool and spa; tennis, racquetball, and volleyball courts; and a pavilion building dubbed the Sportside Club. In addition, the lake, which was required to accommodate stormwater runoff, offers a major amenity.

PLANNING AND PHASING

The first five phases, each including from 40 to 64 units, were designed to establish the project's overall image and to steadily develop the site's northern and eastern portions. The central area around the lake was developed in phase six. Fairfield, pinning its hopes on the recreational amenities, built the club facilities up front.

These five phases were separated from the sixth by a landscaped boulevard connecting two arterial streets on the site's perimeter. Each of these building groups has its own entrance from this roadway. Although the eightplex buildings in phases one through five are large and follow a somewhat uniform layout, they have been sited to protect as many mature trees as possible. The landscape architects con-

Marketing efforts at Players Place focus on recreation.

ducted a complete tree survey; in accordance with local regulations, the developers planted as many trees as were taken down.

In the final phase, the developers were pressed by a need both to increase the project's density and to incorporate the stormwater retention lake. With the lake biting nearly three acres out of the 12-acre phase-six parcel, Fairfield needed a 30 percent boost in density over the first five phases to meet the project's financial target. At the same time, for marketing purposes the new units had to take maximum advantage of the lake.

The phase-six design team proposed changes to both the building forms and the site plan. The new buildings, half of which look out on the lake, incorporate a maximum number of "through" and corner units. As a result, individual units feature more views, light, and air. The new configuration also means better access to units from parking areas and a greater variety of outdoor spaces, including private entry courts and patios for each unit. The overall result: a higher density achieved without compromising the parklike character that the earlier phases had established as the project's trademark.

Some adjacent communities were built at lower elevations and are subject to periodic flooding. The South Florida Water Management District therefore required the developers to retain all runoff on site. The retention lake and a four-acre strip across the street on the site's eastern perimeter are used to meet the standard. This retention system includes underground seepage pits designed to quickly infiltrate the first half-inch of rain before it enters the lake.

RECREATIONAL AMENITIES

Based on the expected market profile, Fairfield knew that the amenities at Players Place would need to cater to both active, fitness-oriented recreation and to informal and organized social gatherings. The resulting complex, located just

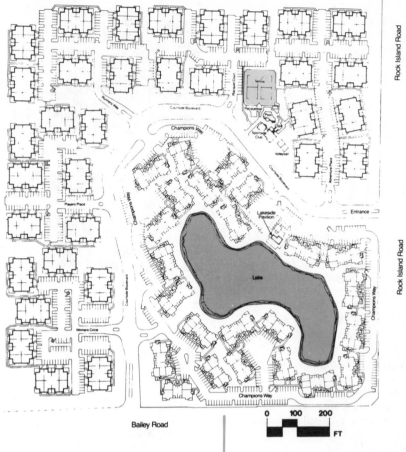

Players Place site plan.

inside the project's main entrance, consists of a party pavilion with bathhouses and a screened room of about 400 square feet. Attached to the pavilion is a canvas-covered barbecue and picnic area. Near the 1,250-square-foot pool is a heated spa that seats 10. The pool includes a tiled lane for lap swimming. Both concrete tennis courts are lighted. A three-side concrete racquetball court and a volleyball court are also available. Along the site's perimeter is a 20-station fitness trail. A smaller pavilion and pool will serve residents of phase six.

All the recreational facilities are the responsibility of the homeowners' association, which will own them when 90 percent of the units are sold. The project is eligible for VA and FHA financing—an important incentive for first-time buyers. Certification for this financing involved an on-site inspection by the agencies' representatives as well as approval of the amenity disposition plan.

A KEY BOOST

According to the developers, the recreational theme has proved a key boost to the fortunes of Players Place. They report that sales prospects have been impressed by the extensive recreational facilities, usually available only in more expensive projects. Also important in the marketing has been a landscape plan that exceeds the local requirements, and the views of the small lake. Many of the buyers are young professionals or managers, about half single and half married, with an average age of 30. Some have moved from other states, attracted by area job prospects. Most, however, have been former renters from within an eight- to 10-mile radius. To advertise the project, the developers used newspaper ads and radio spots, which proved highly effective in this market.

The amenities at Players Place were carefully chosen to reflect the needs of the target market, the space available, the climate, and the need for simple operations and disposition. As a result, the project has enjoyed quick sales. In the longer run, the homeowners' association should be able to avoid major operations or maintenance headaches. And for the foreseeable future, the recreational facilities should receive heavy use.

Tennis courts are supplemented by racquetball and volleyball courts, a fitness trail, and a pool. For the more sedate, the project boasts a three-acre lake.

PROJECT DATA: PLAYERS PLACE

LAND USE INFORMATION:

Site Area: 44 acres
Total Dwelling Units: 440
Gross Density: 10 dwelling units per acre

LAND USE PLAN[1]

	Acres	Percent of Site
Residential Buildings	6.17	26.48%
Parking and Roads	6.63	28.45
Landscaped Open Space	8.30	35.63
Amenities	0.80	3.43
Stormwater Retention	1.40	6.01
Total	23.30	100.00

ECONOMIC INFORMATION

Site Acquisition Cost:	$1,400,000
Site Improvement Costs	
Excavation	$ 335,000
Grading	110,000
Sewer and water	664,000
Paving	395,000
Curbs and sidewalks	27,000
Landscaping	189,000
Entrance	102,000
Total	$1,822,000

Construction Cost per Square Foot:	$30
Amenities Cost	
Sportside Club and Tennis Courts	$ 140,000
Vita Course	10,000
Fountain	5,000
Total	$ 155,000

[1]Data for phases one through five only.

PROJECT CREDITS

Developer:
Fairfield Communities, Inc.
Boca Raton, Florida

Engineer/Planner:
Craven, Thompson & Associates, Inc.
Fort Lauderdale, Florida

Architect:
The Evans Group
Orlando, Florida

Landscape Architect:
Edward D. Stone, Jr. & Associates
Fort Lauderdale, Florida

Phase Six Design:
Rhett Roy Landscape/Planning, P.A.
Ft. Lauderdale, Florida

Wayne Berenbaum Architecture/
Planning, P.A.
Boca Raton, Florida

Conceptual Design
Boca Raton, Florida

LOCHMERE
Cary, North Carolina

In traditional models of amenity-oriented development, the developer assumes nearly all the risk associated with the construction and initial operation of recreational facilities. Often, however, a better approach is to redistribute the risk among other entities, each of which, by responding to its own interest, helps make the overall project successful.

A developer who perceives amenities only as marketing tools, for example, is less likely to prove adept at operating and maintaining them as a project approaches completion. On the other hand, an experienced club operator might view the same amenities as potentially profitable enterprises. In some cases, a sensible arrangement is to place operating and management responsibility in the hands of those best qualified for the job. Although a perhaps inevitable tension exists between a developer's objectives and an operator's objectives, a cooperative arrangement can successfully reduce the risk assumed by both parties. If properly structured, such an arrangement can also enhance the recreational amenities' stability and long-term viability, while still providing significant marketing benefits to the developer.

One project that has successfully employed this delegation-of-risk strategy is Lochmere, a 1,039-acre planned unit development in a suburb of Raleigh, North Carolina. Lochmere contains detached and attached residential neighborhoods, sites for office and retail uses, and an extensive system of trails, parks, lakes, and other recreational amenities. A separate company has built and is operating the Lochmere Golf Club, a daily fee course open to the public, which constitutes an integral part of the surrounding development.

At Lochmere, commercial buildings are also designed to take advantage of lakefront sites.

PROJECT OVERVIEW

A town of about 30,000 residents, Cary has evolved over the last 15 years into one of the state's premier suburban communities. Driven largely by the electronics research and development industry, the Research Triangle—the cities of Raleigh, Durham, and Chapel Hill—has experienced a remarkable rate of economic development. Nestled in the heart of the Research Triangle, Cary has elected to manage a good deal of its growth by encouraging relatively large-scale planned unit developments (PUDs).

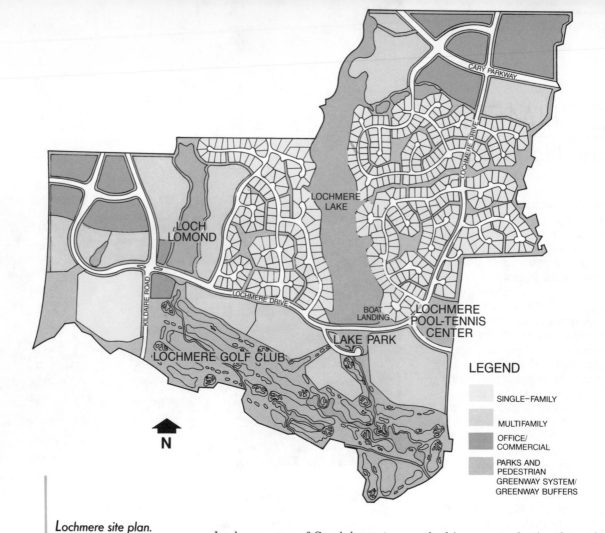

LEGEND

SINGLE–FAMILY

MULTIFAMILY

OFFICE/
COMMERCIAL

PARKS AND
PEDESTRIAN
GREENWAY SYSTEM/
GREENWAY BUFFERS

Lochmere site plan.

Lochmere, one of Cary's largest PUDs, has been the focus of development efforts by the locally based MacGregor Development Company (in conjunction with J. P. Goodson Enterprises on about 150 acres) since the firm began assembling the land in late 1980. MacGregor has offered individual parcels within Lochmere for sale to a select group of builders, most of whom are also based in the immediate area. About one-third of the site is devoted to single-family residential products that will range in price from about $150,000 to well over $300,000. Attached residential neighborhoods will offer a wide variety of units with prices ranging from $100,000 to $250,000. The project's market so far has proven strong and diverse, a mixture of relatively affluent, single-income households with children,

dual-income professional couples, and semiretired people. The multifamily market has been especially responsive, according to the developer, and more products are likely to be targeted to younger buyers in the future, with more options in the $110,000 to $120,000 price range.

Individual Lochmere neighborhoods are stitched together and highlighted by a diverse system of open space and recreational facilities. Chief among these are two large lakes, an 18-hole golf course, a swimming pool and tennis center, and a pedestrian greenway that includes two exercise courses and five small play areas. Also planned are two lakeside parks, one with a small boat docking facility, and a 20-acre public park. When the project is finished, its internal open-space system will connect at the site boundaries with a larger, public trail network that at one corner will offer direct access to an adjacent state park. Overall, the project will include 2,336 dwelling units on 1,039 acres, for a net density of 2.45 units per acre.

THE SITE AND ENVIRONS

Lochmere lies in the southern part of Cary, about 10 miles southwest of Raleigh. The site is completely surrounded by existing or proposed low-density residential areas except at its southwest corner, where it connects with Hemlock Bluffs State Park. Under the former ownership of Davidson College, the site was thought by many to be undevelopable except for extremely low-density housing, because the town had not planned to provide sewer service to that portion of the Swift Creek basin. Swift Creek flows along the site's southern border and was joined, prior to Lochmere's development, by two south-flowing tributaries that effectively divided the property into three nonfloodplain areas. These areas are moderately sloping with nonrestrictive soils, covered by a variety of pines and hardwoods at various stages of maturity. Although part of the land had been sporadically farmed and grazed, the woods on the site are fairly mature.

The two lakes have boosted the value of adjacent lots by as much as 80 percent, report the developers.

In plans for Lochmere's development, the rural character of the surrounding land ranked as important as the natural features of the site itself. Although Cary had grown rapidly in the years preceding Lochmere, many of the town's residents feared that large-scale new development would be incompatible with the area's existing character and would result in irreversible environmental damage.

DEVELOPMENT STRATEGY AND PLANNING PROCESS

MacGregor's design team established an early goal: to reflect in the physical plan, as much as possible, the diverse and sometimes conflicting objectives of the developer, the surrounding residents, and the town itself. To this end, the designers identified and analyzed a number of issues, notably the overall project density, the location and size of nonresidential areas, and the protection of key environmental features—the Hemlock Bluffs State Park and the Swift Creek watershed.

Lochmere's plan reflects these basic concerns by concentrating more intensive uses—commercial and institutional—away from the sensitive areas and by locating open-space buffers around most of the site's perimeter. In response to community concerns, density was lowered to 2.45 dwelling units per acre, although the town's PUD ordinance permits gross densities of up to six units per acre.

The plan deals with the site's hydrological features by turning them into assets. The two north-south tributaries to Swift Creek were dammed to create two lakes: one, Loch Lomond, of 22 acres and the other, Lochmere Lake, of 85 acres. The Swift Creek floodplain was incorporated into the project's 187-acre golf course.

The remaining uplands form the three development cores connected by Lochmere Drive, which in effect bisects the site by connecting the two dams and the site's northern part. An existing thoroughfare, Kildaire Farm Road, has been widened and improved to serve effectively as the project's entrance.

THE ROLE OF AMENITIES

Because the golf course lies in the floodplain along the site's southern edge, frontage opportunities were limited. The two lakes, however, have added a significant premium to single-family lots and multifamily building sites—as much as 80 percent, according to MacGregor. The smaller lake is surrounded by multifamily development, and its shoreline offers an important part of the public open-space system. Most of the frontage on Lake Lochmere, however, is devoted to single-family use. Access is assured, however, by lakefront park developments on a peninsula at the lake's northern end and at the base of the dam to the south. The southern park will offer a boat launching ramp (with parking below the dam) and a small, fixed-pier docking facility.

Cary's PUD ordinance requires 25 percent of the site to be devoted to open space. Of this amount, 20 percent must be designed primarily for active recreation. In Lochmere's case, the addition of exercise courses looping throughout a large por-

tion of the space helped to qualify more open space as active, counterbalancing the relatively large acreage devoted to the lakes. The feeling of low density and open space is enhanced by liberal use of planted medians and by using swales and culverts, rather than curbs and gutters, to accommodate stormwater runoff. The open space, according to the developers, has not only created value in adjacent real estate but has also helped control erosion, eased stormwater drainage problems, and filtered sediments and pollutants.

The project's extensive amenities have played a crucial role in establishing Lochmere's identity and credibility. Many of the facilities, both active and passive, were installed early in the development process, long before they would actually be used at capacity. According to the developer, this timing proved essential to capturing the intended market in a highly competitive region. Even within the project, the relatively early construction of the swim and tennis center, located on the site's eastern edge, helped assure early residents that the project was not being developed piecemeal, but rather as a unified community.

The swim and tennis center has been structured as a membership club. Project residents are not required to join the club, and membership is open to nonresidents. MacGregor expects that ultimately the members will purchase the club and convert it to a more exclusive facility.

THE LOCHMERE GOLF CLUB

The spillway and park below Lake Lochmere's dam.

In an unusual arrangement, Lochmere's golf course was developed by a business entity distinct from MacGregor and Goodson, the overall developers. A separate limited partnership, the Eaglemere Group, was formed to build, own, and operate the course early in the project planning. MacGregor contributed the land and a portion of the course development costs to the effort, and in exchange receives the privilege of marketing the course as part of Lochmere.

The course is open to the public on a daily fee basis. Annual memberships are also available. This arrangement has placed the burden of developing the course on those with particular expertise in golf course design, construction, and management. MacGregor and Lochmere's homeowners' association are also relieved of the formidable long-term costs of maintaining the course. Although the developer has yielded a certain degree of operational control under this arrangement, in Lochmere's case this is less important because of the extensive project amenities beyond golf.

Lochmere's golf course, a core course built largely in the 100-year floodplain of Swift Creek, opened for play in the fall of 1985. Eaglemere, under the direction of Roger Watson and working from the design of Vance Heafner and Gene Hamm, started construction in August 1983. In fall 1984, it planted the greens. Fairway seeding commenced the next spring, and by October the course was ready to play. According to Watson, the floodplain site, suitable for few other uses, posed no particular problems. In many cases, wet sites feature unsuitable organic soils and tricky drainage problems, but at Lochmere the developers found alluvial topsoil up to several feet thick in some areas. This unusual bounty permitted much greater flexibility and the use of less expensive construction techniques. For example, stumps could be buried rather than hauled out.

Five interconnected, spring-fed lakes serve as the primary water supply for course irrigation, boosted by one large pumping station. Unlike many of today's courses, Lochmere has a manual, single-row irrigation system, which under most circumstances means lower capital costs but relatively higher labor expenses.

According to Watson, Eaglemere expects fairly low operating costs due to the relatively simple clubhouse facilities and services, with no dining room, pool, or tennis operation. Course maintenance needs are served from a prefabricated metal structure on a two-acre tract partly leased back to MacGregor for projectwide storage needs. Planned practice facilities are extensive, with a double-teed, 300-yard driving range, indoor and outdoor teaching areas, videotaping capabilities, and so on. Although club membership is not required to play at Lochmere, members do enjoy several benefits: a members-only locker room, starting time preference, a 20 percent pro shop discount, and access to club tournaments and special events.

EVALUATING THE EXPERIENCE

One of the key reasons why the functional separation of Lochmere's golf course from the overall project has worked well lies in the nature of the project's site plan. The flood-

Building in the floodplain, according to the golf course developers, posed few problems and, in fact, may have reduced costs.

plain was virtually undevelopable, except for recreational use. At the same time, by constructing two major lakes and numerous other open spaces, the developer had created higher real estate values in land throughout the project. The golf course was still important in marketing the overall project, but the other amenities help satisfy residents' recreational demands and made boosting land values near the golf course less important.

As a result, the course is more strongly user-oriented than many facilities associated with residential developments. Among other matters, this character is reflected by the combination of a fairly modest clubhouse with extensive teaching capabilities. As a core course, with only limited residential frontage, Lochmere can be marketed as a facility where golf comes first, which should prove a distinct advantage in the Raleigh area's strong golf market.

The trade-offs for the developer are clear. While operational and management control lie mostly with Eaglemere, the golf course developer, the initial agreement between Eaglemere and MacGregor contains several provisions regarding access to memberships, maintenance standards, and so on, all designed to protect MacGregor's interest in the course. So while MacGregor may have yielded some control, it is unlikely that the golf course operators would act against their own interests by failing, for example, to adequately maintain the course.

PROJECT DATA:
LOCHMERE

LAND USE INFORMATION

Site Area: 1,039 acres
Total Dwelling Units: 2,336
Gross Density: 2.2 dwelling units per acre
Net Density: 2.45 dwelling units per acre

LAND USE PLAN

Land Use Type	Acres	Percent of Site
Detached residential	345.5	33%
Attached residential	214.7	21
Office and institutional	62.1	6
Commercial	22.7	2
Open space	329.0	32
School reservation	30.0	3
Streets	35.0	3
Total	1,039.0	100

LOCHMERE GOLF CLUB MEMBERSHIP INFORMATION

Membership Category	Number of Members	Annual Dues
Individual	200	$650
Family	100	$900 (2-member family)
		$1,200 (3-member family)

Green Fee (required for nonmembers) $9 weekends
$14 weekends/holidays

GOLF COURSE INFORMATION
Length: 6,650 yards ("championship" tees)
Par: 72
Acreage: 166
Construction Costs

Course construction	$1,050,000
Irrigation system	200,000
Clubhouse	350,000
Pathways, roads, bridges, etc.	400,000
Total	$2,000,000

Estimated Operating Costs (1986)

Maintenance	$ 220,000
Pro shop	100,000
Food and beverage	50,000
General and administrative	350,000
Total	$ 720,000

Annual Maintenance/Operating Costs per Hole: $40,000
Pro Shop Size: Approximately 9,200 sq. ft., including 3,000 sq. ft. of club storage and repair space and 3,000 sq. ft. of covered outdoor deck.

GAINEY RANCH
Scottsdale, Arizona

For moderately large or complex residential development projects, golf is sometimes used as a kind of catalyst, an organizing force for the physical plan as well as a focal point for marketing efforts. If the project revolves around land development, with land sales to builders, a golf course can become a critically important element of the "infrastructure." In such projects, the developer aims to set the stage for the community's long-term growth and development, and golf is often chosen as an appropriate centerpiece.

At Gainey Ranch, a 642-acre residential and resort community in Scottsdale, Arizona, developer Jim Kilday of Markland Properties, Inc., has taken just such a tack. A key element of Markland's strategy, worked out with land planner Robert Lamb Hart, is to "create great sites," largely by concentrating on the relationships among real estate, golf, and distant mountain views.

At Gainey Ranch, golf provides the major organizing force for the site plan.

PROJECT OVERVIEW

In addition to a series of residential neighborhoods composed of various housing types, Gainey Ranch will contain a "town center" with a 500-room resort hotel, some 120,000 square feet of retail space, and about 35 acres for office development. Setting the tone for this high-end desert project is a private golf club with 27 holes winding through the site.

Markland, a subsidiary of Toronto development company Markborough Properties Ltd. (the land development arm of the Hudson's Bay Company), has been active in the Phoenix area since the late 1970s, when the company became involved in the development of nearby Scottsdale Ranch. About a year later, the company acquired the Gainey Ranch property, a Scottsdale landmark since the early 1940s. In the intervening years, a resort corridor had grown northward from downtown and Camelback Mountain nearly to Gainey Ranch. The affluent community of Paradise Valley had sprouted to the southwest. And recreation and tourism—some $80 million of business annually—had transformed Scottsdale into one of the nation's most important desert resort areas. Gainey Ranch and Scottsdale Ranch were directly in the path of this northward march. By virtue of its size and development concept, Gainey Ranch, in Markland's view, could provide an ideal northern anchor for the maturing resort city of Scottsdale.

Courtesy Robert Lamb Hart

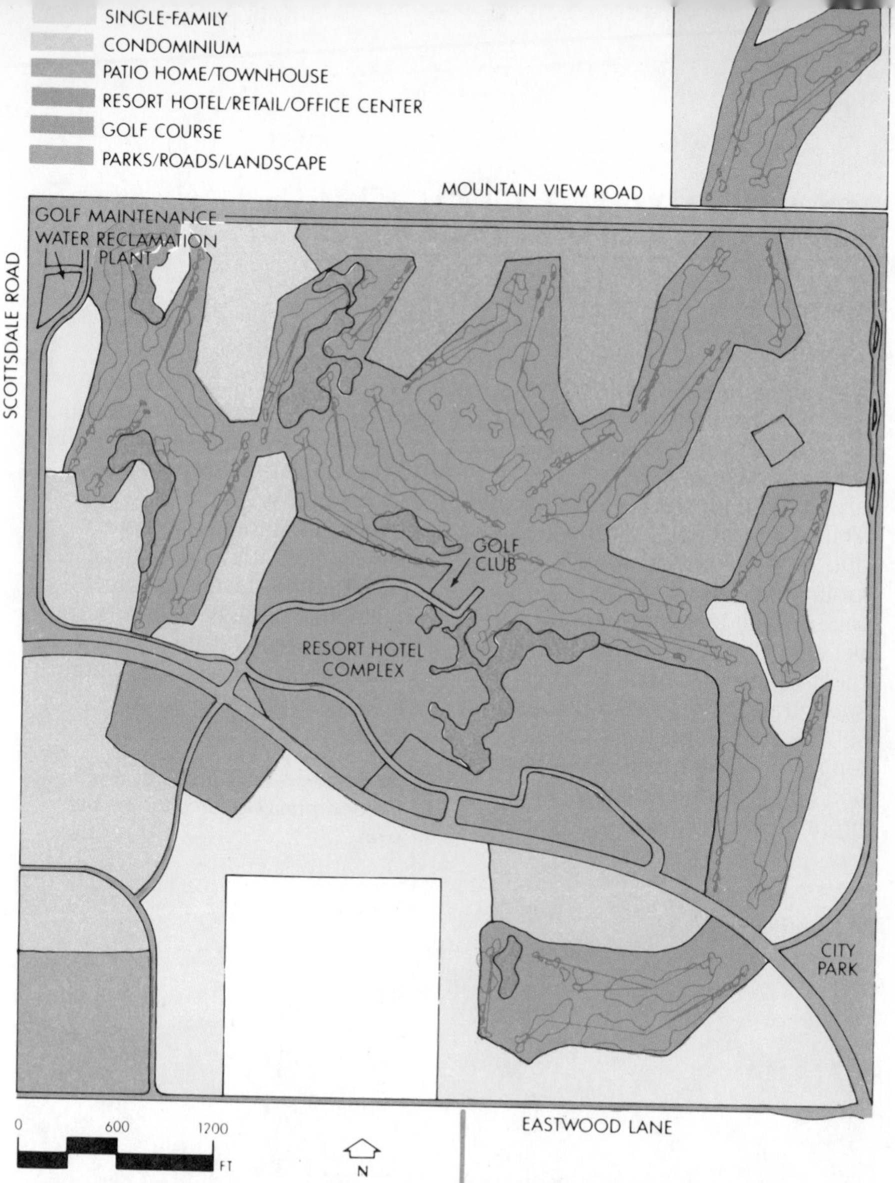

SINGLE-FAMILY
CONDOMINIUM
PATIO HOME/TOWNHOUSE
RESORT HOTEL/RETAIL/OFFICE CENTER
GOLF COURSE
PARKS/ROADS/LANDSCAPE

MOUNTAIN VIEW ROAD

GOLF MAINTENANCE
WATER RECLAMATION
PLANT

SCOTTSDALE ROAD

GOLF CLUB

RESORT HOTEL COMPLEX

CITY PARK

0   600   1200
FT

N

EASTWOOD LANE

Gainey Ranch site plan.

By early 1981, when substantial planning for the project began, Markland had conceived of a community-scale project that, in addition to residential uses, would contain a large resort/conference center and various commercial uses in the functional equivalent of a downtown—an urban-density core within walking distance of most of the project neighborhoods. The golf course would provide the single physical element that would do the most to unify the project.

By late 1985, all the land within Gainey Ranch had been sold or reserved for future development, a Hyatt hotel and luxury office complex were under construction, and the golf course and clubhouse were open. Several attached residential projects were nearing completion.

DEVELOPMENT STRATEGY AND THE ROLE OF AMENITIES

Markland recognized that a sophisticated and competitive real estate market such as Scottsdale's required an unequivocal commitment to major infrastructure and amenities up front; at Gainey Ranch, this involved front-end costs approaching $70 million. Even in Scottsdale's bullish resort market, such a commitment carried considerable risk. Accordingly, Markland aimed to create the highest possible real estate values by attempting to capitalize on Scottsdale's reputation as a resort location and by focusing on the top of the market.

Gainey Ranch has been planned to appeal to a variety of affluent markets, with about 65 percent of its residents living there year-round. Unlike many nearby neighborhoods, it will not be a community composed predominantly of second homes. Markland expects about half the buyers to hail from the Phoenix area, with the rest coming from across the nation. Significantly, the local buyers will include younger professionals and "empty nesters" as well as semiretired or retired residents. The clear intent, says Kilday, is to emphasize variety and options within this top market strata. The dominant product: user-oriented luxury condominiums at densities of 12 to 22 units per acre.

When complete, around 1995, Gainey Ranch will contain just over 2,000 housing units on about 264 acres, for a gross density in residential areas of 7.6 units per acre. The developers intend, however, to ameliorate the relatively high density—high in view of the marketing concept—by concentrating on extremely high-quality products and amenities.

The key amenity in any Scottsdale project, of course, is the desert climate and the spectacular natural setting. To Markland, the primary way to create real estate value is to combine long-range views of the area's mountains with a luxurious, understated foreground landscape, with the golf courses playing a prominent role. Golf at Gainey Ranch thus becomes both a user-oriented recreational amenity and a setting for the entire project. Land planner Robert Lamb Hart adds that the aim was to create a "continuous dominant landscape," using the surrounding landscape in conjunction with site improvements—grading, planting, water, and so on—to shape a spectacular setting for each residential and commercial structure.

Another important element of Gainey Ranch's image and development strategy is the Hyatt hotel, located on 43 centrally located acres adjacent to the golf club. Markland viewed the early construction of a first-class resort hotel and conference center as critical to the project's credibility. A series of steps taken by the developer helped both to boost land values and to secure a commitment by a hotel developer. First, Markland built a water reclamation plant, thereby demonstrating its commitment to the city of Scottsdale. Next, it completed the golf course and site improvements, establishing credibility in the local land sales market. By the time Hyatt came on board, Gainey Ranch was firmly established as one of the premier projects in the region, with high land values as a result. The hotel will become a key organizational entity, helping both to generate early revenues and to absorb the golf club's operating costs. In turn, the hotel will produce a market for retail shops and, to some extent, for real estate as well.

Besides the golf course, recreational amenities at Gainey Ranch include a tennis, swim, and croquet club at the former Gainey family ranch house, tennis and fitness facilities at the resort hotel, and smaller swimming pools and recreation areas in individual neighborhoods throughout the project. All such facilities will be operated as private membership clubs, either by Markland or by independent operators under contract. Markland is keeping its disposition options open for the golf club, with the club's eventual sale likely either to the hotel operator, who has the right of first refusal, to the club members, or to a combination of interests.

Ultimately, Gainey Ranch will contain about 2,000 housing units. Note arroyo—the natural drainage course integrated into the golf course design—in the middle ground.

Peter Lund/Rockrise

Heavy contouring around a Gainey Ranch green.

GOLF AT GAINEY RANCH

The three nine-hole courses at Gainey Ranch reflect Markland's desire to emphasize variety and flexibility. Designed with both the golfer and real estate values firmly in mind, each nine-hole segment reflects a distinctive theme and character, yet each course complements the others. Each segment's theme is also reflected in the landscape architecture of adjacent residential neighborhoods. With as many as four tees on each of its 27 holes, the course poses a number of golfing options. An 18-hole round can be as short as 5,011 yards or as long as 6,805 yards, depending on which nines are played and which tees are used. Between these extremes are several variations. Even off the same tees, the golfer can effectively choose among six different regulation courses. In addition, the operator enjoys exceptional flexibility to manage various users; hotel groups, for example, can be shunted onto one nine for a conference tournament. Maintaining a course is also possible without affecting playability.

Each nine is laid out in a predominantly double-fairway, returning-nine configuration. Holes are generally strategic. With six holes beginning and ending near the clubhouse, along with three practice ranges, this central area features a broad expanse of golf-related open space. From the clubhouse and from many of the residential sites, the view is similar to that of a core golf course.

The Lakes course, measuring 3,089 yards from the middle tees, occupies the site's northwest quarter. As its name suggests, the central feature is a series of interconnected ponds, lakes, waterfalls, and streams. The project's wastewater reclamation plant and irrigation water storage facility are located at the northwest corner; the location of most of the course's water features is based chiefly on their distance from the treatment plant.

The principal design influence on the 3,173-yard Arroyo course, which arcs through the site's southeast corner, was a series of natural drainage courses running from north to south. The reshaped arroyo, which is usually a dry streambed but occasionally runs full, is fully playable and constitutes an important strategic element for the golfer.

The Dunes course, somewhat shorter at 2,949 yards, extends to the northeast, at one point crossing a bordering road. Course architect Mike Poellot minimized turf areas on the Dunes course, emphasizing instead the low native vegetation and undulating, dunelike landforms.

The use of relatively scarce groundwater for golf course irrigation in Arizona has become increasingly problematic. At Gainey Ranch, Markland has set a new standard for large-scale development in the Phoenix area by building a $3.5 million water reclamation plant. To further stretch water resources, the developers have employed alternatives to wall-to-wall turf, including extensive use of native vegetation and a water-conserving, computer-controlled irrigation system. All the lakes are interconnected, and water is recirculated constantly to avoid stagnation. The lakes and ponds store irrigation water and serve as stormwater retention basins.

At the heart of the project sits the Gainey Ranch Golf Club, a 30,000-square-foot clubhouse composed of four major elements, each

Terraces set above practice green at the Golf Club, shown here while still under construction.

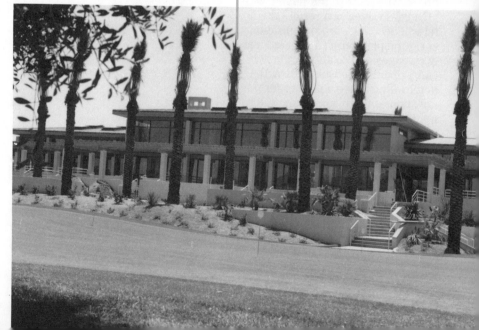

The project's landscape architects paid meticulous attention to the selection of appropriate desert vegetation.

targeted to the needs of a particular user group. Facilities for golf operations include the pro shop, equipment and cart storage and maintenance areas (located under the main building), storage areas, and a golfer's grill. The private club membership, which will probably number about 500, is served by a private locker room, bar and grill, and exercise and game rooms. An additional bar, main dining room, and meeting rooms serve social members as well. In the project's early years, the restaurant will be open to the public. Hotel guests will use a separate set of changing rooms and will have access to a bar overlooking a finishing hole.

Course maintenance facilities are headquartered in the site's northwest corner, adjacent to the reclamation plant. An interesting feature that relates to the overall project is a network of pedestrian pathways, separate from the cart paths, that link project neighborhoods with the town center via the golf course. The pathways are designed so that golfers pose little danger to pedestrians; adequate space allowances are made, and careful attention is given to the location of course hazards. In effect, the course becomes usable by all project residents.

The clubhouse layout highlights the delicate matter of managing access by two distinct user groups: project residents and resort guests. At the cost of some duplication of facilities or functional redundancy, it reflects a desire to provide each group with physically distinct facilities. In addition, Markland is using a variety of management strategies to ensure adequate access to the course. The resort hotel has access to one-third of the starting times. Further, a series of rules govern use privileges—how far in advance, for example, a tee time can be reserved by a club member or hotel guest.

EVALUATING THE EXPERIENCE

Thus far, Markland has been extremely successful in creating a suitable image for a luxury resort and residential community. Markland and the other four builders active on specific parcels are reportedly selling well. Commercial land values are approaching $20 per square foot. The project has been well received by the local community. The developers are committed to creating a high-quality environment and have demonstrated an accommodating attitude toward local values and politics.

This positioning, of course, has involved substantial costs. And while at this stage success is apparent, the project faces some considerable tests. One uncertainty is the depth of the market for extremely high-end condominiums in the Scottsdale area. Another is the precise relationship between these affluent residents and the presence of a major resort hotel, and whether or not, as the developers claim, the course can in fact meet the demand for golf the project will generate.

Nevertheless, Jim Kilday and Markland have demonstrated that, in a strong market and with a carefully considered strategy, money invested in amenities can yield substantial real estate values. At this level, the importance of a clearly articulated strategy is hard to overstate. By carefully defining the specific objectives and expected performance of the golf course, for example, subsequent design decisions fell into place more easily. The massive earthwork required to reconfigure the formerly flat site, for example, resulted in view corridors that directly enhance the value of the real estate. Similarly, a design that respects the native vegetation and desert climate has proven not only to perform better ecologically, but also to lower operating costs. Moreover, the desert image is integral to what Scottsdale, and Gainey Ranch, are all about.

PROJECT DATA:
GAINEY RANCH

LAND USE INFORMATION

Total Acreage: 642.2

Land Use Plan	Acres	Percent of Site
Resort hotel	43	6.9%
Retail	14	2.24
Office	35.5	5.7
Golf course	216.6	34.7
Parks	8	1.3
Water reclamation plant	5.3	0.8
Roads, landscape	55.6	8.9
Residential (no. of units)		
Single-family (264)	85.1	13.6
Single-family attached (98)	24.5	3.9
Patio home (316)	43.3	6.9
Townhouse (325)	36.2	5.8
Condominium (1,025)	75.1	12.0
Total	642.2	100

GOLF CLUB INFORMATION

1985 Green Fee (including cart rental): $38

	Dunes	Arroyo	Lakes
Course length (yards)	2,949	3,173	3,089
Par	36	36	36

Clubhouse size: 30,000 sq. ft.

Estimated Development and Construction Costs (1985)

Course construction	$5.5 million
Irrigation system	1.5 million
Clubhouse	3.0 million
Total	$10.0 million

Estimated Annual Maintenance Cost: $1.25 million
Cost per hole: $46,296

Source: Markland Properties, Inc., and Robert Lamb Hart.

PROJECT CREDITS

Developer/Manager:
Markland Properties, Inc.
Phoenix, Arizona

Planner/Architect/Landscape Architect:
Robert Lamb Hart Planners and
   Architects, Ltd.
New York, New York

Golf Course Architect:
Benz and Poellot
Saratoga, California

Engineer:
Greeley and Hansen Engineers
Phoenix, Arizona

OCEAN EDGE RESORT
Brewster, Massachusetts

In times of economic uncertainty, traditional approaches to amenity-oriented development may involve considerable burdens for a developer. Building amenities up front to establish a marketable image and then selling land or buildings to pay for the facilities has worked well in many cases. This traditional approach, however, becomes more difficult with higher real interest rates that can pose formidable carrying costs. And in uncertain or price-sensitive real estate markets, the risks of such upfront commitments may be unacceptable.

On Cape Cod, Massachusetts, one of the United States' most popular resort areas, the Boston-area development firm of Corcoran, Mullins, and Jennison, Inc., has taken an unconventional approach to minimize the upfront burden and risk associated with recreational amenities. Its project, the 360-acre Ocean Edge Resort, will ultimately consist of 950 detached condominium units situated around an 18-hole golf course, 85 additional bayside condominiums, and numerous other recreational facilities. The Ocean Edge conference center and 90-room hotel occupies a renovated 19th-century mansion and carriage house. A second hotel is also planned.

Located in Brewster on Cape Cod Bay about midway out on the Cape, the site was formerly occupied by an unirrigated, nine-hole golf course. Until early 1984, when Corcoran, Mullins, and Jennison (CMJ) began the project, most real estate activity on the Cape was concentrated on Nantucket Sound. Only a few months later, CMJ started marketing the new units at Ocean Edge, about a year in advance of the start of golf course construction—and more than two years before the course would open.

Hutchins Photography

A conversion and expansion of an older nine-hole course, the Ocean Edge layout has a remarkably mature look for a new golf course.

Throughout the development of Ocean Edge, CMJ has sold units in advance of construction and has never experienced standing inventory of unsold units. The primary market has been Boston-area second-home buyers 35 to 45 years old. Designed as resort units with a single-family, detached feel, the condominiums have sold well to investment-minded buyers. A rental pool has enjoyed strong participation by early buyers, even in the face of the tax reform debate that raged nationally in 1985 and 1986.

The golf course was completed in August 1985 and opened for play the following spring. (Cape Cod has one of the fastest grow-in periods in the nation.) By mid-1986, the developers had sold about 700 units—a pace 75 percent ahead of their projections—and planned to sell out the project in 1987. Strong sales have effectively shortened the period to buildout by two years. Recreational amenities have generally been built in stages corresponding to the pace of real estate sales. By mid-1986, the golf course and two swimming complexes were open. A major golf clubhouse is scheduled to open in spring 1987.

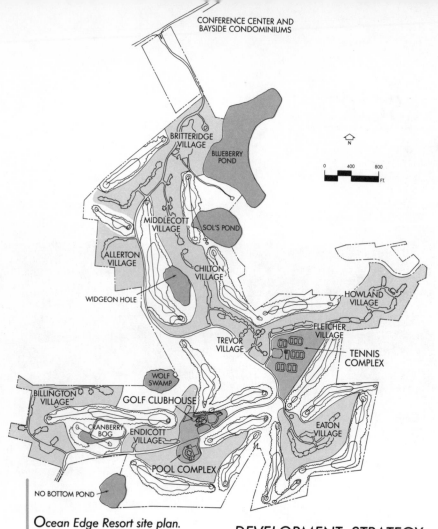

Ocean Edge Resort site plan.

Labels on map: CONFERENCE CENTER AND BAYSIDE CONDOMINIUMS; BRITTERIDGE VILLAGE; BLUEBERRY POND; MIDDLECOTT VILLAGE; SOL'S POND; ALLERTON VILLAGE; CHILTON VILLAGE; WIDGEON HOLE; HOWLAND VILLAGE; FLETCHER VILLAGE; TREVOR VILLAGE; TENNIS COMPLEX; WOLF SWAMP; BILLINGTON VILLAGE; GOLF CLUBHOUSE; CRANBERRY BOG; ENDICOTT VILLAGE; EATON VILLAGE; POOL COMPLEX; NO BOTTOM POND; N

DEVELOPMENT STRATEGY

The most important aspect of CMJ's strategy at Ocean Edge is that the real estate's success has never depended on the presence of the recreational facilities. Ocean Edge is the firm's first foray into recreational real estate. It has approached the project from a background in multifamily rental housing development in greater Boston.

Based on careful market research, the developers determined that substantial demand existed in 1984 for a Cape Cod housing product that looked like a cottage, was owned (or rented) and maintained like a condominium, and sold for

less than $80,000. At that price, the condos could compete with similar projects without extensive recreational amenities. They also knew that, to support the planned conference center and to provide a longer-term draw for a project located away from the beach, they would need to renovate the existing nine-hole course to regulation standards. They recognized, though, that the success of the initial phases should not be contingent on completing the golf course renovation early. Instead, CMJ decided to use the revenues generated from quick early sales of the carefully priced products to pay for the course reconstruction. CMJ determined that it would need to sell about 400 units to break even on the amenity capital expenditures. It reasoned that once the golf course was in, at little upfront risk, the course would help to generate demand for real estate and conferences in the project's later phases.

Further, the golf course, the conference center, and, eventually, the hotel are all structured not as image-enhancers, intended to draw real estate prospects, but rather as facilities that will provide long-term operating income. For the foreseeable future, the golf course will operate as a daily fee course, open to the public.

GOLF AT OCEAN EDGE

The fact that a nine-hole course existed on the site meant little for the overall layout and development of the new course, except that much of the land was already cleared. Very few greens were reused. Those that were required extensive renovation. Most important, the older course was not irrigated. A major expense, therefore, was the drilling of two new wells to supply irrigation water, accounting for nearly 20 percent of the total costs to build the new course and clubhouse.

Otherwise, the site held superb potential for golf, with rolling hills, varied vegetation, easily worked sandy soils, and even an old cranberry bog which, now restored, provides a scenic backdrop for the course's signature 17th hole.

Course architect Brian Silva has created a 130-acre, mostly single-fairway course with returning nines. From the back tees, the par 72 course plays at 6,600 yards. Each hole offers from two to five tees, so the course can be played much shorter and in various configurations. The level of difficulty can be moderated largely through pin position on the greens. The greens, which like all playing surfaces on the Ocean Edge course are of bentgrass, average 5,000 square feet. Tees range in size from 4,000 to 6,000 square feet. The two new wells provide 800 gallons per minute of water to the fully automatic, computer-controlled irrigation system. Cart paths are limited to the area between tees and greens and other high traffic spots.

Silva notes that the Ocean Edge course differs from many Cape Cod courses by virtue of its association with real estate. Features—tees, greens, and hazards—are more dramatic, for example, to provide resort guests with a more memorable round of play and to help catch the eye of real estate prospects. Remnants of the old course, with overgrown sandy rough and eroded mounds covered in wild grasses, contribute considerable character to the new layout.

To help speed up play, and to provide a visually pleasing fairway edge, Silva designed a gradual transition from the closely cut bentgrass to bluegrass and fescue, feathering finally into a pine needle rough before meeting thick forest undergrowth. This edge stratification both defines the fairway as viewed from the tee and helps golfers locate an errant ball. To help control costs, the total amount of clearing and fairway acreage has been minimized. Silva estimates that on a typical course today he will specify 25 percent less clearing and grass coverage than standard practice would have dictated 10 years ago.

Hutchins Photography

Moderately priced townhouse units have proved popular with second-home buyers.

TENNIS FACILITIES

The Ocean Edge tennis complex, planned for a site lying about 600 yards from the central clubhouse, will offer 12 to 14 courts, three of which will be built with a synthetic clay surface. The rest will be nonporous courts. Currently, the developers are planning to light two to three courts and are examining the feasibility of enclosing the same number in a bubble during the winter months. The main clubhouse's 125-seat restaurant will serve tennis members. Initially, the tennis pro shop will be combined with the golf operation under the supervision of the golf pro. Tennis professionals, however, will be available for lessons and will organize and host club tournaments. The developers expect that conference attendees will provide a key source of revenue in the shoulder seasons.

RESULTS

CMJ's basically conservative amenity strategy at Ocean Edge, as viewed with the project more than half complete and proceeding rapidly toward buildout, appears quite successful. In the fall of 1985, with 350 units sold and the golf course just completed but not yet open, the developers needed only about 50 more sales to amortize the capital costs of the course's construction. Their prospects were good: at the time, they had waiting lists of 200 names for new units.

After having reached the point where the amenities were effectively paid for, CMJ changed tacks, responding to rapidly rising property values and the strong demand for Cape real estate. With the success of the project no longer in question, the average price for the standard Ocean Edge condominium jumped from about $76,000 to $115,000. As CMJ vice president Susan Capparell explains, "With the amenities in place and paid for, we could afford a more aggressive aproach to pricing, with prices closer to the overall market and, for us, providing a healthier margin."

Other components of the project are nearly as successful. According to Capparell, the executive conference center in the renovated mansion has enjoyed occupancy levels of 65 percent—quite high, she adds, for the region. The expanded golf course has also been well accepted and is slated to host the New England PGA tournament in 1986, the first time the tournament has been held on a new course.

What accounts for Ocean Edge's success? The bulk of the credit must go to a carefully defined strategy based on straightforward analysis of supply and demand. The developers clearly tapped an unmet need in the market by creating a relatively affordable, flexible, and attractive housing unit. They also refused to take the benefits of recreational amenities for granted. Instead, CMJ viewed the facilities in strict economic terms, linking its amenity expenditures to the projected demand for the facilities by homeowners and resort guests.

Also important, however, were the region's larger economic conditions. In 1985, the Boston metropolitan area enjoyed one of the nation's lowest unemployment rates. This robust economy produced a regional jump in housing prices and land values, belying the nation's low overall inflation at the time. These high values in primary residences, speculate some analysts, led to a wave of refinancing of primary homes to raise capital for second-home purchases. Traditionally, the two strong second-home markets for the Boston area are southern New Hampshire and Cape Cod. As a result of these conditions, these two regional markets remained healthy, even while second-home developers elsewhere saw sales slide in 1985. And well-positioned projects, like Ocean Edge, thrived.

PROJECT DATA:
OCEAN EDGE RESORT

LAND USE INFORMATION

Total Acreage: 360
Number of Housing Units
Golf course condominiums: 950
Bayside condominiums: 85
Gross Density: 2.9 dwelling units per acre

GOLF COURSE INFORMATION

Development and Construction Costs

Construction and irrigation system	$618,000
Wells	417,000
Clubhouse	1,100,000
Cart paths, roadway, bridges	95,000
Total	$2,230,000

Operating Costs (estimated)

Maintenance	$300,000
Pro shop	30,000
Management and administration	50,000
Total	$380,000

Annual Maintenance Costs per Hole	$ 16,666
Green Fee (1986)	$25

Source: Corcoran, Mullins, Jennison, Inc.

PROJECT CREDITS:

Developer:
Corcoran, Mullins, and Jennison, Inc.
Quincy, Massachusetts

Architect/Land Planner:
Sasaki Associates
Watertown, Massachusetts

Landscape Architects:
Frank Todd & Associates
Rowley, Massachusetts

Matarazzo Design
Concord, New Hampshire

Golf Course Architect:
Cornish and Silva
Amherst, Massachusetts

HARBOUR RIDGE
Stuart, Florida

One of the most difficult questions in amenity-oriented development is: How can front-end expenditures for amenities be timed to create the most marketing impact and land value, yet still allow the developer the flexibility to withstand a shifting market or a fluctuating national economy? An additional wrinkle is that early buyers need assurances that the developer will deliver on their expectations of quality.

At Harbour Ridge, an 882-acre planned community in southeast Florida's St. Lucie County, developer John B. Dodge has responded with a two-stage amenity package. In the project's first few years, a small but well-appointed service-oriented facility is intended to establish Harbour Ridge's identity and to help foster a sense of community among early residents. As the project matures, Dodge will build a large, full-service club to support an extensive group of recreational amenities. Interestingly, the new facility will not be merely an extension or enlargement of the initial club. Rather, the two clubs will be located nearly at opposite ends of the site and will cater to different but sightly overlapping user groups.

At buildout, Harbour Ridge is expected to contain 814 detached homes, villas, and garden apartments set among two golf courses, two miles of riverfront, and some 185 acres of preserved natural vegetation, including about 140 acres of wetlands. Other major amenities will include a 10-court tennis and swim complex on eight acres and 152 boat slips in three riverfront clusters. The community's focus will eventually be a 37,000-square-foot clubhouse, expected to open in 1988 at the end of the first development phase.

Leon Corry

Garden apartments, built early in the development process and frequently used for short-term resort rentals, look out over the Golden Marsh course.

After two years of planning, site development began in early 1983. The first golf course and the tennis and swim club were opened, along with limited resort operations, in December 1984. By July 1985, seven of the expected 27 project neighborhoods were complete or under construction.

Harbour Ridge has been planned in two phases. Roughly 40 percent of the housing units will be built in the first phase, lasting until 1987. At buildout, expected in 1991, the project will contain about 60 percent garden apartments, 35 percent villas, and about 5 percent single-family lots.

DEVELOPMENT STRATEGY

John B. Dodge brought a portfolio of recreational development experience to the Harbour Ridge project. His earlier South Florida projects, Delray Dunes and Quail Ridge in Palm Beach County and Piper's Landing, near Stuart, also included golf and tennis facilities. At Harbour Ridge, the strategy aims to tap the growing retiree and semiretiree markets, and to capture some of the primary housing market as well, by developing a multiple-amenity waterfront community in a secluded but readily accessible area.

239

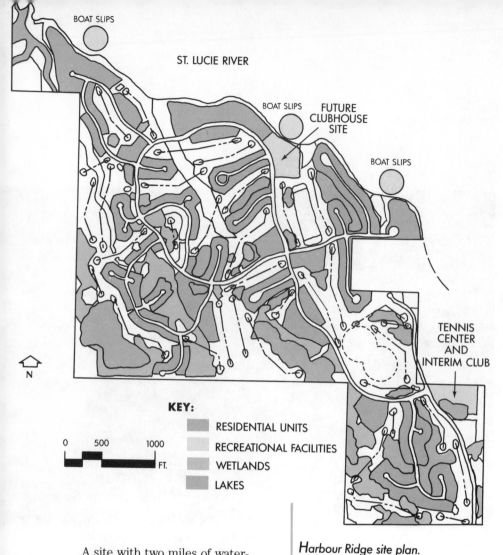

ST. LUCIE RIVER

BOAT SLIPS

BOAT SLIPS

FUTURE
CLUBHOUSE
SITE

BOAT SLIPS

TENNIS
CENTER
AND
INTERIM CLUB

N

KEY:

RESIDENTIAL UNITS
RECREATIONAL FACILITIES
WETLANDS
LAKES

0   500   1000
FT.

Harbour Ridge site plan.

A site with two miles of waterfront and enough acreage for 36 holes of golf is a rare find today in South Florida, especially if the targeted market is not the highest of the high end. But by purchasing the site during the 1981 recession, Dodge was able to keep land costs relatively low and thus to make feasible a gross density of less than one unit per acre.

Although Stuart, a town of about 12,000, lies outside the booming development areas in Palm Beach and Broward counties, the region has experienced a fair amount of growth. The planned completion of Interstate 95 through Martin County north to Ft. Pierce in early 1988 will help extend the boom markets northward and further spur development.

The project is primarily oriented to second-home buyers, who should comprise about 75 percent of Harbour Ridge residents. Of all buyers, 35 percent are expected to relocate from within the state. The remainder will likely hail from the Midwest and Northeast. Seasonal residents will be joined by a combination of retired and semiretired people, "empty nesters," and other families who will use Harbour Ridge as their primary residence. For the first few years of operation, a rental program will be used to both lure investment-minded buyers and to attract resort guests, who may eventually purchase real estate. The 40 Palmetto Village garden apartment units, which owners may place in the rental program, are sold fully furnished.

As in most planned developments in Florida, the recreational amenities will play a fundamental role in defining the project's image. Harbour Ridge's size and projected population dictated two golf courses as the recreational focus and major site features. Dodge saw tennis as a natural and cost-effective adjunct to golf, and the riverfront site in a strong boating market invited some sort of marina or yacht club. This mix, combined with the site's sense of seclusion and natural beauty, would provide the hook upon which Harbour Ridge could hang its competitive hat.

A CHALLENGING SITE

Harbour Ridge lies near the southern edge of unincorporated St. Lucie County on the north fork of the St. Lucie River, just outside the city of Stuart. The nearby Florida Turnpike (and the not-yet-completed Interstate 95 through Martin County to the south) provides access to Palm Beach and its International Airport, about 50 minutes away. Ft. Pierce lies 15 miles to the north. The site's two miles of riverfront are about 10 miles by boat from the Atlantic via the St. Lucie, which crosses the Indian River and the Intracoastal Waterway at the St. Lucie inlet.

At first glance, the site seems quite typical of coastal Florida: pine flatwoods and sand pine scrub, dotted with hardwoods and wetlands. A closer look reveals a number of unusual features. The first, a relatively high ridge (up to 14 feet) that runs along the river, affords fine views of the water and has inspired the project's name. The second distinction, discovered shortly after the purchase of the site in 1981, is an active Southern Bald Eagle nest near the property's eastern edge. The eagles, in a nice bit of timing, hatched a fledgling in the spring of 1985, and the avian family has figured prominently in the project's marketing efforts.

Besides the riverfront, which will play a major role in the remaining phases of Harbour Ridge, the site's overall character derives largely from the 213 acres of wetlands (141 acres of natural wetlands and 72 acres of engineered lakes) and the wildlife and vegetation that they support. The site features three distinct types of wetlands, each with varying hydrological and ecological functions and characteristics. Saltwater and freshwater swamps line the riverfront and extend into the site in several areas known as bayheads and sloughs. Freshwater marshes are located throughout the site as isolated wet prairies and bordering 17.7-acre Mile Lake.

THE AMENITY PLAN

Dodge, building on his previous experience with amenities and clubs, structured the Harbour Ridge package in the early stages of the project as an equity club. Homebuyers are required to purchase an equity interest in the Harbour Ridge Country Club, a nonprofit entity established to operate and maintain the golf courses, tennis center, clubhouses, and docking facilities.

Prospective buyers are required to apply for club membership. At the time of purchase, successful applicants must also buy an equity certificate for either a full membership, which includes golf, or for a more limited social/tennis membership. In addition, they may purchase a boat slip certificate.

When units are resold, the membership may be sold at an appreciated price, but the seller may retain only the original face value. The "profit" is returned to a capital improvement fund, which can only be used to maintain or improve the club facilities. Equity certificates, all of which represent family memberships, range in price from $2,500 for a social and tennis membership to $12,000 for a golf club certificate. Boat slip equity certificates are $12,500. Members must also pay an initiation fee and annual dues. Golf

Surface water management strategies have played a major role in the development of Harbour Ridge.

memberships will be limited to 700, or 350 members per course. Boat slip certificates, of course, will be limited to the number of slips, 152. The boat slip certificate represents the right to dockage, not a fee interest, unlike the golf and the social/tennis certificates. The remaining memberships, if any, will be limited to social/tennis members.

During the project's early years, some revenue-producing nonresident memberships will be available. As units are delivered, these outside members will be replaced by resident equity members. As the project nears completion, the developer must transfer unencumbered all the club facilities and the capital improvement fund to the 814 members. In such an equity structure, this transfer should be relatively smooth, since members will have known the terms of the arrangement all along.

In a project the size of Harbour Ridge, the key issue facing Dodge was how to create a marketable amenity package within an equity club structure without committing himself to massive upfront expenditures. The solution was to carefully design the first golf course and the swim and tennis center so that they could operate as an interim club, serving owners, resort guests, and day visitors. As the first phase is completed, the second golf course and the major club facility will be built, shifting the activity focus to a more central location and a more complete facility.

In the early going, the developers rearranged the sequence of holes on the Golden Marsh course so that golfers would begin and end a round near the interim clubhouse.

GOLF: THE MAJOR SELLING POINT

The Golden Marsh course at Harbour Ridge—so named for the St. John's Wort and other yellow-flowering native vegetation found around Mile Lake—is the first of the two golf courses. The par 72 course measures 6,785 yards from the back tees and occupies about 120 acres, including rough areas. The fairways are laid out continuously, with parallel fairways occurring only in three places. This relatively spacious layout takes great advantage of the site's natural features. Water comes into play on 16 holes.

Golf course architect Joe Lee's familiar sculptured bunkers are less apparent at Harbour Ridge. Lee has noted that the site's unusually rolling terrain enabled bunkers to be carved from existing dunes. Elsewhere, elevated tees and spacious, rolling greens maximize views across lakes, ponds, and marshes. Holes are generally strategic, with numerous mid-fairway bunkers. On the water holes, a player who successfully attempts a more heroic shot will generally be rewarded.

Because the swim and tennis club will serve in the project's first few years as the golf clubhouse, the present hole sequence is temporary. Since the first tee had to be located within a reasonable distance from the smaller club, an imbalance exists between par for the out-nine (38) and par for the in-nine (34). What is now the first hole will eventually be number 12 when the main clubhouse and the second course are finished. At that point the course will have the customary balance of par.

Surface water quality constituted a primary concern for both Dodge and the local planning agency. As a result, a variety of measures have been designed to mitigate the impact of the golf course on water quality. Under Florida law, Harbour Ridge was classified as a Development of Regional Impact. As such, the project approval process was relatively rigorous. Under the terms of the county-granted development approval, the developer had to preserve a buffer zone of upland vegetation around all lakes and wetland habitats. This "ecotone" had to include a minimum of 10 square feet per lineal foot of wetland perimeter and be planned so that at least 50 percent of all wetlands or lake perimeter had at least a 10-foot-wide buffer of native vegetation. Those areas not protected by vegetation were required to be bermed to prevent direct runoff of storm and irrigation water, which could carry fertilizers and herbicides.

The project's irrigation system can use water from up to three potential sources. The principal current supply is from the South Florida Water Management District's C-23 canal, located south of the project. The canal runs directly into the St. Lucie River, and the water now reclaimed was previously wasted to tide. The canal supply is supplemented by treated effluent from an on-site wastewater treatment plant, although this source can only provide up to 15 percent of the project's irrigation needs. The third source, anticipated for use only as a backup supply, is from on-site shallow aquifer wells that will also meet the project's potable water needs.

Although the evidence is not yet conclusive, the designers believe that the course design itself, with large areas of native vegetation, marshes, and lakes, will create a substantially lower demand for irrigation and other maintenance.

The site's vast wetlands required numerous special mitigation techniques.

Leon Corry

Both courses will eventually be served by the current 10-acre practice range, located adjacent to the main clubhouse site. The range has tees at both ends and two pitch and chip practice greens. A large practice putting surface will eventually connect the range to the main clubhouse.

The 37,000-square-foot main clubhouse, slated for completion in 1988, will sit on an 8.5-acre riverfront site in the northeastern portion of Harbour Ridge. The $3.5 million facility will serve as the community's recreational and social focus. Both golf courses will start and end from the club. The Pete Dye–designed St. Lucie course, to be completed by December 1988, will be laid out in two returning nines, thereby speeding up play and offering additional flexibility to members who wish to play only nine holes.

The clubhouse's 19,000-square-foot upper level will contain dining and kitchen facilities, an indoor and outdoor lounge, meeting rooms, and office space. In addition to the standard complement of locker rooms and card rooms, the lower level will feature exercise rooms, a ship's store and dock master, and a pro shop. Also on the lower level but in separate building connected by a breezeway will be the golf car and bag storage area and the golf car staging area.

THE TENNIS AND SWIM CENTER

The club complex at Harbour Ridge currently includes four tennis courts, a 1,400-square-foot pool, a locker room and pro shop building, and a small but elegant dining room and lounge. The complex lies across from the project's main entrance, along the site's eastern perimeter. One key benefit of this location is that nonresident club members can get to the club without having to pass through the main security gate.

The tennis and swim center.

Initially, the main entrance road was to hug the site's eastern boundary. In response to the concerns of neighboring residents, however, Dodge adjusted the road location inward. The remaining parcel near the boundary was well suited for the interim club, which the neighbors were then invited to join.

Since this club is critical to the project's early image, its design was carefully considered. One major requirement was that the club remain residential in scale, because of its close relationship to the nearby neighborhood. The tennis courts are thus separated into two clusters, and the complex is divided into two smaller buildings connected by an elevated wooden walkway.

These structures are complemented by a small lake that includes two islands planted entirely with native vegetation. To the north and east, 50- and 150-foot buffer zones with heavy forest cover and dense undergrowth help reduce the complex's impact on the neighboring properties. In the early stages of development, Dodge agreed not to light the courts located adjacent to an existing residential area.

Fast-Dry, the synthetic clay surface used at Harbour Ridge, was suggested by the tennis management firm retained by the developer. It was chosen for its appeal to a wide range of players, and out of consideration of the likely age of the majority of club members. Most clubs in the area have similar surfaces, and the tennis pro, also supplied by the management firm, intends to develop league programs that will compete with these other clubs.

THE MARINA

The marina planned at Harbour Ridge illustrates the degree of compromise necessary to satisfy current regulatory requirements and yet maintain a fairly substantial boating amenity. Harbour Ridge will offer 152 slips in three docking pods along the St. Lucie. The river measures about a mile wide at the site's location, providing excellent small boat sailing and fishing. Under power, the St. Lucie inlet to the Atlantic is about an hour away. Boaters also have access to the Gulf of Mexico through the Okeechobee Waterway.

The marina site along the St. Lucie River.

The decentralized layout of slips in three pods of 40 to 50 slips each is not only in tune with regulatory requirements but will also be convenient for club members, who are likely to reside throughout the project. Each pod will be composed of fixed piers on PVC-encased concrete piles with a main walkway ending in a tee. Finger walkways will permit access to each slip. The three pods will collectively cover about 115,000 square feet. This simple and economical design is possible because of the low tidal fluctuation, the mild climate, and the simple dockside services planned at Harbour Ridge. Outer slips will accommodate boats with up to a six-foot draft. Dockside services will include electric, telephone, and cable television hookups.

The Harbour Ridge riverfront, while providing superb access for residents, includes a number of characteristics that constrain marina development. The north fork of the St. Lucie at Harbour Ridge's location is designated by the state as an Outstanding Water/Aquatic Preserve, which precludes dredging and imposes other conditions for development. The configuration and location of any marina at the site are thus restricted by the existing bottom profile.

Other mitigation measures are also required under the terms of the permit issued by the Florida Department of Environmental Regulation. First, the permit specifies a schedule for completion of the first two pods and requires that the first be fully occupied before the second is opened. Dock master's logs must be submitted quarterly to monitor slip occupancy patterns. Before Dodge can build the third pod, at least two full years of water-quality monitoring data must be made available to the agency. Further development permission remains, of course, contingent on adequate water-quality performance. The state requires monitoring quarterly for water quality and annually for sediment.

The physical facilities are also limited under the terms of the permit. No transient slip rentals or fueling facilities are allowed. Pump-out stations are required at each docking pod, and floating, absorbent, oil-and-grease containment booms must be installed around the perimeter of each facility. Wave arrestors of hollow PVC pipe will extend from the pier stringers to about two feet above the river bottom.

Another condition of the permit is that the developer must produce a detailed shoreline stabilization and revegetation plan for the 75-foot-wide riverfront preservation zone. This plan should include removing exotic species of trees and using native, salt-resistant vegetation to check erosion along the shore. If such measures fail to fully control the erosion that might result from increased boat traffic, the developer will turn to structural solutions such as revetments.

OTHER AMENITIES

Each villa and garden apartment grouping at Harbour Ridge will include a small neighborhood pool, with a barbecue grill, sink, and cabinets. Mailbox clusters will also be located here. Apartment projects will have bicycle storage shelters.

In the 75-foot riverfront preservation zone, the developer has begun building a nature trial and boardwalk. This trail will connect with a network of bicycle and golf car trails that will run throughout the project. Private golf cars will be permitted and encouraged as an alternative to automobile use.

A variety of small boats—Sunfish and Hobie Cats on the river and electric-powered prams or rowboats on Mile Lake—will be available for hourly rental. According to the developer, prior experience has shown that the market expects these amenities and will look for such small touches as an indicator of the entire project's quality.

Other notable additions, new to the developer, are an exercise trail or parcourse and Nautilus-equipped exercise rooms planned for the main clubhouse. Dodge notes that these amenities are in direct response to the national interest in health and physical fitness.

EVALUATING THE EXPERIENCE

Harbour Ridge demonstrates an intriguing solution to the dilemma of amenity phasing and timing. Building the kind of club facility that is ultimately planned for this sizable project upfront would have placed an excessive burden on the developer. But by creating early in the timetable a facility capable of serving as an interim club, the developer has been able to meet the market's amenity expectations while permitting himself considerable flexibility later on. During the first year of operation, the swim/tennis/golf club was extremely well received by real estate buyers, resort guests, and outside members. Two factors deserve mention.

First, the complex, although relatively modest, was carefully designed to project the kind of ambience and quality the targeted market expects. Architectural design, interior details, and landscaping received close attention. Second, a more modest physical facility than might be found elsewhere has been balanced by high levels of services and programs for the club members. It was important to the developer to create a social focus for the new community, and the most likely vehicle was the club. Management issues are thus critical, even with a smaller membership in the project's early years. To this end, Dodge has been pleased with the kind of professional amenity management provided by the tennis management firm. The wide variety of activities and programs available at Harbour Ridge has also attracted many outside members, who are helping to produce needed revenues early on.

One of the problematic aspects of an interim club is that golf car storage and operations can quickly overwhelm the smaller facility. At Harbour Ridge, the developer therefore paved a portion of a future tennis court, located close enough to the starting area but far enough away from the club to be unobtrusive. Electric cars, typically used in this region, would have required an expensive installation to keep the 30 to 40 cars charged. The members thus drive gasoline-powered golf cars that Dodge leases from a local firm. The main clubhouse, when built, will house a fleet of club-owned electric cars.

At Harbour Ridge, the developer considered postponing the extensive golf practice range until he built the second course and the clubhouse, since the range site lies fairly distant from the interim club. Surprisingly, however, it has received considerable use and is considered by the members a valuable feature, regardless of its location.

The marina proposals at Harbour Ridge illustrate the regulatory constraints that developers can expect in many areas of the nation. In this case, the permitting process has required many modifications and concessions from the developer. Doubtless in some instances the agencies have also compromised. Nevertheless, the market profile of the South Florida boat owner remains a powerful incentive for the developer to create such a facility if at all possible. In this case, the developer has consciously taken a cooperative, even conciliatory, posture in hopes of obtaining approval.

PROJECT DATA:
HARBOUR RIDGE

ECONOMIC INFORMATION

Land Acquisition	$7.5 million
Infrastructure[1]	$1.8 million
Construction Costs[2]	$53 to $68 per square foot
Land Planning	$2.5 million
Marketing and Sales	$2.5 million
General Administration and Overhead	$3.2 million
Golf Course	
Construction[3]	$1.2 million
Irrigation system	$351,000
Clubhouse (projected)	$3.5 million
Annual operating costs	
Maintenance	$405,000 ($22,500 per hole)
Pro shop	$156,000
Administration	$197,000
Tennis Club	
Construction (4 courts)	$63,000
Clubhouse	$940,000
Annual operating costs[4]	
Maintenance	$12,000
Pro shop	$12,000
Food and beverage	$110,000

[1]Includes water and sewage treatment plant.
[2]Includes landscaping and irrigation, neighborhood amenities (pools, bicycle shelters, etc.), and architecture and engineering.
[3]Includes clearing and grading, greens and tees, roads, pathways, and bridges.
[4]Tennis club administrative costs included under "Golf Course, Administration."

HARBOUR RIDGE COUNTRY CLUB MEMBERSHIP INFORMATION (1985)

Membership Type	Resident Members[1]	Nonresident Members	Members Projected at Buildout	Equity Certificate Cost	Initiation Fee	84–85 Annual Dues
Golf	83	21[2]	700	$12,000	$3,000	$1,600
Tennis/Social	2	103	up to 114	$ 2,500	$ 500	$ 400
Boat Slip[3]	—	—	152	$12,500	—	—
Total	85	124	814	$27,000	$3,500	$2,000

[1]"Resident member" indicates equity participation.
[2]Includes 15 general or limited partners in Harbour Ridge, each of whom also retains an equity interest in the club. Fifty-nine nonresident summer golf memberships are not included in the table.
[3]Boat slip certificate may be purchased in addition to a golf membership or tennis/social membership. Boat slip members are not included in the total equity membership figure of 814.

PROJECT CREDITS

Developer:
John B. Dodge
Harbour Ridge Ltd.
Stuart, Florida

Planner/Landscape Architect:
Edward D. Stone, Jr. & Associates
Fort Lauderdale, Florida

Golf Course Architect:
Joseph L. Lee
Boynton Beach, Florida

SPINNAKER ISLAND AND YACHT CLUB
Hull, Massachusetts

Many marinas designed as part of real estate ventures are not truly marinas in the strict sense. According to the National Marine Manufacturers Association, the term is usually reserved for those facilities that offer boaters a comprehensive range of services and facilities, from restaurants to rigging repairs. For a real estate developer, a marina can provide an important link in an overall project concept aimed at marketing a certain lifestyle. Even for nonboaters, the sight of yachts in the water adds an undeniable distinction to a project. Less distinctive and desirable for many, however, are the fumes, noise, and equipment needed to fully service resident boats. As a result, these more industrial aspects of marinas, while essential for boaters, are often not included in marinas built as real estate amenities. Such a limited-service marina, however, usually depends on nearby full-service facilities to be truly attractive to a serious boating market.

At Spinnaker Island and Yacht Club, along the Massachusetts coast, a simple, attractive marina offers an example of such an amenity—an essential part of its overall project, yet clearly dependent on the local marine infrastructure to fully serve its market. Also notable are the Spinnaker marina's engineering, with a floating breakwater, and its marketing concept, with slips sold as "condominiums."

Spinnaker Island and Yacht Club is a 102-unit attached residential development on an 8.5-acre island near the coastal town of Hull. One of the Boston Harbor Islands, the site was formerly used for military purposes. Spinnaker Island now contains townhouses, a five-story building with condominium units and structured parking, a 102-slip marina, and other recreational facilities. In the process of imaginatively recycling surplus federal property, Spinnaker Island has provided a key boost to the credibility of the real estate market in Hull, a faded but reviving resort town about 22 miles south of Boston.

By early 1986, local developers Paul and Francine Townsend of Sandcastle Associates, Inc., had completed two of the project's four phases, initially planned for a five-year buildout. Forty-nine units were occupied in early 1986. Based on booming area property values and the project's strong market acceptance—the 22-unit first phase pre-sold within 11 days—the Townsends now predict an April 1987 completion. The 102 total units will include 77 townhouses ranging in size from 900 to 1,620 square feet and 25 mid-rise condominiums of 1,050 to 1,520 square feet. Thus far, about half the buyers have treated their purchases as second homes.

In addition to the 102-slip marina, the project also offers a waterfront swimming pool and cabana, a health club, and a natural barrier beach. The island is connected to the mainland of Hull, which arcs northward into Boston Harbor, by a 300-yard-long causeway built in the 1940s.

The view across Hull Bay from above the Spinnaker Island Yacht Club.

Spinnaker, née Hog, Island.

DEVELOPMENT STRATEGY

Sandcastle Associates' project prior to Spinnaker Island had been the conversion of a beachfront Hull guesthouse to condominiums. Based on this experience, however, they were convinced of a nascent area market for luxury vacation housing. And as longtime Hull residents, the Townsends believed that a highly visible residential project was required before the town's property values could begin to catch up with the rest of the Boston metropolitan area.

Sandcastle based its development strategy principally on the features of the site itself. The real estate products, intended to attract both primary- and second-home markets, were designed to take maximum advantage of the island setting, capitalizing both on its sense of isolation and on its convenience to Boston and other nearby attractions. With an especially strong local demand for boat slips, Sandcastle decided to match the number of slips to the number of housing units and then offer them for sale as so-called "condominium" slips. Selling the marina as it was being developed, the Townsends surmised, would maintain a healthy cash flow and help smooth the transition from developer to owner control at buildout.

Based on the advice of its marketing consultants, the Codman Company of Boston, Sandcastle planned four phases so that the most desirable products—those with the best views—would be offered in the first and last phases. The less certain condominium units would be built after the project's credibility had been established.

THE SITE

Long before it was Spinnaker Island, the site was known as Hog Island, a U.S. Army base that had helped guard the New England coast since World War I. When the base closed in 1975, the town of Hull opened extra school classrooms on the island, an arrangement that lasted only until tax-cutting legislation squeezed the local education budget. Desperate for economic development, the town issued a request for proposals to develop the island into a residential community.

Although the prospect generated considerable interest, two major factors were unclear. Left from the Army's stay was a massive concrete bunker, almost entirely underground, that covered most of the island. Would it prove an obstacle or an opportunity? To its credit, the bunker raised the elevation of the naturally flat island to 60 feet above the water at its highest level. The resulting views stretch for miles.

Second, the island's value was unknown. Because of legal restrictions, the town could only sell the island for its appraised value, and prospective developers were asked to submit plans without a definite figure for land coats. As a result, only three firms submitted proposals. The Townsends' plan, with a much lower density than the others, won the development rights. Natural features on the island included a saltwater marsh on the east side, a natural location for a marina. Moreover, common terns, a protected bird species, had nested in a rotting, 50-year-old pier on the site.

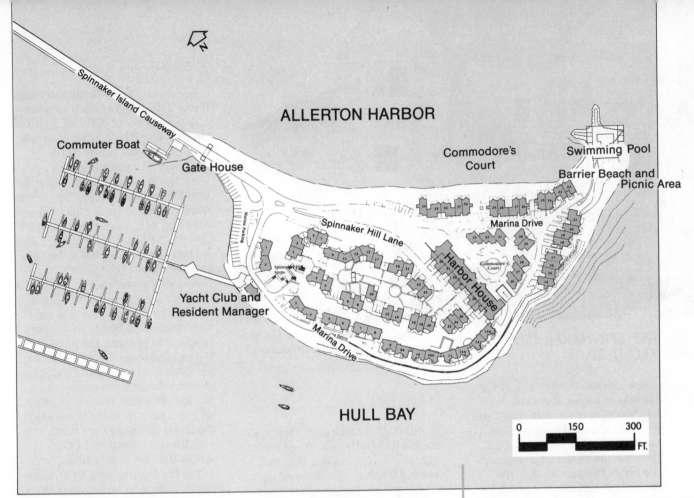

ALLERTON HARBOR

Commuter Boat

Gate House

Spinnaker Island Causeway

Commodore's Court

Swimming Pool

Barrier Beach and Picnic Area

Spinnaker Hill Lane

Marina Drive

Harbor House

Commodore's Court

Spinnaker Hill Steps

Yacht Club and Resident Manager

Marina Drive

HULL BAY

0   150   300
FT.

Spinnaker Island site plan.

SITE PLANNING AND ARCHITECTURE

Spinnaker Island's site plan, designed by Grazado Velleco Architects, reflects a desire to combine tightly clustered housing with views of the water, to take advantage of the rugged topography while maintaining easy access and circulation, and to establish a coherent set of common open spaces. The old Army bunker, an I-shaped cavern capped by an 18-inch concrete slab, essentially provided a platform for the first and most prominent phase of the project. Reached by a curving road that climbs to the top of the island, this phase consists of four groups of townhouses clustered around landscaped motor courts. Garages face into these "piazzas." Living areas face out toward the water. Arched gateways connect each cluster, and paving patterns, landscaping, and mailbox pavilions reinforce the fact that these spaces are primarily meant for pedestrians, not cars.

On the island's lower slopes at the bunker's edge, the developers constructed another building platform. This one, however, houses a 51-space parking garage. At the garage's west end rises the five-story Harbor House, which will contain the 25 condominiums. Ingeniously, the top two floors of the mid-rise buildings will become the foundation for Phase IV's last six townhouse units at the top of the hill.

The parking garage's roof provides the base for eight townhouses that, along with the taller building, will enclose a landscaped court. The remaining townhouse units are sited along the shoreline, with 16 separated from the water by a perimeter roadway. The marina and swimming pool occupy opposite ends of the island, with the pool built on piles at the easternmost tip. In the most pragmatic use of the bunker's interior space, the health club is located at its southeast end, accessible from the mid-rise building lobby or through the bunker corridor.

THE SPINNAKER ISLAND YACHT CLUB

Townhouses in the first phase are organized around a series of "piazzas."

The marina, the key amenity at Spinnaker Island, is notable both for its engineering technology and its ownership and management. Located on the island's west side at the juncture of the causeway and the project's main portion, the facility will ultimately contain 102 slips that will accommodate boats up to 50 feet long. Thus far, about 50 percent of the craft are power boats and 50 percent are sailboats. Although the marina is intended for use mostly by project residents, 35 slips are targeted for purchase by outsiders. Permitting authorities reduced the total number of slips, initially planned at 120, to reflect the total of housing units. Realizing that not all homebuyers would want a boat slip, the developer set aside the 35 slips. Even though more slips could likely be sold to outsiders, expansion is limited by a lack of space for additional visitor parking.

Although a more protected marina site lies on the island's opposite side in Allerton Harbor, the presence of a salt marsh dictated the siting on Hull Bay, where the bottom had already been disturbed by the Army's activities. This decision, however, meant that a breakwater would be required. It also meant that the construction would disturb the terns' nesting site in the old pier.

Based on the rugged conditions—a large tidal fluctuation and severe winters—the developers chose a system of floating piers manufactured by Pontona, a Swedish firm. These concrete piers, with polystyrene floats and wood decking, are arranged in three parallel rows, all accessible from a 12-foot-wide, fixed access pier. The basin ranges in depth from seven to 10 feet.

Interestingly, the breakwater also floats. This 429-foot-long structure is anchored about 120 feet south of the end pier. The marina is largely protected to the north by the causeway. Manufactured by Pontona, the breakwater was nearly finished when, in October 1985, a hurricane caused considerable damage. Based on new, more rugged specifications, the breakwater and remaining piers were expected to be back in place by the 1986 season.

Sandcastle was able to obtain the required marina permits in about 14 months. The process was expedited somewhat by the developer's proposal to mitigate the impact on the nesting terns. In exchange for permission to remove the old Army pier that housed the nests, Sandcastle built a new nesting platform on fixed piles in water of the same depth on the causeway's north side.

Spinnaker Island Yacht Club is one of the first condominium marinas in the Boston area. In arrangements similar to acquiring parking spaces in some urban residential condominium projects, boat slip buyers purchase a deed of easement, which guarantees passage across the access pier and entitles them to use the slip and all available services. Spinnaker Island's slip prices, initially set at $9,500, are now at $24,000. In addition, owners pay an annual maintenance and management fee, currently $700. Those project residents who do not own slips can belong to the yacht club for a dollar a year. Club programs, such as racing or social events, will be left up to club members, according to Sandcastle, and will probably be relatively limited. Only project residents (not outside slip owners) can use the pool and health club. Residents are free to sell their boat slips along with their houses or separately, either to fellow residents or to outsiders, as long as the 35-slip allotment is not yet filled.

As is typical for a residential amenity, the marina's services are quite limited. A dock master, on duty six months each year, manages the yacht club and assures security when the boats are in the water. Grounds maintenance is the responsibility of the resident manager. To assure a variety of other services such as fueling, supplies, and maintenance, the developers purchased a nearby full-service marina and boatyard. This facility was recently sold to a Spinnaker Island resident, who will continue to cater to the yacht club members.

EVALUATING THE EXPERIENCE

To date, Spinnaker Island's transformation from a rugged Army outpost to an exclusive coastal enclave has proven extraordinarily successful. As a local developer, Sandcastle Associates was able to recognize both an emerging market for luxury housing and the great potential of the underused island site. Moreover, the strong demand for boat slips, coupled with the condominium marina concept, has demonstrated the wisdom of Sandcastle's $1.5 million marina investment.

The existing network of local boat supply and service firms plays an integral part in the marina's success. Slip owners at Spinnaker Island can enjoy both an extremely attractive place to keep their boats—for many owners, almost on their doorstep—and relatively easy access to full-service boatyards nearby. Because of the climate, owners must store their boats on land anyway, which enables them to take advantage of the off-season for repairs and service.

By selling the slips early in the project, Sandcastle has placed a good deal of management responsibility squarely on the shoulders of the yacht club's members. At the same time, the developer will maintain strong influence as long as slips remain unsold.

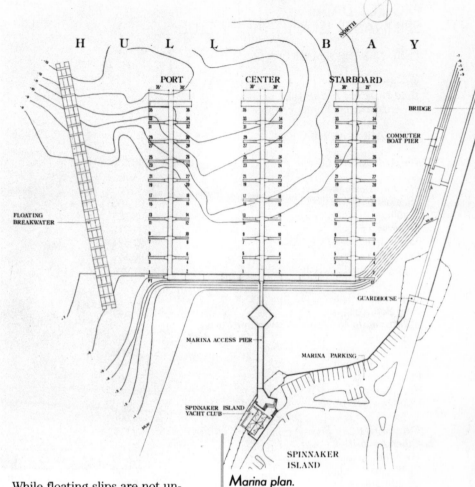

Marina plan.

While floating slips are not unusual in New England, floating breakwaters are seldom seen. Perhaps fortuitously, Spinnaker Island's breakwater was tested soon after construction by Hurricane Gloria. The resulting redesign should prove sufficient. The more protected site for a marina, where a breakwater would not have been required, was undevelopable because of the salt marsh. Sandcastle wisely moved the marina to the island's other side. Although the breakwater made this site more costly to develop, the developer received the marina permits relatively quickly and avoided extensive mitigation requirements.

PROJECT DATA:
SPINNAKER ISLAND YACHT CLUB

LAND USE INFORMATION

Site Area: 8.5 acres
Total Dwelling Units: 102
Gross Density: 12 units per acre

ECONOMIC INFORMATION

Site Acquisition Cost	$300,000
Site Improvement Cost	
Excavation	$1,201,108
Grading	408,187
Sewer/water	224,712
Landscaping	397,624
Demolition	90,141
Total	$2,321,772
Total Hard Costs	$16,113,911
Total Soft Costs	$4,243,845
Approximate Marina Construction Costs	
Dredging	$ 70,000
Shoreline stabilization	100,000
Fixed-access pier	150,000
Floating piers	750,000
Breakwater	350,000
Utilities	70,000
Total	$1,490,000
Capital Cost per Slip	$ 14,607
Other Amenities Costs	
Pool and cabana	$ 165,000
Yacht club building	135,000
Health club	45,000
Commuter boat pier	56,000

Source: Sandcastle Associates.

PROJECT CREDITS:

Developer:
Sandcastle Associates, Inc.
Hull, Massachusetts

Architect/Planner:
Grazado Velleco Architects
Marblehead, Massachusetts

Marketing and Management:
The Codman Company
Boston, Massachusetts

NOTES

Chapter One

1. Eric Smart, *Recreational Development Handbook* (Washington, D.C.: Urban Land Institute, 1981), p. 14.

2. Geoffrey S. Cornish and Ronald E. Whitten, *The Golf Course* (New York: The Rutledge Press, 1981), p. 49.

3. Dorice Taylor, "Sun Valley: The Beginning," *SKI* 50: 5 (1986), p. 24.

4. Clinton J. Chamberlain, *Marinas: Recommendations for Design, Construction, and Management* (Chicago: National Association of Marina Manufacturers, 1983), p. ii.

5. Colleen Grogan Moore, *PUDs in Practice* (Washington, D.C.: Urban Land Institute, 1985), p. 4.

6. Smart, *Recreational Development Handbook*, p. 15.

7. See Richard Ragatz, *Recreational Properties* (Eugene, Ore.: Richard Ragatz Associates, Inc., 1974).

8. Smart, *Recreational Development Handbook*, p. 15.

9. Remarks by J. Richard McElyea of Economics Research Associates before ULI's Recreational Development Council, May 1985.

10. Carlton S. Van Doren and Associates, ed., *Statistics on Outdoor Recreation* (Washington, D.C.: Resources for the Future, Inc., 1984), p. 293.

11. Doris Walsh, "A Healthy Trend," *American Demographics*, July 1984, p. 4.

12. Remarks by Henry Kelly, U.S. Congressional Office of Technology Assessment, before a policy forum on recreation and tourism, June 1985.

13. Ragatz, *Recreational Properties*, p. 440.

14. William Lazer, "How Rising Affluence Will Reshape Markets," *American Demographics*, February 1984, p. 16.

15. "Demographic Forecasts," *American Demographics*, October 1984, p. 46.

16. "Demographic Forecasts," *American Demographics*, August 1984, p. 46.

17. Remarks by David Pearson before the Recreational Development Council, May 1985.

18. Bryant Robey, *The American People* (New York: Truman Talley Books, 1985), p. 219.

19. "Demographic Forecasts," *American Demographics*, July 1984, p. 50.

20. James Chaffin, "The Snowmass Club," *Urban Land*, March 1985, p. 20.

21. J. Richard McElyea, personal communication, January 28, 1986.

22. See *Lake Tahoe*, Panel Advisory Service Report (Washington, D.C.: Urban Land Institute, 1985).

23. Douglas Wrenn, "Barrier Island Development: The Federal Government's Changing Role," *Urban Land*, January 1983, p. 36.

24. Charles Siemon and Wendy Larsen, "Florida: Grappling with Growth II," *Urban Land*, September 1985, p. 36.

Chapter Two

1. Ralph Bowden, "Residential Amenities: Long-Term Lessons Lead to Long-Term Financial Planning." *Urban Land*, October 1985, p. 36.

2. Much of the material on equity membership plans in this chapter is based on remarks by William Wernersback of Pannell Kerr Forster in Fort Lauderdale, Florida, and James Wanless, Esq., of Gunster, Yoakley, Criser, and Stewart in Palm Beach, Florida. Their presentation, entitled "The Disposition Question: Options for Long-Term Ownership and Operations," was made to the ULI Professional Development Seminar on Recreational Amenities in St. Thomas, U.S. Virgin Islands, December 13, 1985.

Chapter Three

1. Much of the organization and content of this chapter is based on ULI's 1974 book *Golf Course Developments* (ULI Technical Bulletin 70, now out of print), by golf course architect Rees Jones and landscape architect Guy Rando. Many of the standards and guidelines, particularly those regarding golf course design, planning, and construction, have been drawn from this earlier work.

2. See National Golf Foundation, *Statistical Profile of Golf in the United States: 1983 Annual Review* (North Palm Beach, Fla.: National Golf Foundation, 1984).

3. For a thorough review of the history of golf course architecture, see Geoffrey S. Cornish and Ronald E. Whitten, *The Golf Course* (New York: The Rutledge Press, 1981).

4. Harry C. Eckhoff, "What's Happening in Golf Course Development?" *Urban Land*, March 1974, p. 18.

5. National Golf Foundation, "Guidelines for Planning and Building a Golf Course," Information Sheet GC-1, February 1986.

6. John W. McGrath and Patrick Mulligan, "The Golf Course of the Future: Economic Realities," *Urban Land*, December 1975, p. 3.

7. Interview with John Cole, Town of Breckenridge Department of Community Development, November 26, 1985.

8. Rees Jones and Guy Rando, *Golf Course Developments* (Washington, D.C.: Urban Land Institute, 1974), p. 36.

9. McGrath and Mulligan, "Golf Course of the Future."

10. See Jones and Rando, *Golf Course Developments*, pp. 8–25.

11. National Golf Foundation, *Statistical Profile*, 1983.

12. McGrath and Mulligan, "Golf Course of the Future."

13. "The Short Ball: Is It a Nicklaus Masterstroke or Folly?" *The Wedge*, April 1985, p. 10.

14. Jones and Rando, *Golf Course Developments*, p. 30.

15. Ibid., p. 32.

16. Ibid., p. 47.

17. Ibid., p. 49.

18. Ibid., p. 50.

19. Ibid., p. 52.

20. Ibid., p. 53.

21. "Reclamation: A Piece of the Water Management Puzzle," *Urban Land*, November 1985, p. 32.

22. Jones and Rando, *Golf Course Developments*, p. 53.

23. Cornish and Whitten, *The Golf Course*, p. 18.

24. Jones and Rando, *Golf Course Developments*, p. 54.

25. See Karla Heuer, *Golf Courses: A Guide to Analysis and Valuation* (Chicago: American Institute of Real Estate Appraisers, 1980).

26. National Golf Foundation, "Guidelines for Planning and Building a Golf Course."

27. Carlton S. Van Doren and Associates, ed., *Statistics on Outdoor Recreation* (Washington, D.C.: Resources for the Future, Inc., 1984), pp. 359–360.

28. Heuer, *Golf Courses*, p. 12.

29. National Golf Foundation, *Statistical Profile*, p. 2.

30. Ibid., p. 3.

31. Ibid., p. 3.

32. National Golf Foundation, "Guidelines for Planning and Building a Golf Course."

33. Remarks by Robert Trent Jones, Jr., at ULI's Professional Development Seminar on Recreational Amenities, St. Thomas, U.S. Virgin Islands, December 13, 1985.

34. Urban Land Institute, *Residential Development Handbook* (Washington, D.C.: Urban Land Institute, 1978), pp. 216–217.

35. Jones and Rando, *Golf Course Developments*, p. 4.

36. Cornish and Whitten, *The Golf Course*, p. 24.

37. Jones and Rando, *Golf Course Developments*, p. 28.

38. Ibid., p. 36.

39. Ibid., p. 37.

40. See National Golf Foundation, *Planning and Building the Golf Course*, rev. ed. (North Palm Beach, Fla.: National Golf Foundation, 1981).

41. McGrath and Mulligan, "Golf Course of the Future."

42. See National Golf Foundation, *Planning and Building the Golf Course*.

43. Ibid.

44. Jones and Rando, *Golf Course Developments*, p. 59.

45. National Golf Foundation, *Planning and Building the Golf Course*, p. 19.

46. Erling Speer, remarks at St. Thomas ULI seminar, December 13, 1985.

47. Remarks by Richard Diedrich at St. Thomas ULI seminar, December 13, 1985.

48. Remarks by Gary Sandor of the Vintage Club made before the Executive Group of ULI's Recreational Development Council, Phoenix, Arizona, October 10, 1985.

49. Jones and Rando, *Golf Course Developments*, p. 91.

50. Ibid., p. 99.

51. Personal communication with J. Richard McElyea, June 24, 1986.

52. Remarks by Richard Diedrich at St. Thomas ULI seminar, December 13, 1985.

53. Personal communication with Rodney Slifer, October 11, 1985.

54. The organization and basic content of this section on construction is based on that contained in Jones and Rando, *Golf Course Developments*. See also National Golf Foundation, *Planning and Building the Golf Course*; and Joachim Tourbier and Richard Westmacott, *Lakes and Ponds* (Washington, D.C.: Urban Land Institute, 1976).

55. Remarks by Robert Trent Jones, Jr., at St. Thomas ULI seminar, December 13, 1985.

56. See National Golf Foundation, *Golf Course Maintenance Report: 1985 Biennial Review* (North Palm Beach, Fla.: National Golf Foundation, 1985).

57. Remarks by Robert Trent Jones, Jr., at St. Thomas ULI seminar, December 13, 1985.

58. National Golf Foundation, *Golf Course Maintenance Report*, p. 9.

59. *Clubs in Town and Country 1984* (Houston: Pannell Kerr Forster, 1985), p. 4.

60. Personal communication with J. Richard McElyea, June 25, 1986.

61. National Golf Foundation, *Golf Course Maintenance Report*, p. 8.

62. Pannel Kerr Forster, *Clubs in Town and Country*, p. 13.

63. Personal communication with Rodney Slifer, October 11, 1985.

Chapter Four

1. For a comprehensive historical and factual overview of tennis, see *The Encyclopedia of Tennis* (New York: Harper and Row, 1979). This 487-page reference may be ordered for $10 from the USTA Education and Research Center, 729 Alexander Road, Princeton, N.J. 08540.

2. Interview with Miles Dumont, United States Tennis Association, February 13, 1986.

3. Carlton S. Van Doren and Associates, ed., *Statistics on Outdoor Recreation* (Washington, D.C.: Resources for the Future, Inc., 1984), p. 273.

4. Arthur E. Gimmy, *Tennis Clubs and Racquet Sport Projects: A Guide to Appraisal, Market Analysis, Development, and Financing* (Chicago: American Institute of Real Estate Appraisers, 1978), p. 7. See also Van Doren, *Statistics on Outdoor Recreation*, p. 273.

5. James Chaffin, "The Snowmass Club," *Urban Land*, March 1985, p. 20.

6. Remarks by Paul Pastoor of John Gardiner's Tennis Ranch at ULI's Professional Development Seminar on Recreational Amenities, St. Thomas, U.S. Virgin Islands, December 13, 1985.

7. See Gimmy, *Tennis Clubs and Racquet Sport Projects*.

8. See USTA Education and Research Center, *Lighting Outdoor Tennis Courts* (North Palm Beach, Fla.: Tennis Foundation of North America, 1978).

9. Natalie Gerardi, "Should You Get into the Tennis Racket?" *House and Home*, July 1974, p. 86.

10. United States Tennis Association (USTA), *Tennis Courts 1986–1987* (Lynn, Mass.: H. O. Zimman, Inc., 1986), p. 20. *Tennis Courts* is the most complete and concise guide to the physical aspects of tennis facilities and forms the basis for several sections of this chapter.

11. USTA, *Tennis Courts 1986–1987*, p. 26.

12. Ibid., p. 12.

13. Remarks by Lou Ellen Wilson of Sunmark Communities Corporation at St. Thomas ULI seminar, December 13, 1985.

14. Gerardi, "Should You Get into the Tennis Racket?"

15. USTA, *Tennis Courts 1986–1987*, p. 62.

16. USTA Education and Research Center, *Lighting Outdoor Tennis Courts*, p. 17.

17. USTA, *Tennis Courts 1986–1987*, p. 75.

18. Michael J. Keighley, ed. *A Guide to Tennis Club Planning, Building, and Financing* (North Miami, Fla.: Industry Publishers, Inc., 1979), p. 9.

19. Gerardi, "Should You Get into the Tennis Racket?"

20. USTA, *Tennis Courts 1986–1987*, p. 84.

21. Gerardi, "Should You Get into the Tennis Racket?"

22. Remarks by Paul Pastoor at St. Thomas ULI seminar, December 13, 1985.

23. Keighley, *Guide to Tennis Club Planning*, p. 57.

24. Remarks by Paul Pastoor at St. Thomas ULI seminar, December 13, 1985.

25. *Clubs in Town and Country 1984* (Houston: Pannell Kerr Forster, 1985), p. 14.

26. Allen Brown, "Tennis and Other Rackets" (paper prepared for ULI's Publications Division, 1978).

27. Remarks by Paul Pastoor at St. Thomas ULI seminar, December 13, 1985.

28. USTA, *Tennis Courts 1986–1987*, p. 27.

Chapter Five

1. C. R. Goeldner, T. A. Buchman, and K. P. Duea, *Economic Analysis of North American Ski Areas* (Boulder: University of Colorado Business Research Division, 1983), p. 13.

2. Goeldner, Buchman, and Duea, *Economic Analysis*, p. ii.

3. Ski Industries America (SIA), "White Paper on Skiing" (unpublished report, 1984), p. 2.

4. Charles R. Goeldner and Stacy Standley, "Skiing Trends" (paper prepared for a national symposium on outdoor recreation trends, New England Center, Durham, N.H., April 20–23, 1980), p. 8.

5. Goeldner and Standley, "Skiing Trends," p. 18.

6. Ibid., p. 21.

7. SIA, "White Paper," p. 4.

8. Ibid., p. 23.

9. Goeldner and Standley, "Skiing Trends," p. 27.

10. See Robert G. Enzel and John Urciolo, *The White Book of Ski Areas: U.S. and Canada* (Washington, D.C.: Inter-Ski Services, Inc., 1978).

11. Goeldner, Buchman, and Duea, *Economic Analysis*, p. 3.

12. Marvin W. Kottke and National Ski Areas Association (NSAA), *1984–1985 NSAA End of Season National Business Survey* (Springfield, Mass.: National Ski Areas Association, 1985), p. 10.

13. Goeldner, Buchman, and Duea, *Economic Analysis*, p. 134.

14. James Branch, "Developing an Urban Ski Facility," *Ski Area Management*, January 1986, p. 102.

15. Goeldner, Buchman, and Duea, *Economic Analysis*, p. 17.

16. Ibid., p. 11.

17. Ibid., p. 11.

18. "Varied Real Estate 'Menu' Is the Spice in Purgatory's Ambitious Expansion Plan," *Resort Development*, January 1986, p. 13.

19. Carl Burlingame, "Fractionals Take Off; Strongest New Trend Today in Resort Real Estate," *Resort Development*, April 1986, p. 8.

20. James Branch, "Classification of Resort Areas by Type" (unpublished paper, n.d.).

21. Much of the information in this section is based on material in *SKI* magazine's 50th anniversary issue, published in January 1986.

22. Dorice Taylor, "Sun Valley: The Beginning," *SKI*, January 1986, p. 22.

23. SIA, "White Paper," p. 23.

24. Interview with Harry Frampton, June 5, 1986.

25. Remarks by James Chaffin at Executive Group meeting of ULI's Recreational Development Council, Phoenix, October 10, 1985.

26. Branch, "Developing an Urban Ski Facility."

27. Remarks by James Branch at ULI's Professional Development Seminar on Recreational Amenities, St. Thomas, U.S. Virgin Islands, December 13, 1985.

28. Interview with Robert W. Ross, Jr., chief landscape architect, U.S. Forest Service, January 10, 1985.

29. U.S. Department of Agriculture, Forest Service, *National Forest Landscape Management: Ski Areas*, vol. 2, chap. 7, Agriculture Handbook No. 617 (Washington, D.C.: U.S. Department of Agriculture, 1984), p. 18.

30. Goeldner, Buchman, and Duea, *Economic Analysis*, p. 38.

31. Interview with James Branch, October 2, 1985.

32. Remarks by James Branch at St. Thomas ULI seminar, December 13, 1985.

33. Remarks by Robert Parker at St. Thomas ULI seminar, December 13, 1985.

34. Interview with Branch, October 2, 1985.

35. *SKI*, January 1986, p. 194.

36. Goeldner and Standley, "Skiing Trends," p. 34.

37. Branch, "Developing an Urban Ski Facility."

38. Interview with Branch, October 2, 1985.

39. I. William Berry, "They Build the Trails You Ski On," *SKI*, March 1978, p. 47.

40. Branch, "Developing an Urban Ski Facility."

41. Interview with Branch, October 2, 1985.

42. Remarks by James Chaffin at Executive Group meeting of ULI's Recreational Development Council, Orlando, Fla., May 8, 1986.

43. Remarks by James Branch at St. Thomas ULI seminar, December 13, 1985.

44. Branch, "Developing an Urban Ski Facility."

45. Personal communication with James Branch, May 27, 1986.

46. Remarks by Robert Parker at St. Thomas ULI seminar, December 13, 1985.

47. Kelly Roark, "Wachusett Mountain," *Project Reference File*, vol. 14, no. 20 (Washington, D.C.: Urban Land Institute, 1984).

48. Branch, "Developing an Urban Ski Facility."

49. Goeldner, Bachman, and Duea, *Economic Analysis*, p. 112.

50. Interview with Branch, October 2, 1985.

51. Interview with staff at Sno-Engineering, Inc., October 2, 1985.

52. Interview with Branch, October 2, 1985.

53. Kottke and NSAA, *End of Season Survey*, p. 10.

54. Remarks by Christine Johns and Robert Parker at St. Thomas ULI seminar, December 13, 1985.

55. See USDA, *National Forest Landscape Management*.

56. Ibid., p. 13.

57. *National Ski Areas Association News*, November 2, 1986.

58. SIA, "White Paper," p. 22.

59. Goeldner, Bachman, and Duea, *Economic Analysis*, p. 27.

60. Interview with William Shanahan, October 2, 1985.

61. Goeldner, Bachman, and Duea, *Economic Analysis*, p. 81.

62. Ibid., p. 29.

63. Michael Janofsky, "Rising Insurance Rates Pose Concern for the Ski Industry," *New York Times*, February 15, 1986, p. 1.

64. SIA, "White Paper," p. 21. See also Richard Houlihan, "Report on Liability Insurance Premiums, Trends, and Recommendations" (unpublished NSAA report, August 1985).

Chapter Six

1. Carlton S. Van Doren and Associates, ed., *Statistics on Outdoor Recreation* (Washington, D.C.: Resources for the Future, Inc., 1984), p. 290.

2. National Marine Manufacturers Association (NMMA), Marketing Services Department, *Boating: A Statistical Report on America's Top Family Sport* (Chicago: National Marine Manufacturers Association, 1984).

3. James W. Dunham and Arnold A. Finn, *Small Craft Harbors: Design, Construction, and Operation. Special Report Number 2* (Fort Belvoir, Va.: U.S. Army Corps of Engineers, Coastal Engineering Research Center, 1974), p. 248.

4. Dunham and Finn, *Small Craft Harbors*, p. 258.

5. Ibid., p. 259.

6. See Douglas Wrenn, *Urban Waterfront Development* (Washington, D.C.: Urban Land Institute, 1984).

7. Donald W. Adie, *Marinas: A Working Guide to Their Development and Design*, 3rd ed. (New York: Nichols Publishing Company, 1984), p. 45.

8. NMMA, *Boating*.

9. Dunham and Finn, *Small Craft Harbors*, p. 252.

10. Douglass G. Norvell et al., *Financial Profiles of Five Marinas* (Chicago: National Marine Manufacturers Association, 1984), p. 25.

11. Clinton J. Chamberlain, *Marinas: Recommendations for Design, Construction, and Management* (Chicago: National Marine Manufacturers Association, 1983), p. 1.

12. Adie, *Marinas*, p. 133.

13. Chamberlain, *Marinas*, p. 8.

14. Adie, *Marinas*, p. 98.

15. Ibid., p. 111.

16. Dunham and Finn, *Small Craft Harbors*, p. 249.

17. For an extensive discussion of the complex topic of dredging see Adie, *Marinas*, p. 173, and U.S. Army Corps of Engineers, *Shore Protection Manual*, 3rd ed. (Fort Belvoir, Va.: U.S. Army Corps of Engineers, 1984).

18. Adie, *Marinas*, p. 123.

19. Department of Defense, "Regulatory Programs of the Corps of Engineers," *Federal Register*, July 19, 1977, as cited in Chamberlain, *Marinas*, p. 117.

20. See U.S. Environmental Protection Agency, Region IV, *Coastal Marinas Assessment Handbook* (Atlanta: U.S. Environmental Protection Agency, 1985).

21. Adie, *Marinas*, p. 337.

22. Ibid., p. 340.

23. Chamberlain, *Marinas*, p. 100.

24. Remarks by Bruce Blomgren at ULI's Professional Development Seminar on Recreational Amenities, St. Thomas, U.S. Virgin Islands, December 12, 1985.

25. Chamberlain, *Marinas*, p. 48.